Fifth Edition

MUSIC
The Art of Listening

Jean Ferris

Arizona State University, Tempe

McGraw-Hill College

Boston Burr Ridge, IL Dubuque, IA Madison, WI New York San Francisco St. Louis
Bangkok Bogotá Caracas Lisbon London Madrid
Mexico City Milan New Delhi Seoul Singapore Sydney Taipei Toronto

McGraw-Hill College

A Division of The **McGraw·Hill** *Companies*

MUSIC THE ART OF LISTENING, FIFTH EDITION

Copyright © 1999, by The McGraw-Hill Companies, Inc. All rights reserved. Previous editions © 1985, 1991, 1995 by Wm. C. Brown Communications, Inc. All rights reserved. Printed in the United States of America. Except as permitted under the United States Copyright Act of 1976, no part of this publication may be reproduced or distributed in any form or by any means, or stored in a data base or retrieval system, without the prior written permission of the publisher.

This book is printed on acid-free paper.

1 2 3 4 5 6 7 8 9 0 QPD/QPD 9 3 2 1 0 9 8

ISBN 0–697–29384–X

Editorial director: *Phil Butcher*
Sponsoring editor: *Christopher Freitag*
Developmental editor: *JoElaine Retzler*
Marketing manager: *David S. Patterson*
Senior project manager: *Marilyn Rothenberger*
Production supervisor: *Deborah Donner*
Freelance design coordinator: *Mary L. Christianson*
Photo research coordinator: *John C. Leland*
Supplement coordinator: *David A. Welsh*
Compositor: *Shepherd Inc.*
Typeface: *10/12 Times*
Printer: *Quebecor Printing Book Group/Dubuque, IA*

Freelance designer: *Kristyn A. Kalnes*
Cover image: *Musee d'Art Moderne de la Ville de Paris, France/Giraudon, Paris/SuperStock*

The credits section for this book begins on page 359 and is considered an extension of the copyright page.

Library of Congress Cataloging-in-Publication Data

Ferris, Jean.
    Music : the art of listening / Jean Ferris. — 5th ed.
      p.   cm.
    Includes bibliographical references (p.) and index.
    ISBN 0–697–29384–X   (book)
    1. Music appreciation. I. Title.
MT6.F394M9   1999
781.1'7—dc21

           97–42495
           CIP
           MN

www.mhhe.com

MUSIC
The Art of Listening

In loving memory of Sue

Contents

PART ONE
Basic Concepts   2

Color Plates

Listening Examples

Preface

Music: The Art of Listening is a practical, concise textbook for the beginning student of music history and appreciation, written in language readily understandable by a student with no previous music experience. Throughout the text, music is presented in its broad cultural and historical context, never as an isolated phenomenon divorced from the world surrounding it. Relationships are drawn between music and the other arts, with which students may have more familiarity, and between the music characteristic of one period and music of the distant past and of modern times.

American music is addressed throughout the text. We discuss, for example, the manner in which the Protestant Reformation profoundly affected music in the United States. Students learn that W. A. Mozart and Benjamin Franklin were eighteenth-century contemporaries who shared a classical taste, and that the trend toward nationalism, so strong in late nineteenth-century Europe, was slow to affect American music. Brief discussions of the lives of great European and American composers provide not only human interest but also a sense of musicians' positions in society, their aesthetic ideals and practical intentions, and the influence of their personal experience on the works for which they are revered. The chapters on vernacular music emphasize its relation to so-called art music and the mutual exchange of influence enjoyed by musicians in both fields.

Occasional references throughout the fifth edition to the music of non-European cultures, and the last section's brief Musical Encounters with African, Indian, Islamic, Japanese, Chinese, and Native American music, are intended not so much to teach these music traditions as to broaden students' understanding of music, discourage the misconception that the familiar is necessarily "right," and stress the increasingly significant impact upon Western music of non-Western concepts.

Appreciation of much of the music in the West's contemporary concert and vernacular repertoires is greatly enhanced by awareness of the cultural traditions—sometimes ancient, sometimes foreign, often mixed—upon which the repertoire is based. While the format of the text makes it possible for students to avoid the Musical Encounters, I hope many will find that they greatly enrich the introductory music experience. Instructors might well assign these sections for supplemental reading (no Terms to Review are listed).

Professors who have used earlier editions of this text will find the organization of material more logical and effective here, largely due to helpful suggestions by reviewers. Every effort also has been made to enhance the students' listening experience. New listening examples include Vivaldi's "Primavera" from The Four Seasons, a Verdi recitative and aria, Wagner's Liebestod (instead of the Prelude to Tristan), and an ensemble scene from Leonard Bernstein's West Side Story. Listening selections also include a delicate lute dance piece by John Dowland and a charming and humorous harpsichord piece by François Couperin, offering highly attractive selections from two periods that are often underrepresented, though of strong appeal to many listeners today. Detailed listening guides written by Professor Vicki Curry of the University of Utah provide far more listening support than that afforded by earlier editions of the text.

The following ancillary items can be used with this text (please consult your local McGraw-Hill representative for policy, prices, and availability). There are three cassettes or CDs containing all of the music for which listening guides are printed in the text. Also, a set of two supplemental compact discs, containing some of the Optional Listening Examples and Suggestions for Further Listening referred to in the Instructor's Manual, is available to instructors. Listening guides for all of the optional selections, printed in the Instructor's Manual, *may be copied and distributed to students,* greatly increasing the flexibility of choice of examples to be studied. The Instructor's Manual also offers chapter outlines, resource lists, and test questions, and testing software for both Macintosh and Windows formats is available.

I am extremely grateful to my colleagues at Arizona State University, on whose expertise I continually impose in the quest to improve this text. For this edition (as for the fourth), I particularly thank Dr. Theodore Solis for his suggestions concerning listening examples,

Dr. J. Richard Haefer for advice concerning Native American Music, and Dr. James DeMars, whose *Tapestry V* (Listening Example 53) so beautifully illustrates the sharing of Western, Native American, and African concepts.

To Christopher Freitag, McGraw-Hill acquisitions editor, whose creativity, music expertise, good nature, and unflagging hard work are constant sources of stimulation and support, I express the deepest admiration and warmest thanks, while my gratitude to my resourceful, diligent, creative, hardworking developmental editor, Joey Retzler, knows no bounds. I'm extremely grateful as well to Professor Vicki Curry for her outstanding work on the listening guides, and to Tom Laskey of SONY for producing the fine set of recorded music examples. Project manager Marilyn Rothenberger expertly coordinated all of our efforts, and I feel fortunate indeed to have been in her capable hands.

The following prepublication reviewers have made valuable contributions to the improvement and refinement of this text through five editions, and to them I express my warmest appreciation: William R. Baldridge, University of Texas; Cosmo A. Barbaro, Edinboro University of Pennsylvania; Laurence E. Barker, University of Texas at San Antonio; Adrienne Fried Block, Hunter College, City University of New York; Jane Bowers, University of Wisconsin at Milwaukee; Thomas D. Brosh, Community College of Aurora; Doris Burbank, Alvin Community College; Allen Cannon, Bradley University; James W. Clark, Anderson College; *Judith Cline, Hollins College; Dorothea Cromley, Eastern Montana College; Ronald L. Douglass, Jackson Community College; *Ervin Ely, Bismarck State College; Judith Fanning Hunt, University of Alaska; *Mark R. Jelinek, Bloomsburg University; William Johnson, Laramie County Community College; Richard Kassel, City College, City University of New York; Ken Keaton, Florida Atlantic University; Richard L. Kennedy, Alice Lloyd College; Jerome Laszloffy, University of Connecticut; *Timothy Lynch, College of the Sequoias; John P. Manchester, Jr., Hinds Community College; *John C. Metcalf, Kutztown University; Robert F. Nisbett, Colorado State University; Dennis N. Pitcock, University of Wisconsin at Oshkosh; Jerry E. Rife, Rider College; Richard Robinette, Southwestern College; Charles F. Schwartz, East Carolina University; Roger Ward Scott, Phillips County Community College; Ronald J. Sherrod, Grossmont College; *Stephen Shore, Bunker Hill Community College; Mary Alice Spencer, South Dakota State University; *Alan E. Stanek, Idaho State University; James A. Starr, Emporia State University; Edward Szabo, Eastern Michigan University; Joan Thompson, Moorpark College; Edward Turley, College of St. Benedict/St. John's University; *Elizabeth Weber, Chicago State University.

*took part in reviewing the most recent revision

Overture

We in the Western world are blessed with music in great variety, including music to accompany drama, music for instruments and/or the singing voice, music for dancing, music for worship, music for exercising, and music for "easy listening." Radio, television, records, tapes, CDs, and live performers bring folk, popular, and art music to us from all over the world, each kind of music offering something to, and requiring something of, the listener. The demands placed upon listeners and upon those who perform, or interpret, music vary greatly from one kind of music to another.

Popular music, primarily a source of entertainment and relaxation, may require little if any formal training on the part of performers or listeners. But while the best popular music of any age has quality and substance, and perhaps—as the reflection of a particular culture at a given time—important sociological significance as well, the very characteristics that render music "popular" may tend to make it short-lived. Thus, many popular songs soon sound dated, their appreciation by later generations as dependent upon nostalgic considerations as upon purely aesthetic ones.

Some kinds of music serve a purpose or elicit a specific response. For example, it is easier to exercise, row a boat, dance, march, or perform any rhythmic task with music to set the pace and synchronize movements. The background music in a movie intensifies emotional reactions, covers awkward pauses in the film's dialogue, and provides a sense of continuity between scenes. Music in a religious service enhances the spirit of worship. Listening to pleasant, undemanding music relieves tension or lessens boredom.

Art music, on the other hand, does not necessarily serve any functional purpose, but may simply express an abstract concept the composer had in mind and thought worth sharing. The famous writer and art critic John Ruskin (1819–1900) defined art as "the expression of one soul talking to another," and most composers of art music (also called *classical,* or *concert,* music) have tried to communicate to their listening audience something of their experience, their personality, their mind, or indeed their soul.

Listening to art music is itself an art, as the title of this text implies, and good listening constitutes an active, creative experience. The prepared listener applies a fair measure of knowledge and experience as his or her part in the successful cycle of creation, performance, and appreciation of serious music. Art music challenges composer, interpreter or performer, and listener alike. The rewards for all three lie in the lasting value of great music and in the intense pleasure it evokes. A Beethoven symphony, for example, stirs the same emotions and evokes the same thrills in listeners today that it did when it was introduced over a hundred years ago.

As you practice the art of listening, you may expect to experience greater pleasure from every type of music—popular and art, old and new, Western and non-Western, religious and secular—than ever before. The highly sensuous pleasure we experience while listening to great music is our emotional reward for an intellectual effort well made.

From ancient if not prehistoric times, music has been conceived as an integral component of all of the arts. In this engraving of Robert Fludd's Temple of Music we see related harmony to architectural proportions.

The Bettman Archive

Shopping mall patrons enjoying an orchestral performance.
American Symphony Orchestra League (Carter & Burry Photography)

PART ONE
Basic Concepts

M usic is an art of organized sounds. Therefore, we begin the study of music history and appreciation with a discussion of the characteristics of *musical sounds.* High or low, loud or soft, sung or played upon an instrument, musical sounds form a varied and provocative world rich in intellectual and aesthetic pleasures.

This section of the text introduces the various *elements of music* that composers combine in particular ways to form musical compositions. Listeners seldom consider the individual elements while enjoying a piece of music, appreciating instead the effects of their skillful combination. However, recognition of the elements of music immeasurably enhances the capacity to understand and enjoy music of every kind.

The *formal design* of a musical composition, as of any work of art, also contributes to its beauty and value. But a listener, unlike a viewer of painting or sculpture, cannot hold music in place for leisurely observation, but must memorize it *as it happens* in order to recognize repeated and contrasting sections. This poses for listeners a challenge unique in the world of art. Our introductory discussion of form in music will offer simple techniques for developing basic listening skills.

Part I concludes with a discussion of several types of *music performance.* You should begin attending live performances early in this course and continue to do so throughout it. To fully enjoy your earliest listening experiences, apply your ever-expanding knowledge of musical sounds, of the elements of music, and of

patterns of design and organization to participate actively and creatively in the

experience of great music.

Maximilian ("Weisskunig") listening to a concert. Woodcut by Hans Burgkmair, sixteenth century.
Calmunn & King Archives London

1
Sound

Music, which is meant to be heard, necessarily involves sound. Some people distinguish between "noise" and "musical sound," but such distinction is avoided by many contemporary musicians, who define music simply as "organized sound," and consider sounds of all kinds valid material for the composition of music.

The characteristic tone quality of a sound is determined by the voice or instrument that produces it. A sound is also affected by the manner of its attack and release, and by other sounds with which it may be combined.

Among the characteristics of sound are its highness or lowness, called the **pitch** of the sound, and its loudness or softness, called its **dynamic level.** Composers often utilize changes in level of pitch and dynamics to organize musical material and to achieve expressive effects.

Pitch

The pitch of a sound is its highness or lowness, which depends upon the rate of vibration, or **frequency,** of the sound-producing medium. If we pluck a guitar string, depress a piano key, or blow across the top of a bottle, the resulting sound is caused when something—a string on the guitar or the piano, the column of air in the bottle—vibrates. Depressing the guitar string with a finger before plucking it, or adding water to the bottle before blowing across it, changes the size of the vibrating medium, causing it to vibrate at a different rate of speed and therefore to produce a different pitch. A faster rate of vibration causes a higher pitch, and a slower rate of vibration causes a lower pitch.

As a pianist sits at the piano, the keys on the left-hand side of the keyboard produce tones comparatively low in pitch. You can see when looking inside a grand piano that the strings to the pianist's left are much longer and thicker, and therefore vibrate more slowly, than the strings on the right, which produce the high tones.

Naming Pitches

A **tone** is a *specific* pitch, produced by sound waves with a constant rate of vibration (as opposed, for example, to the sound of a gong, which includes a wide range of pitches). We refer to specific pitches, or tones, with letter names, using the letters A through G, a system best explained by referring to a piano keyboard (see figure 1.1). The keyboard consists of a simple pattern of white and black keys, each key representing one tone. Depressing a key causes a hammer to strike a specific set of strings inside the piano, sounding a particular tone.

Each of the seven different white keys bears one of the seven letter names. The black keys have the same letter names as the white keys, but each is qualified as **sharp** (higher in pitch than the corresponding white key) or **flat** (lower in pitch than the corresponding white key). For example, the black key that falls between C and D on the keyboard (figure 1.1) may be called C sharp (C♯) or D flat (D♭), depending on the composer's intention.

A grand piano. The long, thick strings at the pianist's left produce lower tones than the short strings at the right.

Figure 1.1

A portion of a piano keyboard.

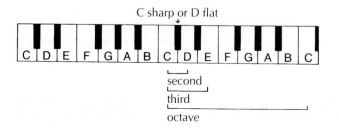

Notating Pitches

Music is written, or *notated,* on a **staff** of five lines and four spaces. The staff forms a kind of "ladder," with each line and each space representing a particular pitch arranged in ascending order from the bottom line to the top. A sign called a **clef,** placed at the beginning of the staff, indicates that a particular line represents a specific pitch, and thus fixes the position of all of the pitches on the staff. The bass clef (𝄢), sometimes called the F clef, indicates that the fourth line of the staff is (a particular) F (see figure 1.2). The treble clef (𝄞), also called the G clef, indicates that the second line of the staff represents (a particular) G (see figure 1.2).

E F G A B C D E F G A B C* C* D E F G A B C D E F G A

*Several pitches, including the "middle C", may be notated in either the bass or the treble clef.

Figure 1.2

Pitches notated in the bass and treble clefs.

Intervals

The distances, or **intervals,** between two tones have number names. For example, the interval from any note (notated pitch) to its nearest neighbor, as from C to D, is called a *second,* because it involves two adjacent notes, C and D (figure 1.1). The interval from C to E is a *third,* notated on alternate lines or alternate spaces of the staff; from C to F is a *fourth,* and so on.

The interval of an *eighth,* as from C to C, is called an **octave.** The two notes of an octave look alike on the keyboard and also sound quite similar, due to the simple relationship of their frequencies: the higher tone is produced at twice the rate of vibration of the lower tone.

Dynamics

In the seventeenth century, when composers first indicated degrees of loudness or softness in their music, Italian musicians were the most widely respected and emulated in the Western world. Thus, Italian terms for dynamic expression came into the music vocabulary and have been generally accepted since then. Table 1.1 includes the terms most commonly used, their abbreviations as they usually occur in written music, and their English meanings. It is important to distinguish between terms that indicate levels of volume, such as **forte** ("loud") and **piano** ("soft"), and those that indicate the process of changing levels, such as **crescendo** ("becoming louder") and **decrescendo** or **diminuendo** (both of which mean "becoming softer").

creh-shen´-doh
deh-creh-shen´-doh
dee-mih-nyu-en´-doh

Table 1.1   Dynamics

	Levels of Volume	
Italian Term	**Abbreviation**	**English Meaning**
pianissimo	*pp*	very soft
piano	*p*	soft
mezzopiano	*mp*	moderately soft
mezzoforte	*mf*	moderately loud
forte	*f*	loud
fortissimo	*ff*	very loud
	Processes of Changing Levels	
crescendo		becoming louder
decrescendo		becoming softer
diminuendo		becoming softer

1 □   LISTENING EXAMPLE 1   1A 1

Pitch/Dynamics

Composer: Richard Strauss (1864–1949)

Title: Introduction to *Also sprach Zarathustra (Thus Spake Zarathustra)*

Composed: 1896

Timbre: Orchestra and organ

□	0:00	**Theme** (represents "nature") Begins very softly (*pianissimo*) and at a relatively low level of pitch.
□	0:37	**Theme,** second statement This statement begins at a moderate dynamic level (*mezzoforte*) and ends at a slightly higher pitch level than the first statement.
□	0:52	**Theme,** third statement The third statement begins at a loud dynamic level (*forte*), yet the music expands still further by getting louder (*crescendo*), increasing the number of instruments, and rising to a climactic pitch.

Changes in dynamic level during the performance of a composition may be achieved in two ways:

    a. the instruments or voices may simply play or sing more loudly or more softly; or
    b. a number of instruments or voices may be added or taken away.

Composers often indicate changes in pitch and dynamic levels for expressive or emotional purposes. This is the case in Listening Example 1, the short but highly effective introductory section to *Also sprach Zarathustra,* by Richard Strauss. Strauss intended this expressive piece to depict the development of the superman envisioned by the philosopher Friedrich Nietzsche. Here the dramatic crescendo and corresponding rise in pitch level suggest the great heights of power to which the imagined hero might rise.

Summary

Sound constitutes the raw material of which music is composed. One characteristic of musical sound is its pitch, which is determined by the rate of the sound waves' vibration. A constant rate of vibration produces a specific pitch called a tone. Tones, represented by letter names, are notated on a staff, preceded by a clef sign indicating which tone is represented by each line and space.

    Expressive effects often are achieved by changes in the dynamic level (loudness or softness) of musical sounds.

Critical Thinking

The Critical Thinking questions at the end of each chapter are intended to stimulate your thinking and to help you recognize relationships between the arts and everyday life. There are no right or wrong answers to them, but you should be able to support whatever position you choose on each topic.

- How do our voices change in terms of pitch and dynamics when we are excited? Angry? Frightened?

- Can you suggest any examples of popular or concert music that evoke emotional responses by changes in pitch levels and/or dynamics?

pitch   The highness or lowness of a sound.

frequency   The rate of a sound wave's vibration.

dynamic level   Level of volume.

tone   A sound with specific pitch, produced by a constant rate of vibration of the sound-producing medium.

sharp   A sign (♯) that indicates that a tone is to be performed one-half step higher than notated.

flat   A sign (♭) that indicates that a tone is to be performed one-half step lower than notated.

staff   Five lines and four spaces upon which music is notated.

clef   A sign that fixes the tone represented by each line and space on the staff.

interval   The distance between two pitches.

octave   The interval of an eighth, as from C to C.

forte   Loud.

piano   Soft.

crescendo   Becoming louder.

decrescendo or **diminuendo**   Becoming softer.

2
Rhythm

Rhythm concerns the arrangement of long and short sounds in music. Since music is never static but continually moves in time, it always has rhythm—the earliest and most basic of the building materials, or **elements,** of music. We somehow feel rhythm "inside," and respond to it both physically and emotionally.

Music notation indicates proportionate note durations. For example, a half note (♩) is held twice as long as a quarter note (♩), just as $\frac{1}{2} = 2 \times \frac{1}{4}$. The *cessation* of musical sound is also notated, by the use of signs called **rests.** (See table 2.1.) However, rhythmic notation does not indicate the rate of speed, or **tempo,** at which a piece is to be performed.

Tempo

The nineteenth-century invention of the *metronome,* an instrument that may be set to sound regular beats within a wide range of fast and slow tempos, made it possible for composers to indicate tempo as exactly as they notate pitch. Many compositions also include verbal tempo indications, such as "fast" or "very slow," often expressed in the Italian terms shown in table 2.2. While metronome markings primarily interest musicians, verbal descriptions of each movement's tempo usually appear in printed concert programs and in liner notes accompanying cassettes and CDs, making familiarity with the most common terms useful to the interested listener.

Meter

Musical sounds vary in intensity as well as duration, some sounding strong and others weak; but while we may think of rhythm as the "pulse" of music, its **beats** do not always occur in such regular patterns as those of a healthy heart. Music in which strong and weak beats are not arranged into patterns may be compared with literary prose, as opposed to poetry. The rhythm of much early music, such as Gregorian chant (p. 59–61) and Renaissance choral music (p. 75–77), is often based on the

Table 2.1				Rhythmic Notation

This table assumes that the quarter note equals one beat. Any other note may equal one beat instead, and the other note values then change proportionately.

Notated Symbol	Name	Rest	Number of Beats per Note	Number of Notes Equal to 4 Beats
o	Whole note	▬	4	1
♩	half note	▬	2	2
♩	quarter note	𝄽	1	4
♪	eighth note	𝄾	½	8
♪	sixteenth note	𝄿	¼	16

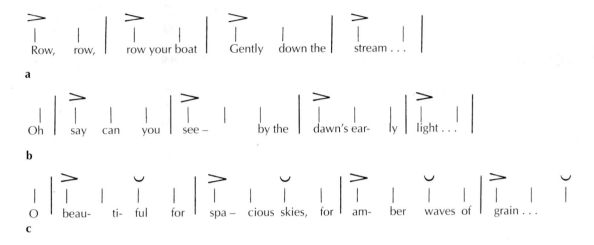

Figure 2.1

(a) Duple meter, two beats per measure. (b) Triple meter, three beats per measure.
(c) Quadruple meter, four beats per measure.

Table 2.2	Some Common Tempo Indications

Italian Term	English Meaning
largo	slow; "broad"
adagio	slow; "at ease"
andante	moderately slow; "walking" tempo
moderato	moderate
allegro	fast; cheerful
presto	very fast
vivace	lively
molto	very (allegro molto = very fast)
non troppo	not too much (allegro non troppo = not too fast)
con brio	with spirit

rhythm of the text as it would be spoken, rather than on a system or pattern of strong and weak beats.

In much music, especially that of the Western world, rhythm is **metered,** or organized into metrical patterns. Metered music is notated in units called **measures** (sometimes called **bars**), each containing a certain number of beats. A piece may begin on the first beat, or on or between any other beats of a measure. The duration of a tone may be worth more or less than a beat. For example, if you tap the beats of "America the Beautiful" as you sing the first phrase, you will notice that the second syllable of "beautiful" and of "spacious" come between taps or beats, and that the word "grain" is held for three beats.

The common or regular meters, or measured beat patterns, are **duple** (two beats to the measure, figure 2.1a), **triple** (three beats to the measure, figure 2.1b), and **quadruple** (four beats to the measure, figure 2.1c). Composers also sometimes use *irregular* meters, such as those containing five or seven beats per measure. They also may change meter during a piece or even during a section of a composition, or combine two or more meters at the same time.

1 4   # LISTENING EXAMPLE 2   1A 2

Syncopation

Composer: Scott Joplin (1868–1917)

Title: "Maple Leaf Rag"

Published: 1899

Rhythm: Duple meter; highly syncopated

Timbre: Piano

Form: A A B B A C C D D

4	0:00	**A—First strain**

The syncopated melody in the right hand is accompanied by steadily marching octaves and chords in the left.

0:19	0:19	**A—***repeat*
5	0:47	**B—Second strain**

Similar to the first section in style and melody, this strain begins at a higher level of pitch, which then steadily descends.

0:19	1:06	**B—***repeat*
6	1:23	**A—First strain** returns
7	1:41	**C—Third strain**

This strain, called the *trio*, is of a contrasting character, yet still syncopated.

0:19	2:00	**C—***repeat*
8	2:18	**D—Fourth strain**

Yet another melodic, and of course syncopated, rhythmic idea is presented.

0:19	2:37	**D—***repeat*

Accent

Stressed beats, or **accents,** occur in music as they do in spoken language, varying the intensity with which sounds are produced. Accents may be achieved, or implied, in at least three ways: by *stress* (striking a note harder or playing or singing it louder than adjacent tones); by *duration* (holding a tone longer than those around it); or by *position* (placing a tone significantly higher or lower than others).

It is the custom in most metered Western music to accent the first beat of each measure, as indicated by the symbol > in figures 2.1a, b, and c. (When there are more than three beats per measure, there is a secondary, or weaker, accent [∪] on another beat, as in figure 2c.) To achieve rhythmic variety, however, musicians sometimes place accents where they are not expected, achieving the rhythmic effect called **syncopation.**

This contradiction of the usual placement of strong and weak beats is a noteworthy characteristic of jazz, and of a precursor of jazz called **ragtime.** A **rag** (as a ragtime piece is called) is a piano piece in duple meter, composed of a number of sections, or **strains,** each of which is repeated at least once. The left hand of the pianist articulates the two beats per measure, with an accent on the first beat.

Meter	Accents	Conducting Pattern
Table 2.3		*Standard Conducting Patterns*
Duple: 2 beats per measure ("Row, row, row your boat")	STRONG-weak	
Triple: 3 beats per measure ("My country, 'tis of thee")	STRONG-weak-weak	
Quadruple: 4 beats per measure ("Yankee Doodle")	STRONG-weak-*strong*-weak	

Meanwhile, the right hand plays a syncopated melody, in which many accented notes occur *between* beats. (As you hear Listening Example 2, tap the beats and notice the accents that occur between taps.) It is this frequent "anticipation" of the beat that gives ragtime its distinctive style.

Conducting Patterns

The conductor of a performing group, or *ensemble,* such as a chorus, band, or orchestra, bears many responsibilities and has ultimate control over a performance. Besides directing entrances and cutoffs and establishing tempos, the conductor indicates accents, crescendo and decrescendo, and many subtle changes in musical expression.

Following standard conducting patterns, such as those of the regular meters shown in table 2.3, the conductor indicates the first beat of each measure, normally the strongest, by bringing the arm down; thus, the first beat of a measure is called the **downbeat.** The conductor indicates the last beat of a measure, usually the weakest, by raising the arm in an **upbeat,** bringing it into position to give the downbeat of the next measure. While professional conductors often modify these basic patterns, they remain recognizable to the performers following the conductor's direction, and to experienced concertgoers.

Summary

Rhythm, which organizes time in music, may be free and flexible, based upon the inflections of a text, or organized into metered patterns. In metered music, each measure contains a pattern of strong and weak beats, the strongest accent normally occurring on the first beat of the measure. Composers sometimes syncopate rhythm by accenting normally weak beats.

Metronome markings, and/or verbal tempo indications, often expressed in Italian terms, give the speed at which a piece should be performed. Using standardized conducting patterns, a conductor controls the tempo of an ensemble performance, as well as the metrical patterns, various changes in expression, and any unusual accents.

Critical Thinking

- Can you suggest functions of everyday life that involve measured rhythm? (Two examples are walking and breathing.) Besides talking, which of our everyday experiences involve nonmeasured rhythm?

- What examples of rhythm (measured or free) are found in nature?

- How do artists achieve "rhythm" in their paintings?

Terms to Review

rhythm   The arrangement of time in music.

elements of music   The basic materials of which music is composed: rhythm, melody, harmony, timbre.

rest   A sign that indicates silence, or the cessation of musical sound.

tempo   Rate of speed at which a musical piece is performed.

beat   The basic rhythmic pulse of music.

metered music   The rhythm is organized into patterns of strong and weak beats.

duple meter   Two beats per measure.

triple meter   Three beats per measure.

quadruple meter   Four beats per measure.

measure (bar)   A unit containing a number of beats.

accent   A strong sound. Accents may be achieved by stress, duration, or position of a tone.

syncopation   The occurrence of accents in unexpected places.

ragtime   A popular piano style in which the syncopated melody in the right hand is accompanied by regular beats in the left hand.

rag   A piece in ragtime.

strain   A melodic section of a march or rag.

downbeat   The first beat of a measure.

upbeat   The last beat of a measure.

3 Melody

A **melody** is a succession of tones logically conceived so as to make musical sense. Just as words are arranged in a particular order to form a sentence, the tones of melodies, too, must be organized in order to be meaningful. Western music lovers particularly listen for melody in music, responding to a fine melody's sensuous appeal and indefinable power to stir emotions. Simple folk and popular tunes lighten our cares, and many of us find our lives immeasurably enriched by appreciation for the great melodies of the world.

As figure 3.1 indicates, a written melody forms a linear pattern on the music staff. We could, in fact, trace a melody's distinctive shape or contour by drawing a line on the page from note to note; indeed, we think of melody as horizontal, or linear, and often speak of a "melodic line." The pitches of some melodies, such as "Yankee Doodle" (figure 3.1a), lie close to one another on the staff; such melodies form a smooth, or stepwise, contour. In contrast, wide skips between the pitches in melodies such as "The Star Spangled Banner" (figure 3.1b), yield a melodic contour that is more angular, or disjunct.

A melody consists of one or more **phrases,** punctuated with stopping points called **cadences** that, like commas, semicolons, and periods, indicate varying degrees of pause or finality. The melody of "Row, Row, Row Your Boat," for example (figure 3.2a), consists of two unlike phrases (*a* and *b*), the first generally ascending and the second generally descending in pitch. For the chorus of "Jingle Bells" (figure 3.2b), which has four lines of text, the first phrase is repeated for the third line of text, and the second phrase is altered for the fourth line (*a b a b*). The melodic phrases of "Deck the Halls" (figure 3.2c) occur in the order *a a b a*. Perhaps you can think of other simple melodies and identify their phrase patterns using letters of the alphabet.

Examples of melodic **sequence,** or the repetition of a melodic phrase pattern at different levels of pitch, abound in all kinds of music. The second phrase of "Three Blind Mice" ("See how they run") is a repetition of the first melodic pattern at a higher level of pitch; the four-note pattern at the beginning of Beethoven's Symphony no. 5 (*da-da-da-DUM*) is repeated at a lower pitch level; and the phrase "Land where my fathers died" in "America" is succeeded by "Land of the pilgrim's pride," sung to the same melodic pattern at a lower level of pitch.

Figure 3.1

(a) "Yankee Doodle," a conjunct melody line.
(b) "The Star Spangled Banner," a disjunct melody line.

Figure 3.2

Three ways of setting simple texts to music.

a   Row, row, row your boat gently down the stream.

b   Merrily, merrily, merrily, merrily, life is but a dream.

(a)

a   Jingle bells, jingle bells, jingle all the way.

b   Oh what fun it is to ride in a one-horse open sleigh.

a   Jingle bells, jingle bells, jingle all the way.

b   Oh what fun it is to ride in a one-horse open sleigh.

(b)

a   Deck the halls with boughs of holly, fa la la la la, la la la la

a   'Tis the season to be jolly, fa la la la la la, la la la la

b   Don we now our gay apparel, fa la la, la la la, la la la la

a   Troll the ancient yuletide carol, fa la la la la la, la la la la

(c)

Figure 3.3

Motivic principal theme of Beethoven's Symphony no. 5.

Melodic Types

While all melodies share certain characteristics, each is distinguished by its particular rhythmic patterns, phrase structure, contour, and other characteristic qualities, which combine to form a wide variety of melodic types. For example, we sometimes refer to a melody that seems complete in itself, and is easily remembered and sung, as a **tune.** Folk and popular songs are generally tuneful, as are also some famous melodies from great symphonies, operas, and other serious works. A tuneful melody may consist of any number of phrases, and its contour may be either smooth or disjunct.

A **theme** is a melody—tuneful or not—that recurs throughout a piece in its original form or in altered forms. For example, consider the manner in which the musical theme of a movie is changed to suit the moods or situations of the film.

A **motive,** or **motivic melody,** is a short melodic phrase that sounds fragmentary or incomplete in itself, but is suitable for many kinds of variation and development. The most famous example is the four-note motive beginning Beethoven's Symphony no. 5 (figure 3.3). These four tones hardly constitute a tune, and they seem too fragmentary to be called a theme; yet Beethoven found in them the rich source of much of the melodic (and rhythmic) material of this famous symphony.

A **lyrical melody,** longer than a motive, is songlike in character. In a composition of some length, a lyrical melody is usually repeated, with or without variation, rather than developed in the intellectual manner of a motive. Some lyrical melodies are tuneful, while others are too long and complex to be considered tunes. The melodic lines of Samuel Barber's lovely *Adagio for Strings* (Listening Example 41) exemplify the concept of lyrical melody.

Scales

Melodies are built upon the tones of a series or pattern of pitches, within the range of an octave, called a **scale.** The word *scale* is derived from the Italian word for "staircase," and a scale, like a staircase, is an ascending or descending pattern of *steps.*

A **half step** is the distance from any note on a keyboard to its nearest neighbor in either direction, and the smallest interval traditionally used in Western music. Two half steps comprise one **whole step,** just as 2 x 1/2 = 1 (figure 3.4). The number of possible scale patterns, defined according to the number and pattern of their half and/or whole steps, is virtually unlimited.

Major and Minor Scales

The two scales most commonly used in Western music—the *major* and *minor* scales—each contain five whole and two half steps, arranged in particular order. The ascending pattern of steps in the **major scale** is *whole, whole, half, whole, whole, whole, half* (see figure 3.5). That is, starting anywhere on a keyboard, you may play a major scale by following that particular pattern of steps. The tones of most melodies do not occur in the same order as the scale on which they are based. However, "Joy to the World" begins with a descending major scale, and "Do, Re, Mi" from *The Sound of Music* describes the ascending version of the scale. (The syllables *do, re, mi, fa, sol, la,* and *ti* heard in that song refer to the seven notes of the major scale.)

The ascending **minor scale** pattern of steps is as follows: *whole, half, whole, whole, half, whole, whole* (see figure 3.6). The Civil War song "When Johnny Comes Marching Home Again" is based upon the minor scale.

The most significant difference between the major and minor scales is the third step, which is a *whole step* in the major scale and a *half step* in the minor scale. The words "Johnny comes marching home" in the first phrase of that song are sung to the

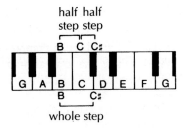

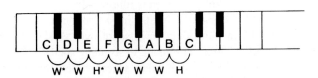

*Whole steps   *Half steps

Figure 3.4

Keyboard showing half steps and whole steps.

Figure 3.5

The white notes of the octave from C to C on the keyboard correspond to the pattern of the major scale.

Figure 3.6

The white notes of the octave from A to A on the keyboard correspond to the pattern of the minor scale.

Figure 3.7

The chromatic scale consists of twelve half steps.

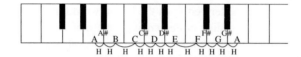

first three pitches of the minor scale, while "Doe, a deer" from the song "Do, Re, Mi" are sung to the first three pitches of the major scale. Try singing the word "home" (from "Johnny") a half step higher, or the word "deer" (from "Do, Re, Mi") a half step lower, to hear how much the particular scale affects the sound of the music.

Tonic Note

The first and last note of either the major or the minor scale is called the **tonic.** Thus, C is the tonic note of the major or minor scale that begins and ends on C. The tonic note of the scale upon which a composition is based is also the name of the **key** in which that piece is composed. In other words, a piece that is based upon the C major scale is said to be in the key of C major.

The tonic usually is heard more often than any other note in a composition based on the major or minor scale, and as you play or sing up or down either scale, you will feel a kind of magnetic pull to the tonic. For this reason, major and minor melodies, like the scales they are based upon, sound incomplete until the tonic note is sounded. To illustrate this, try singing the last phrase of "Row, Row, Row Your Boat," omitting the last note.

Chromatic Scale

While the major and minor scales are most familiar to Western ears, much music, popular and classical, is based on other scales instead. The **chromatic scale** (see figure 3.7), composed entirely of *half steps,* often lends a poignant emotional effect to music. We can hear this in Listening Example 3, an *aria,* or song, from the opera *Samson and Delilah,* by the French composer Camille Saint-Saëns. The beautiful Delilah sings this seductive aria to weaken the moral defenses of Samson, leader of the enemies of her people. She intends to trick him into confiding the secret of his superhuman strength.

The aria is in **strophic form,** the most common song form, in which two or more verses of text are set to the same music. The repetition of music gives strophic form symmetry, or balance, while the new text of each verse provides variety. Sometimes each verse of a song in strophic form is followed by a **refrain,** a recurring section of text and melody that often becomes the most familiar part of a song.

Listening Example 3 includes only the first (of two) verses and the famous refrain, which begins with a highly chromatic descending melodic line (to the words "Ah! réponds à ma tendresse!"), delicately accompanied by the harp and other strings. Soaring to a dramatic climax, this ardent expression of Delilah's love and longing moves Samson to passionate declarations of his love for her.

LISTENING EXAMPLE 3

Chromatic Melody

Composer: Camille Saint-Saëns (1835–1921)   *sanh-sahns´*

Title: "My heart opens to your voice," from *Samson and Delilah*

Composed: 1877

Melody: Chromatic

Form: Strophic aria

Timbre: Soprano voice with orchestra

	Dalila (Verse 1)	Dalilah	
9	0:00	*(The orchestra begins with a tender, throbbing accompaniment.)*	
0:05	0:05	Mon coeur s'ouvre à ta voix comme s'ouvrent les fleurs	My heart opens to your voice as the flowers open
. . . .		Aux baisers de l'aurore!	to dawn's kisses!
0:21	0:21	*(orchestra expressively echoes the melodic phrase)*	
0:26	0:26	Mais, o mon bien-aimé, pour mieux sécher mes pleurs,	But, o my beloved, the better to dry my tears,
. . . .		Que ta voix parle encore!	let your voice speak once more!
0:42	0:42	*(orchestra expressively echoes the melodic phrase)*	
. . . .		Dis-moi qu'à Dalila tu reviens pour jamais!	Tell me that you are coming back to Delilah for ever!
. . . .		Redis à ma tendresse	Remind me once again
. . . .		Les serments d'autrefois, ces serments que j'aimais!	of the promises of bygone days, those promises I loved!
. . . .		**(Refrain)**	
10	1:16	Ah! réponds, résponds à ma tendresse!	Ah! answer my tenderness,
. . .		*(a highly chromatic descending melodic line, accompanied by the harp and other strings)*	
. . .		Verse-moi, verse-moi l'ivresse!	fill me with ecstasy!
. . .		Réponds à ma tendresse,	Answer my tenderness,
. . .		Réponds à ma tendresse,	Answer my tenderness,
. . .		Verse-moi, verse-moi l'ivresse!	fill me with ecstasy!
1:03	2:19	*(Samson begins to sing in response.)*	

(see figure 3.8)

Whole-Tone Scale

The **whole-tone scale,** on the other hand, divides the octave into six *whole steps* (see figure 3.8). The absence of half steps, whose proximity to the next tone implies a "leading" or "leaning" toward it, gives whole-tone music a quality of "endlessness," which composers often exploit to achieve a dreamy, ethereal effect. In Listening Example 4, Claude Debussy depicts in musical terms a lazily relaxed scene of sails (*voiles*) on the water on a calm day.

Pentatonic Scale

While any five-note pattern within the range of an octave may be called a **pentatonic scale,** the particular pattern formed by playing the five black notes on a keyboard is a very popular scale upon which many simple melodies are based (see figure 3.9). The "gaps" occurring in these melodies, due to the step and a half between some tones, seem to lie comfortably in our voices and are characteristic of many folk tunes and children's songs. "Merrily We Roll Along," "Nobody Knows de Trouble I've Seen,"

1 [11]

LISTENING EXAMPLE 4

 1A 4

Whole-Tone Melody

Composer:	Claude Debussy (1862–1918)	*Deh-bū-see´*
Title:	"Voiles," from *Préludes,* Book 1	*Vwahl*
Composed:	1910	
Melody:	Based on the whole-tone scale	
Timbre:	Piano	

[11]	0:00	The falling melodic figure that begins the piece and recurs throughout is composed of a series of whole tones.	
1:28	1:28	Crescendo from *pp* to *ff* (perhaps a breeze passes by).	
2:06	2:06	Calm returns, as a high-pitched whole-tone melody is accompanied by repeated leaps from a low bass note to the octave lower. (Such a repeated accompanying pattern is called an *ostinato.*)	*ahs-tin-ah´-toh*
2:40	2:40	The piece ends quietly (*pp*) as the sails float off into the distance.	

Figure 3.8

The whole-tone scale consists of six whole steps.

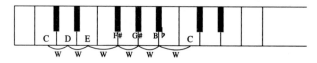

Figure 3.9

This pentatonic scale may be played, starting a half step higher, on black keys only.

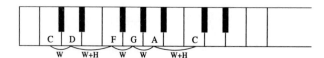

"Oh! Susanna," and "Old Folks at Home" are among the innumerable tunes that may be played entirely or for the most part using only the black notes on a keyboard.

Listening Suggestion

Just as it is not necessary to count beats to enjoy rhythm in music, neither must you necessarily analyze the scale on which a melody is based. Rather, as you expand your awareness of the materials of which music is made, you will probably find yourself noticing, with less effort as your experience increases, rhythmic, melodic, and other effects that enrich the pleasure of the prepared listner.

Summary

The meaningful succession of pitches we call "melody" provides the linear aspect of music. Melodies have distinctive outlines or contours, which may be conjunct (stepwise) or disjunct (with wide skips between tones) in shape. Tuneful melodies are easy to recognize and to sing. Fragmentary or motivic melodies offer rich potential for development. Lyrical melodies are songlike and seem relatively complete in themselves. A theme is a melody that recurs, in the same or in altered form, through-out a piece or a section of a piece of music. The scale upon which a melody is based affects the emotional as well as the aesthetic character of the music.

- Compare a melody you like with one you don't care for. How do they differ? What is pleasing to you about one of the melodies and unsatisfactory about the other?

- Why do some melodies sound sad and others sound happy?

- Why are some melodies easy to memorize and others difficult even to recognize when your hear them again?

melody A meaningful succession of pitches.

phrase A section of melody, comparable to a section or phrase of a sentence.

cadence A stopping point.

sequence A melodic phrase repeated at different levels of pitch.

tune A melody that is easy to recognize, memorize, and sing.

theme A melody that recurs throughout a section, a movement, or an entire composition.

motive, motivic melody A short melodic phrase that may be effectively developed.

lyrical melody A relatively long, songlike melody.

scale An ascending or descending pattern of half and/or whole steps.

half step The smallest interval on a keyboard.

whole step An interval equal to two half steps.

major scale The ascending pattern of steps as follows: whole, whole, half, whole, whole, whole, half.

minor scale The ascending pattern of steps as follows: whole, half, whole, whole, half, whole, whole.

tonic The first and most important note of the major or minor scale, to which all other notes in the scale bear a subordinate relationship. The tonic is represented by the Roman numeral I.

key The tonic note, and the major or minor scale, upon which a composition is based.

chromatic scale The twelve consecutive half steps within the range of an octave.

strophic form The most popular song form, which has two or more verses set to the same music.

refrain A section of melody and text that recurs at the end of each verse of a strophic song.

whole-tone scale The six consecutive whole steps within the range of an octave.

pentatonic scale A five-note scale.

4
Harmony

Two or more different tones sounded together produce **harmony** in music. It has been suggested that harmony is to music as *linear perspective*—the technique of intersecting lines on a flat surface so as to imply their convergence at a distant point—is to painting, since both harmony and perspective add "depth" to their respective arts. Supporting this analogy are the facts that linear perspective in painting and harmony in music both developed during the historical period known as the Renaissance, and that both are characteristically Western concepts of little significance in the art and music of other cultures.

Melody and harmony work closely together. A singer's melody is sometimes accompanied by instrumental harmony. One voice in a quartet sings the melody of a song while the other three voices "harmonize." While the crowd at a football game sings the national anthem, the band on the field plays both the melody and the harmonic accompaniment.

In everyday English, the word *harmony* implies a pleasant or desirable condition. However, in music, harmony has neither positive nor negative connotations; it refers simply and objectively to meaningful combinations of tones.

Consonance and Dissonance

In our everyday conversation, *dissonance* implies a negative or undesirable situation. But musicians use this term and its counterpart, *consonance,* with different connotations. When two or more tones are sounded simultaneously, the resulting harmony may be active, with a sense of tension or drive; in contrast, it may be *passive,* or at rest. In music, the active type of sound is considered **dissonant** in comparison with the passive sound, which is called **consonant.** Dissonant combinations provide interesting variety and sometimes a sense of tension and drive or direction in music, while consonant sounds resolve the tension created by preceding dissonances.

Consonance and dissonance are relative, rather than absolute, terms, meaningful only when used in comparison with each other. Both are essential components of Western harmony, and neither type of sound is inherently good or bad. The sound produced by any combination of intervals has elements of both consonance and dissonance. Some sounds are merely more dissonant, or less consonant, than others. The most consonant interval is the octave, since the close relationship of the frequencies of the two tones creates a very stable sound (see p. 7). Other intervals can be measured to determine their relative degrees of consonance or dissonance, but the standards by which sounds are labeled "consonant" and "dissonant" change through time; they also differ from culture to culture, and even from one individual to another.

Chords

A **chord** is a combination of three or more pitches sounded simultaneously and conceived as a meaningful whole. Just as random successive pitches do not constitute a

Figure 4.1

Triads on each note of the
C major scale.

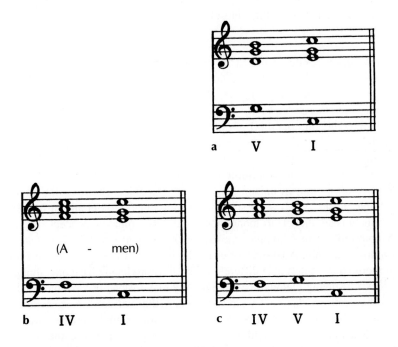

Figure 4.2

Cadence formulas. (a) V
(dominant) to I (tonic).
(b) IV (subdominant) to I.
(c) IV–V–I.

melody (or random successive words a sentence), so random combinations of pitches do not constitute chords.

Chords may be built of any combination of intervals, as twentieth-century composers have shown in their daringly innovative harmonic conceptions; however, Western harmony traditionally has built chords by combining a number of thirds. The chord most commonly found in traditional Western music, called a **triad,** consists of one third piled on top of another (see figure 4.1). Melodies often "outline" chords, implying appropriate accompanying harmonies: for example, the triad outlined by the first six notes of "The Star Spangled Banner" (figure 3.1b, p. 15) generally provides the harmonic accompaniment for that portion of the piece.

Tonality

The system of harmony prevalent in the West for the last three hundred years is called major/minor **tonality,** or the **tonal system.** The word *tonality* refers to the dominance of the tonic note over the other pitches in the major or the minor scale. Each note within the scale bears a specific relationship, distant or close, to the tonic, and each of the triads built upon the notes of the scale leads systematically away from or toward the tonic triad (represented by the Roman numeral I, as in figure 4.1).

The strongest relationship exists between the tonic triad and the triad built upon the fifth step of the scale, called the **dominant** (V). In the context of a composition, the dominant triad seems to lead or pull toward the tonic, and many compositions end with the harmonic cadence V–I (see figure 4.2a and c).

The next-closest chord to the tonic is the triad built upon the fourth, or **subdominant,** step of the scale, which provides a somewhat weaker sense of drive toward the tonic chord. The subdominant triad may resolve directly to tonic, as in the "Amen" at the end of a hymn, or it may lead through V to I (see figure 4.2b and c).

The I, IV, and V chords have particular importance not only at cadence points, but throughout traditional Western music. As demonstrated in simple accompaniment charts for guitar or piano, a musician can effectively accompany many melodies by using just these three closely related chords.

Texture

As a fabric maker combines threads to create material of a particular *texture,* a composer uses melody lines—singly, combined with one another, or accompanied by harmony—to create texture in music. Music **texture** is defined in terms of its predominantly *melodic* or *harmonic* conception. There are three basic textures—two primarily melodic, and the third primarily harmonic in concept. Remember to think of melodic "lines" as the "threads" of musical texture.

mah-nah´-fō-nee

A single, unaccompanied melodic line, whether sung or played on one or more musical instruments, is **monophonic** in texture. Gregorian chant (see Listening Example 5, p. 60.), sung in unison by an unaccompanied choir, is one example of monophonic music. A folk song sung by an individual without any instrumental accompaniment is another. Thus monophony is clearly a melodic concept.

poh-lih´-fō-nee

A composition that involves melody *in more than one line simultaneously* is **polyphonic** in texture. A **round,** for example, is a melody that may be performed by two or more voices entering at different times, thus producing harmony, though all of the voices are singing melody lines. Polyphony may instead involve the combination of melodies entirely different from each other: the well-known spirituals "Swing Low, Sweet Chariot" and "All Night, All Day," for example, create attractive harmonies when sung together. Although the combination of melodic lines in rounds or "partner songs" produces harmony, polyphony, like monophony, is primarily a melodic concept. That is, the harmony results from the combination of *melodies,* rather than from the addition of chords to one melody line.

hoh-mah´-fō-nee

On the other hand, a melody accompanied by other voices that are producing harmony, but are not primarily of melodic significance themselves, produces the texture called **homophony.** Hymns are usually accompanied by chords on a piano or organ; folk singers often play chords on an instrument to accompany themselves; a band provides harmonic accompaniment while the crowd sings "The Star Spangled Banner"; one section of a choir sings a melody with which the other voices harmonize. All of these are examples of homophonic texture, or homophony, in which a melody is accompanied by chordal harmony, a concept we consider essentially harmonic.

Listening Suggestion
The complex subject of texture includes a wealth of implications and stimulates controversy even among music experts. Polyphonic music, while melodically conceived, produces harmony, and primarily chordal or homophonic compositions often have melodic implications in more than one voice. To further complicate the situation, the term *texture* sometimes refers in a more general sense to the relative density or transparency of the musical sound. With experience, one learns to understand in what way the term is being used by its context.

The choir Gospel Inspirations perfoming in New Orleans. Choirs may sing in unison, but most choral music is homophonic or polyphonic in texture

Summary

Harmony is a sophisticated, and relatively late, development in the history of Western music. However, while barely implied, or purely incidental, in the music of most non-Western cultures today, harmony is an essential element of most Western music of the last five hundred years.

Harmony in music is accomplished by the simultaneous sounding of two or more different tones. Active, or dissonant, combinations work together with passive, or consonant, sounds to produce varied effects in Western music. A meaningful combination of three or more tones is called a chord, and the most basic chord is called a triad.

There are three textures in music: monophony (a single melody line with no harmony), polyphony (the result of the simultaneous combination of melodic lines), and homophony (a melody accompanied by chordal harmony). Such intellectual definitions, however, only point the way to discriminating, perceptive—indeed, creative—listening, which may lead individuals to analyze their hearing experiences in different terms. An understanding of these and other basic principles will enhance, but should not dominate, the art of listening.

Critical Thinking

- Do you recognize and can you describe relationships between the concepts of harmony in music and linear perspective in painting? Can you suggest reasons these may have more relevance to Western art than to the art of other cultures?

- Why do composers include dissonance in their music? Why do you think the proportion of dissonant to consonant sounds has steadily increased in music (popular and classical) through the ages?

- Can you think of any melodies (from popular, folk, religious, or concert music) that begin with the outline of a triad?

Terms to Review

harmony   The simultaneous sounding of two or more different tones.

dissonance   An active, unsettled sound.

consonance   A passive sound that seems to be "at rest."

chord   A meaningful (as opposed to a random) combination of three or more tones.

triad   A chord with three tones, consisting of two superimposed thirds.

tonality or **tonal system**   The system of harmony, based upon the major and minor scales, that has dominated Western music since the seventeenth century.

dominant (V)   The fifth note of the major or minor scale.

subdominant (IV)   The fourth note of the major or minor scale.

texture   The manner in which melodic lines are used in music.

monophonic texture (monophony)   One unaccompanied melodic line.

polyphonic texture (polyphony)   The simultaneous combination of two or more melodic lines.

round   A melody that may be performed by two or more voices entering at different times, producing meaningful harmony.

homophonic texture (homophony)   A melodic line accompanied by chordal harmony.

5 Timbre

tam´-breh

Timbre is the quality of sound characteristic of a particular voice, instrument, or ensemble. For example, although the range of pitches played by a flute is quite similar to the range of an oboe, the distinctive qualities of the sounds—the *timbres*—of the two instruments make one readily distinguishable from the other. Similarly, brass instruments, such as trumpets and trombones, produce a quality of sound quite unlike the sound of string instruments or woodwinds. It has been said that timbre is to music as color is to art, and indeed we sometimes speak of the "color" of a sound when referring to its distinctive timbre.

Timbre is largely determined by the shape of the sound waves produced by a voice or instrument. It is affected by the material an instrument is made of and by the manner in which it is played. Pitch, too, affects timbre: the highest notes on the piano, for example, have a different quality of sound from those at the lower end of the keyboard. In addition, the timbre of a particular tone may be affected by those that precede and follow it melodically, or by those that sound together with it harmonically. The range of "colors" in music is as broad as the range of colors in the visual arts and as great a source of interest and pleasure.

Many pieces are specifically intended for performance on one or more particular musical instruments. Some are meant to be sung, with or without instrumental accompaniment. Even so-called "nonmusical" sounds such as bird calls, train whistles, the whirr of machinery, or the patter of falling rain are sometimes recorded and used by composers in music compositions. Indeed, the diverse realm of timbre offers modern composers many resources from which to choose.

Vocal Timbres

Women's voices generally are classified as **soprano** (high range of pitches), **mezzo-soprano** (medium range), and **alto** or **contralto** (low range). (See table 5.1.) The voices differ not only in their ranges but also in their characteristic timbres, or qualities of sound. For example, a soprano's voice is often lighter and thinner than a contralto's, which may be comparatively full and rich, as well as lower in pitch. Even between singers with similar vocal ranges—two sopranos, for example—there are distinct differences in timbre.

Table 5.1	Classifications of the Singing Voice
Soprano	High female voice
Mezzo-Soprano	Medium-range female voice
Contralto (Alto)	Low female voice
Tenor	High male voice
Baritone	Medium-range male voice
Bass	Low male voice

base

Men's voices include **tenor** (high), **baritone** (medium), and **bass** (low); these terms refer to vocal timbre as well as to the range of pitches. Thus, a high baritone may sing in the tenor range, but with the richer, or "darker," quality characteristic of the baritone voice. In fact, any individual voice, whatever its range or category, has a distinctive quality of sound. Perhaps you have heard concerts performed by the celebrated "three tenors" (Luciano Pavarotti, Placido Domingo, and Richard Carreras) and have noticed the differences in their highly distinctive voices. Similarly, any vocal ensemble or combination of voices has a timbre that is unique.

Instruments of the Orchestra

The word *orchestra* refers to a large ensemble of instruments from different "families," as opposed to a small group consisting of all brass, woodwind, string, or percussion instruments. The members of a family of instruments share certain characteristics, such as the method by which they are played (bowed, plucked, blown, or struck). In some cases, they also resemble one another in timbre. As in any family, the members come in various shapes and sizes, and each has particular capabilities.

The orchestra familiar to Western music lovers, known as a **symphony orchestra,** includes members of all four of the instrument families named above, but is dominated by strings (see fig. 6.1).

String Instruments

vē-o´-lah
chel´-lo

The **string** family is represented in the orchestra by the *violin,* a rather small instrument that may be held comfortably under the chin; the *viola,* slightly larger, but also held under the chin; the *cello* (or *violoncello*), a large, heavy instrument propped on the floor in front of the seated player; and the *double bass,* or *string bass,* which is so large that the player must stand or lean against a high stool to play it. Each of these instruments usually is played with a bow drawn across the strings, although it may be plucked (a technique called **pizzicato**), strummed, or tapped with the wood of the bow for special effects.

The *harp,* another kind of string instrument sometimes included in an orchestra, is constructed differently from the other string instruments: its strings are perpendicular to the instrument rather than parallel to it. The strings are plucked rather than bowed. Each string on the harp produces one pitch, and several pedals at the base of the instrument enable the player to make the tones sharp or flat when necessary.

The string family includes many other instruments not normally included in an orchestra, such as the guitar, banjo, dulcimer, and ukelele.

Woodwinds

The **woodwind** family includes the tiny *piccolo,* the *flute,* the *oboe,* the *English horn,* the *clarinet,* and the *bassoon.* The piccolo and the flute are held horizontally; the player activates the column of air inside the instrument by blowing across a hole near one end. Each of the other woodwinds has in its mouthpiece one or two "reeds" (small, flexible pieces of material) that the player causes to vibrate, thus activating the column of air inside.

The *saxophone* is a reed instrument that comes in several sizes, classified, in the manner of singing voices, as soprano, alto, tenor, and bass. It traditionally has been utilized in the realm of popular music, especially jazz, but recently the saxophone has been included in some important modern orchestral literature.

Violin   Viola   Cello   Double bass

Orchestral string
instruments.

Brass
Instruments

The members of the **brass** family, also wind instruments, include the *trumpet,* the *trombone,* the *French horn,* and the *tuba,* as well as other instruments less frequently included in the symphony orchestra. The range of pitches is determined, of course, by the size of the instrument. The characteristic "brassy" timbre derives from the metal of which these instruments are made, the vibration of the player's lips on the mouthpiece, and the flared "bell" that all brass instruments have at one end.

Percussion
Instruments

tim´- pah-nē

The **percussion** section of the orchestra includes all of the instruments played either by shaking or rubbing the instrument, or by striking the instrument with an implement (such as a mallet or drumstick) or with another like instrument (as with *cymbals*). Some percussion instruments produce definite pitches; these include the *timpani* (kettledrums), the *chimes,* and mallet instruments such as the *xylophone.* The irregular vibrations of other percussion instruments, such as the *tambourine,* the *triangle, cymbals,* and *drums* (other than the timpani), produce sounds of indefinite pitch; that is, we cannot identify specific tones from their sound.

The modern harp is equipped with pedals with which the player may raise or lower the strings a half or whole step, enabling the harpist to play the instrument in any key.

Increased interest in both rhythm and timbre during the twentieth century has led to enormous expansion of the percussion section of the orchestra. In fact, members of the percussion family produce the widest variety of timbres within the orchestral ensemble. Instruments from other areas of the world, which used to be considered exotic and of no practical use for Western purposes, increasingly are included in performances of contemporary orchestral music. In addition, new instruments sometimes are invented for special effects as the demand arises. The crash of the cymbals, ring of the chimes, swish of the maracas, snap of the whip, and boom of the bass drum are only a few of the sounds produced by the percussion family.

Several attractive, famous, and readily available compositions effectively demonstrate the sounds of orchestral instruments. The best-known include Benjamin Britten's *A Young Person's Guide to the Orchestra* (Instructors' Supplemental CD1, track 81), and *Peter and the Wolf* by Sergei Prokofiev.

Saxophone

Piccolo

Flute

Oboe

English horn

Clarinet

Bassoon

Woodwinds.

Trumpet

French horn

Tuba

Trombone

Brass instruments.

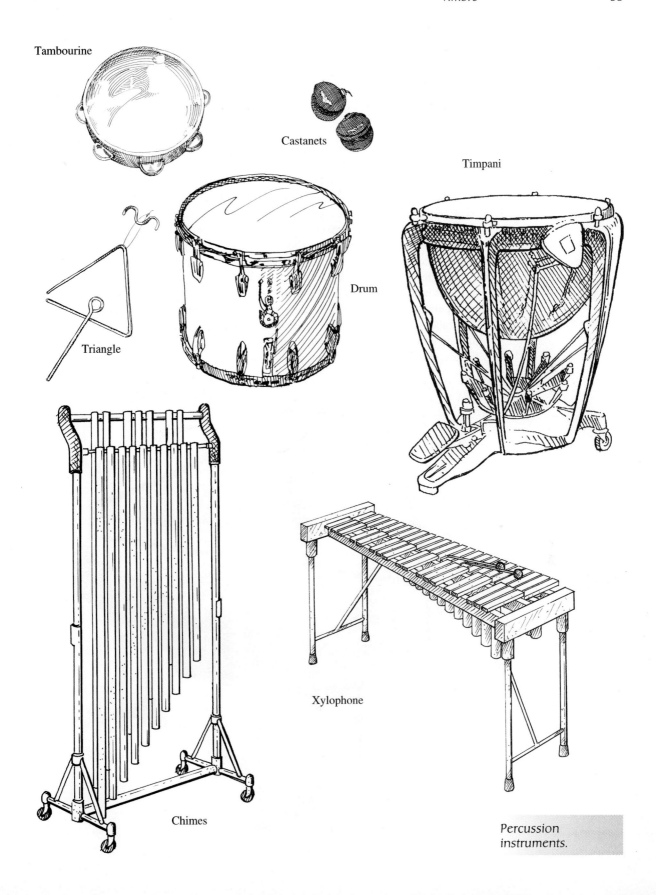

Tambourine

Castanets

Timpani

Triangle

Drum

Chimes

Xylophone

Percussion instruments.

Keyboard Instruments

A **keyboard instrument** is one that produces sound when the player presses keys on a keyboard. Keyboard instruments may be included in the orchestral ensemble, or featured as solo instruments playing together with the orchestra. They also are used to accompany voices or other instruments and, of course, to perform solo compositions.

Harpsichord

When the *harpsichord* player depresses a key, a small piece called a *plectrum* plucks one of the strings above the soundboard, causing the distinctive sound of the instrument; as soon as the key is released, a tiny piece of felt falls to stop the vibration of the string, causing the sound to cease. Thus, the tones of the harpsichord, unlike those of the piano or organ, cannot be sustained for more than a brief moment. However, the many embellishments characteristic of much harpsichord music help to connect one sound to the next. Though smaller and lighter than the piano, a good harpsichord has a great deal of resonance and produces a rich sound.

Of great importance during the sixteenth, seventeenth, and early eighteenth centuries as both a solo and an accompanying instrument, the harpsichord was eclipsed in popularity by the piano for nearly two hundred years. Recently, however, musicians and music lovers have rediscovered the beautiful timbre and charming style of harpsichord music, and today the instrument is becoming increasingly popular in homes, churches, and concert and recital halls.

An elaborately decorated harpsichord.

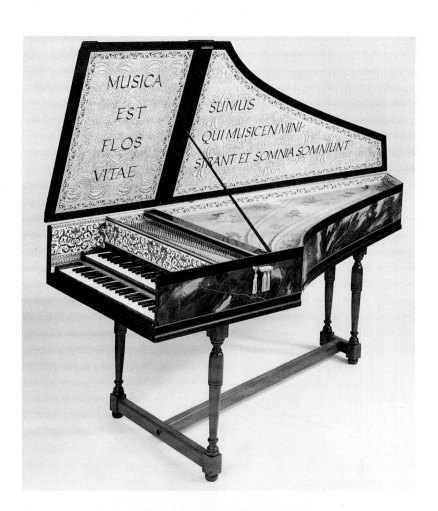

Piano

Although the sound of the *piano,* like that of the harpsichord, is produced by vibrating strings, the piano is technically a percussion instrument, since depressing its keys causes hammers inside the piano to strike the strings. An amazingly versatile instrument, the piano is capable of producing connected singing tones or bright, percussive sounds, according to the sensitive touch of the player. The two or three pedals on a piano enhance the pianist's ability to affect the sound produced. The damper pedal (on the right) allows the pianist to sustain tones (for a limited time) after the keys have been lifted, and the soft pedal (on the left) softens the dynamic level. If there is also a middle pedal, it sustains selected tones while others are released.

Pipe Organ

The *pipe organ* is a keyboard instrument whose tones are produced by wind. It consists of sets of pipes of various lengths and materials that are mechanically or electrically supplied with air. Unlike the sounds of the harpsichord or the piano, which fade more or less quickly, organ tones are sustained as long as a key or a pedal is depressed and air is passing through the corresponding pipe.

    The pipe organ, called the "king of instruments," presents a grand appearance as well as a glorious sound. The organ seen in Color Plate 1 replicates many found in the cold northern countries of Europe, where the brilliant colors of the musical instrument liven the atmosphere in a dark church. There may be as many as five keyboards (most organs have two or three), as well as a pedalboard, which is played, sometimes with great virtuosity, by the organist's feet. The organist adjusts levers, buttons, or handles called **stops** to change the timbre or the dynamic level of the sound by either "stopping" or releasing the air flow through particular pipes. (So dramatic is the effect of "pulling out all the stops" that this expression has entered our colloquial speech!) Other effects are achieved when the player moves from one keyboard to another, or uses the pedalboard. Many organs also have a *swell* pedal, which allows a gradual increase or decrease in dynamic level.

Electronic Instruments

The broad contribution of electronic techniques to contemporary music is one indication of the unprecedented significance of timbre to the modern composer. Many composers from the 1960s to the present have appreciated the immediacy and accuracy of performance and the variety of sounds that electronic instruments provide.

    The electronic piano and guitar are played much like the conventional (also called natural, or *acoustic*) versions of those instruments, though their timbres differ markedly from the acoustic instruments they represent. Electronic organs, also widely available today, resemble pipe organs in their appearance and method of performance. Technically, though, they are not organs at all, but electronic sound generators worthy of consideration as unique, rather than imitative, musical instruments. Much of the great organ literature can be performed effectively on them (although it will not sound the same as it does when played on a pipe organ). It is perhaps more significant that composers now are writing for the electronic instrument itself.

Electronic Synthesizer

The **electronic synthesizer** is an instrument that allows a composer to produce imitative, altered, or original sounds. When combined with the resources of the magnetic tape recorder and computer technology, the synthesizer provides a wide array of new composing techniques. Synthesizers were introduced in Germany about 1950, but it was nearly a decade before Americans had even limited access to synthesizers in their own country. Since that time, the technology has vastly improved, and synthesizers are now widely available for the composition and performance of both popular and art music.

Pitch, timbre, and virtually every other aspect of sound may be electronically controlled on the synthesizer. Parts of a sound may be filtered out, entirely altering the effect. The sound produced by traditional instruments, too, may be fed through microphones into the synthesizer and electronically altered. The synthesizer also can imitate the sounds of instruments, of voices, or of "natural" sounds such as thunder and rain. Pitches between scale steps can be sounded on the "fingerboard" of the synthesizer, unstopped by keys or frets. Composers sometimes use computers to aid them in creating on the synthesizer such complex effects as the complicated rhythms and extremely rapid tempos characteristic of some contemporary music.

Further, composers may, if they desire, record each step of their work for instant replay; this allows them to hear their work immediately, make any necessary changes, and preserve satisfactory results. Recording their own compositions also enables composers to bypass the interpretation of their work by someone else, eliminating the need for rehearsals and assuring an accurate presentation.

MIDI

Resources for the composition and performance of electronic music recently have been broadened considerably through the Musical Instrument Digital Interface, or **MIDI,** a remarkable system that enables composers to manage quantities of complex information and allows synthesizers, computers, sound modules, drum machines, and other electronic devices from many manufacturers to communicate with each other. MIDI-based systems were originally of interest only to composers of concert music; but today they are used to write and perform film scores, teach music theory, create rhythm tracks for rap music, and provide music for computer games. The number of ways in which the electronic synthesizer may serve composers, and the variety of timbres available for their exploration and use, seem limited now only by the boundaries of human initiative and perception.

Figure 5.1

A sophisticated electronic music workstation in Nashville. An important advance for professional musicians, the MIDI standard also has made it easy for anyone with a personal computer to explore the art of music composition.

Summary

Voices and instruments differ not only in the pitches they produce, but also in the quality, or "color," of their sound, which is called their timbre. Men's singing voices differ from women's; but even among men's or women's voices, the timbre of a high voice is significantly different from that of a low one.

Each of the four families of orchestral instruments—strings, woodwinds, brass, and percussion—is distinguished by characteristic timbres. The instruments within each family also vary in timbre as well as in range of pitch. The string instruments provide the backbone of the symphony orchestra; woodwinds and brass instruments add color to the orchestral sound, as do the percussion instruments, which also emphasize rhythmic effects.

The wide variety of sounds produced by traditional keyboard instruments is greatly expanded today by the availability of electronic instruments, including the versatile synthesizer. Sophisticated MIDI techniques afford today's composers even further resources for producing a virtually limitless array of varied timbres.

Critical Thinking

- Why do you suppose the word "color" is often used for "timbre" in music?

- How would you compare the "color" of a trumpet to that of a flute?

- Can you imagine the theme from "Star Wars" played by string instead of brass instruments?

Terms to Review

timbre   The characteristic quality of the sound of a voice or instrument.

soprano   High female singing voice.

mezzo-soprano   Medium-range female voice.

alto (contralto)   Low female voice.

tenor   High male voice.

baritone   Medium-range male voice.

bass   Low male voice.

symphony orchestra   An instrumental ensemble consisting of members of the four families of instruments, dominated by strings.

string instruments   Instruments that may be bowed, strummed, struck, or plucked. Orchestral string instruments include the violin, viola, cello, string bass (or double bass), and harp.

pizzicato   The technique of plucking string instruments.

woodwinds   Wind instruments, that include the piccolo, flute, oboe, English horn, clarinet, bassoon, and saxophone.

brass   Wind instruments that include the trumpet, trombone, French horn, and tuba.

percussion   All instruments that may be played by shaking, rubbing, or striking the instrument itself. These include the timpani (tuned kettledrums), other drums, chimes, tambourine, triangle, cymbals, and various mallet instruments, such as the xylophone.

keyboard instruments   Instruments on which sound is produced by pressing keys on a keyboard.

stops   Levers, handles, or buttons that allow an organist to change timbres at will.

electronic synthesizer   A highly versatile electronic sound generator capable of producing and altering an infinite variety of sounds.

MIDI   A system allowing composers to manage quantities of complex information, and making it possible for unrelated electronic devices to communicate with each other.

6
Attending Performances

Since we must hear music to experience it fully, no amount of reading or talking about music can substitute for our listening to it. Records, tapes, and compact discs allow repeated hearings of great music at a modest cost; they are invaluable for purposes of study, analysis, and enjoyment in the home.

Even more satisfying, however, is the experience of music in live performance, where *performers* and *listeners* actively complete the chain of events that a *composer* has begun. Both performing music and listening to music are highly subjective processes: One performer's technique differs from another's; the timbre of each fine musical instrument is unique; a tempo preferred by one conductor may seem too fast or too slow to someone else; each listener has favorite composers and pieces. Taste and experience influence dynamics, tempo, and emotional expression in a performance, as do the size of the concert hall, the climate, and other variable circumstances. Awareness on the part of performers and audience alike that they are sharing a once-in-a-lifetime experience heightens the excitement of a great concert.

On the other hand, attendance at live performances poses challenges easily avoided by simply listening to recorded music. Repeated exposure to the same recording of a piece affords a comfortable familiarity, as relaxed—even lazy—listening replaces the more demanding challenge of hearing something for the first time. Such listening also can dull the listener's objectivity, as the familiar interpretation becomes accepted as "correct." Listening to *different* recordings of the same work does encourage active listening, and awareness of the quality of the performance as well as that of the composition. However, even in this situation the listener plays only a passive role, whereas the listener at a live concert is an active participant who shares in the responsibilities and rewards of the performance. Therefore, concert attendance is the best way to experience great music. The hall may be a gymnasium or a high school auditorium; the performers may be gifted amateurs rather than well-known professionals; but the music will be *live,* and *you* will have had a part in making it.

Performance Procedures

The term **concert** usually refers to the "concerted" effort of a large group, while a **recital** is performed by a soloist or a small ensemble, often in a small chamber or hall. For any music performance, you should plan to arrive early, allowing yourself time to be seated, glance through the program, and absorb the atmosphere as audience and performers prepare for the event about to begin. The members of a band or an orchestra come onto the stage quite early, arrange their music on their stands, and "warm up" by practicing passages from the compositions they are about to perform. The resulting cacophony, as many instruments play different music at the same time, is a normal part of the preconcert atmosphere that adds to the pleasant feeling of expectancy.

Orchestral Performances

Shortly before an orchestral performance is to begin, the first violinist, who serves as the conductor's assistant and is known as the **concertmaster,** enters the stage, and the audience usually claps. The concertmaster calls the orchestra to attention and then gestures to the first oboist to play an A, the pitch to which the orchestra tunes. (If a keyboard instrument is included in the ensemble, however, the other instruments must tune to it, since the tuning of a piano or an organ cannot be quickly adjusted.) At the concertmaster's signal that the orchestra is in tune, the orchestra settles down and the conductor enters the stage, greeted by applause from the audience. The conductor bows, turns to face the orchestra, raises the baton, and begins the performance—often by playing the national anthem, for which the audience stands and may sing along.

Since the late eighteenth century, the instruments of the orchestra have been arranged on the stage much as they are today. The smaller strings, providing the dominant "color," or timbre, of the symphony orchestra, are seated across the front of the stage. Violins are usually to the conductor's left, violas toward the center, and cellos to the conductor's right, with the double basses lined up against the wall to the conductor's right. Members of the other three families of instruments are suitably placed where they will best enhance the overall sound of the ensemble. The woodwinds usually are behind the strings toward center stage, the brass are behind them, and percussion instruments are placed widely across the rear stage area. Research into early music performance practice and advanced studies in the science of sound, or *acoustics* (see p. 53), occasionally has led conductors to vary this basic seating pattern for practical and aesthetic reasons; figure 6.1 shows one of many possible alternative adaptations of this basic seating arrangement.

Figure 6.1
A symphony orchestra.

The size of the orchestra also varies according to the style of the music being performed. Eighteenth century orchestras were quite small, but during the nineteenth century, several new instruments were added to the ensemble, necessitating the addition of more violins and other "traditional" instruments for a balanced sound. A twentieth-century trend toward restraint and control of resources has led many composers to write for a smaller ensemble once more. Therefore, instrumentalists may enter or leave the stage between compositions, depending on the style of the next work to be performed.

Formal design, based upon principles of repetition and contrast, is essential to every art; *repetition* lends unity, symmetry, and balance to a work, while *contrast* provides variety. But music is unlike literature or the visual arts, whose forms may be analyzed in any order and at leisure; music poses the challenge of continuing relentlessly once its performance has begun. Of course, a student or scholar may examine the written **score,** as a music manuscript is called; however, the everyday listener must learn to memorize passages as they occur, so as to appreciate repetition and contrast throughout the performance.

We will discuss the important forms of orchestral music in detail in later chapters, but will introduce them briefly here to enhance your early orchestral concert experiences.

A **symphony** is an orchestral piece that has several sections, or **movements,** separated from one another by a brief pause but related to each other in much the same way as the acts of a play, the chapters of a novel, or the verses of a poem are related. The movements differ from one another in tempo, mood, thematic material, and sometimes key; however, a symphony is conceived as an integrated work, and a performance seldom is interrupted by applause between movements.

A **concerto,** also a multimovement work, represents a "concerted" effort between the orchestra and an instrumental soloist, who stands or sits at the front of the stage near the conductor. The solo instrument is named in the title of the work; thus a piece titled Violin Concerto is a multimovement compositon for orchestra and solo violin. A concerto contains some passages performed by the orchestra alone, others played by the soloist, and still others that the orchestra and the soloist perform together. The concerto soloist is not a member of the ensemble but a featured guest, whose name figures prominently in publicity for the program.

Program music is instrumental (as opposed to sung) music that is based upon a literary or extramusical subject; it purports to tell a story or describe a scene, an idea, or an event by solely instrumental means (since there is no text). Orchestral program music usually has a descriptive or literary title. In "Spring Symphony," for instance, the instruments might suggest the sounds of birds or a storm. But a piece titled "Romeo and Juliet," while still considered program music, probably would require an explanation in the concert program of the series of events depicted in the music.

The printed concert program gives the name of each piece to be performed and its composer. Further, the tempo, mood, or title of each movement of a multimovement work is indented under the title of the piece. (See figure 6.2.) A program of several pages sometimes includes information about the history and style of the music to be played, and about the performers' backgrounds and experience. It also often contains a description of any program music included in the concert.

Referring to the concert program in figure 6.2, you can already recognize some of the indented tempo markings (*andante, allegro, moderato*); and you might well

Orchestral Forms

arrive 10-15 min early

The Printed Program

Figure 6.2

The printed program. As in many orchestral performances, this concert began with a brief opening work, continued with a concerto with a featured soloist, and concluded with the performance of a symphony.

The Phoenix Symphony Orchestra

Theo Alcantara, Music Director and Principal Conductor

THE CLASSICS

April 20 & 21 — Phoenix Symphony Hall — 8:00 p.m.

Theo Alcantara, Conductor
Max Wexler, Violin
The Phoenix Symphony Orchestra

Rimsky-Korsakov	**Russian Easter Overture, Opus 36**
Prokofiev	**Violin Concerto No. 1, Opus 19 in D Major** Andantino Scherzo: Vivacissimo Moderato Mr. Wexler

INTERMISSION

Schumann	**Symphony No. 1, Opus 38, in B-Flat Major, "Spring"**
	   Andante—Allegro molto vivace
	   Larghetto
	   Scherzo
	   Allegro animato e grazioso

guess the meaning of others, such as *andantino* (a diminutive form of *andante*). The term **opus,** included in the title of all three pieces here, means "work," and refers to the chronological order in which a piece was written or published: that is, Opus 1 would indicate a composer's first major work. The work of certain composers is organized according to particular catalogue numbers: Mozart's music is identified by K numbers, J. S. Bach's by the catalogue initials BWV, and so on.

Band Performances

Many orchestral customs and procedures apply as well to symphonic **band** concerts, though the band sounds quite different from an orchestra, since it has few, if any, strings. To the traditional marching band, consisting of members of the woodwind, brass, and percussion families, the **concert** or **symphonic** band, which plays orchestral literature, often adds to its ensemble one or two string basses, occasionally a harp, and (very rarely) a cello.

The atmosphere at a band concert is often less formal than that at an orchestral performance, and there is less standardization of concert procedure. The symphonic band is an evolving medium, no longer confined to playing transcriptions of orchestral, keyboard, or vocal music, but gradually acquiring an expanding repertoire of its own. A typical performance includes some light or popular pieces (such as marches or **transcriptions** of popular or patriotic songs), as well as serious orchestral and band literature. When a transcription of a work is performed, the name of the individual who altered the original instrumentation to that of the band appears on the printed program after the name of the composer. For example, "J. S. Bach/William Smith" after the title of a composition indicates that Bach composed the music, and that Smith rendered it suitable for performance by a band.

Your live music experiences should, if possible, include many other kinds of performance; music theater, dance, choral concerts, jazz, chamber music, and solo recitals offer listening, visual, intellectual, and emotional delights. We will cover all of these forms in some detail as we pursue the adventure of exploring the wide and wonderful world of music.

You will find that the knowledge you gain about our Western music traditions will also enhance your encounters with the music of other cultures, which is becoming increasingly present and appreciated in the United States. An early such encounter might involve the music of India, for example; this has increasing influence upon both our popular and our classical music. The Musical Encounter with India in Part VI of this text indicates that the manner in which this rich music tradition considers such basic elements as melody and rhythm differs markedly from the way they are conceived in the West.

Other Performances

Alvin Ailey American Dance Theater in a 1992 production of District Storyville for the English National Opera.

Summary

The experience of attending live performances, essential to the understanding and appreciation of great music, is greatly enhanced by some familiarity with the basic concepts of various kinds of music. Symphony orchestras play symphonies, concertos, and various kinds of program music. Bands perform literature written for their unique sonorities, exclusive of string instruments, and occasionally play transcriptions of pieces written for other performance groups as well.

The printed concert program provides much of the information needed to follow the events of the concert. You are encouraged to apply the information you learn throughout this course as you become familiar with American and European concert customs and procedures, and if time and interest allow, to compare our music traditions with those of other cultures as well.

Critical Thinking

- In what ways do the members of a concert audience actually affect the performance?

- How might you prepare to become an active audience participant in an orchestral concert?

- Aside from the quality of the performance and the quality of the music being performed, what else would you consider in forming an opinion of a particular concert?

Terms to Review

concert   A term describing any music performance, but usually one by an orchestral, band, or choral ensemble.

recital   A performance by a soloist or small ensemble.

concertmaster   The conductor's assistant, who is also the orchestra's first, or principal, violinist.

score   The notated parts for all the voices and/or instruments of a music composition.

symphony   A multimovement orchestral form.

movement   A section of a large work, such as a symphony or concerto. *usually* **4**

concerto   A multimovement work for orchestra and an instrumental soloist.   *20-30 min*

program music   Instrumental music that purports to tell a story or describe a scene, idea, or event.

opus   "Work." An opus number indicates the chronological order in which a piece was composed or published.

band   An instrumental ensemble consisting of woodwind, brass, and percussion sections. A **concert** or **symphonic** band may include a few string instruments as well.

transcription   An arrangement of a piece so that it may be played by a different instrument or ensemble than that for which it was written.

PART TWO

Ancient Greece, the Middle Ages, the Renaissance

M usic reflects the social, economic, and religious climate in which it is conceived, as well as the personal inclinations and artistic ideals of its creator. Therefore, the music characteristic of one historical period differs in important respects from the music of another era. A study of music history reveals that during a given significant period of time there has been a consensus—or at least a sharing of artistic ideals—among the majority of important artists in the West. We refer to the manner in which this majority expressed themselves as the *style* of that period of art.

The style characteristic of the music of any period derives from the manner in which the elements of music were combined, from the approach to dynamics, form, and texture, and from the relative degree of consonance and dissonance that appealed to that time's discriminating ears. Other factors also influencing musical style include the purposes of music, the social and financial status of important composers of the time, nationalistic concerns, the character of the contemporary audience, and the available means of disseminating new music.

Certain dates with convenient round numbers are generally applied to the major stylistic periods, as follows:

Medieval period (or Middle Ages)	500–1450
Renaissance	1450–1600
Baroque	1600–1750
Classical period	1750–1820
Romantic period	1820–1900
Twentieth century	

Performers study style in an effort to learn something of a composer's expectations and of the manner in which music was performed during the era in which it was composed. Listeners, too, can best appreciate a composition and the quality of its performance if they understand the style in which it was conceived. We must listen to early music with expectations different from those we bring to more familiar styles. Listeners always have faced the challenge of adjusting to the new music of their day; our growth in knowledge and experience as listeners can in effect "stretch our ears" and lessen the shock of the new.

The music produced during the historical periods covered in Part II of this text predates the music most commonly recorded and heard in our concert halls today. We know little of how the music of ancient Greece sounded, although we have written descriptions of its concepts, which have much in common with our own understanding of music. The Renaissance, which experienced a profound "rebirth" of interest in the artistic ideals of ancient Greece, produced delightful dance pieces, a great body of sacred and secular songs, and some of the most glorious choral music the world has known. And the period falling between the ancient culture and its rebirth in the Renaissance, ignominiously dubbed the Middle Ages or Medieval period, achieved its own astonishing heights of beauty and innovation in all the arts.

7
The Music of Ancient Greece

Ancient Greece has been called the cradle of Western civilization, for many aspects of our culture were born and nurtured there. Though we are not often reminded of the Greeks' contributions to the music we enjoy today, they were in fact many and significant. Western musicians owe much to that early culture's theoretical and practical accomplishments, and share with it many important concepts that continue to shape the development of music in the Western world.

Having conquered Greece more than a century before the birth of Christ, Rome assimilated many of the theories and practices of Greek culture, disseminating them throughout the Roman Empire. When, in the fifth century C.E., Rome was finally overthrown and Europe plunged into a long period of turmoil and instability, artistic endeavor and appreciation necessarily declined as people struggled simply to survive. (Scholars increasingly replace the letters B.C. (for Before Christ) and A.D. (for Anno Domini, or Year of the Lord) with B.C.E. (Before the Common Era) or C.E., to avoid religious association or connotation in the dating of historical events.) From the tenth century on, however, the arts flourished once more, encouraged and supported by the Christian church. The fifteenth century experienced a strong resurgence of interest in the ancient Greek and Roman culture, as people turned to what they knew and believed about those civilizations for inspiration and instruction in the arts and humanities.

Ever since that time, relics of ancient art of all kinds have provided models to be studied and copied. Excavations of the Roman cities Pompeii and Herculaneum, begun in the eighteenth century and still in progress today, reveal yet further examples of the arts and artifacts of ancient Greece and Rome, which we continue to admire and emulate.

Few of these examples have to do with music, however; modern architects, sculptors, painters, poets, and dramatists avidly study ancient examples of their respective arts, but musicians are much less fortunate. Greek musicians often **improvised,** or simultaneously invented and performed their music, leaving no manuscript for later scholarly perusal. Even composed pieces sometimes were passed from master to pupil orally, as they are in some cultures today, rather than notated for future reference. Further, many written compositions were destroyed or simply allowed to disappear as the young Christian church zealously eradicated such vestiges of pagan influence. While several notated examples of ancient Greek music have been discovered, some of them quite recently, many are incomplete, or so worn with time they are difficult to decipher; and even when the notation is clear, music authorities differ in their interpretations of the ancient systems.

Thus, although we know a good deal *about* Greek music, we really do not know how the music actually sounded. It is one of the frustrations of modern times that all of our technological expertise has been incapable so far of restoring that lost art.

Pompeii street, paved with polygonal blocks of various shapes and sizes. The large cut stones crossing the road allowed people to cross without getting wet when rainwater flooded the road, while allowing the wheels of vehicles to pass through the spaces between the stones.
Halton Getty/Tone Stone Images.

Music in Greek Life

Music was included in the general education system, and constituted an important part of Greek drama and certain religious rites. Both Plato (427–347 B.C.E.) and his pupil Aristotle (384–322 B.C.E.) wrote profoundly about music, which they agreed had moral and ethical properties essential to the complete education of young scholars.

Musicians entertained social gatherings, accompanied outdoor athletic games, accompanied the recitation of poetry, and formed the chorus in dramatic presentations. Contemporary commentary indicates that the music of ancient Greece was generally monophonic in texture, consisting simply of a melody line sung and/or played upon music instruments; pictures show singers accompanying themselves with instruments that apparently doubled, and perhaps embellished, the melody line, but singing or playing in harmony seems not to have occurred. Instruments also may have provided introductions, interludes, and closing sections for vocal compositions. Detailed descriptions of Greek music instruments, such as those in figures 7.1 and 7.2, have supported attempts to reconstruct many of them, but we have few of the original instruments themselves.

The Greeks' Lasting Influence

The Greeks' aesthetic, scientific, and philosophical concepts concerning music, articulated in ancient articles, treatises, pictures, and reports of conversations, have profoundly influenced the history of Western music. The words we use for many music concepts, our systems for tuning musical instruments, our understanding of the science of sound, and our belief that music has the power to evoke emotional response and affect behavior, are part of the rich legacy we have inherited from the ancient Greeks.

Music and Words

Our modern music vocabulary reflects the influence of ancient Greece in such words as *melody, rhythm, harmony, orchestra, organ, symphony,* and *chorus,* all of which

Figure 7.1

"Alkaios and Sappho with Lyres," detail of red-figure vase, ca. 450 B.C.E. Glyptothek und Museum Antiker Kleinkunst, Munich. Standing as tall as her colleague, the poet Alkaios, Sappho is depicted as a poised and beautiful woman, fully the equal of a male poet-musician.

Antiken Sammlung Munich/Blow Up.

not only are Greek in origin, but express Greek concepts of the meaning and purpose of music. To the Greeks, the word **music** meant "the art of the Muses," the goddesses of all the arts, and had a much more general meaning than we ascribe to music today. That is, music as we understand it normally was combined in ancient Greece with other arts, especially drama, poetry, and dancing, the Muses presiding equally over all. A "musical" person was refined and well educated in a general sense.

In particular, the Greeks equated music and poetry, considering them nearly synonymous terms. The nature of the ideal relationship between words and music has intrigued musicians for centuries, and it is tantalizing to know that the Greeks believed they had achieved their perfect union. Did they truly accomplish this—and if so, how? Many composers, including some we will discuss in this text (Claudio Monteverdi in the seventeenth century, Christophe Willibald Gluck in the eighteenth, and Richard Wagner in the nineteenth) also strove to achieve the ideal marriage of words and music.

Stories and Myths

Ā-yu-re-DEE-chay

Greek mythology contains many delightful, and often thought-provoking, tales about the origin and purposes of music, which was thought to have been invented by the gods for their own pleasure. There are also stories about the invention of musical instruments. And many tales describe the overwhelming, even magical, powers of music. One tells of Orpheus, the half-mortal son of the god Apollo, who played a string instrument called the lyre (shown in figures 7.1 and 7.2) so divinely that even the rocks were moved by his music. The story of his pursuit of his young wife, Euridice into Hades, and of his efforts to bring her back from the realm of the dead, has been set to music many times.

Other Greek myths on many other subjects have inspired works of visual, literary, and musical art through the ages. One example is the story of Pygmalion, a gifted sculptor who brought his statue of a beautiful woman to life. This myth inspired a play by George Bernard Shaw that later became the hit Broadway musical *My Fair Lady*.

The Philosophy of Music

Ee-thos

The ancient Greeks had many theories about the philosophical nature of music, its place in the universe, its effect upon human behavior, and its proper use in society. They espoused the doctrine of **ethos** concerning the moral and ethical aspects of music: they believed that listening to particular kinds of music affected not only one's mood, but one's very self, for better or worse. They thought music capable of healing the sick and accomplishing other miraculous feats as well.

Western civilization no longer attributes magical properties to music, but the doctrine of ethos remains meaningful in a more general sense. Music therapists effectively relieve certain kinds of physical and emotional distress, for example. The doctrine of ethos has affected the development of religious music in particular. Believing, for example, that certain types of music caused undesirable effects, the early Christian church forbade performance of music surviving from the "pagan" Greek society. Such influential figures as St. Augustine, John Calvin, and Martin Luther expressed concern about the effects of music upon themselves and their congregations. Members of the sixteenth-century Council of Trent felt that some of the current music practices in the Roman Catholic Church detracted from the worship experience and from proposed reforms. The Puritans arriving in America in the early seventeenth century specified which type of music was proper for worship and which was suitable for entertainment only. Worshipers today, in Western and other cultures as well, usually both prescribe the qualities they desire in their religious music and proscribe the use of music they deem unsuitable.

Scientific Theories of Music

The Greeks left systematic descriptions of their theories of music composition. Pythagoras, who lived in the sixth century B.C.E., was the first individual we know to have made important discoveries concerning the scientific basis of music. He explored the science of sound—called **acoustics**—and of the tuning of musical instruments, and he measured intervals in terms of their relative consonance and dissonance. His demonstration that plucking two lengths of string, one twice as long as the other, produces tones an octave apart, and that plucking lengths of string in other simple ratios also produces significant intervals—the fifth (3:2), the fourth (4:3), and so on—provided the foundation upon which the Greeks based their theory of music.

Using the Pythagorean interval measurements, the Greeks developed a system of seven-note scales, or **modes,** whose names, at least, musicians refer to yet today. Medieval musicians, in fact, thought *their* modes related to those of the ancient Greeks, though certain misconceptions led to discrepancies between the ancient and Medieval systems. Close relationships do exist, however, between the ancient Greek modes and some Eastern scale systems, such as those of India, which are still in use today, and which recently have become of increasing significance to Western musicians. Indeed, much that was discovered and scientifically explained by the ancient Greeks remains valid and important to our understanding of the art of music today.

Classicism versus Romanticism in Art

Di-oh-NYE-sis
OW-los

Two important rival religious cults vied for approval in ancient Greece, and a particular style of music was associated with each. One sect was represented by the god Apollo, who, according to Greek mythology, played the "respectable" lyre and preferred music of a calm, orderly, and spiritually uplifting nature. The other musical god, Dionysus, played a rather raucous wind instrument called an *aulos* and promoted music suitable for drama, revelry, and competitive games. Both lyre and aulos are shown in figure 7.2.

It has become customary to refer to the first type of music—restrained, objective, and emphasizing form and balance—as **classical** in style, and to the other type—emotional, dramatic, and more concerned with expression than with balance or formal design—as **romantic.** Classicism and romanticism have alternately dominated artistic expression in Western culture until the twentieth century, which has produced significant works in both styles.

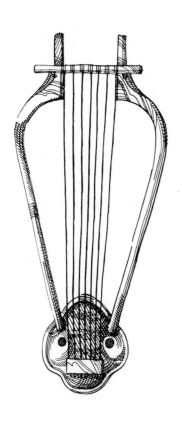

Figure 7.2

Ancient Greek
instruments: lyre (left),
and aulos (right).

Summary

Music was very important to the ancient Greeks, for whom it embodied broader concepts than we afford it today. Greek music, generally monophonic in texture, often was improvised at the time of performance. It involved voices or instruments or both.

The language of Western music is enriched by many derivations from Greek, and the Greek concept of the relationship between words and music remains of great interest to musicians today. While the doctrine of ethos is less significant now than it was in ancient times, elements of the basic concept remain of concern today. The ancient Greeks' research into the theories of music scales, the tuning of instruments, and the science of acoustics produced information that continues to be of value to modern musicians.

Finally, a comprehensive survey of the development of music in the Western world is inconceivable without reference to two terms rooted in ancient concepts: *classical* (suggesting objectivity and restraint) and *romantic* (suggesting intense emotionalism). These terms describe two basic approaches to art.

Critical Thinking

- How has the style of clothing changed within your lifetime? The style of cars? The style of popular music? Can you apply the terms *classical* and *romantic* to any of the styles you have mentioned?

- Why does popular music change in style more frequently than serious, or concert, music?

- Can you think of any ways other than those mentioned in the text in which the doctrine the Greeks called ethos is applied in modern society? (Consider movements to censor or ban certain recordings or art works, for example.)

- It is often said that Americans tend to have romantic personalities. Do you agree? Can you suggest specific examples of romantic behavior in American history? In contemporary American life?

- Do you consider yourself to be more a romantic or a classicist? Why?

Terms to Review

improvisation   The process of simultaneously composing and performing music.

music   In ancient Greece, "the art of the Muses," blending poetry, drama, and the visual arts with what we consider to be musical sounds.

ethos   The moral and ethical qualities of music.

acoustics   The science of sound.

modes   Seven-note scales within the range of an octave.

classical style   A restrained, objective style of art.

romantic style   An emotional, subjective style of art.

8
Medieval Music

Two important periods of Western *art* (sometimes called *concert,* or *serious*) music seem particularly challenging to the contemporary listener. One is the oldest music of which we have extensive knowledge, the music of the **Medieval period,** or the **Middle Ages.** The other (paradoxically) is the music of our own time.

Perhaps the most intimidating aspect of the music and art of the Middle Ages is that it occurred so long ago—between 500 and 1450 C.E. However, time is relative; people, after all, do not change a great deal in five hundred or even fifteen hundred years. Art, religion, entertainment, family, and the problems of war and peace were all part of life in the Middle Ages, as they are today, and composers, artists, and listeners of that time were people like ourselves, with problems and experiences similar to our own.

Then why was their music so different from that to which we are accustomed today? And what relevance can Medieval art have to our study of contemporary artistic styles?

As a matter of fact, relationships between the music of the Middle Ages and that of our own time form the very basis of the study of music appreciation, for Western art music has evolved in a logical way. Each age has taken what it could use from previous artistic styles and techniques and added characteristics that appealed to contemporary tastes. We recognize continuity from one age to the next, but over a long period of time significant changes in artistic style become apparent. Naturally, there have been many changes in the five centuries since the close of the Medieval period. Still, Western music developed from the music of the Middle Ages. Composers, performers, and listeners in our time are more interested in and attracted to the music of that early period than have been the music lovers of any period between then and now.

Historical Perspective

With the fall of Rome, Western Europe entered a chaotic period of social and political unrest. Religious and political differences between and within regions led to nearly constant warfare; long periods of drought followed by devastating floods caused widespread famine and disease; and material comforts were few, and unavailable to all but the noble classes. Despairing of hope for a better life on earth, the people of the Middle Ages put their faith in a blissful eternal life in Paradise.

Even during these long and dismal "Dark Ages," religious choirs expressed this faith in beautiful chanted melodies; and by the thirteenth century, magnificent works of painting, sculpture, architecture, and music appeared.

Artistic Style

The art of the Middle Ages was strongly affected by the mystic, fatalistic persuasion of the time. Medieval painted and sculpted figures, for example, appear weightless, or almost disembodied. One explanation for this is that the religious climate of the time precluded the scientific study of anatomy necessary for a realistic portrayal of

Figure 8.1

The cathedral at Reims,
France—an example of
Gothic architecture.

James Austin, Cambridge

the human figure; but a more important reason is that such mystic, ethereal represen-
tations of saints and martyrs suited the aesthetic and religious ideals of the period.

The visual arts of the Middle Ages were highly decorative and refined, their colors sensitively applied and details meticulously drawn. Beginning about the twelfth
century, churches in the architectural style called **Gothic** raised incredibly delicate
walls and towering spires toward heaven (see figure 8.1). The sculptures, frescoes,
and stained-glass windows of these late Medieval churches illustrated Bible stories
that could be "read" by people who were unable to read written words (see Color
Plate 2).

Most Medieval art, in fact, was based upon a religious subject, and served both
to enhance the worship experience and to instruct the illiterate faithful. In Simone
Martini's exquisite painting of the Annunciation (figure 8.2), in which a radiant
angel announces to the shrinking young Mary that she must prepare to become the
mother of Christ, we see the great beauty of line and decorative quality characteristic
of much Medieval art.

The people of the Middle Ages expected music, as well, to contribute to the expression of religious devotion and never to distract from it.

Figure 8.2

Annunciation, Simone Martini. **In this famous altar painting of 1333, a radiant angel announces to the young Mary that she is to be the mother of Christ.**

Art Resource, NY/Alinari, Florence

Early Christian Music

After the fall of Rome in the fifth century C.E., the Christian church became the only effective unifying force in the Western world, disseminating learning and culture throughout Europe. Yet the Church was responsible as well for the loss of much of our rich musical heritage. Christians suppressed performances of music addressed to Greek and Roman gods, struggling to focus people's minds entirely on the Christian deity. Only vocal music with a religious text was considered worthwhile, and many notated copies of purely instrumental early music were destroyed or simply allowed to disappear. A great deal of ancient music that had not been written down was lost as well, as the Church discouraged performances by those steeped in its practice.

Nevertheless, the earliest Christians had, after all, been Jews themselves in Roman society; the Christian culture was affected by ancient Jewish rites, as well as by those of the ancient Greeks, and by other Eastern influences. The daily prayer hours, singing of psalms in the worship service, and chanting of parts of the liturgy were all ancient customs that the Christian church carried over and adapted to its own purpose.

Modes

Medieval melodies were based upon modal scales (see p. 53), most of them relatively unfamiliar to most twentieth century listeners. You may play a **Medieval mode** by starting on any white note on the keyboard and playing up or down an octave, using white keys only. The different patterns of half and whole steps formed by the seven tones of each mode give the music based upon each a characteristic "flavor," or sound (just as we have already heard that music based on the *major* scale, or mode, sounds different from music that is *minor*). The particular modes beginning on A and on C (figures 3.6 and 3.5) came to be used more frequently than the others; in fact, these two modes eventually became, respectively, the minor and major scales of the tonal system.

Although the tonal system of harmony replaced the modal system as the predominant means of organizing Western music, composers in more recent periods often have used Medieval modes for refreshing variety in their music, for programmatic purposes (to suggest the era that introduced them), or simply in the search for something "different." The modes have been a particularly rich source of inspiration to rock musicians, who may or may not have known the history of the scales they have found so appealing.

Further Characteristics of Medieval Music

Medieval polyphony consisted of relatively independent melodic lines, intended to be heard in a *linear* rather than a *vertical,* or harmonic, fashion; that is, the sounds resulting from the combinations of melodic lines were not conceived as chords, and should not be heard as such. This **linear polyphony** challenges modern ears, which are accustomed to rich harmonies accompanying a single melody line, to hear independently two or more lines of music and to appreciate the effects of their simultaneous sounding.

The timbres attractive to Medieval ears were softer and more delicate than many of those to which we have become accustomed—including, for example, the rich sonorities of the symphony orchestra. The light timbres of this early music actually make it easier to follow the characteristic independent melodic lines.

Obviously, then, we must approach the music of the Middle Ages with expectations different from those we bring to the music of more recent periods. But because many contemporary composers are turning once again to modal scales and other Medieval concepts, an understanding of Medieval music has value not only for its own sake, but also as the source of insight into some of the most provocative styles of the twentieth century.

Gregorian Chant

One of the most pervasive religious practices around the world and through the centuries has been the chanting of religious texts to simple melodies, with rhythms replicating those of the text as it would be spoken. (For a brief discussion of Islamic chant, for example, see "Musical Encounter 3: Music of Islam," p. 322.) This type of singing, performed in **unison** (all of the voices singing the same melody at the same time) and **a cappella** (unaccompanied by instruments), is called **plainsong, plainchant,** or simply **chant.**

A great body of Christian chants eventually was collected, and in the sixth century C.E., Pope Gregory I organized and codified the chants for more convenient and systematic use by Christian churches throughout the Western world. Although Gregory's personal involvement in this important work is uncertain, this large collection of music has been called **Gregorian chant** ever since.

The melodies of Gregorian chant, based upon the Medieval modes, are commonly sung a cappella and in unison by men and boys, or by women in female religious institutions such as convents. The rhythm, like the rhythm of speech, is free and flexible. The text of a chant may be treated in a syllabic manner, with one note of music corresponding to each syllable of text. In such a **syllabic** chant, each of the *sih-la´-bik* syllables of a word ("alleluia," for example) has one note of music (see figure 8.3), and the rhythm is similar to that of the text as it would be spoken.

1 12

LISTENING EXAMPLE 5

 1A 5

ANONYMOUS

Title: Kyrie IV from "Cunctipotens Genitor"

Composed: Middle Ages

Genre: Chant

Rhythm: Free, flexible, unmetered

Texture: Monophonic

Timbre: Voices (in unison)

The melody, based upon a modal scale, is narrow in range and smooth in contour.

12	0:00	Kyrie eleison,	Lord have mercy upon us,
. . . .		*(heard three times)*	
0:45	0:45	Christe eleison,	Christ have mercy upon us,
. . . .		*(heard three times)*	
1:27	1:27	Kyrie eleison.	Lord have mercy upon us.
. . . .		*(heard three times; the third time, though, is varied and expanded)*	

Figure 8.3

Syllabic chant.

Al - le - lu - ia

Figure 8.4

Melismatic chant.

Al - - - - - - - - le - - - - - etc.

meh-lis-ma´-tik

    Listening Example 5 is a more florid type of chant, called **melismatic,** which sets one syllable of text to several notes (see figure 8.4). Such a setting, because of the manner in which it stretches the expression of a syllable of text, is appropriate for such a short text.

    It is paradoxical indeed that Gregorian chant, forming the very nucleus of our study of Western art music, represents almost the antithesis of art music itself; for the purpose of plainchant is to draw attention *away* from itself, to God. Its beauty lies in its strength, purity, and simplicity, and in the indefinable "religious" atmosphere it imparts. (Equally paradoxical is the commercial success of several recent recordings of Gregorian chants, beginning with one by the Benedictine Monks of Santo Domingo de Silo produced by Capital Records in 1994.)

Rise of Polyphony

During the ninth century, Christian monks began to vary the traditional performance of Gregorian chant by adding a line of melody parallel to the original chant, much as singers in some African and other non-Western cultures do today in informal music performance. (African music is discussed in "Musical Encounter 1" on pp. 314–317.)

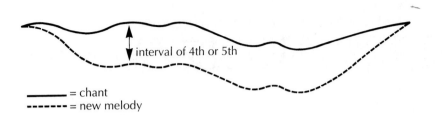

Figure 8.5
Parallel organum.

Eventually the monks combined more melodic lines with given chants, and the new melodies became increasingly independent of the original lines. When at least one entirely independent melody was combined with a plainchant, polyphony had been invented.

We can hardly exaggerate the importance of the development of the earliest form of polyphonic texture, called **organum** (figure 8.5). Non-Western cultures have shown only minimal interest in polyphony: melodic embellishments, **drone** or single-tone accompaniments, and the custom of singing parallel melody lines at various intervals hardly alter the essentially monophonic character of most non-Western music. On the other hand, polyphony is a basic characteristic of much music in the Western cultures.

or´-ga-num

By the thirteenth century, composers were adding more than one new voice above a plainchant, creating three- and four-voice compositions of rich and varied texture called **motets.** For these compositions, the original chant was organized into regular metric patterns and probably played on an instrument, and the new melodic lines were provided with texts to be sung.

Secular Music

More religious than secular music has survived from the Middle Ages, for secular songs of a popular nature were often improvised at the time of performance, and little of this music was written down. Besides, popular music tends to be short-lived. Even today, with our access to sheet music, records, and tapes, we have probably forgotten most of the popular songs of two decades ago.

However, the texts and music that do survive provide evidence of a strong and thriving Medieval secular tradition.

Song

Motets were composed for secular as well as religious purposes, and both types of texts were freely juxtaposed, for secular and religious concepts were not as clearly separated then as they are today. One composition might mix secular and religious texts, French and Latin languages, and unlike voices and instruments. Such a mixture, which strongly enhanced the independence of the melodic lines, appealed to the aesthetic ideals of that time, and lends a distinctive charm to the Medieval motet today.

A Medieval manuscript discovered early in the nineteenth century in a monastery in the Bavarian Alps contained the words to a number of songs written for entertainment by a group of wandering students and clerics. These youthful verses of wine, women, and satire reveal the Medieval propensity for unabashed frankness of speech, as they tell of love, the religious life, virtue, and vice in Latin, Low German, and a mixture of the two languages. Some songs are sad, others are bitter, and many are outrageously funny. Alternately tender and bawdy, they indicate the talent and wit of those early wandering musicians, as well as the probable cause of their academic and clerical displacement.

tru´-ba-dors
tru-vares´

Beginning at least in the twelfth century, certain French noblemen produced another kind of secular song. These were talented poets and composers who had accumulated the financial and social security allowing them to live a relatively gracious and leisurely life. Called **troubadours** in the south of France and **trouvères** in the north, they hired scribes to write down their songs, and resident entertainers called **minstrels** to perform them.

Troubadours, trouvères, and minstrels flourished in the twelfth and thirteenth centuries, their combined talents producing a wealth of delightful songs that survive in large number today. The texts, written in the flowery language of chivalry, often dealt with affairs of the heart, for marriage was a matter of social, political, and economic convenience, and people assumed that romantic love existed only outside of official alliances. Some of these poems are superficial while others are of literary quality, quite charming and expressive.

Other countries, too, had their secular song traditions of a popular or a more serious order. The art of the French troubadours and trouvères was emulated in Germany by noble poet-musicians called **Minnesinger;** Spain, Italy, and England also fostered traditions of monophonic secular songs throughout the Medieval (and Renaissance) periods.

The English Sound

The history of music in England has followed a curiously independent path. Even very early English art music shows a strong folk influence; it often sounds "major" or "minor," since much of it was based upon the Medieval modes that later would be adopted as the scales of the tonal system. Early English music has a fresh, youthful sound and a blended sonority not at all characteristic of the intellectually conceived Medieval French polyphony.

The melody lines of the twelfth- or thirteenth-century English piece "Sumer is icumen in" (Listening Example 6) form what we think of today as consonant harmonies. The piece is a **canon,** a polyphonic composition in which all of the voices perform the same melody, beginning at different times, to achieve attractive harmonies. "Sumer is icumen in" also may be called a *circular canon,* or round (see p. 24), since each voice, as it finishes the melody, may return to the beginning and start again without altering the meaningful harmonic combinations.

ahs-ti-nah´-to

As four voices sing this canon or round, they are accompanied by two other voices singing a repeated bass motive, or bass **ostinato** (see Listening Example 4, p. 20), to the words "Sing cuckoo."

Instrumental Music

Though Medieval musicians had access to a variety of musical instruments, little music was composed specifically for instrumental performance. Instruments often accompanied singers by doubling their melody lines, and perhaps provided preludes, interludes, and postludes for their songs as well. However, Medieval manuscripts did not specify particular instrumentation. The only purely instrumental music surviving from the Middle Ages comes in the form of various popular dances.

vee-ell´

The string family had the greatest variety of instruments, including the *vielle,* the most important string instrument of the twelfth and thirteenth centuries, and the ancestor of the Renaissance viol and the modern violin. All of these are bowed instruments on which the strings extend from a "neck" at one end over the body to a "bridge" at the other end. Other common string instruments included the harp and

sahl´-tur-y

the *psaltery,* whose strings, stretched from one end to the other on a simple body—often just a board or stick—were either plucked or struck.

LISTENING EXAMPLE 6

 1A 6

English Round

Composer: ANONYMOUS

Title: "Sumer is icumen in."

Composed: c.a. 1310

Genre: Secular song

Texture: Polyphonic. The combinations of melody lines produce consonant sounds with the effect of chordal harmony characteristic of early English music.

Timbre: Four-voice canon accompanied by a two-voice bass ostinato

Form: Circular canon

13	0:00	Sing cuccu nu, sing cuccu nu *(2-voice bass ostinato)*
0:05	0:05	Sumer is icumen in,
0:07	0:07	*Lhude sing cuccu,
0:09	0:09	*Groweth sed and bloweth med,
0:11	0:11	And *springth the wude nu;
. . . .		Sing cuccu;
. . . .		Awe bleteth after lamb, Lhouth after calve cu;
. . . .		Bulloc sterteth, bucke verteth, Murie sing cuccu,
. . . .		Cuccu, cuccu
. . . .		Wel singes thu cuccu, Ne swik thu naver nu.

Asterisks (*) are located where the second, third and fourth voices enter.

Early French harp.
Stock Montage, Inc., Chicago

Medieval wind instruments included flutes, *recorders* (which were end-blown, as today, through a whistle mouthpiece), and *shawms* (reed instruments related to the modern oboe). Each came in several sizes, covering a wide range of pitches.

A different kind of wind instrument was the *bagpipe,* a common folk instrument of the Middle Ages, as it still is in many parts of the world today. The bagpipe, which appeared in many forms and had several different names, consisted of one or more reed pipes attached to a windbag that supplied the pipes with air. At least one of the pipes was a drone (that is, capable of producing only one pitch), giving the instrument its characteristic whining timbre.

Brass instruments were used less frequently than strings and woodwinds, although trumpets and horns, deemed suitable for outdoor music, sometimes accompanied festive or military occasions. By the twelfth century, drums of several types and sizes marked the beat for singing and dancing.

Pipe organs, too, were important in the Medieval period. Aside from the full-sized organs found in many churches, two types of small portable organs performed secular music.

The Role of Women

Women of the noble classes were admired for their ability to sing and play instruments. Certain art works of the Medieval period portray women participating in informal music making in the home, or as minstrels or other professional performers of secular music.

Although women were excluded from singing in church congregations or choirs, in accordance with the apostle Paul's instruction that women should "keep silence in the church," women living in convents sang in their worship services, and some composed music for that purpose. In the twelfth century, the Abbess **Hildegard of Bingen** (1098–1179) developed a reputation as a composer of sacred song and chant in an age when most accomplishments of this nature were anonymous. She wrote both the texts and the music of her songs, and she was also an influential teacher and advisor on assorted subjects. Recent researchers have discovered generous quantities of her music, examples of which are readily available on CDs or cassettes.

The Ars Nova

While most changes in artistic style occur gradually over long periods of time, at the beginning of the fourteenth century a deliberate move toward modernity occurred, producing a conscious effort to write music in a new style. An essay entitled ***Ars Nova*** (*The New Method,* or *The New Way*), published early in the century, indicated awareness of and appreciation for the new approach to music. This title then was applied to the French-dominated style that characterized the music of the fourteenth century, replacing the ***ars antiqua,*** or Old Method, of the thirteenth century.

Historical Perspective

Fourteenth-century Europe witnessed social, political, religious, and artistic changes of many kinds, as increasing urbanization caused significant changes in taste and living style. Although still ruled by absolute monarchs, the common people now demanded a voice in social and political affairs. Secularization was growing as well, the power and influence of the Church, weakening as it struggled to settle internal dissent. Newly aware of inherent differences between sacred and secular concepts, people came to consider certain forms and styles of art better suited to one or the other.

Life in the fourteenth century continued to be difficult, dangerous, and generally brief; the French and English began what became the Hundred Years' War, and a recurring plague known as the Black Death eventually destroyed a third of the

Figure 8.6

Virgin Enthroned. Giotto, from the Church of Ognissanti. In Giotto's humanistic painting, the angels look with warmth and reverence directly at Mary, whose womanly figure is—for the first time in Western art—apparent beneath her graceful robes.

Art Resource, NY/Alinari, Florence

European population. Yet fourteenth-century Italy ushered in the **Age of Humanism,** characterized by a new respect for and faith in humankind. The arts gloriously reflected the new, optimistic, human-centered outlook.

Artistic Style

Romantic dramas, stories, and poems abounded, written in the flowery language of the age of **chivalry,** a period when various customs and conventions associated with knighthood affected many aspects of life and art. Chaucer's witty *Canterbury Tales* and Dante's epic poem *Divine Comedy* are important literary works of the fourteenth century. The outstanding painter of the period, an Italian named Giotto (ca. 1266–1337), abandoned the formal, flat, unrealistic approach of Medieval artists to represent people and objects in a new, more natural manner (figure 8.6). For the first time in Western art, painted figures were afforded a three-dimensional representation, appearing solid and real in their stylized settings.

Joh´-toh

Music

Music, too, became somewhat more expressive—that is, slightly more romantic—in the fourteenth century. As Giotto added *depth* to his paintings, composers were paying more attention to a seemingly related concept: the *vertical combinations* that resulted from the simultaneous sounding of two or more melodic lines. However, music was not yet governed by harmonic considerations but remained basically linear, with composers combining modal melodies in polyphonic compositions of increasing complexity and sophistication. Appreciation—that is, understanding and enjoyment—of the music of the *ars nova* depends upon the listener's ability to hear in a melodic rather than a chordal fashion.

Although proportionately more secular music was composed during the fourteenth century than in the earlier Middle Ages, one form of religious music became increasingly important at this time: the setting to polyphonic music of portions of the Roman Catholic Mass.

The Mass

The **Mass** is the main worship service of the Catholic church. Parts of the Mass change according to the seasons of the church year; for example, certain texts and responses are appropriate at Easter, and others at Christmastime. These variable portions of the Mass are called the **Proper,** since they are "proper," or appropriate, only at certain times.

Other sections of the service may be celebrated at any season or time of day, and these form the **Ordinary** of the Mass. There are five sections in the Ordinary: the *Kyrie* ("Lord have mercy upon us"), *Gloria* ("Glory be to God on high"), *Credo* ("I believe in one God"), *Sanctus* ("Holy, holy, holy"), and *Agnus Dei* ("Lamb of God, who takest away the sins of the world").

Although Greek was the original language of the words, or **liturgy,** of the Mass, Latin became the language of the Catholic church in the third century and remained so until the 1960s, with the exception of the *Kyrie,* which continued to be spoken or sung in Greek. Since 1965, the Mass has been celebrated in vernacular languages, although a small number of congregations continue to prefer the use of Church Latin. In any case, the text of the Mass has remained essentially unchanged since the Middle Ages.

Portions of the Proper and the Ordinary of the Mass often had been set to music before the fourteenth century, and various musical settings were chosen for performance in church regardless of any musical relationship among them. However, the first complete setting of the entire Ordinary of the Mass by one composer is thought to be the *Missa Notre Dame (Mass of Our Lady),* by a fourteenth-century poet and musician, **Guillaume de Machaut.**

Mah-sho´

Summary

Medieval musicians preserved what they could use of ancient music traditions. The early Christian church adopted the practice of chanting portions of the worship service, eventually acquiring a large collection of Gregorian chants, usually sung in unison with no instrumental accompaniment. Chants may be syllabic in style, with one note of music per syllable of text, or melismatic, with several notes per syllable.

In the thirteenth century, musicians created the motet by providing texts for two or three melody lines added above a plainchant. Musical instruments were varied and plentiful, but little music was composed specifically for instrumental performance. Vital secular music traditions evolved, however, as troubadours, trouvères, Minnesinger, and other talented amateurs produced a rich body of songs on the themes of noble or chivalric life.

Ars nova is the term applied to the prevalent style of music in fourteenth-century Europe, reflecting an increasing urbanization and secularization of society, as humanism replaced the mysticism and pessimism of the thirteenth century. Literature flourished, and the paintings of Giotto were more natural and realistic than those of any earlier time. Many composers set portions of the Mass to music, but Machaut was the first known composer to produce a complete polyphonic setting of the five parts of the Ordinary.

Critical Thinking

- It seems paradoxical that we are more comfortable today with the music of the seventeenth, eighteenth, and nineteenth centuries than with the music of either earlier or more recent times. Can you suggest some reasons why this is so?

- Can you suggest some effective means of developing familiarity with and understanding of very old and very modern music?

- The historian Barbara Tuchman titled her book about the fourteenth century *A Distant Mirror,* because she recognized many similarities between that era and ours. If you are interested in pursuing this idea, her book is an excellent and stimulating source.

Terms to Review

Medieval period or Middle Ages   The period from about 500 to 1450 C.E.

Gothic   Thirteenth century style of architecture, characterized by lofty spires and pointed arches.

Medieval modes   Seven-note scales modeled on, but differing somewhat from, those of the Greeks.

linear polyphony   Polyphonic music conceived without the intention that the combined melody lines should form chordal or harmonic combinations.

unison   Production of music by several voices or instruments at the same pitch, performed at the same or at different octaves.

a cappella   Unaccompanied group singing.

plainsong, plainchant, chant, Gregorian chant   Music to which portions of the Catholic service are sung. The texture is monophonic, the timbre that of unaccompanied voices.

syllabic chant   Chant with one note of music for each syllable of text.

melismatic chant   Chant with several notes of music for each syllable of text.

organum   The earliest form of polyphony.

drone   A sustained tone.

motet   A polyphonic vocal form, usually consisting of two melodic lines, each with its own text, above a plainchant melody.

troubadours, trouvères   Noble French poets and composers of art (as opposed to popular) songs.

minstrel   Traveling or resident entertainers and music performers.

Minnesinger   Noble poet-musicians of Medieval Germany.

canon   A polyphonic composition in which all of the voices perform the same melody, beginning at different times.

ostinato   A persistently repeated melodic and/or rhythmic pattern.

ars nova   The prevalent musical style of the fourteenth century.

ars antiqua   The musical style of the thirteenth century.

Age of Humanism   A period, characterized by a new optimism, that began in fourteenth-century Italy and spread throughout western Europe during the Renaissance.

chivalry   A Medieval code of customs and behavior associated with knighthood.

Mass   The Roman Catholic worship service.

> **Proper**   Portions of the Mass performed only at certain times.

> **Ordinary**   Portions of the Mass appropriate any time of the church year: the Kyrie, Gloria, Credo, Sanctus, and Agnus Dei.

liturgy   The words of the Mass.

Key Figures

Literary Figures	*Chaucer*
	Dante
Artists	*Giotto*
	Simone Martini
Composers	*Hildegard of Bingen*
	Machaut

9
The Renaissance: General Characteristics

The optimism and self-confidence already apparent among the late fourteenth century humanists increased and became more widespread during the next two hundred years. The people of the **Renaissance** sought to understand the world as it had never been understood before. Their curiosity led artists to dissect cadavers, explorers to travel around the world, clerics and laypeople to question the authority of the Church, and Leonardo da Vinci to question nearly everything. By 1450, music had joined the other arts by adopting the Renaissance style.

Reh-neh-sahns´

Lay-oh-nar´-doh da Vin´-chi

So numerous, prolific, and talented were the artists in every field during the period we call the Renaissance that we are tempted to think of this long and productive period as a historical phenomenon unique unto itself. But like every other stylistic period, the Renaissance developed from cultural seeds planted and roots strongly imbedded in the period that came before it.

Historical Perspective

The trend toward secularization begun during the *ars nova* became ever more apparent in the early fifteenth century; although the Church remained the most important patron of the arts, it was no longer the only one. Even works of art commissioned by popes during this period show a curious mixture of pagan and Christian influence; angels sometimes look like Roman figures of Victory, and cherubs resemble Cupid, the Roman god of love. Increased wealth accompanied by political and social stability allowed members of the nobility to commission works of art and financially support the artists of their choice. Whereas Medieval art was intended primarily to enhance the worship experience, citizens of the fifteenth century appreciated art for its own sake.

In the early fifteenth century, the Italian city of Florence became the center of business and cultural activity in Europe. The merchants and bankers of Florence represented a new class, freed from blind allegiance to the Church by the spirit of humanism, and from dependence upon temporal rulers by their own wealth. In response to its generous support of scholarship and the arts, the gifted from other nations flocked to Florence, which they found receptive to their talents and ideas. The invention of movable-type printing by Johannes Gutenberg in 1440 made possible the wide dissemination of many new concepts; soon the Renaissance spirit spread from Florence to the rest of Italy, and then to other European countries as well, causing profound changes in nearly every area of life.

As returning travelers introduced Western Europeans to many foreign luxuries, the desire for increased trade stimulated the search for navigable waterways around the world. Thus, during the fifteenth and sixteenth centuries, Spanish, Portuguese, and English adventurers sailed far and wide to establish new settlements, spread Christianity, and search for gold. Christopher Columbus, John Cabot, Amerigo Vespucci, Hernan Cortés, Vasco Núñez de Balboa, Francisco Pizarro, Ponce de León, and Ferdinand Magellan were all Renaissance men who discovered, explored, and settled new lands.

The Age of Humanism led to a civilization centered on human beings rather than on God, as people assumed responsibility for the state of affairs on earth. Faults within the Catholic church became increasingly apparent even to devout believers, and by the early sixteenth century conditions were ripe for the movement known as the Protestant Reformation.

The Reformation

The **Protestant Reformation** erupted in Germany in 1517 when Martin Luther, a modest German scholar and monk, dared to criticize the excesses and abuses he observed within his beloved Church. Luther brought to public attention 95 "theses," or articles of complaint, expressing his desire for reform within the Church, rather than rebellion against it. However, the Reformation gained unforeseen momentum and soon spread to other countries, dividing Western Christianity as it did so.

Luther believed that the repertoire of church songs should include some in the vernacular language as well as those sung in Latin, and he introduced a new kind of hymn, called a *chorale* (pp. 78–79). Several years later, in Switzerland, John Calvin established a Protestant (protesting) sect even more radical and further removed from Catholicism than Luther's. Music in the Calvinist service consisted *only* of unaccompanied psalm tunes (p. 79).

Hyu´-geh-noz

When the Roman church refused to grant King Henry VIII of England a divorce he passionately desired, the king declared Catholicism illegal in his country; in 1534, he established the Church of England. Soon other Protestant sects appeared in that country, too, while in France the Protestant Huguenots rapidly increased in number, despite vengeful persecution by Roman Catholics. Some Huguenots escaped from France to Holland, sowing the seeds of Protestantism there as well.

The Counter Reformation

As Protestantism spread in northern Europe, Italy remained staunchly Catholic; but by the middle of the sixteenth century, even Italian Catholics felt threatened by the strong Protestant movements. Many left the Roman church to join the new sects, and even faithful Catholics could not with impunity deny the need for reforms. A Catholic group known as the Council of Trent spent nearly twenty years (1545–1563) formulating recommendations for improvements in Church procedures. The movement they represented, called the **Counter Reformation,** was the Catholic response to the Protestant movement begun by Martin Luther. In the spirit of the Council's recommendations, the devout Catholic composer Palestrina (pp. 76–77) wrote serenely beautiful choral music indicating sensitivity to some of the criticisms of Catholic church music voiced by Protestants.

Artistic Style

By the late fourteenth century, artists and intellectuals were already experiencing a rebirth—a *renaissance*—of interest in the arts of ancient Greece and Rome. As many important works of antiquity were rediscovered, greatly admired, and widely copied, a deep appreciation, even glorification, of the human and the natural replaced the otherworldly mysticism and idealism of the Middle Ages. Painters and sculptors avidly studied human anatomy by dissecting corpses, and fifteenth-century artists painted the human body, often nude, not merely as a manifestation of God's goodness, but because the body was both natural and beautiful in itself.

Several new materials and techniques enhanced the natural, realistic, "representational" style of art preferred in the Renaissance. High-quality paints existed in a wide array of long-lasting colors. Painters mastered linear perspective and used it to achieve a "natural" effect in their work. Their landscape backgrounds and foregrounds reflect the Renaissance love of nature, and many paintings from this period fairly glow with natural light. Madonnas and saints, for whom attractive girls and handsome youths posed as models, appear warm and breathing in Renaissance paintings, in contrast to the characters in beautifully decorative but quite unrealistic Medieval art. We view this not as an *improvement,* in any sense, but simply as a change in artistic taste and style.

Mature Renaissance art is classically restrained and generally religious in nature, imparting a sense of serenity and repose. Emotional expression is carefully controlled and formal design of primary importance in the art of this amazingly productive period. Renaissance painters often used a pyramid design, placing the principal object near the center of the picture and balancing it with smaller figures to each side and slightly lower, as in Leonardo da Vinci's *Madonna of the Rocks* (see Color Plate 3). Raphael's famous *School of Athens* (figure 9.1), also balanced and symmetrical in design, illustrates the Renaissance interest in classical antiquity. Under the arch, Plato points to heaven and Aristotle to earth, indicating their respective concepts of the source of all human knowledge, while Socrates, Euclid, and Pythagoras discuss their various theories with rapt and reverent students. The viewer's eye is carried through the building to the distant sky rather than resting on a flat and decorative surface, as would be typical of the art of the Middle Ages. Classical columns, Grecian garb, and statues of Greek gods all testify to Raphael's ancient source of inspiration.

Rah-fay-el´

Figure 9.1

School of Athens, Raphael.

Art Resource, NY/Alinari, Florence

The great Italian painters Michelangelo, Leonardo, Raphael, Botticelli, and Bellini are only a few of the many Renaissance artists whose names are familiar—perhaps more familiar than those of any other artists of any period—to art lovers all over the world. The northern countries, too, produced a wealth of extraordinary artists during the fifteenth and sixteenth centuries, but by the end of the Renaissance, Italy was the acknowledged center of artistic activity. Women, who seldom received instruction in arts other than music and needlework, are little represented among the artists of this period; but one woman, Sofonisba Anguissola (ca. 1535–1625), whose well-to-do father made the unusual decision to educate his six daughters as well as his son, produced outstanding portraits, religious paintings, and scenes from everyday life.

Architecture

Buildings of the period also exhibit Renaissance repose: their graceful columns support without obtruding, and their façades are calm and smooth. Clear windows rather than stained glass allow restful natural light to fill the interiors.

In line with the increasing secularization of the period, Renaissance architects devoted as much time and talent to palaces, public buildings, and private residences as to places of worship. Rooms for living and working in were beautifully decorated and made as comfortable as the facilities of the day allowed; for whereas Gothic thought and architecture had been aimed toward heaven, the new style was meant to enhance the comfort of human life.

Sculpture

Mē-kel-ahn´-je-lo

Appreciation for the beauty of the human form, along with the newly acquired knowledge of anatomy, led to great interest in sculpture during the Renaissance. The greatest sculptor of the period was Michelangelo (1475–1564), whose *David* (figure 9.2) is a handsome, muscular youth, poised and lifelike. Typical of the period is the boy's careful contemplation of his proposed action, which he will not undertake without due reason and consideration.

Figure 9.2

David, Michelangelo.

Art Resource, NY/Alinari, Florence

The renaissance of art and literature began in Italy, but the renaissance of music began in the part of Europe that today includes Belgium and parts of Holland and northern France, variously referred to in that early period as the **Netherlands,** or **Flanders.** By 1450 a great pool of talent existed in that northern region, where artists of various nationalities enjoyed the generous patronage of the wealthy Burgundian (French) dukes.

Music

For nearly a century after that time, most of the important music positions in Europe were held by Netherlanders (Flemish) lured from their home by offers of generous wages and prestigious positions. Their northern style, which they composed, performed, and taught in the regions they visited, became the norm of Western music for the first hundred years of the Renaissance. The variety of religious and secular vocal and instrumental music produced during this fertile period offers a rich source of entertainment and inspiration for today's listeners.

Most Renaissance music, like most Renaissance art, was religious in nature, and most was conceived for vocal performance. Renaissance musicians generally preferred the homogeneous sound of a cappella, or unaccompanied, choral singing, although one or more voice lines might be doubled with an instrument on occasion.

Timbre

So prevalent and so magnificent was polyphonic music that this period is known as the **Golden Age of Polyphony.** However, the sound preferred by Renaissance musicians was quite different from the three independent melodic lines typical of Medieval linear polyphony. Sometimes a predominant melody in the highest (soprano) voice was supported by the other, less prominent, melody lines; but more frequently, all of the voices shared similar melodic material and were of equal importance.

Texture

Eventually, the lowest (bass) voice assumed more and more responsibility for supporting the harmonies above, clearly intimating an imminent change of style.

Though melodies composed during the Renaissance were modal in concept, composers and/or performers often altered pitches to imply the increasingly preferred "major" or "minor" sounds. The system of major/minor tonality was not actually formed until the seventeenth century, but Renaissance ears gradually became accustomed to some of its sounds.

Renaissance Modes

Summary

The Protestant Reformation was a movement critical of certain practices, including some concerning music, within the Roman Catholic church. The Catholic response, or Counter Reformation, included recommendations for specific changes in the use of music in the Church.

In the early fifteenth century, as the trend toward secularization increased, art began to be appreciated for its own sake, as well as for its worship-enhancing properties. Paintings and sculpted figures appeared more natural than they had in earlier works, and buildings were designed to be comfortable as well as beautiful. There was also a strong rebirth, or "renaissance," of interest in the classical arts of ancient Greece and Rome.

Although musicians had no Greek and Roman models to imitate, they sought to emulate the ideals of the ancient periods as they understood them. Their music, predominantly polyphonic in texture, was based on modal scales, though "major" and "minor" sounds became more and more characteristic as the Renaissance continued.

Critical Thinking

- In your opinion, was the Renaissance appreciation and emulation of the arts of ancient Greece and Rome a progressive or a reactionary phenomenon?

Terms to Review

Renaissance   The term, meaning "rebirth," refers to the period of renewed interest in the classical arts of ancient Greece and Rome. The Renaissance began in the early part of the fifteenth century and dominated the style of Western music from 1450 to 1600.

Protestant Reformation   A protest movement, led by Martin Luther, against certain tenets of the Catholic church.

Counter Reformation   The Catholic response to the Protestant Reformation; it proposed certain reforms, including some related to church music.

Netherlands, Flanders   Area of northern Europe where the musical Renaissance began.

Golden Age of Polyphony   Term for the Renaissance, when polyphonic texture was prevalent and particularly beautiful.

Key Figures

Inventor	*Johannes Gutenberg*
Religious Leaders	*Martin Luther*
	John Calvin
Artists	*Michelangelo Buonarroti*
	Sandro Botticelli
	Leonardo da Vinci
	Raphael (Raffaello Sanzio)
	Giovanni Bellini

Plate 1

Historically inspired new mechanical-action organ built for
Arizona State University by Paul Fritts and Co. Organ Builders,
Tacoma, Washington.

Paul Fritts, Tacoma WA

Plate 2

South Rose window, Chartres cathedral.
Christ sits enthroned at the center,
surrounded by angels and the four beasts
of the Apocalypse, with twenty-four
Elders (of the Apocalypse) in the outer
circles. The reference is to the Book of
Revelation.

Sonia Halliday, West on Turville, UK

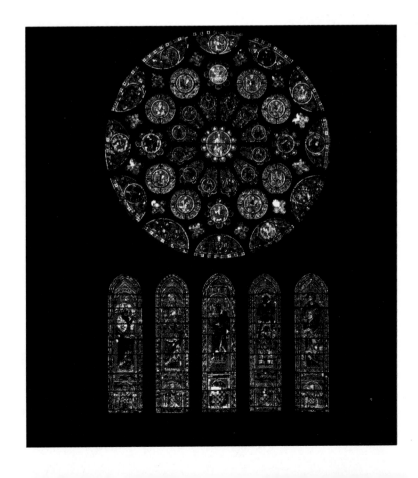

Plate 3

Leonardo da Vinci, *Madonna of the Rocks,* c. 1485. The religious subject, pyramid design, deep perspective, idealized nature, warm facial expressions, and restful mood all exemplify art of the Renaissance. Oil on panel, 6 ft 3 ins × 3 ft 6 ins (1.9 × 1.09 m). Louvre, Paris.

E. T. London Archive

Plate 4

Michelangelo, *The Last Judgment*, 1534–41. Christ directs the good souls on His right toward heaven, while the wicked on His left plunge to hell. Fresco, 48 × 44 ft (14.6 × 13.4 m). Sistine Chapel, Vatican, Rome.

Scala/Art Resource, NY

Plate 5

Antoine Watteau, *Le Mezzetin,* 1718. Among Watteau's favorite subjects were Italian theater musicians and comedians. Here he depicts a well-known entertainer playing the guitar, a popular instrument of the period. Oil on canvas, 21³/₄ × 17 ins (55.2 × 43.2 cm) Metropolitan Museum of Art, New York. Munsey Fund, 1934. [34.138]

Photograph © 1988 The Metropolitan Museum of Art

10
Religious Music of the Renaissance

The rise of humanism notwithstanding, most of the music of the Renaissance was conceived within a religious context. The expressive motets and the glorious polyphonic settings of the Mass produced during this period remain unrivaled for sheer perfection of choral writing.

While the **Renaissance motet,** like that of the Medieval period, is a polyphonic vocal composition, the differences between the motets characteristic of the two periods are striking:

a. The Medieval motet might be either sacred or secular, but the Renaissance motet, though sometimes based on a folk or popular tune, is invariably a religious piece. Regardless of the source of the preexisting melody line around which the composer created a new composition, a Renaissance motet always has a reverent, worshipful character.

b. The Renaissance motet never mixes texts and languages (as sometimes occurs in Medieval motets) but expresses the single motet text in Church Latin.

c. While instruments may have doubled one or more voice parts on occasion, ideal to the Renaissance was the homogeneous sound of a cappella performance.

d. No line in the Renaissance motet has more significance than another; each enters in imitation of the preceding voice until all have treated one phrase of the text, then each phrase receives similar imitative treatment by all of the voices in turn.

The words of a Renaissance motet might be entirely original or taken from verses in the Bible, offering composers a much wider range of expression than the liturgical Mass text afforded. Thus, although the Renaissance motet is invariably reverent in mood, even composers of quite conservative Mass settings often exhibited innovative techniques when writing motets. For example, they dramatized descriptive words or phrases in musical ways, such as setting a phrase like "my heart leaps up" to a melody "leaping" from a low to a high pitch. Such **word painting,** which included harmonic and rhythmic as well as melodic techniques, greatly increased the emotional impact of the music.

The Renaissance motet is **through-composed** in form, meaning that each phrase of text is set to new melody. The texture, called **imitative polyphony,** differs from that of a canon or round (see p. 62) in that the imitation here is only similar to, rather than literally the same as, the preceding voice. The entrance of each new phrase of text is called a **point of imitation.**

Motet (and Mass) composers varied the sonority of their compositions with certain passages in which the voices move together in the same rhythm, producing a chordal effect. Nevertheless, since each line was melodically conceived, and the concept of tonal harmony (in which the composer intends the combinations of tones to constitute chords) yet to be developed, the term **homorhythmic,** rather than *homophonic,* best describes the texture of these passages of Renaissance choral music.

Josquin des Prez (ca. 1445–1521)

Jhos-kanh´ da Prã

Considered by his contemporaries to be the greatest composer who had ever lived, **Josquin des Prez** is recognized yet today as a creative genius whose art represents a peak in the history of Western music. Josquin's music is of the Renaissance in style and technique, but it is timeless in its beauty and artistic expression.

Josquin was born in the French Netherlands, but his special talent soon caused him to be lured away to challenging and lucrative positions elsewhere. A fine singer as well as a great and prolific composer, he spent much of his adult life composing, performing, and teaching in Italy. Like most progressive composers of religious music during this period, Josquin developed innovative techniques in his motets, but remained essentially conservative in the composition of Masses. His frequent use of word painting and his occasional pungent dissonances for emotional effect render his motets exquisitely personal expressions of religious devotion.

More than any other composer of the early to mid-Renaissance, Josquin perfected the techniques of imitative polyphony. He often treated his voices in pairs, having them enter two at a time instead of singly. Occasionally he thinned the texture by having one or more voices drop out, and he created a smooth, "seamless" effect by overlapping the end of a phrase in one voice with the beginning of a new phrase in another. Versatile and imaginative, he set his texts beautifully, creating wonderful effects within the framework of the imitative motet.

Renaissance Mass

Polyphonic settings of the Mass Ordinary underwent significant changes during the Renaissance. Many Masses composed early in the period were based upon secular tunes and involved highly complex polyphonic relationships between the melody lines; but many later Renaissance composers responded to complaints of the Council of Trent, which deemed inappropriate the use of secular tunes, and held that polyphonic complexities made it difficult to understand the sacred text. These later composers abandoned secular sources and skillfully organized the lines of music so that the words could be clearly understood. The great Mass settings of the late Renaissance period, thus imbued with classical order and serenity, constitute choral music of unprecedented and unsurpassed beauty.

Giovanni Pierluigi da Palestrina (ca. 1524–1594)

pal-es-trē´-nah

During the early and mid-Renaissance periods, young Italian composers studied and absorbed the style and techniques of the Flemish or Netherlander musicians working in Italy, and by the last half of the sixteenth century, Italians had come to dominate the musical as well as the visual arts of Europe. The outstanding composer of the late Renaissance was the Italian **Giovanni Pierluigi da Palestrina.**

Having assimilated and perfected Josquin's techniques, Palestrina adapted them to his own personal style, which was more conservative than that of the innovative Josquin. Known by the name of the town where he was born, Palestrina soon acquired another nickname: "Prince of Music."

Palestrina, who devoted most of his career to writing religious music, was particularly sensitive to the recommendations of the Council of Trent. With no attempt to

1 14

LISTENING EXAMPLE 7

  1A 7

Palestrina

Composer: GIOVANNI PALESTRINA (ca. 1525–1594)

Title: "Agnus Dei I" from the *Missa Papae Marcelli* (Mass for Pope Marcellus)

Composed: 1557

Genre: Mass

Form: Through-composed

Texture: Mostly imitative polyphony, with homorhythmic passages

Timbre: Six voices (soprano, alto, tenor I and II, and bass I and II). Palestrina divided the full choir into smaller groups and wrote passages for different combinations of voices. He generally reserved the full six-voice texture for emphasis in significant passages.

Melody: The modal lines are long, predominantly stepwise, and confined within a modest range of pitches. Although not based upon a Gregorian chant, the character represents the essence of Gregorian style.

Rhythm: The lines are rhythmically as well as melodically independent. A gentle pulse prevails, but there is no sense of rhythmic drive, nor are there regularly recurring accents.

Harmony: Although this music sounds almost entirely consonant to twentieth-century ears, Palestrina skillfully alternated areas of tension and release. The many thirds and sixths provide a full, rich sonority. Notice that Palestrina included the third in the final cadence.

14	0:00	Agnus Dei,	Lamb of God,
0:51	0:51	qui tollis peccata mundi,	who takest away the sins of the world:
. . . .			
1:59	1:59	miserere nobis.	have mercy upon us.

be artful or complex, he gave his polyphonic Mass settings and motets a "transparent" texture that allowed the words to be clearly understood. His melodic lines are quite easy to sing; combined, they produce pure and simple harmonies that lie easily on the ears. The use of many thirds and sixths gives his music a fuller, richer sonority than that of earlier Italian religious music. Rhythms, adapted to the flow of the text, seem perfectly natural, adding to the restful effect of the music. Occasional passages written in a homorhythmic or syllabic style enhance the articulation of the words and provide interesting textural variety; yet each line of music retains melodic interest. Indeed, although the "chordal" effects Palestrina achieved imply homophonic texture, his music remained primarily modal and polyphonic (linear) in concept.

Palestrina was a composer who avoided extremes. Blessed with genius, he confined his talent to suit the needs of his church and the taste of his generation. The cool, objective, elegant sound of "Agnus Dei I" from Palestrina's *Missa Papae Marcelli* (Listening Example 7) is the very embodiment of Renaissance balance, order, and repose.

When Martin Luther presented his 95 theses to the Catholic church, some of the issues he raised concerned the practice of church music. For example, Luther believed that people should be able to *participate in,* rather than merely observe, their worship

Protestant Worship Music

Martin Luther and his family. Chorales were sung at home in harmony and with instrumental accompaniment.

service; he therefore criticized the exclusive use of Latin, a language that only a few well-educated people understood. He did not advocate eliminating Latin from the service entirely; in fact, his complaints were modestly expressed and his suggestions for reform quite moderate. He simply believed that some music should be appropriate for singing by the congregation, with texts in the vernacular tongue and tunes easy to learn and sing. This music would be in contrast to Gregorian chant and polyphonic Masses and motets, which required performance by trained choirs.

As we have seen, Luther's ideas influenced Protestants in other countries as well as Germany, and several new forms of religious music evolved for use in the various Protestant church services.

Chorale

The **hymn,** or congregational song, introduced into the worship service by Martin Luther is called the Lutheran **chorale.** Chorale texts, newly written or adapted from religious poems, were set in strophic form: that is, all of the verses of a chorale were set to the same music.

Some chorale tunes were newly composed, and others were adapted from Catholic church music or from folk or popular songs. Their strong, stirring melodies have inspired many types of church and concert composition.

In church, chorales were probably sung unaccompanied and in unison throughout most of the sixteenth century, but polyphonic arrangements and four-voice harmonizations soon appeared for use when singing chorales at home or elsewhere for social and entertainment purposes. By the seventeenth century, it was common for the church organ to play a four-part harmonization while the congregation sang the chorale melody, as in most Protestant churches today.

Psalm Tunes

The Swiss reformer John Calvin proposed church music reforms far more rigorous than those of Martin Luther. Eliminating Latin from his service entirely, Calvin insisted that the only music appropriate for use in worship was the unaccompanied singing, in the vernacular language, of the Biblical verses called *psalms.* Thus, the chorale, with its freely written text (not necessarily based on a verse from the Bible), did not serve the Calvinists, who created for their purposes instead the **psalm tune.**

The Book of Psalms, found in the Old Testament of the Bible, contains 150 songs or poems of praise written in free verse—that is, with no set number of syllables per line and no rhyme scheme. To render them suitable for congregational singing, Calvin and his associates translated each of the 150 psalms into metered and rhymed verses in their vernacular language (French) and printed them in a **psalter:** a collection of psalms in versions suitable for singing.

The psalm texts, like the verses of a chorale, were set to strong, attractive melodies, either newly composed or borrowed from religious or even secular sources. Like chorales, the psalm tunes were strophic in form. It was not considered necessary to provide a separate tune for each psalm, since all psalms with identical metrical patterns could be sung to one tune. Calvin's psalter included tunes in several meters, but some later psalters contained no music at all, directing congregations to sing the metered, rhymed psalm verses to particular familiar tunes.

During the sixteenth century, the singing of the psalms, both in the worship service and at home, became the prevalent form of Protestant music everywhere except in Germany, where the Lutheran chorale predominated. Many early psalm tunes survive in the hymnals and psalters of Protestants around the world, and, like chorales and Gregorian chant, as the rich source of melodic material for composers of art music.

Summary

Josquin des Prez was born in the Netherlands, where the musical Renaissance began; he spent much of his life in Italy composing secular and religious music of superb quality. His varied use of imitative polyphony is particularly effective, and he imbued his motets with a warm, personal expression unprecedented in earlier music.

Italian composers gradually absorbed the Netherlanders' style, which had become the dominant influence in Western music by the late sixteenth century. The greatest composer of the late Renaissance was Palestrina, who assimilated Josquin's techniques in his restrained, conservative religious compositions. The purity of the Gregorian ideal is apparent in Palestrina's superb motets and Mass settings.

Martin Luther, the leader of the Protestant Reformation, introduced a new form of congregational song, the chorale; it was marked by tuneful melodies and vernacular texts. Calvinists limited their worship music to the unaccompanied unison singing of psalm tunes, which differed from chorales primarily in the source of their text. Soon Protestants in several countries published psalters containing metered and rhymed versions of the psalms in their own languages.

Critical Thinking

- In what ways did the Protestant Reformation reflect the tastes and the needs of sixteenth century society? Would such a movement have been possible during the Middle Ages? Explain your answer.

Terms to Review

Renaissance motet   A religious vocal composition that is through-composed, polyphonic in texture, sung in Latin, and invariably serene and worshipful.

word painting   Musical illustrations of verbal concepts. *descending from h to L pitch or from L to high*

through-composed   A song form containing new music throughout.

imitative polyphony   A technique in which each phrase of a composition is addressed by all of the voices, which enter successively in imitation of each other.

point of imitation   The introduction of a new phrase in imitative polyphony.

homorhythmic style   Polyphony in which all the voices move in the same rhythm, producing a chordal effect. (The chordal effect is achieved by the combination of melodic lines rather than by the addition of chords to one melody, as in homophonic texture.)

hymn   A religious song, with nonliturgical text, appropriate for congregational singing.

chorale   A characteristic hymn introduced by Martin Luther.

psalm tunes   Tuneful settings of the 150 psalms in versions suitable for congregational singing.

psalter   A collection of psalms in rhymed, metered verse.

Key Figures

Composers   *Josquin des Prez*
                   Giovanni Pierluigi da Palestrina

Religious leaders *Martin Luther*
                   John Calvin

11
Secular Music in the Renaissance

As the secular interests of the Renaissance led to the composition of a significant quantity of secular music, certain stylistic differences between religious and secular music and between vocal and instrumental music became apparent. In particular, a new kind of solo song introduced in Italy, the *madrigal,* became an important source of entertainment.

Though the **madrigal,** like the motet, was through-composed in form and mostly polyphonic in texture, several significant differences become apparent between the motet and the madrigal.

Madrigal

mad'-ri-gul

a. *Language.* Because the madrigal was a secular composition, it was written in the vernacular language rather than in Church Latin.

b. *Text.* Most madrigals have a secular text, describing picturesque pastoral scenes, for example, or poignant affairs of the heart. The words, often written by renowned poets of the day, may be particularly appropriate for dramatic word painting.

c. *Expressive style.* Even composers who wrote conservatively for the Church allowed themselves considerable emotional leeway in their madrigals. Their extreme examples of word painting, called **madrigalisms,** vividly depict dramatic extramusical concepts in musical terms. Sighs and cries, for example, were literally interpreted, and extreme emotional states dramatically portrayed.

d. *Purpose.* Unlike Renaissance motets, which were performed to enhance the worship experience, madrigals were sung at social gatherings in homes or at private meetings, primarily for the entertainment of the performers themselves.

e. *Performance practice.* While effective performance of Renaissance motets required a relatively sophisticated degree of music training and experience, madrigals could be performed by anyone able to read music and sing—accomplishments expected of all members of the refined society of the period. There does not seem to have been a standard method of performing these songs, but generally they were sung by small groups, with only one or two voices for each melody line. On occasion, some of the vocal lines might have been played upon instruments.

Italian madrigals soon became very popular in England, and by the late sixteenth century the English were writing madrigals of their own. Although the English madrigal had much in common with the Italian form, the English compositions had a certain flavor of their own—less emotional, lighter in mood, whimsical, gently humorous, sentimental, or festive. All of these qualities are exemplified in Thomas

1 15

LISTENING EXAMPLE 8

 1A 8

English Madrigal

Composer: Thomas Weelkes (ca. 1575–1623

Title: "As Vesta Was from Latmos Hill Descending"

Composed: 1601

Genre: English madrigal

Rhythm: Duple meter, with occasional irregularities in the alternation of strong and weak beats.

Texture: Polyphonic, with some homorhythmic passages

Melody: The melodic lines are based upon the notes of the major scale—still considered, however, a mode, since the major-minor system (tonality) had not yet been articulated.

Timbre: Six voices

Form: Through-composed

Note: Several madrigalisms are italicized

15	0:00	As Vesta was from Latmos *Hill descending,*
. . . .		(*high pitch—"hill"*) (*descending scales*)
0:13	0:13	She spied a maiden queen the same *ascending,*
. . . .		(*ascending scales*)
. . . .		Attended on by all the shepherds swain,
16	0:49	To whom Diana's darlings came *running down amain,*
. . . .		(*descending scales; imitative polyphony*)
17	1:11	first *two by two,* then *three by three together,*
. . . .		(*2 voices only*) (*3 voices only*) (*all voices together*)
18	1:20	*Leaving their goddess all alone,* hasted thither;
. . . .		(*minor mode; slow*) (*highest voice alone*)
. . . .		And mingling with the shepherds of her train,
. . . .		With mirthful tunes her presence entertain.
19	1:54	Then sang the shepherds and nymphs of Diana.
. . . .		(*all voices; homorhythmic texture*)
20	2:04	Long live fair Oriana!
. . . .		(*Note the longer note values in the lowest voice; staggered polyphonic entrances of upper voices represent cheering members of a crowd*)

Weelkes's famous madrigal "As Vesta was from Latmos Hill Descending" (Listening Example 8).

Instrumental Music

Renaissance musicians availed themselves of a variety of musical instruments, and although Renaissance composers remained primarily concerned with setting religious texts to worship music, they increasingly appreciated instrumental music for its own sake. Much secular instrumental music from the Renaissance, whether for court or commoner, had a distinctly popular character. For example, many instrumental pieces were in the forms and rhythmic patterns of popular dances of the day. These were *stylized* dance pieces, having the rhythms and character of particular dances but intended to be listened to rather than to accompany dance. Dance pieces organized in

Figure 11.1
A woman playing the lute.
Stock Montage, Chicago

pairs or sets of three we recognize now as prototypes of the longer and more complex *dance suites* of the Baroque period (see p. 121).

Renaissance composers sometimes indicated that a piece might be "either played or sung"; they did not specify which instruments were to play given parts in ensemble music until late in the sixteenth century, when instrumental timbres became significant in their own right. (Still, it was not until the seventeenth century that composers customarily wrote music for specific voices or instruments.)

String Instruments

The most widely used instrument in the sixteenth century was a pear-shaped plucked string instrument called the **lute** (see figure 11.1), on which one could play difficult, virtuosic compositions as well as simple pieces intended for home entertainment. The lute was also well suited to accompany singing and to play transcriptions of vocal music. Also popular was the guitar, on which musicians could play all but the most virtuosic lute compositions.

Bowed as well as plucked string instruments enjoyed popularity during the fifteenth and sixteenth centuries. Prevalent among the bowed instruments was the **viol,** a six-stringed precursor of the modern violin. The viol, however, was constructed

1 [21]   # LISTENING EXAMPLE 9   1A 9

Lute Piece

Composer: John Dowland (1563–1626)

Title: "Queen Elizabeth's Galliard"

Published: 1610, London from "Varietie of Lute Lessons"

Rhythm: Lively triple meter

Texture: Homophonic

Genre: Court dance (galliard)

Timbre: Lute solo

[21]	0:00	**Section A**
		Simple, tuneful melody consisting of two phrases
0:16	0:16	Varied repeat of the first two phrases; melody is elaborated with shorter note values
[22]	0:33	**Section B**
		Change to a more spirited melody in a compound meter (beats are subdivided by 3); *hemiolas* (alternation between duple and triple meter) create lively syncopations
		As in Section A, the melody consists of two phrases.
0:17	0:50	Varied repeat

The great Irish lutenist John Dowland produced a large repertoire of songs, sung in parts or accompanied by lute and viol, as well as many charming pieces for solo lute. "Queen Elizabeth's Galliard" (Listening Example 9) illustrates the manner in which he often adapted dance forms, such as the fast-tempo galliard, to the solo lute repertoire.

with ridges in its neck to indicate where the player should stop the string. Its soft and delicate tone made the viol an ideal instrument for accompanying the singing voice during the Renaissance, when music lovers did not require the wide range of dynamic levels preferred in later periods.

Keyboard Instruments

Keyboard instruments also were available, on which musicians accompanied singing and played music composed specifically for keyboard performance. Depressing a key on the **clavichord** (figure 11.2) causes a metal piece to strike a string and to maintain contact until the player releases the key. The instrument has a softer sound and is somewhat more sensitive to individual touch than the harpsichord (pictured on p. 34). Moreover, the clavichord player is able to control subtle changes of volume and even to create a slight **vibrato,** or rapid variation of pitch, when desired.

The tone decays more rapidly on the harpsichord, the strings of which are plucked rather than struck. Large harpsichords sometimes have stops that provide a change in timbre and allow abrupt changes of dynamic level. Harpsichord cases made during the Renaissance, when the instrument was extremely popular, were often elaborately carved and painted, rendering the instrument a source of visual as well as aural beauty. Some harpsichord cases were even inlaid with precious stones.

Renaissance composers also produced a quantity of organ music. Sixteenth-century pipe organs had several stops, offering a wider variety of timbres than earlier instruments afforded. Some even had a few pedals, although the full pedalboard of the modern pipe organ was not yet available.

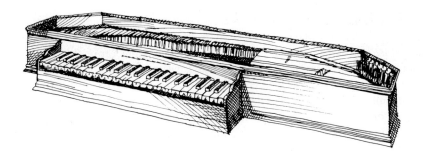

Figure 11.2
A sixteenth-century
clavichord.

A brass consort.

Renaissance music lovers enjoyed a variety of wind instruments. The **recorder,** which was especially popular, came in several sizes, providing a wide range of pitches. The Renaissance trumpet and trombone produced softer sounds than their modern counterparts, but were loud enough to furnish entertainment at outdoor banquets or festive affairs.

Wind Instruments

Ensembles

Mixed string and wind ensembles, formed according to the instruments' dynamic capabilities, sometimes played together, with or without keyboard accompaniment. These were considerably smaller than the modern symphony orchestra.

Instrumental ensembles more often consisted of members of the *same* instrument family. Such groups, called **consorts,** consisted of three or more instruments of related timbre but of different sizes, and therefore with different ranges of pitch. Consorts of instruments were organized much like vocal choirs, with soprano, alto, tenor, and bass ranges, the combination of instruments of like timbre satisfying the Renaissance taste for a blended sonority.

Women Musicians

During this long, productive period, young girls were not thought to need much education, and only the wealthy and those reared in religious institutions received formal music lessons. Though forbidden to sing in church, women in Renaissance convents sang motets and polyphonic Mass settings, as well as Gregorian chant, in their cloistered grounds; and in certain convents, women played a variety of musical instruments as well. Some of the music they played and sang was composed by their sisters in the religious community.

Ladies of the nobility (such, perhaps, as the handsome woman in figure 11.1) and those having positions at the various courts of Europe were expected to include musical abilities among their accomplishments and were often afforded appropriate educational opportunities to develop their talents; but only certain instruments were considered suitable for women to play. These included the viol, lute, psaltery, harp, clavichord, harpsichord, and small organs, all of which required no change of facial expression and could be played in "graceful" positions.

Very late in the Renaissance, the high female singing voice achieved a certain vogue, and professional as well as amateur female ensembles performed madrigals and other secular songs. Counts and cardinals, kings and dukes enjoyed the entertainment provided by these talented, privileged women.

Summary

Secular music, both vocal and instrumental, became increasingly appreciated throughout the Renaissance, though religious music remained predominant. The madrigal, a vocal piece similar in form and texture to the Renaissance motet, had a secular text sung in the vernacular language. Created by Italians, the madrigal soon became popular in England, where it assumed a lighter, more frivolous character.

Renaissance musicians, both male and female, played a wide variety of instruments, either to accompany singers by doubling voice lines, or in solo or ensemble performances. Women also sang in religious, professional, and amateur ensembles. The increasingly subjective and dramatic qualities of secular music, especially the madrigal, foretold the approach of a new artistic style as the seventeenth century drew near.

Critical Thinking

- In the sixteenth century, after-dinner entertainment often involved the informal but proficient singing of madrigals. Why do you think such participatory entertainment has been largely superseded by passive experiences (watching television, attending a concert or a movie) today? What has been gained and what has been lost by this change?

madrigal A secular song introduced in Italy that became popular in England as well. Polyphonic in texture and expressive in mood, madrigals are written in the vernacular language.

madrigalism Word painting used to enhance the expression of madrigal texts.

lute A plucked string instrument; the most widely used instrument of the sixteenth century.

viol The most popular bowed string instrument of the Renaissance.

clavichord A keyboard instrument capable of subtle changes of volume and able to produce a slight vibrato.

vibrato A rapid variation of pitch that lends "warmth" to the tone of a voice or instrument.

recorder An end-blown wind instrument, sometimes called a "whistle" flute, developed in the Middle Ages and very popular in the Renaissance. The tone is soft and slightly reedy.

consort An ensemble of several members of the same instrument family.

Composers   *Thomas Weelkes*
             John Dowland

PART THREE

The Baroque, Classical, and Romantic Periods

This section of our text will introduce the composers and the music most familiar to today's concert audiences and today's listeners to our various recorded media. As you study this music, you might wonder why it has served to please so many generations of music lovers, even through radical changes of taste in art, literature, fashion, and design. What seemingly universal values does it represent? Has it become familiar because we like it—or do we like it because we have heard it so frequently on recordings and TV and in the concert hall?

We shall see that the preference for either classical or romantic art continued to alternate throughout these long and productive periods. The art of the Baroque abandoned the serene classicism of the period it succeeded for passionate and personal artistic expression; the eighteenth century so conformed to the classical ideals of ancient Greece and the Renaissance that we call it the Age of Classicism; and the nineteenth century similarly is called *the* Romantic period, so closely did its artists emulate the Dionysian characteristics of drama, subjectivity, and union of the arts.

Remember to approach the music and art of each period as much as possible in the spirit in which it was conceived. No matter how fine the music, each score is, in a sense, an unfinished work, dependent upon a great performance—and great *listening*—to fully achieve its composer's goals.

12
Toward the Baroque

The evolution from the Renaissance to the Baroque occurred in the visual arts before it affected music, and in southern Europe before it reached the north; but gradually, throughout Western Europe, the classical ideals of balance, order, and repose generally were replaced by a romantic preference for drama and a highly personal expression in art.

The Baroque hardly sprang full-blown upon unsuspecting artists; nor was the transition between Renaissance and Baroque a cultural vacuum of sorts. Rather, artists seeking new means of expressing new ideas produced striking works of art bearing relation both to what came before and to what lay ahead. The late works of Michelangelo, the paintings of El Greco, the later madrigals of several sixteenth-century Italians, and the *polychoral* works of Venetian composers all showed signs of the coming change.

Historical Perspective

The Reformation initiated a long and tragic period of religious warfare, when Protestants stormed Catholic churches to destroy beautiful works of art and music instruments they considered profane, and Catholics used the infamous court of the Inquisition to try and condemn dissenters according to its own harsh rules. As feelings ran equally high among Protestants in the north and Catholics in the south, the cool, detached emotional atmosphere of the Renaissance soon gave way to the vivid, passionate expression of the **affections,** the Baroque term for human emotions, or "states of the soul."

Artistic Style

As artists increasingly discarded the boundaries controlling expression in classical art, distortion and exaggeration enhanced their newly dramatic approach. Even Michelangelo, whose early paintings and sculptures are models of grace, serenity, and balance, responded in his later years to the political, social, and ecclesiastical changes of the sixteenth century. Whereas his *David,* finished about 1504 (figure 9.2) depicts a confident young man poised and at peace with himself, the Youthful Captive of 1513 (figure 12.1) twists in a terrible struggle to break his bonds. The figures of "Night" and "Day" (1519–1534), part of the famous Medici tomb in Florence, are also twisted and contorted in a manner that is physically unrealistic but emotionally expressive. And Michelangelo's late fresco, *The Last Judgment* (1536–1541) (Color Plate 4), seems the very antithesis of the serene painting he applied to the ceiling of the Sistine chapel many years earlier.

Another famous artist who developed an emotional and personal style is known as El Greco (The Greek), due to his birth on the island of Crete, though he lived most of his life in Spain. El Greco (1541–1614), whose unrealistically elongated figures stretch expressively toward heaven, painted not only his models' faces and figures, but also their very souls and personalities. Sometimes referred to as mannerism, El

Figure 12.1

Youthful Captive, Michelangelo.

Art Resource, NY/Alimari Florence

Greco's style defies labels, but its drama, emotion, and mysticism are closer in spirit to the Baroque than to the Renaissance.

Music

Jehs-wal'-dō

Carlo Gesualdo (ca. 1560–1613)

During the late sixteenth century, while some musicians continued to compose in the Renaissance style, others eloquently propounded new ideas in articles, discussions, and new types of musical composition. One of many composers whose music exhibited characteristics of both old and new styles was **Carlo Gesualdo.**

Gesualdo, Prince of Venosa, displayed a penchant for melodrama in life as well as music: discovering his wife and her lover together, he promptly murdered them both.

Obviously an emotional man, Gesualdo intended his madrigals to enhance, indeed to exaggerate, the emotional impact of their text. His madrigals were unusual (though not unique) in his day for their wide vocal range and varied rhythms. However, Gesualdo is particularly remembered for his extreme **chromaticism,** or use of notes *other* than the seven tones of the mode in which he was working. That is, without abandoning the Renaissance system of modal scales, Gesualdo frequently included in his music notes foreign to a particular mode, thus creating poignant melodic effects, as well as unusual and often startling dissonances between voices. Once considered curiosities, Gesualdo's madrigals now are appreciated as works of intrinsic aesthetic value, historically provocative, but also beautiful in their own right.

Resurrection,
El Greco.

1 [23]   # LISTENING EXAMPLE 10   1A 10

Gesualdo Madrigal

Composer: Carlo Gesualdo (ca. 1560–1613)

Title: "Moro Lasso"

Composed: 1611

Genre: Madrigal

Rhythm: Duple meter

Texture: The alternation of imitative polyphony with homorhythmic passages contributes to the unsettled, emotionally charged atmosphere of the setting.

Melody: The polyphonic sections are based upon modal scales, while the homorhythmic passages contain highly chromatic melodies.

Harmony: Chromaticism and expressive dissonance are characteristic. Notice that the third is included in the final cadence.

Timbre: Five voices

Form: A A′ B

		A section	
[23]	0:00	Moro lasso al mio duolo,	Wearily I die in my pains,
. . . .		*(note the descending chromatic line; homorhythmic texture)*	
0:13	0:13	E chi mi può dar vita.	And she who could give me life,
. . . .		*(imitative polyphony; modal)*	
0:32	0:32	Ahi, che m′ancide e non vuol darmi	Alas, she gives me death and will
. . . .		aita,	not give me help,
. . . .		*(dramatic change in harmony)*	
		A′ section (same three lines of text set to similar music; fourth line of text added)	
[24]	0:55	Moro lasso al mio duolo,	Wearily I die in my pains,
. . . .		E chi mi può dar vita.	And she who could give me life,
0:31	1:26	Ahi, che m′ancide e non vuol darmi	Alas, she gives me death and will
. . . .		aita,	not give me help,
0:54	1:49	O dolorosa sorte,	Oh dolorous fate,
. . . .		**B section** (last line of text set to entirely different music)	
[25]	2:09	Chi dar vita mi può, ahi, mi da	She who can give me life, alas,
. . . .		morte.	gives me death.

The descending chromatic line that begins "Moro Lasso" ("Wearily I die," Listening Example 10), presages the madrigal's essence of tragedy and despair, which is heightened by several stark utterances of "ahi!" ("alas!"), dramatically sudden changes in harmony, and the use of pungent dissonances. All these unorthodox techniques combine to lend excruciatingly emotional expressiveness to this fine madrigal.

Venetian School

Several Italian cities, politically independent and with diverse economic situations, developed significant individual styles during the latter part of the sixteenth century. In Venice, the center of much secular as well as religious activity, the beautiful church of St. Mark was designed on the plan of a cross, with a full organ in each of the two opposing arms. Both solemn and festive occasions were celebrated at the

Figure 12.2

Figure 12.2

The glorious sounds of vocal and instrumental choirs performing polychoral music resounded from choir galleries variously located around the spacious interior of the Basilica St. Marco (St. Mark's) in Venice.

Alinari/Art Resource, NY

church, which, by nature of its architectural design, lent itself to the performance of music by several choirs of voices and/or instruments (figure 12.2). Called **polychoral music,** this festive style contributed to the pomp and pageantry of celebrations of every kind.

Two characteristics of the Venetian polychoral style bore particular significance for future generations of composers:

a. The several choirs of four or more voices and instruments each, when performing simultaneously, were better served by a chordal or homorhythmic texture than by the complex polyphony of the Renaissance. Venetian polychoral works therefore include large sections composed of massive chordal combinations, vertically conceived, and moving in a homorhythmic fashion. The concept was still modal, but it pointed toward the homophonic texture of much tonal music in the Baroque.

con-chār-tah'-tō

b. Contrasting sonorities of various voices and instruments had strong appeal to the Baroque imagination. Known as the **concertato principle,** this was destined to become one of the underlying concepts of the Baroque style.

Giovanni Gabrieli (1557–1612)

Gah-brē-el'-ē

Giovanni Gabrieli, a famous organist, teacher, and composer, wrote many compositions for St. Mark's cathedral and also participated in performances there. His motets were written for two to five choirs (of voices or instruments), which responded to one another antiphonally from various positions in the church. The vocal choirs usually were accompanied by an organ, by string instruments such as the viol, or by brass instruments such as cornets or trombones.

Gabrieli wrote one polychoral instrumental piece of particular historical interest. Even its title, *Sonata Pian'e Forte,* was innovative. At that time, the word **sonata**

LISTENING EXAMPLE 11

Polychoral Music

Composer: Giovanni Gabrieli (1557–1612)

Title: Sonata Pian'e Forte

Composed: 1597

Rhythm: Moderately slow; Duple meter

Texture: Homorhythmic

Timbre: Choir I—Three trombones and cornetto; Choir II—Three trombones and viola

26.	0:00	Choir I (*piano*)
		Phrase 1 (4 measures)—introduced by solo trombone
0:13	0:13	Phrase 2 (5 measures)
0:28	0:28	Phrase 3 (4 measures)
27	0:43	Choir II (*piano*)
. . . .		Lower in pitch; more mellow in tone
0:33	1:16	Sudden brightening from minor to major
28	1:20	Combined Choirs (*forte*)
. . . .		Running passages add to the drama of this passage.
0:19	1:39	Alternating Choirs/Combined Choirs
. . . .		Brief conversational exchanges between the choirs (*piano*) are interspersed with *forte* passages for all instruments.
0:47	2:07	Combined (*forte*)
0:56	2:16	Alternating (*piano*)
1:21	2:41	Combined (*forte*)
1:33	2:53	Alternating (*piano*)
1:45	3:05	Syncopated, fanfare-like statements (*forte*)
1:56	3:16	Bold *forte* statement
2:11	3:31	Bold *forte* statement heard again
2:23	3:43	Increased use of shorter note values makes the music seem to move faster, and this sense of heightened activity is enhanced by occasional sharp dissonances.
2:50	4:10	The splendid piece ends, as it began, with the emphatic tones of a solo trombone.

indicated a piece to be played upon instruments rather than sung; but the idea of contrasting *piano* (soft) and *forte* (loud) passages was relatively new, having been of little significance to serene Renaissance music. These dynamic terms appear not only in the title of Gabrieli's piece, but throughout the score; *piano* indicates those sections to be played by one choir alone, and *forte* those sections to be played by combined ensembles. Such contrasting dynamic levels were to become a highly important characteristic of Baroque music.

Gabrieli's sonata (Listening Example 11), scored for two choirs of instruments, is also the first known piece to have specified which instrument was to play each line of music. Here each choir is a *broken consort,* meaning that it contains one instrument of a timbre different from the others in the group. By indicating that one choir consisted of three trombones and a *cornetto* (an ancient instrument similar to a recorder and played with a trumpet mouthpiece), and the other of three trombones and a viola, Gabrieli foretold the style-conscious Baroque, when composers were to write consistently for specific voices and instruments.

Florentine Camerata

mah'nō-dē

Another Italian city, Florence, housed a group of intellectuals collectively known as the **Florentine Camerata,** who avidly discussed and promoted changes in artistic style. Specifically, they sought a mode of expression more subjective and more dramatic than that of the Renaissance.

One of their most significant contributions was a new type of solo singing, called **monody.** Solo songs, accompanied by the lute or other instruments, had been popular in the sixteenth century. Even compositions intended for ensemble singing, including the polyphonic madrigal, sometimes were performed as solo songs, with instruments playing the other voice lines.

The Florentine Camerata, however, found existing vocal forms unsuitable for the clear and dramatic expression of a text, which they deemed ideal, for the following reasons:

a. The combination of melodic lines in the polyphonic madrigal interfered with the understanding of the words.

b. The melody lines of the typical Renaissance madrigal were unrelated to the natural declamation of the words.

c. The use of the same melody for several verses of a strophic song belied any relationships between words and music.

d. Madrigalisms seemed to the new intellectuals naive and unnatural.

Appreciative of the ideals (though unable to know the practice) of the ancient Greeks, the members of the Camerata envisioned a style of melody that would approximate spoken inflections in the dramatic declamation of a text. They wanted singers to avoid extreme vocal ranges as they are avoided in speech, and to make every effort to express the words as clearly as possible.

The new solo singing style—monody—was accompanied by simple instrumental chords that supported, but never interfered with, the vocal delivery. This approach implied the homophonic texture—a predominant melody supported by simple harmonies—that was destined to become one of the important musical innovations of the Baroque.

Summary

During the late sixteenth century, as a desire for drama and personal expression in art replaced classical ideals, musicians and other artists foretold in their works the style we call Baroque. Painters and sculptors used distortion and exaggeration to create dramatic effects, while musicians cultivated a newly emotional approach to their art. Gesualdo's madrigals have wide vocal ranges, great rhythmic variety, and extreme chromaticism. Composers of the Venetian school exploited the concertato principle, writing grand polychoral works that contrasted sonorities and dynamic levels with stunning effect. The increasing importance of instrumental music, and the specification of which instrument was to play each part, were also signs of a coming change; Gabrieli's *Sonata Pian'e Forte,* is a good example of this.

A group of artists and intellectuals known as the Florentine Camerata introduced a solo singing style, called monody, that was particularly suited to expressing a dramatic text. Both monody and the Venetian polychoral style implied a new texture of music eventually known as homophony.

By the turn of the seventeenth century, the Baroque period was well under way.

- The late sixteenth century was one of several periods in which the arts experienced a gradual transition from one style to another. Today, prevalent artistic styles change rapidly, and numerous contrasting styles are concurrently significant. Can you suggest some social, political, religious, and technological developments that have encouraged this multiplicity of artistic styles?

affections   The Baroque term for human emotions or states of the soul.

chromaticism   The use of notes that are not in the scale upon which a composition is based.

polychoral music   Music for two or more vocal and/or instrumental choirs, performed antiphonally. A characteristic feature of music of the Venetian school.

concertato principle   The principle of contrasting the sonorities of different performing ensembles.

sonata   In the fifteenth and sixteenth centuries, an instrumental composition to be "sounded" upon instruments rather than sung.

Florentine Camerata   A group of scholars and intellectuals in Florence around the turn of the seventeenth century who promoted changes in the prevailing style of art.

monody   Music for one voice with a simple accompaniment, introduced by the Florentine Camerata.

Artists	*Michelangelo*
	El Greco

Composers	*Carlo Gesualdo*
	Giovanni Gabrieli

Monastery Church,
Melk—an example of
Baroque architecture.
Art Resource, NY/Marburg

13
The Baroque:
General Characteristics

In contrast to the serenely balanced works of the Renaissance, the art of the **Baroque** teems with drama and activity. The period, which musicians date from about 1600 to about 1750, was one of vivid contrasts and contradictions, an age of paradox, in fact. Eighteenth-century Classicists applied the term *baroque,* generally considered to mean distorted or irregular, to the impassioned art of the period preceding them; yet that which seemed so strange to them affords rich pleasure and inspiration today.

The Baroque vigorously affirmed both sides of almost any question. For example, religion had vital importance, profoundly affecting the literature, philosophy, science, art, and music of the period; Milton's *Paradise Lost,* Bernini's adornment of St. Peter's Church in Rome, the Passions of Bach, and the oratorios of Handel were all personal expressions of strong religious faith.

However, the secular side of life was also more important than ever before in the Christian era, and much Baroque art had a decidedly popular character. As the seventeenth century witnessed the opening of the first public opera house and the presentation of the first public concerts, composers found themselves no longer exclusively dependent upon acceptance of their works by a small, aristocratic audience, and increasingly they sought public approval. Handel's first love was the opera, which depended more and more upon public support, and Bach's secular concertos, suites, toccatas, and fugues are as impressive as his religious works.

Scientific research made great strides during the seventeenth century, though superstition was rampant and the belief in witchcraft, alchemy, and astrology remained firm. Science and religion, knowledge and faith—all had their place in the colorful, dramatic, style-conscious period we call the Baroque.

Religion

The controversy between Catholics and Protestants far exceeded anything envisioned by either Martin Luther or John Calvin. The long and terrible religious wars of the sixteenth and seventeenth centuries had left south and central Europe largely Roman Catholic and the northern countries largely Protestant. Now the center of intellectual activity moved north, out of reach of the terrible Spanish and Italian Inquisitions.

Religious persecution was not confined, however, to the Catholic south, for in England the Anglican church, under the aegis of the Crown, mercilessly harassed the Puritans, who espoused many Calvinist ideals. A desperate group of Puritans, who became known as Separatists, fled to Holland; from there they sailed to the New World in 1620. Today we refer to them as the Pilgrims. Other Puritans sailed directly from England to settle in the new colonies, enduring great physical hardship in their pursuit of spiritual, though not yet political, independence.

The first book printed in America (1640) was a psalter called the *Bay Psalm Book,* designed for use by the Puritans and other psalm-singing colonists.

Science and Philosophy

The day in 1564 when the great artist Michelangelo died also witnessed the birth of the great scientist Galileo Galilei. The son of an influential member of the Florentine Camerata, Galileo was inclined toward the arts; but he found his true calling in the rapidly expanding world of scientific research and discovery. He fell victim, however, to one of the most curious contradictions of the seventeenth century, when his scientific discoveries ran headlong into a rigid wall of religious dogma. The Church steadfastly refused to accept that the earth—the "center of the universe"—in fact revolved around the sun. Galileo's sophisticated instruments supported his contention, but the Inquisition supported the Church, and Galileo was forced to recant.

On the day in 1642 when the Italian Galileo died, the English scientist Isaac Newton was born. Fascinated, like Galileo, with the relationships between planets and stars, Newton studied the effects of gravity and performed important experiments on the measurement of time. His studies of the pendulum eventually led to advances in measuring time in music, including the nineteenth-century invention of the metronome.

Many other seventeenth-century scientists also invented new instruments and improved old ones for the purposes of observing, measuring, and recording scientific data. As Galileo and Newton contemplated the circulation of heavenly bodies, the Englishman William Harvey studied the circulation of the blood. And in keeping with the Baroque appreciation for opposite extremes, both the telescope and the microscope were inventions of the period. The Baroque also produced the English philosopher and scientist Francis Bacon and the Frenchman René Descartes, the epitome of the thinking man.

Re-nā′ Dā-cart′

Artistic Style

The art of the Baroque is filled with tension, drive, activity—in a word, drama. Baroque painters often direct the viewer's eye right off the canvas, as if resisting, in the romantic way, the boundaries of measured space. Sculpted figures no longer pose with classical grace and poise, but seethe with tension and strain, caught in the midst of some dramatic action. Baroque buildings jut and protrude, projecting a sense of dramatic instability, and the decorative ornamentation of the period is so elaborate and complex that it is almost dizzying in effect.

Literature

Baroque literature, which like the other arts sought to achieve maximum emotional impact, included one of the greatest novels of all time, *Don Quixote de la Mancha,* by the Spaniard Miguel de Cervantes. The novel's two main characters exemplify Baroque contradictions: the spiritual, whimsical Don Quixote ignores or simply transcends reality, while the earthy Sancho Panza prefers the practical to the ideal.

France, basking under the beneficent patronage of the Sun King, Louis XIV, excelled in the production of dramatic works. The comedies of the great playwright Molière poked unbridled fun at the foibles and hypocrisies of contemporary French society, and his stage designs and special effects provided the visual thrills Baroque audiences adored.

Seventeenth-century painters shared with contemporary scientists a fascination with the properties and effects of light, contriving brilliant effects that lend high drama to their works. Often a shaft of light streams from a window, an open doorway, or an unseen source, illuminating an object or figure surrounded by the deepest shadows. In one famous painting, *The Conversion of St. Paul* (figure 13.1), the Italian painter Caravaggio (like Gesualdo a murderer in real life) captures the very moment when Saul, blinded by a heavenly light as he heard the Lord call his name, has

Figure 13.1

Conversion of St. Paul,
Caravaggio.
Alinari/Art Resource, NY.

fallen from his horse, his servant looking on in astonishment. The blinding light, religious fervor, dramatic action, and personal nature of the divine communication all are characteristic of the Baroque.

The works of northern artists Frans Hals, Rembrandt van Rijn, Jan Vermeer, and Peter Paul Rubens share many characteristics of style and technique with the religious paintings of the Italian Baroque. But while religious subjects dominated the art of Catholic Italy and other southern and central European countries, the artists of Protestant Holland produced art for their homes, of which they were very proud, instead of the church, where Calvinists considered art to be idolatrous. The late seventeenth century in Holland was an age of the eye for artists as well as scientists: the telescope and the microscope revealed what previously had been beyond normal sight, and the Dutch masters proved especially gifted at painting light and all of its effects.

Figure 13.2

David, Giovanni Bernini.

*Art Resource, NY/Alinari,
Florence*

Sculpture
Bur-nĕ́-nē

One of the greatest sculptors of the Baroque period, Gianlorenzo Bernini (1598–1680), was also a fine painter, architect, dramatist, and composer. In vivid contrast to Michelangelo's *David,* (figure 9.2, p. 72), who quietly contemplates in the Renaissance way the action he plans to take, Bernini's *David* (figure 13.2) is portrayed in the very act of hurling his stone at Goliath. This young man's muscles and veins bulge with tension as he twists his body, frowns in concentration, and bites his lips in the strain of violent activity.

An even more dramatic example of the Baroque ability to capture a violent event in progress is Bernini's *Apollo and Daphne* (figure 13.3). According to a Greek myth, as Apollo frantically pursued the lovely nymph, her father, the river god, changed her into a laurel tree at the moment of impending capture. The subject is classical, but Bernini's expressive rendition, in which we see Daphne transformed before our very eyes, is entirely romantic. Unrestrained by emotional *or* physical boundaries, Bernini seems to have denied the technical limitations of working with marble, and the effect is nearly magical.

Figure 13.3

Apollo and Daphne,
Giovanni Bernini.

*Art Resource, NY/Alinari,
Florence*

Music

The composer's status continued to evolve during the seventeenth and early eighteenth centuries. The Church, the courts, and the city-state governments remained artists' primary employers, but some composers resisted submission to the taste and will of a patron. Handel, for example, abandoned his secure position as a court musician to compose operas and oratorios for the English public, and Bach even went to prison for a month in defiance of his patron's refusal to release him from service.

Contrasts

The contrasts and contradictions of seventeenth-century life are apparent as well in the music of the Baroque, when composers contrasted earlier styles and techniques with new means of expression, finding both old and new of value. Secular music appeared in equal quantity and quality with music having religious connotations. There were as many fine instrumental compositions as vocal pieces. Homophonic texture now assumed equal importance with polyphony. Further, contrasts of timbre, alternation of free and metered rhythms, and abrupt changes of dynamic levels were also characteristic of the music of this period.

Appreciation for contrasts also led to the composition of new kinds of multi-movement works—that is, works consisting of several sections, or **movements,** each one complete in the sense that it conforms to some formal design, but each conceived as only one part of a whole. Movements generally contrast with one another in tempo, mood, key, melodic material, texture, and perhaps timbre and other characteristics as well. However, according to the Baroque doctrine of the affections, only one mood (affection) was to be expressed within one composition, or at least within one movement of a multimovement work. In performance, one movement is usually separated from another by a pause, but the audience customarily holds applause until the entire work is completed. The *sonata, concerto, symphony,* and *dance suite* are examples of multimovement works.

Texture

Toward the end of the sixteenth century, both the Venetian polychoral style and Florentine monody demonstrated the harmonic and dramatic potential of a new texture—homophony—in which a melody in one voice was supported by chords in the others. Soon the Renaissance "sound ideal" of four or more melodic lines of nearly equal importance was replaced by the preference for one melody, in the highest voice or voices, supported by a strong bass line, with the disposition of the inner voices left largely to improvisation.

This new concept of texture in music constituted a profoundly significant change between the music of earlier periods and that of the Baroque. You will recall the linear polyphony of the Middle Ages, and the imitative polyphony of the Renaissance; in both of these, despite increasing appreciation for the combinations of sound resulting from simultaneous lines, each line retained equal melodic significance. Although the Baroque bass line had strong melodic implications even in homophonic sections, it served primarily to support the harmonies underlying the principal melody. This was clear evidence that composers had a new vertical, or harmonic, orientation. Now they were contrasting polyphony, which was strongly governed by harmonic considerations, with passages in homophonic style.

Rise of Tonality

By the end of the Renaissance, two of the modes—those beginning on A and C—were being used more often than the others; but it was not until the seventeenth century that composers developed and theoreticians articulated the **tonal system, in** which every note of the major or minor scale bears a specific relationship to every other note, and all of the pitches are more or less closely related to the tonic. It was at this time that composers recognized and utilized the chord we call a triad (see p. 23) as an entity; it was no longer the result of a combination of passing voice lines, but a meaningful and consonant unit of sound. The increasing use of triads built upon all the degrees of the major or minor scale gave a sense of stability and harmonic direction to tonal music that had not been inherent in modality.

Thus, the tonal system of harmony, implied in some early English music and approached by composers in the late Renaissance, was wholly adopted during the seventeenth century. By the late 1600s, tonality had replaced modality as the means of organizing the composition of Western music.

Summary

The preferred style of music during the seventeenth century and the first part of the eighteenth was the dramatic, emotional style we call Baroque. During this age of contrasts, secular art assumed equal importance with religious works, as scientists and philosophers vied with clerics for the attention and faith of the people. Paintings of this period were vivid in color and filled with activity; sculpture and architecture also were dramatic instead of serene. Literature, too, achieved a strong emotional impact.

By the late seventeenth century, the Baroque style of music had fully evolved; the replacement of modality by the tonal system of harmony affected every aspect of music composition. As concerned with harmonic as with melodic aspects of their music, Baroque composers organized their works "vertically" as well as "horizontally."

Critical Thinking

- Why do you suppose that the modes we recognize as the major and minor scales came to be preferred over the other modes for a very long historical period? How do the major and minor modes sound different from each other? From the other modes? Why do you think many composers today use modal instead of, or as well as, tonal effects in their music?

Terms to Review

Baroque The term, originally meaning irregular, now applied to the dramatic, emotional style of seventeenth- and early-eighteenth-century art.

movement A section of a complete work that has its own formal design and a degree of independence, but conceived as a part of the whole; usually separated from other movements by a pause.

tonal system The system of harmony based upon the major and the minor scales.

Key Figures

Scientists	*Galileo Galilei*
	Isaac Newton
Philosophers	*Francis Bacon*
	René Descartes
Literary Figures	*Miguel de Cervantes Saavedra*
	Jean Baptiste Poquelin Molière

Artists	*Caravaggio (Michelangelo Merisi)*
	Frans Hals
	Rembrandt van Rijn
	Jan Vermeer
	Peter Paul Rubens
	Gianlorenzo Bernini
Composers	*Johann Sebastian Bach*
	George Frideric Handel

14
Dramatic Vocal Music of the Baroque

At the beginning of the seventeenth century, even those composers who exploited the expressive characteristics of monody in their solo madrigals and other secular songs often found Palestrina's polyphonic style of composition more suitable than monody for church music. Thus, in the style-conscious manner of the Baroque, they used the old style (Palestrina's) for one purpose and the new (monody) for another.

The composer who referred to these two styles respectively as the "first" and "second" practices of music was **Claudio Monteverdi,** whose music was admired in his own time and is still performed and appreciated today.

Mon-te-vär'-dē

Claudio
Monteverdi
(1567–1643)

For thirty years, Monteverdi served as choirmaster at St. Mark's in Venice, where Giovanni Gabrieli had composed and performed great works in the Venetian polychoral style. As choirmaster, Monteverdi composed motets and other religious compositions using Renaissance techniques.

However, Monteverdi shared Gesualdo's taste for dramatic and emotional settings of madrigal texts. He avoided Gesualdo's extreme chromaticism, but nevertheless startled his contemporaries with his use of dissonance for expressive purposes. Dissonant combinations long had been used for dramatic emphasis, but composers had accepted certain conventions regarding their use: dissonances were to be approached and resolved according to rather strict rules, and they normally occurred on weak beats.

But Monteverdi allowed the text of his songs, rather than the prevailing rules of music theory, to determine his use of dissonance—thereby offending conservative individuals who listened to music with Renaissance ears. He suggested that the conventional rules constituted the **first practice** of music and should be respected in the composition of serious or conservative pieces; but he considered the **second practice,** as he called his dramatic style of madrigal composition, more suitable for the setting of secular songs.

By the term first practice (sometimes called the *stile antico*), Monteverdi referred to Palestrina's style of choral polyphony, in which all of the voices were nearly equal in importance and the music, although sensitive to the expression of a text, was nevertheless the composer's priority. Many musicians continued to find this style appropriate for church music for two reasons:

a. The texts of religious compositions, usually taken from familiar biblical or liturgical sources, were easily recognized, even in a complex polyphonic setting.

b. The cool emotional atmosphere of this style was considered to enhance worship.

First and
Second
Practice

Table 14.1	Comparison of First and Second Practices
First Practice	**Second Practice**
Polyphonic texture	Homophonic texture
Music dominates text	Text dominates music
Often used for church music	Often used for secular songs

Many of the same composers, however, possessing the Baroque love for drama, often reversed the relationship between music and text in their secular songs, allowing the emotional content of the words to determine the means of expression. This expressive style, which Monteverdi referred to as the second practice or the *stile moderno,* was generally homophonic in texture. (See table 14.1.)

Thus, according to the first practice, in which the music was more significant than the text, the established rules of music theory were observed and the texture was predominantly polyphonic. In the second practice, the text dominated the music, and rules might be broken for the purpose of better expressing the words. Here the texture was usually homophonic.

Although the system of tonality was not fully established when Monteverdi wrote his first madrigals in the new expressive style, he observed certain tonal principles. Monteverdi's bass line was an organizing and stabilizing element; it supported the melody or melodies above, and gave his music a sense of direction, of harmonic drive. He and other early Baroque composers used the triad as a chord and recognized rudimentary relationships between triads, thus producing music with a new sense of stability. As tonality became more firmly established, both chromaticism and dissonance were used more freely, supported by the reliable movement of the bass voice and by the systematic use of logical chord progressions.

Early Opera

The ancient Greeks had combined music with drama; in the Middle Ages, music accompanied liturgical plays; and in the sixteenth century, short but spectacular music dramas called *intermedii* had entertained audiences between the acts of a play. Madrigals sometimes constituted mini–music dramas in themselves, with different voices or combinations of voices answering each other in dialogue form.

However, with the possible exception of the Greeks, musicians prior to the Baroque period had not produced a type of vocal music suitable for the presentation of a full-length music drama. The polyphonic madrigal, with its several equal voices, precluded the rapid and efficient articulation of a text, and even the solo madrigal, a late-sixteenth-century solo song with instrumental accompaniment, remained too dependent upon musical considerations to effectively express a lengthy text.

On the other hand, the new type of vocal writing introduced by the Florentine monodists was eminently suited for dramatic recitation. Thus, the earliest **operas—** music dramas sung throughout—consisted almost entirely of monody.

Early operas, composed around 1600, were actually less elaborate than some of the earlier intermedii. The same **librettos,** or texts, based upon Greek mythology, were set to music over and over again and performed by small casts accompanied by a few music instruments. Yet these early operas were enthusiastically received by audiences, who were moved not only by the expressiveness of the new singing style, but also by the sheer beauty of the highly trained singing voice.

The invention of monody was of unparalleled importance to the history of Western music, for it demonstrated that a solo singer could express a text clearly and dramatically while singing beautiful music. However, composers soon recognized two distinct types of solo singing, each implied, but not achieved, by monody: the *recitative* and the *aria*.

The word **recitative** (from the same root as *recitation*) refers both to a particular style of singing and to a particular piece of music. The style is closely related to spoken declamation, and the piece is a section of music sung in that style.

Several characteristics of recitative render it particularly suitable for the rapid exchange of dialogue or the efficient and economical presentation of a long text:

Recitative
res-i-tah-tēv′

Melody
The melody of a recitative reflects something of the natural inflection that would occur in a spoken presentation of the text. Although extremely high or low pitches may be used for descriptive or dramatic purposes, the vocal range of a recitative is usually rather narrow, as it is in speech.

Rhythm
The rhythm of recitative is free or flexible, the words normally set in syllabic style. The rhythm may be metered, but in performance the singer freely adapts the rhythm to that of the text.

Form
Recitative is flexible in form, adaptable to the demands of the text.

Texture
Recitative is generally homophonic in texture, consisting of a vocal line supported by an instrumental accompaniment.

   a. *Dry recitative* is accompanied by occasional chords played on a keyboard, or by the small group of instruments called a *continuo*. (See p. 121.)

   b. *Accompanied recitative* is accompanied by the orchestra.

An **aria** (in English works sometimes called an "air") is more closely related to musical than to textual concerns. It often corresponds to a dramatic soliloquy, providing the opportunity for reflection upon, and emotional reaction to, events that have occurred in the drama. In this sense, the aria was well adapted to the Baroque doctrine of the *affections,* since it was confined to the expression of a particular mood or emotional state. The text of a Baroque aria is usually rather short, with words and phrases repeated for dramatic emphasis and for musical organization.

Arias differ from recitatives in melody, rhythm, form, and accompaniment.

Aria
metered structured rhythm, homophonic backed by orchestra became so popular that the term bel canto "beautiful voice"

Melody
Arias often have soaring melody lines, designed to move the emotions and display the beauty of the singing voice. Since the text is of secondary importance, there is often ample opportunity for vocal display. During the Baroque, singers were expected to add elaborate embellishments to the melody, especially during the repetition of a section of the piece.

Rhythm

An aria has metered rhythm and is performed with less distortion of the rhythm that is typical of recitative.

Form

An aria has a formal design. One frequently used form is the **da capo** aria, which has an *A B A* design. The first section (*A*) and the second (*B*), usually contrasting in mood, melodic material, and key, are presented; then the singer repeats the *A* section, usually adding vocal embellishments.

Accompaniment

An aria is accompanied by the orchestra, which not only supports the vocal line and enriches the sonority, but often has melodic responsibility as well, introducing or imitating phrases of the vocal line and providing instrumental preludes and interludes.

Monteverdi was the first composer to realize that successful music drama requires a skillful blending of the literary, visual, and performance arts. His 1607 opera *Orfeo,* based on the Greek myth of Orpheus and Euridice, included recitatives, arias, duets, other vocal ensembles, and even dances, all colorfully accompanied by a forty-piece orchestra. A great success in its day, *Orfeo* is still performed in opera houses around the world.

"Tu se' morta," (Listening Example 12) is a famous example of Monteverdi's style. It is generally referred to as a recitative, though it has the emotional expressiveness later associated more often with an aria. We may view it as a seminal work having elements of both kinds of solo singing.

The first public opera house opened in Venice in 1637, and soon there were opera houses in other Italian cities and other countries as well. But by the early eighteenth century, the classical ideals of the Florentine Camerata had been overturned. No longer did opera purport to simply and naturally express a dramatic text. The drama now had become a mere framework around which composers and stage designers created marvelous musical and visual effects. Staging, costumes, and scenery grew ever more elaborate. With the aid of complicated machinery, gods flew to earth, people ascended to heaven, and earthquakes, fires, and tempests added to the entertainment. At an opera staged by Bernini in Rome, a "fire" on the stage appeared so real that the audience fled from the theater!

It seems paradoxical indeed that the classically inspired monody led very soon to the extravagant, flamboyant, romantic form we call Baroque opera.

Bel Canto

Arias reigned supreme in late Baroque Italian opera, their simple, repetitive, and familiar texts providing effective vehicles for virtuosic vocal display. The singing voice attained artistic levels never before conceived, and audiences flocked to the opera house to hear their favorite soloists sing their favorite arias. People chatted, ate, and drank during the recitatives, interested only in the beautiful melodies and vocal display of the arias. The term **bel canto** (Italian for "beautiful singing") is applied to this type of opera, which emphasizes the beauty and virtuosity of the singing voice, even at the expense of dramatic integrity.

For the first time, clear distinctions were drawn between music that was instrumentally conceived and music intended to be sung; moreover, *how* one sang (or played an instrument) was as important as *what* one performed. Heated disputes occurred between composers, who wanted their melodies sung as they were written, and singers, who took increasing liberties with the melody lines. Differences between those who believe that the text of an opera is most important ("opera is primarily a

1 [29] 1A 12

LISTENING EXAMPLE 12

Early Recitative

Composer: Claudio Monteverdi (1567–1643)

Title: "Tu se' morta," from *Orfeo,* Act II

First performed: 1607

Genre: Recitative from an opera

Rhythm: Flexible; follows the pattern of speech

Texture: Homophonic. The bass line indicates the chords to be filled in by the accompanying keyboard instrument.

Harmony: Basically tonal. Dissonance is used for expressive effect.

Melody: The chromatic, declamatory melody line appears motivated by textual concerns more than by purely musical ones.

Timbre: Solo tenor voice accompanied by continuo (a portable organ and bass lute)

When Orpheus (Orfeo) learns of Euridice's death, he vows in despair to follow her to the underworld.

[29]	0:00	Tu se' morta, se' morta,	Thou art perished, art perished,
....		*("Tu"—emotional pause)*	
....		mia vita.	beloved,
....		ed io respiro,	and I yet linger
....		tu se' da me partita,	thou art from me departed,
....		se' de me partita per mai più,	art from me departed forever,
....		mai più non tornare,	yea never returning,
0:68	0:68	ed io rimango nò! nò!	and I remain here—no! no!
....		*("rimango"—emotional high pitch)*	
....		che sei versi alcuna cosa ponno,	for if verses may have any power,
1:01	1:01	n'andrò sicuro al più profondi	then shall I seek the most profound
....		abissi,	abysses,
....		*("abissi"—dark, low pitch)*	
....		e in tenerito il cor del rè del	and with my song entreat the king
....		l'ombre,	of shadows
1:20	1:20	meco trarotti a reverder	to let me bring thee to see again the
....		le stelle,	heavens,
....		*("stelle"—high, climactic)*	
....		o se ciò negherammi empio destino,	or if this cruel fortune still denies me,
....			
1:35	1:35	rimarò teco in compagnia	I shall stay with thee within the
....		di morte!	realm of shadows!
....		*("morte"—dark, low pitch)*	
1:49	1:49	Addio terra,	Farewell earth, then,
....		*("terra"—dark, low pitch)*	
....		addio cielo,	farewell heavens,
....		e sole, addio.	and sunlight, forever.
....		*("sole"—high tone)*	

Lyrics reprinted from *Masterpieces of Music Before 1750.* Compiled and Edited by Carl Parrish and John F. Ohl, by permission of W. W. Norton & Company, Inc. Copyright 1951 by W. W. Norton & Company, Inc. Copyright renewed 1979 by John F. Ohl and Catherine C. Parrish.

dramatic form") and those who believe that the text may be sacrificed for musical effect ("opera is primarily a musical form") began with the earliest operas and persist today.

Although male singers known as **castrati** (eunuchs) were extravagantly admired for the extreme range and power of their voices, a taste for women's voices developed during the seventeenth and early eighteenth centuries, leading to the decline of the castrato and the rise of the *prima donna,* or virtuoso female singer. (The term *prima donna,* meaning "first lady," originally referred to the singer of the principal female role in an opera.) Schools for destitute girls in Venice and other cities provided advanced music instruction in singing and playing instruments, and noble families encouraged their daughters to become accomplished musicians. Soon there was a demand at courts, castles, and various private occasions for performances by professional as well as amateur female musicians. Women were largely denied the professional opportunities available to men as directors of court or church music ensembles; but a few gifted women attained prestigious posts, composing and directing as well as performing music to generous acclaim.

Ballad Opera

By the 1720s, audiences were beginning to tire of the highly stylized Baroque opera. The librettos were not terribly interesting, little effort was put into acting, and first French, then German and English audiences lost interest in performances sung in Italian. A new dramatic form called the **ballad opera,** which adapted familiar catchy tunes to present an amusing story in English, quickly became popular in England. In 1728, English poet and playwright John Gay produced *The Beggar's Opera* in this style, ridiculing some of the more obvious limitations of Italian Baroque opera, to the huge enjoyment of English audiences, who soon abandoned the opera house in favor of Gay's hilarious entertainment.

George Frideric Handel was thereby forced to abandon the form that had made him a rich man and turn—with enormous success—to another new dramatic vocal form, the oratorio.

George Frideric Handel (1685–1759)

Handel, who was born in Germany, spent considerable time in Italy, and eventually became a British citizen, was the prototype of the Baroque composer. A religious man and one of the greatest organists and harpsichordists of his day, Handel nevertheless composed more music for the theater than for the church. Even his religious music had a decidedly dramatic flair, for drama was in his soul. Having spent three years in Rome, Handel proceeded to compose a large number of highly successful Italian operas.

In 1710, Handel was appointed court musician to the Elector of Hanover, Germany. But soon, possessing the independent personality characteristic of romantics, Handel requested a leave of absence to visit England and left the Elector's court—never to return. Handel liked England, where he wrote and produced many Italian operas for the appreciative English audience.

Handel was slow to realize, however, that changing public taste meant the end of the Italian opera's reign in England. Having made a sizeable fortune, he literally faced bankruptcy before finally—to his good fortune and ours—abandoning Italian opera to compose oratorios instead.

The **oratorio,** like the opera, developed early in the Baroque period, and the two forms share many characteristics. Both are vocal dramatic works originally conceived for popular entertainment. However, an oratorio is based upon a religious subject, often with a story derived from the Old Testament of the Bible. Some early oratorios were costumed and staged in the manner of operas, but by Handel's time oratorios were conceived for concert performance, as they are today.

There is proportionately less recitative in Handel's oratorios than in his operas, and the arias are less flamboyant and generally require less virtuosity. The chorus—a composition for a group of singers with several voices on each part—is used extensively. Like an aria, a chorus has formal design, metered rhythm, and an orchestral accompaniment. It may be either homophonic or polyphonic, and often includes sections of both textures.

Handel's *Messiah,* the world's best-known and best-loved oratorio, is in some ways uncharacteristic of the oratorio form, for it is a series of contemplations on the life of Christ rather than a story with an integrated plot. Its subject is drawn from the New Testament rather than the Old, and its soloists comment upon dramatic events in which they do not participate.

Messiah has three long sections, each dealing with a particular period in the life of Christ. Handel composed this long and powerful work in the incredibly short time of about three weeks. Amazed at the power and the beauty of his own oratorio, Handel believed it to have been divinely inspired.

Handel's other oratorios, also enthusiastically received by his English audience, continue to thrill listeners around the world today. They are based upon familiar Bible stories, are performed in English, and have stirring choruses that especially appealed, as choral music does today, to the English. (King George II was so enthralled by the glorious "Hallelujah" chorus in *Messiah* that he rose from his seat, and since then it has become traditional for the audience to rise whenever that chorus is performed.)

Johann Sebastian Bach (1685–1750)

Johann Sebastian Bach was born the same year as Handel, and although Handel lived several years longer, the date of Bach's death is generally accepted as the end of the Baroque period. By that time many composers had already left the heavy drama and fervent religious expression of the Baroque and turned to the lighter, more graceful, and more secular Rococo and Classical styles.

Although Bach was Handel's contemporary, there were many important differences between them. Both men wrote religious and secular music, but Bach was essentially a man of the church, and Handel a man of the theater. Handel was a great impresario who won and lost fortunes during his turbulent career; Bach was a practical and methodical musician who dutifully composed and performed for the Church. Handel never married; Bach was a dedicated family man who married twice and fathered a large number of children. Handel demanded professional independence; Bach generally served the will of his employers. While Handel's music was intended primarily to entertain, much of Bach's music was composed for purely practical purposes, to teach or to fulfill his obligations as a church musician.

Oratorio

or-a-tor'-ē-ō

Messiah

In the style-conscious manner of his period, Bach wrote many kinds of music, each suitable for a particular purpose. He wrote quantities of choral music for the churches he served, as well as two large choral works called **Passions,** oratorios based upon the events leading to the crucifixion of Christ. Although a Protestant, Bach also wrote a long and very beautiful Mass, hoping to attract the favorable attention of an influential Catholic Elector. The position Bach sought was not awarded him for several years, but his *B Minor Mass* contains some of the most glorious music ever written.

Cantata

Among Bach's many compositions are nearly two hundred dramatic vocal works, some religious, some secular, called **cantatas.** (The term *cantata* originally meant a piece to be sung, as opposed to the instrumental *sonata.*) The Baroque religious cantata was specifically a vocal dramatic work, based upon a religious story, with recitatives, arias, and choruses sung in the vernacular and accompanied by an organ and usually a small orchestra. Since the cantata was intended for church rather than concert performance, its style is often somewhat restrained, and it is considerably shorter in length than an oratorio.

1 30 # LISTENING EXAMPLE 13   1A 13

Oratorio Chorus

Composer: George Frideric Handel (1685–1759)

Title: "And the glory of the Lord," from *Messiah,* Part I

Composed: 1741

Genre: Chorus from an Oratorio

Rhythm: Allegro; Triple meter

Timbre: 4-part chorus; 2 oboes, strings, and continuo

30	0:00	**A** Orchestral introduction
0:11	0:11	"And the glory, the glory of the Lord" *(homophonic texture; introduced by the altos)*
0:19	0:19	"shall be revealed" *(imitative polyphonic texture; introduced by the tenors)*
0:44	0:44	Brief orchestral interlude
31	0:50	**B** "And all flesh shall see it together"
0:09	0:59	"For the mouth of the Lord hath spoken it" *(sung with "And all flesh shall see it together")*
32	1:25	**A and B combined**
33	2:04	**A** "And the glory, the glory of the Lord shall be revealed"
0:15	2:19	**B** "And all flesh shall see it together"
0:22	2:26	"For the mouth"
34	2:41	**Coda**—"Hath spoken it" *(Adagio tempo; homophonic texture)*

Morning hymn: Bach at home with his family.
Stock Montage, Inc., Chicago

Those cantatas intended for performance in the Lutheran church service were based upon chorale tunes that suggested a dramatic and musical subject for the work. The chorale also provided a unifying element throughout the multimovement composition, recurring in several sections. The congregation often joined the choir in singing the familiar chorale tune in the last movement of the cantata.

Summary

Monteverdi recognized the values of both the Renaissance polyphonic and the new homophonic styles of composition, referring to them as the first and second practices, respectively. Composers of the Baroque period combined these techniques to introduce three new dramatic vocal forms: opera, oratorio, and cantata. Each of these new forms included speech-related recitatives, songlike arias, and elaborate choruses, and each was accompanied by an orchestra.

By the late seventeenth century, Italian opera, dominated by arias in the bel canto style, had achieved wide popularity. However, the English audience eventually tired of foreign operas and responded enthusiastically to ballad operas in their own language. Having lost the fortune he had made as a composer of Italian operas, Handel turned to the composition of oratorios instead. His *Messiah* remains the best-known and best-loved oratorio in the world today.

Bach lived at the same time as Handel, but the two composers were quite different in temperament and experience. Bach was a church musician and a teacher, primarily dedicated to the service of his employers. His vocal music includes a large number of cantatas, two long Passions, and the famous *Mass in B Minor*.

Critical Thinking

- What do you consider the ideal relationship between words and music in vocal music?

- Do you always listen to the words of popular songs?

- If you have experience with opera, oratorio, the Broadway musical, and/or operettas, do you think the words or the music should be of more importance in each case?

- Do you think Handel's *Messiah* will continue to be as popular in the twenty-first century as it has been in the twentieth? Explain your answer.

Terms to Review

first practice or *stile antico*   The polyphonic, conservative style of the late Renaissance.

second practice or *stile moderno*   The homophonic, expressive style introduced by Monteverdi.

opera   A dramatic vocal form blending visual, literary, and musical arts, performed in a theater or opera house.

libretto   The text of a dramatic vocal work.

recitative   A speechlike setting of a text, with homophonic accompaniment by a keyboard (dry recitative) or an orchestra (accompanied recitative).

aria   A songlike setting, musically expressive, accompanied by the orchestra; generally homophonic in texture.

da capo **aria**   An aria with an *A B A* design.

bel canto   The eighteenth-century Italian singing style that emphasized the beauty and virtuosity of the voice.

castrato   A castrated male singer.

ballad opera   An English dramatic form in which comedy and satire were set to popular tunes.   *Handel developed*

oratorio   A dramatic vocal work on a religious subject, performed in a concert hall or church.

Passion   An oratorio based on the events leading to the crucifixion of Christ.   *Bach*

cantata   A multimovement dramatic vocal work on a religious or secular subject, performed in concert style.

Composers   *Claudio Monteverdi*
John Gay
George Frideric Handel
Johann Sebastian Bach

Key Figures

15
Baroque Instrumental Music

Baroque composers of instrumental music benefited from advances made in instrumental styles and techniques during the Renaissance; and since they did not have to be concerned with setting a text, they were at an advantage compared with composers of vocal music. Many music instruments and instrumental techniques became extraordinarily advanced during the Baroque, when for the first time instrumental music became equal, in quantity and quality, with music for the voice.

Renaissance forms continued to be used, along with a number of new instrumental forms. Keyboard music increased in variety and quantity, as the lute declined in popularity and the harpsichord and organ became more important.

Music for Keyboards

Many of the kinds of pieces that had made up the lute repertoire were now played on the harpsichord instead. The harpsichord also was used to accompany performances of many kinds. The pipe organ's ability to produce a variety of timbres, dynamic levels, and pitches made it well suited to the Baroque taste for dramatic contrasts. Organists were able to achieve the abrupt change of dynamic levels called **terraced dynamics,** a distinctive feature of Baroque music, while changing stops and moving from one keyboard to another also provided a wide range of sonorities.

Although some organs have been made larger since the time of Bach and Handel, and although electric and electronic features, more pedals, and different stops have been added in modern times, the organ has not been improved since the early eighteenth century. As a matter of fact, today's organ builders often endeavor to build organs, such as the beautiful mechanical-action pipe organ shown in Color Plate 1, with the same mechanical principles and qualities of sound as the magnificent organs of the Baroque.

Several important forms of music intended for performance on a keyboard instrument were introduced or advanced during the Baroque.

Fugue

The **fugue** is a polyphonic composition with three to five melodic lines, or voices. The first voice presents the *subject,* or principal melody, which is then imitated by each of the other voices in turn. The entrances alternate between the tonic and dominant keys, with those in the dominant called the *answer* (see figure 15.1).

Whereas the imitation in a round or canon is literal (with each voice performing the same melody in turn), the imitation in a fugue is merely similar, since the answer begins on a different tone from the subject. Also, in the fugue—unlike the canon or round—each voice proceeds with independent material after it has entered. There are usually references to the subject and answer throughout a fugue, but the form is quite flexible after the opening section, or *exposition,* of the fugue is completed.

Soon fugues were being written for instruments other than the lute or keyboard, and they are also very effective in choral music. Some keyboard fugues, such as Bach's "Little" Fugue in G Minor (Listening Example 14), constitute independent

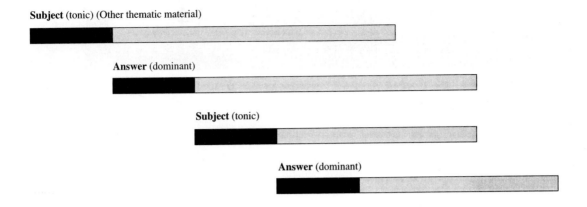

Figure 15.1

Diagram of the exposition of a four-voice fugue.

compositions, some are the second of a contrasting pair of pieces, and some form one movement of a multimovement work.

A **prelude** is a relatively short keyboard piece that may be either an independent composition or the introduction to another piece or set of pieces. Preludes often are improvisatory in style, suggesting that the performer is testing the instrument, or "warming up" for the more structured and virtuosic piece or pieces to follow. The prelude and fugue were a common pair during the late Baroque.

One of Bach's greatest legacies was a set of forty-eight preludes and fugues called the *Well-Tempered Clavier,* which included preludes and fugues in each of the major and minor keys. (*Well-tempered* is a method of tuning keyboard instruments, and *clavier* is a general term for keyboards.) Even during the century after his death, when Bach's music was generally unknown or out of favor, this set of preludes and fugues, together with a second similar volume, remained in print and was highly valued.

The **chorale prelude** is a religious keyboard composition based upon the melody of a Lutheran chorale. Like much of the music of the Baroque, the chorale prelude served a practical purpose: it allowed a church congregation to hear a chorale melody played on the organ before singing it themselves.

A **toccata** is a virtuosic keyboard piece that exploits the technical brilliance of the performer. The toccata was a popular form for lute or keyboard during the Renaissance, and became of major importance for harpsichord and organ during the Baroque. Like the prelude, the toccata often has an improvisatory character, with a flexible rhythm and elaborate embellishment of the melody lines. The melodies of a toccata tend to be more rhapsodic than tuneful, in keeping with the improvisatory quality of the piece.

Toccatas often featured a favorite melodic device of the Baroque: the use of melodic **sequence.** This is the repetition of a melodic phrase at different levels of pitch. Examples abound in all kinds of music from every period. The second phrase of "Three Blind Mice" ("see how they run") is a repetition of the first melodic pattern at a higher level of pitch; the four-note pattern at the beginning of Beethoven's

Prelude

Toccata
show off talents of preformer

₁ 35   # LISTENING EXAMPLE 14   1A 14

Fugue

Composer: Johann Sebastian Bach (1685–1750)

Title: "Little" Fugue in G minor

Composed: ca. 1709

Form: A fugue

Rhythm: Quadruple meter

Timbre: Organ

Texture: Imitative polyphony

Exposition

Voice I :	**subject**	countersubject (rest)	free counterpoint
Voice II:	**answer**	countersubject (rest)	
Voice III:		**subject**	countersubject
Voice IV:			**answer**

	35	0:00	**Subject**	(tonic, g minor)	
	. . . .		Begins with a *broken triad* (played one note at a time instead of simultaneously) in the order 1–5–3; enters in Voice I (soprano range)		
	0:18	0:18	**Answer**	(dominant, d minor)	
	. . . .		Voice II (alto range) enters with the **answer** in the dominant key as Voice I continues with the *countersubject* (new thematic material that follows the subject and is treated by each voice in turn).		
	0:41	0:41	**Subject**	(tonic, g minor)	
	. . . .		Voice III (tenor range) enters with the subject as Voice II continues with the countersubject.		
	0:59	0:59	**Answer**	(dominant, d minor)	
	. . . .		Voice IV (bass range) enters with the answer as Voice III continues with the countersubject. (End of exposition)		
	36	1:15	Episode (note the sequences used in the episodes)		
	0:10	1:25	**Subject** (begins in Voice III; moves to Voice I)		(tonic, g minor)
	0:30	1:45	Episode	(modulates)	
	0:38	1:53	**Subject** (Voice II; now in the major mode)		(Bb major)
	0:52	2:07	Episode		
	1:05	2:20	**Subject** (Voice IV)	(Bb major)	
	1:21	2:36	Episode	(modulates)	
	1:39	2:54	**Subject** (Voice I)	(c minor)	
	1:55	3:10	Episode (much longer than the other episodes)		(modulates)
	2:25	3:40	**Subject** (Voice IV)	(tonic, g minor)	

Symphony no. 5 is repeated at a lower pitch level; the phrase "Land where my fathers died" in "America" is succeeded by "Land of the pilgrim's pride," the same melodic pattern at a lower level of pitch.

Sequence often occurs in showy toccatas, providing a simple technique for moving rapidly through many keys. Remember that tonality was a relatively new concept for composers in the Baroque, and they delighted in experimenting—sometimes to extremes—with changing keys. They always returned, however, to the security of tonic.

Just as the speechlike recitative is often succeeded by an aria in vocal music, the flexible and improvisatory toccata is often followed by a tightly structured fugue. Such contrasts eminently suited the baroque taste for contrast.

Suite

The short sets of dance pieces for lute or keyboard that were popular during the Renaissance were expanded in the Baroque to multimovement works consisting of several dance pieces, called **suites.** A suite sometimes was introduced by a short prelude or overture, after which each section had the characteristic style, tempo, and rhythmic patterns of a particular dance, highly stylized and intended for listening rather than dancing.

The Continuo

Except for solo lute and keyboard pieces, all other kinds of Baroque solo and ensemble music were accompanied by a small group of music instruments called the **continuo.** This important new performance practice derived from the emphasis on the strong bass voice, called the **thoroughbass,** which sounded continuously throughout Baroque ensemble compositions, and had functional as well as aesthetic significance. The continuo included at least one sustaining bass instrument, such as a cello, a bassoon, or a string bass, that played the all-important bass line. It also contained a lute or keyboard instrument that played the bass line as well and the melody as notated by the composer, while "filling in" the unwritten middle voices, thus completing the harmonies implied and supported by the bass. Keyboard (or lute) players improvised the inner parts according to the rules of tonality, completing the triad built upon each bass note—unless the composer indicated otherwise by using a system of musical shorthand called the *figured bass.*

The **figured bass** allowed composers to indicate the desired interval or intervals above a bass note, should they be other than the third and the fifth (the triad built upon the bass note). The composer simply wrote above or below the bass note the number or "figure" representing the interval required, leaving it to keyboard players to *realize* (complete the harmonies above) the figured bass line. This system of notation and improvisation, exemplifying the vertical, or chordal, orientation of the Baroque musician's thought process, was so important in the Baroque that the period is sometimes referred to as the "Age of the Figured Bass."

Chamber Music

A good deal of **chamber music** was written during the Baroque, when several music instruments were brought to a peak of perfection. The flute, greatly improved in quality, greatly gained in popularity as well. The period also produced the world's finest violins, including those made by the famous Stradivari and Guarneri families. The new violins differed in several respects from the viols of the Renaissance; new methods of construction and new bowing techniques produced a louder sound better suited to the romantic taste of the Baroque music lover.

Sonata

The **sonata,** a multimovement form for one or more solo instruments accompanied by a continuo, became an important form in the seventeenth century. Unfortunately, inclusion in the continuo of more than one instrument led to some confusion in terminology concerning the Baroque sonata. The **trio sonata,** for example, was so called because it had three written lines of music—two melody lines and a bass—though it required a minimum of four performers, one for each of the two melody lines and at least two for the continuo.

Arcangelo Corelli, an Italian violin virtuoso and composer. Engraving by Van Der Gucht.
The Bettman Archive, NY

There were two types of Baroque sonatas:

a. The **sonata da camera,** similar to the dance-related keyboard suites, was intended for concert (secular) performance.

b. The **sonata da chiesa,** for performance in church, was somewhat more serious, yet generally included dance movements that simply were not labeled as such.

Antonio Vivaldi.
The Bettman Archive, NY

Arcangelo Corelli was famous in his own time as a virtuoso violinist and an out-standing composer of music for the instrument he played so beautifully. Apparently never tempted to write for the singing voice, he frequently treated the violin as a singing instrument instead. In his beautiful trio sonatas, Corelli perfected the achievements of earlier composers; and his solo sonatas and concertos made advances of immeasurable value to composers who followed.

The Renaissance consort of instruments of similar timbre was generally replaced in the Baroque with the mixed ensemble we call an **orchestra.** Early orchestras were

*Arcangelo
Corelli
(1653–1713)*

Orchestral
Music

basically string ensembles with a few wind instruments to add color and variety to the sound. Baroque composers often required great virtuosity of the players in these small orchestras.

The concertato principle, described in chapter 12, appealed strongly to Baroque musicians, who particularly enjoyed the effect of contrasting sonorities. In fact, the orchestral form called a **concerto**—a multimovement composition for orchestra and one or more solo instruments—was based upon "concerted" effort by two or more opposing elements. Like the sonata, the concerto also afforded Baroque composers the variety they appreciated in tempo, mood, and key.

The most prolific composer of Baroque concertos was Antonio Vivaldi.

Antonio Vivaldi (1678–1741)

Though ordained a priest, **Antonio Vivaldi** spent most of his life as a professional musician. He taught at a Venice orphanage-conservatory for girls, and traveled to other European cities as a guest conductor of opera and orchestra performances. He wrote vast numbers of choral and orchestral compositions, as well as many operas, responding to the demand in his day for quantities of new music.

Among the most famous and best-loved Baroque compositions is Vivaldi's set of four violin concertos titled *The Four Seasons*. Scored for a string orchestra and three solo violins, each of these concertos includes dramatic virtuoso passages for solo violin. Vivaldi prefaced each concerto by a sonnet, the words of which are repeated in the score in passages where the music is intended to express a particular programmatic idea. These attractive pieces abound with colorful references to the sounds and effects of nature, revealing Vivaldi's gift for achieving varied orchestral sonorities. Listening Example 15 features the "Spring" Concerto from *The Four Seasons*.

Concerto Grosso

The Baroque also produced an abundance of the kind of concerto called a **concerto grosso**: a composition for string orchestra plus a small *group* of solo instruments. The

 1 37   # LISTENING EXAMPLE 15   1B 1

Solo Concerto

Composer: Antonio Vivaldi (1678–1741)

Title: "Spring" Concerto (from *The Four Seasons*), first movement

Composed: c. 1725

Genre: Concerto

Form: Ritornello

Rhythm: Allegro; Quadruple meter.

Dynamics: Some tutti sections are played *forte* and then *piano*, providing an echo effect. There are no crescendos or diminuendos between loud and soft.

Melody: The theme presented at the beginning consists of two contrasting phrases. Each is presented *forte* and then immediately repeated *piano*. Only the second phrase returns throughout the remainder of the movement.

Timbre: *Concertino*—violin (occasionally joined by two other solo violins)
    Tutti/ripieno—violins, violas, and double bass
    Continuo—cello and harpsichord

Key: E major

Program: Following is the introduction Vivaldi wrote for this concerto:

I.   *Spring has come, and the birds greet it with happy songs, and at the same time the streams run softly murmuring to the breathing of the gentle breezes. Then the sky being cloaked in black, thunder and lightning come and have their say; after the storm has quieted, the little birds turn again to their harmonious song.*

II.   *Here in a pleasant flowery meadow, the leaves sweetly rustle, the goatherd sleeps, his faithful dog at his side.*

III.   *Nymphs and shepherds dance to the festive sound of the pastoral musette under the bright sky that they love.*

37	0:00	**Ritornello—Main theme ("Spring has come")** (tonic, E Major)	

The bold main theme is presented in two phrases (a) and (b).
a   *forte*
a   *piano* (as an echo)
b   *forte*
b   *piano* (as an echo)

38	0:34	**"Songs of the Birds"**

The solo violin along with two additional violins play various ornaments (such as trills) in a high range. These are meant to imitate various bird songs. The other instruments are silent during this section.

0:37	1:11	**Ritornello—Main theme (phrase b only)** (tonic, E Major)	

b   *forte*

39	1:20	**"Murmuring Streams and Gentle Breezes"**

Gently flowing lines in the orchestra, *piano*

0:25	1:45	**Ritornello—Main theme (phrase b only)** (B Major)

The main theme returns, now at a lower pitch in the key of B major.

40	1:54	**"Storm"**

Thunder is depicted by a tremolo in the orchestra and is heard intermittently throughout this section. The violins play a fast ascending scale to depict lightning. A different figure representing lightning as well (perhaps lightning jumping from cloud to cloud) is played by the solo violin.

0:28	2:22	**Ritornello—Main theme (phrase b only)** (c# minor)

After the storm, the main theme is now heard in the minor mode.

41	2:30	**"Return of the Bird Songs"**

The solo violin is joined again by two other solo violins in a musical representation of various bird songs.

0:18	2:48	The tutti enters with material that is reminiscent to the main theme.
0:30	3:00	This section ends with one last passage for the solo violin.
0:44	3:14	**Ritornello—Main theme (phrase b only)** (tonic, E Major)

b   *forte*
b   *piano* (as a final echo, bringing the movement to a satisfactory ending)

solo ensemble of a Baroque concerto grosso often consisted of two violins and continuo, but many other combinations also were used late in the period. Just as in the solo concerto, passages alternate between those for full orchestra (called **tutti,** or **ripieno**), those for solo group (called **concertino**) alone, and those for tutti and ripieno together. A concerto grosso usually has three movements, in the order fast–slow–fast.

Corelli is said to have virtually invented the concerto grosso, and Vivaldi and Handel wrote many concertos of this kind for a wide variety of solo combinations and an orchestra augmented by several wind instruments. But J. S. Bach's *Brandenburg* Concertos No. 2 and No. 5 are surely the best-known and most popular concerti grossi today.

1 42

LISTENING EXAMPLE 16

 1B 2

Concerto Grosso

Composer: Johann Sebastian Bach (1685–1750)

Title: *Brandenburg* Concerto No. 2 in F Major

Composed: before 1721

Genre: Concerto grosso

Timbre: Concertino—trumpet, flute, oboe, and violin
Tutti/ripieno—violins, violas, and double basses
Continuo—cello and harpsichord

First Movement

Rhythm: Allegro; Duple meter. Notice the strong rhythmic drive and consistent tempo characteristic of music of the Baroque. The continuo marches steadily along, supporting the harmonies and having melodic interest as well.

Dynamics: Contrast is accomplished mainly by alternating solo and tutti passages, though some tutti sections are played *forte* and then *piano,* providing an echo effect. There are no crescendos or diminuendos between loud and soft.

Melody: Try to distinguish motivic figures tossed between instruments and played at different levels and in different keys (melodic sequence). Perhaps you will sense that Bach moves away from the tonic, exploring rather remote keys, but returning securely to the tonic as expected.

Key: F major

42	0:00	**Tutti—Main theme**	(tonic, F Major)
. . . .		The brilliant main theme is played in unison by the flute, oboe, solo violin,	
. . . .		and violins of the *ripieno,* accompanied by the solo trumpet, other strings and continuo.	
0:20	0:20	**Solo** (short solo for violin)	
43	0:26	**Tutti—Main theme**	(tonic, F Major)
0.06	0:32	**Solo** (oboe, trumpet, flute)	
44	0:46	**Tutti—Main theme**	(C Major)
0:05	0:51	**Solo** (trumpet)	
45	1:16	**Tutti—Main theme**	(d minor)
. . . .		Heard briefly in violins accompanied by a trill in the solo trumpet.	
0:05	1:21	**Solo** (lengthy section featuring all members of the concertino; begins with legato	
. . . .		sequences between trumpet and oboe)	
46	2:50	**Tutti—Main theme**	(c minor)
0:10	3:00	**Solo** (section *ends* with sequences)	
47	3:08	**Tutti—Main theme**	(g minor)
0:23	3:31	**Solo**	
48	4:18	**Tutti—Main theme**	(tonic, F major)
0:10	4:28	**Solo**	
49	4:48	**Tutti—Main theme**	(tonic, F major)
. . . .		Notice the slightest relaxation in tempo, or **ritardando,** at the very end.	

Second Movement

Tempo: Andante

Meter: Triple

Key: D minor (relative minor)

The lovely, emotionally expressive slow movement is performed by the solo flute, oboe, and violin accompanied only by the continuo. Imitative entrances of the solo instruments enhance the poignancy of the main melody, and the emotional intensity is further heightened by the relentlessly consistent pulse of the accompaniment. The minor mode also contributes to the sense of pathos. There is ample opportunity to appreciate the timbres of the solo instruments, for each treats the tender theme with delicacy and sensitivity.

Third Movement
Tempo: Allegro assai (quite fast)
Meter: Duple

Key: F major

The joyful, strongly accented main theme is introduced by the trumpet in the tonic key, the brilliant effect enhanced by the extremely high level of pitches. The oboe answers in the dominant key (C major), and as the movement continues, the violin (tonic) and flute (dominant) take turns with the joyous melody.

A bright motive including the distinctive rhythmic pattern "short, short, long" is introduced by the orchestra, and the main theme and motivic figure are then effectively tossed between the solo instruments, ripieno, and continuo. The movement ends with a gloriously triumphant statement of the main theme by the trumpet.

Summary

During the Baroque, instrumental music became of equal importance with music for the voice. New forms developed for keyboard and other instruments, organized according to rules of the recently adopted tonal system of harmony, revealed appreciation for dramatic contrasts of timbres, tempos, and dynamic levels. Most instrumental and vocal compositions were accompanied by the continuo, an ensemble that included at least one sustaining instrument and a keyboard or lute player who realized the harmonies above a figured bass.

The Baroque also produced many beautiful sonatas for a variety of solo instruments accompanied by a continuo, while the concerto, pitting orchestra against one or more solo instruments, seemed especially suited to express the Baroque appreciation for contrasts of sound.

Critical Thinking

- The concerto grosso, replaced in popularity by the solo concerto throughout the nineteenth and early twentieth centuries, has had particular appeal for a number of recent and contemporary composers. Why do you suppose this form lost and then regained such favor?

- Instrumental and vocal music were of approximately equal interest in the Baroque. Do you think that instrumental or vocal music appeals more to today's audience? Explain your answer.

Terms to Review

terraced dynamics   Abrupt changes of dynamic level.

fugue   An imitative polyphonic composition.

prelude   A short independent or introductory piece for keyboard.

chorale prelude   A prelude based upon a Lutheran chorale melody.

toccata   A rhapsodic and virtuosic keyboard form.

sequence   Repetition of a melodic phrase at different levels of pitch.

suite   A collection of stylized dance pieces.

continuo   A group of instruments, including a lute or a keyboard instrument and one or more sustaining bass instruments, that accompanied Baroque ensemble compositions.

thoroughbass   The strong bass line that sounded continuously throughout Baroque ensemble compositions.

figured bass   A system of musical shorthand by which composers indicated intervals above the bass line with numbers (figures) rather than with notated pitches.

chamber music   Music for a small instrumental ensemble with one instrument per line of music.

sonata   In the Baroque, a multimovement composition for one or two solo instruments, accompanied by continuo.

> **trio sonata**   A sonata in either of the styles below for two solo instruments and continuo.
>
> **sonata da camera**   Lighter in mood, intended for concert performance.
>
> **sonata da chiesa**   Serious in mood, intended for performance in church.

orchestra   A mixed ensemble of string and wind instruments, conceived in the Baroque.

concerto   A multimovement composition for orchestra and one or more solo instruments.

concerto grosso   A multimovement composition for orchestra plus a small group of solo instruments.

> **tutti, ripieno**   Terms used for the orchestral group in a concerto grosso.
>
> **concertino**   The group of solo instruments in a concerto grosso.

ritardando   A gradual slowing in tempo.

Key Figures

Violin Makers	*Antonio Stradivari*
	Giuseppe Guarneri
Composers	*J. S. Bach*
	Arcangelo Corelli
	Antonio Vivaldi

16
Toward Classicism

The early eighteenth century experienced an important "sub-period," the **Rococo** The French (also known as the *stile galant,* or gallant style), which exhibited stylistic characteristics of both the earlier (Baroque) and the later (Classical) styles, yet had a distinct character of its own. The dates are vague, but the Rococo prevailed in France from 1715 to 1740, and its influence spread far beyond the country of its origin. Thus, for well over twenty-five years, the arts of the Rococo combined the ornateness of the Baroque with the delicacy of the Classical style.

In the visual arts, the Rococo represented a final flowering of the Baroque, as ornamentation became even more ornate and manners and dress even more elaborate than in the seventeenth century. The move to Classicism (called "Neoclassicism" in the visual arts) would occur later in the eighteenth century. (Since music had no significant ancient models to imitate, the prefix *neo,* meaning "new," is unnecessary to distinguish the music of the eighteenth century from that of the ancient Greeks.)

This richly decorated interior is typical of the extravagant Rococo style.
Calmann & King Archives, London

However, while the visual arts exaggerated Baroque characteristics, the music of the Rococo was in many ways a reaction *against* the Baroque, eschewing the heaviness and drama of the earlier style and adopting new concepts of melody, texture, and performance practice. During the Rococo, in fact, music evolved to the less complex, more "natural" style we call Classical.

The Rococo did not produce outstanding art of the quality of either Baroque or Classical masterpieces, as the light works of the Rococo adhered to the French concept that the purpose of art is to amuse and entertain rather than to edify or improve. Indeed, this delightful music and art well retains its power to please ear and eye.

Historical Perspective

In 1715, Louis XIV died, leaving a child heir to the French throne, and for the next eight years the Duke of Orléans reigned as regent. More attracted to the privileges than to the responsibilities of his position, the duke encouraged the enthusiastic pursuit of pleasure. Now the social life of the French aristocracy moved away from the formal and austere court at Versailles to intimate Paris salons and comfortable country lodges, where gifted hostesses presided over intellectual conversation, witty gossip, and the performance of elegant music. During the period of the Regency, France was a secular, materialistic, somewhat lawless society: morals were loose, the emphasis was upon the here rather than the hereafter, and the elite pursued temporal happiness with verve and abandon. Among the nobility, marriage was purely a formal arrangement intended not to interfere with one's social, or love, affairs. Dress and manners became elegant in the extreme.

At its best, French society during the Regency cultivated the beautiful and pleasurable; at its worst, the artificial and trite. We are indebted to the former for some lovely paintings, artifacts, and music.

Visual Arts

Appreciation for elegant decoration led to the creation of beautiful ornaments made from many rich materials. Gold- and silversmiths produced extravagant candlesticks, salt and pepper shakers, and snuffboxes; tapestry art reached its peak during this period; and the porcelain ware was superb. Furniture, elaborately carved and decorated—often with the "natural" lines of flowers and seashells, favorite decorative themes of the Rococo—was comfortable as well as beautiful. Even the fashionable dress of the day reflected the new elegance, as members of the aristocracy adopted the lace cuff and powdered wig.

Many paintings of this period portray elegant men and women, beautifully dressed or gracefully nude, pursuing love and pleasure in idyllic pastoral surroundings. The picturesque setting and graceful pose of Le Mezzetin (Color Plate 5) correspond to the refined music with which the charming musician entertained his audiences. This and other paintings of the finest artist of the period, Antoine Watteau (1684–1721), have a warmth and sensitivity raising them above the triviality and artificiality of their subject matter. Watteau's most famous painting, called *Pilgrimage to Cythera* or *Embarkation for Cythera* (figure 16.1), portrays a group of well-to-do men and women who have spent an idyllic afternoon on a mythical island of love. The subject is Rococo, but the sensitive facial expressions and the intimation of delicate relationships between individuals make this a work of timeless beauty.

Figure 16.1

Embarkation for Cythera, Antoine Watteau.

Art Resource, NY/Alinari, Florence

Music

The pleasant, sophisticated music of the Rococo, primarily instrumental, was often quite witty, with hidden jokes readily recognized by those who knew the latest court gossip. One piece or movement now frequently introduced more than one melody, in contrast to the Baroque inclination to present one melodic idea and one mood (or *affection*) at a time. Some Rococo melodies contained two balancing phrases, anticipating the antecedent ("question") and consequent ("answering") melodic phrases of much of the music to come in the Classical era.

The texture of Rococo music was homophonic; the bass lost its prominent position as leader of the harmonic direction and joined the inner voices to support the melody line, which was often highly embellished. Harmonies conformed with the rules of the tonal system, but harmonic changes occurred less often than they had in the more intellectually conceived music of the Baroque. The powerful emotional effect of seventeenth-century music was replaced by sentiment during this period, which came to be known as the "age of feeling."

The French Rococo style influenced composers in several other countries as well. In Italy, **Domenico Scarlatti** (1685–1757), a contemporary of Bach and Handel, composed charming keyboard sonatas in the Rococo style. His melodies are often two-fold, foretelling the "question and answer" duality typical of the Classical melodic phrase. Scarlatti's music provides ample opportunity for virtuosic display, yet avoids the heavy, complex contrapuntal writing of the Baroque.

1 52   # LISTENING EXAMPLE 17   1B 3

Rococo Keyboard Piece

Composer: François Couperin (1668–1733)

Title: "Le tic-toc-choc" (from *Ordre 18*)

Composed: 1722

Rhythm: Fast; duple meter; even-note rhythm representing the constancy of a clock

Melody: Located in the left hand (lower pitch), while the right hand plays a steady rhythmic accompaniment

Genre: Movement from a suite

Form: Rondeau

Timbre: Harpsichord solo

Key: F major

This charming piece, consisting of repetitive phrases, elaborately ornamented, was meant to provide enjoyment and easy
   listening rather than an intellectual or spiritual experience. As the title suggests, it also illustrates the fascination with
   clockworks characteristic of the period.

52	0:00	**A**	F major
		Left-hand melody with '**long**–short–**long**–short' rhythm; right-hand accompaniment with even-note rhythm	
		Ornamented cadence	
0:16	0:16	**A** (repeated)	
53	0:32	**B** (1st Couplet)	C major
		Texture similar to the main theme; longer note values in the melody at first, but moving to a similar rhythm as heard in the main theme	
0:16	0:48	**A**	F major
54	1:02	**C** (2d Couplet)	d minor
		Slightly longer than the main theme	
0:25	1:27	**A**	F major
55	2:08	**D** (3rd Couplet)	g minor
		Another slightly longer section; occasionally both hands move together, creating a bit more contrast in this section	
0:27	2:35	**A**	F major
0:45	2:53	**Ending**	
		Varied repeat of the last few measures of the main theme	

The most important composer of the period, however, was a Frenchman named
François Couperin (1668–1733). He, too, wrote many kinds of instrumental music,
including several sets of pieces similar in structure to Baroque suites, often with fan-
ciful titles such as The Benevolent Cuckold or The Soul in Sorrow. Couperin is best
remembered, however, for his keyboard pieces in the Rococo style, such as "Le tic-
toc-choc" from *Order 18,* Listening Example 17.

Expressive Style

Germany, also affected by the Rococo, introduced a style of its own, called **expressive.** Combined with elements of the Rococo, this style provided a wealth of ideas to
composers in the latter part of the eighteenth century. Unlike the aristocratic French

Rococo, the German expressive style represented a middle-class taste. It shared with the Rococo a preference for simple, "natural" melodies unobtrusively supported by other voices, and the intention to be pleasant rather than profound. However, composers of music in the expressive style avoided the elaborate embellishment of the Rococo; they used instead subtle changes of melody, harmony, dynamic level, rhythmic patterns, and keys to produce delicate tugs at the heartstrings. The expressive style was more serious than the frivolous Rococo, with more chromaticism, more use of expressive dissonance, and more modulation to distant keys; but clearly there was not the desire to evoke the deep emotion of the Bach Passions or the Handel oratorios.

The most famous composer in the expressive style was **Carl Philipp Emanuel Bach** (1714–1788), whose father, Johann Sebastian, was already considered a composer of old-fashioned music.

Summary

Certain characteristics of the aristocratic Rococo style affected all of the arts of the second quarter of the eighteenth century. The unsettled political climate, the turn away from organized religion, the morality (or lack thereof) of the time—all required an art to please, but not provoke; to stir emotions, but gently so. While Bach and Handel continued to compose in the Baroque style, and while some artists, especially those concerned with literature, had already adopted the Classical style of expression, much of the painting, sculpture, architecture, and music of the early eighteenth century reflected the ideals of the Rococo. This French-inspired, elegant, frivolous, witty, and sophisticated style survived in some form, in fact, throughout much of the century.

The German expressive style, inspired by the middle class, was more concerned with the expression of sentiment than with elaborate embellishment of a melodic line. More serious than the frivolous Rococo, it pointed toward the German Romanticism destined to dominate art in the nineteenth century.

While representing a reaction against the solemnity, emotionalism, and heaviness of the Baroque, the Rococo and expressive styles also offered many positive ideas that bore fruit later in the century as the Classical style evolved. The preferences for homophonic texture, for simpler harmonies and less frequent harmonic change, for a "singing" melody line, and for clarity and elegance as opposed to drama and overwhelming emotion would prevail through the Classical period.

Critical Thinking

- Although elements of earlier and later styles are apparent in the arts of the Rococo, the style seems to represent primarily a reaction against the past in the visual arts and an intimation of the future in music. Can you suggest some reasons for this difference?

- Why do the characteristics of a stylistic period generally appear later in music than in the other arts?

Terms to Review

Rococo   An elegant, sometimes frivolous, style of art introduced during the French Regency and prevalent in France during the second quarter of the eighteenth century.

expressive style   An emotional style of music inspired by the German middle class of the second quarter of the eighteenth century.

Key Figures

Artist   *Antoine Watteau*

Composers   *Domenico Scarlatti (Rococo)*
                François Couperin (Rococo)
                C. P. E. Bach (expressive style)

17

The Classical Period: General Characteristics

During the eighteenth century, prevailing social, political, and economic conditions led many countries to abolish rule by divine right, and from about 1750 to 1825 democratic, republican, and revolutionary causes affected every phase of European life and art. Yet this Age of Revolution coincided, paradoxically, with a period of classical restraint in the arts. Of course, revolutionary fervor affected some individuals and some countries more than others, so there was actually a greater diversity of styles during this period than ever before. But the two outstanding composers of the late eighteenth century, Franz Joseph Haydn and Wolfgang Amadeus Mozart, were consummate Classicists. Haydn wrote pleasant, good-natured music throughout his long life even as revolutionary events swirled around him. And Mozart, who invested much of his music with a degree of emotional expression unusual for his time, never allowed emotion to dominate his art.

Historical Perspective

During the seventeenth century, England exhibited astonishing defiance of Europe's political status quo by beheading a king, making a commoner head of a Puritan regime, and finally establishing a solid and prosperous constitutional monarchy. France, scandalized by such revolutionary events, was at the same time highly impressed by them, for Louis XIV's extreme authoritarianism had demoralized the French and his lavish spending had left them nearly bankrupt. When he died in 1715, the French also deemed it time for a change, effectively articulating and defending the ideas that led to the Age of Reason; but they freely acknowledged their debt to the English for pointing the enlightened way.

The Enlightenment

Intellectuals of the latter 1700s generally concurred with the secular and antiestablishment trends of the early years of the century. Voltaire (1694–1778), one of the leaders of the intellectual movement called the French **Enlightenment,** wrote essays bitterly attacking French society, politics, and religion, and was beaten and twice imprisoned for his heretical views. Denis Diderot (1713–1784) compiled a great dictionary intended to make universal knowledge accessible to all.

Proponents of the Enlightenment, distrusting emotions as a guide to truth, abandoned the mystic and supernatural beliefs of the previous century. Voltaire, Diderot, and their cohorts advocated reliance upon reason and upon humanity's natural goodness to improve the quality and conditions of life. They resisted mistreatment of the middle and lower classes, and initiated significant humanitarian reforms. They held knowledge to be universal, truth absolute, and reason the pathway to enlightenment.

Although primarily a secular movement, the Enlightenment propounded religious tolerance as one of its goals. Several Protestant sects—democratic movements that stressed the values of a private faith and constructive good works over creeds, nationalities, or social ideas—joined the cause. In Britain, Quakers relieved victims of poverty, disease, and unjust imprisonment, while in America, members of the same sect actively opposed slavery. Methodists in both the Old and New Worlds revived the Protestant ethic of hard work and pure morality.

The Enlightenment had a profound effect upon America, in fact. The great American Thomas Jefferson represents the prototype of the classical man: intelligent and well educated, he was with varying degrees of excellence a linguist, scientist, mathematician, architect, musician, and statesman. Jefferson, George Washington, and Benjamin Franklin certainly were revolutionaries, but how very classical was the style of their revolt.

In the effort to replace power with reason, repression with tolerance, despair with hope, ignorance with knowledge, and political and social abuse with justice, Western Europeans turned increasingly to what they knew of the ancient Greek and Roman civilizations; they were strongly drawn to the pure and simple beauty of Greek art and the social and political ideas of republican Rome. The same ideas that brought about many changes in society, religion, and politics inevitably affected the arts as well.

Artistic Style

The frivolous, aristocratic art of the Rococo was hardly suitable to express the enlightened, democratic, and revolutionary views of the late eighteenth century. The French Enlightenment having dampened the playful spirits of the Rococo, art soon reflected the more serious nature of the new morality. The products of excavations of the time led painters, sculptors, and architects to turn increasingly to ancient Greece, republican Rome, or Renaissance replicas of the arts of these civilizations for inspiration.

Many of their works gave visual expression to the same ideals imbued in the great music of the Classical period.

Painting

The greatest painter of mid-eighteenth-century France, J. B. S. Chardin (1699–1779), had an exquisite sense of both color and design. Shunning the rich drawing rooms and elegant dress of Rococo society, Chardin depicted the sensible middle and working classes of France, making plain people—a new source of interest!—appear warm and real. The design, form, and texture of objects as well as those of people intrigued him, and Chardin's pots, plates, glasses, and bowls, as seen in figure 17.1, are among the loveliest ever painted.

Jacques-Louis David (1748–1825), a Neoclassicist whose revolutionary sympathies imbued his later works with romantic characteristics, preferred form and design over color, in the Neoclassical way. Greatly impressed by antique sculptures, including the relics recently discovered at Pompeii and Herculaneum, David frequently clothed his modern figures in classical garb and placed them in classical settings. A moralist like Voltaire, David often used Roman tales of conquest and virtue to preach the new morality; for example, *Brutus Returning from Condemning His Sons to Death* (1789) (figure 17.2) depicts a Roman father who has had his sons killed for participating in a royalist conspiracy. French authorities at first refused to exhibit this grim painting, whose political implications seemed threatening to them, but the art public insisted it be shown, and the picture actively stirred the revolutionary zeal already blazing in the French.

Figure 17.1

Kitchen Maid, Jean-Baptiste-Siméon Chardin.

The Englishman William Hogarth (1697–1764), another moralist, tempered his visual sermons with satire and caustic wit. His engravings, such as *Gin Lane* (figure 17.3), ridiculed English society much as the operettas of Gilbert and Sullivan would more than a century later.

One of England's greatest painters during this period, Sir Joshua Reynolds (1723–1792), preferred instead to paint the rich and elegant, stressing line over color in the classical manner. While Hogarth depicted life as he saw it with all its imperfections, Reynolds believed it proper for art to improve upon nature.

Sculpture and Architecture

Sculpture perhaps constituted the ideal art of the Neoclassical period, for it is literally composed of line and form. The greatest sculptor of the age was Jean-Antoine Houdon (1741–1828), a Frenchman who studied in Italy and created beautiful

Figure 17.2

Brutus Returning from Condemning His Sons to Death, Jacques-Louis David.

RMN, Paris

figures based upon Greek and Roman lore. Like the painters of his day, Houdon made his living from portraiture, but unlike Reynolds, he made every effort to produce accurate portrayals. Houdon accompanied Benjamin Franklin on a trip from France to America in 1785, adding a number of American figures to his already famous collection of French notables. The likenesses of Washington, Franklin, and Jefferson that appear on American coins today (figure 17.4) were done by Houdon.

The ornate façades and twisted columns of Baroque architecture seemed outmoded when compared to the grace and simplicity of the Neoclassical style. All signs of frivolity having disappeared, the new buildings imparted a sense of classical dignity and proportion. Plain cornices, simple columns, and spacious domes suited the late-eighteenth-century taste.

Classicists (of any age) believe in universal values, and the eighteenth-century Neoclassical style spread far beyond western Europe. The new nation across the sea, for example, produced a cool and reasoned Declaration of Independence (note this tone in its opening words: "When in the course of human events it becomes necessary for one people to dissolve the political bonds which have connected them with another . . ."). Washington, D.C. (figure 17.5) was designed in the 1790s to become a city of Neoclassical buildings, grassy parks, and long, wide avenues, America's founders apparently believing that cool and simple lines of graceful beauty offered the best possible setting for the calm and reasoned governing of the new republic.

Figure 17.3

Gin Lane, William Hogarth.

Lady Cornewall, Sir Joshua Reynolds. (National Gallery of Art, Washington/ Widener Collection).

Figure 17.4

A fifty-cent piece, a nickel, and a quarter bearing the images of Franklin, Jefferson, and Washington, by Jean-Antoine Houdon.

Literature

The decline of religion, mystery, fantasy, and romance combined with the triumph of reason, knowledge, and classical restraint to produce more prose than poetry in the eighteenth century. England experienced literary activity of more quantity and variety than ever before, producing novels, histories, plays, tracts, pamphlets, and speeches in abundance, as biographers, satirists, compilers of dictionaries, and humorists vied for the public's attention, and newspapers and magazines proliferated. Lively arguments were conducted in print, with readers actively taking sides and even coming to blows when they met in the streets. The English theater achieved unprecedented importance.

Figure 17.5
Washington, D.C.
National Park Service/Dept. of Interior.

Men and women from all walks of life, of various means, and with different tastes participated as producers or consumers of prodigious quantities of all kinds of literature in the Classical style.

Music in Europe

Before the eighteenth century, serious music generally was heard only in church and perhaps the opera house; but as public concerts became more common in the eighteenth century, the average person's experience with and appreciation for music increased. The system of royal, ecclesiastical, or noble patronage that had weakened during the Baroque became even less tenable as the public began to attend concerts in greater numbers, and some composers learned to rely upon general, rather than private, support.

By the middle of the century, even a middle-class family usually had a harpsichord or other musical instrument in the home. Composers augmented their meager incomes by offering music lessons, printing important books of music instruction, and writing relatively simple pieces for amateurs to play, while concerts were programmed to include music that would please the eager, but inexperienced, audience. Mozart in particular enjoyed and wrote many compositions for the new keyboard instrument called the **fortepiano,** named for its range of dynamic levels from loud to soft. Because of its wide dynamic range for the time and its ability to accomplish gradual changes in dynamic level according to the touch of the performer, the fortepiano was particularly well suited for the expressive music of the eighteenth century, and became more and more popular.

Women became more involved in the art of music making in the home, often taking lessons and practicing diligently to entertain their families, suitors, and close friends. Gifted female amateurs were admired for their performances on the piano, harp, or guitar, or as singers of simple songs. Late in the eighteenth century, a significant number of women became professional musicians, braving criticisms of impropriety and often winning recognition for their accomplishments. Touring as singers, pianists, violinists, or performers on other instruments, these talented and accomplished women sometimes played music they had composed. At least one young woman, Marianne von Martinez (1744–1812), studied with the famous composer Franz Joseph Haydn and later composed a large number of full-length works. Her singing and harpsichord playing were very well reviewed by at least one prestigious critic.

Composers in the Classical period rejected the intensity of religious feeling and the dramatic contrasts of the Baroque style; but though it was more restrained, their emotional expression was no less sincere than that of composers in the style of Bach and Handel. They were less prosperous than they might have been under the old patronage system, but most composers treasured their new independence and enjoyed even greater esteem than ever before. Even Haydn, who accepted employment at an Austrian court, wore livery, and ate with the servants for much of his life, became increasingly independent as his reputation spread. Paradoxically, the younger Mozart steadfastly refused bondage to a patron, yet achieved neither the widespread reputation nor the financial independence enjoyed by Haydn during his lifetime.

General Characteristics

A simple appraisal of the manner in which later-eighteenth-century composers approached the elements of music, formal design, and emotional expression indicates the wide expanse the stylistic pendulum covered in its swing from the Baroque to the Classical period.

Form
Finding beauty in order and in the symmetry of design, Classicists clearly organized their music according to old or new principles of musical form. Much as painters, sculptors, and architects emphasized line over color and design over subjective or emotional content, so composers stressed form, balance, and control in their music.

Melody
Classical themes often showed duality even within themselves; they often consisted of an antecedent and a consequent phrase (similar to a "question-and-answer" effect), or were constructed of two or sometimes more contrasting sections.

Texture
Homophony, having assumed equal importance with polyphony in the Baroque, now became the predominant texture, with melodies generally placed in the top line. The bass, which supported the harmonies above, had less melodic interest than it had carried in the music of the Baroque.

Dynamics
The range of dynamic levels increased in the latter part of the eighteenth century, and changes between them became more subtle, and at the same time more dramatic. Crescendos, for example, were longer and more expressive.

Timbre
Instrumental music, which during the Baroque had achieved virtually the same significance as music for the voice, dominated during the Classical period, when secular music surpassed music for worship in quantity, if not in quality as well. Orchestral music was particularly important, while the piano, appreciated for its ability to

achieve expressive dynamic effects, replaced the harpsichord as the primary keyboard instrument.

Thus the imaginary pendulum that hovered in precarious balance during the Baroque between vocal and instrumental, polyphonic and homophonic, and religious and secular orientations finally swung far from the position it had held in the Renaissance.

Viennese Style

The music of Haydn, Mozart, and the young Beethoven sometimes is referred to as **Viennese** in style, since all three composers lived in, worked in, and drew inspiration from the spirit and culture of eighteenth-century Vienna, where music was an essential part of nearly everyone's life. Some critics prefer the term *Viennese* because it is more specific than the ambiguous term *classical*. Over the ages the latter term has acquired several meanings: it is used with reference to the arts of ancient Greece and Rome, to distinguish art music from popular or folk styles, and to describe an objective, emotionally restrained approach to art, as opposed to the more subjective "romanticism." In still another sense, a "classic" is an art work that has survived for a long period of time.

Yet, three characteristics of the late eighteenth century's artistic style render the term Classical particularly applicable to that period: frequent references to the arts of Greece and Rome, intense concern with clarity of form and with balanced design, and the pervasive quality of emotional restraint characteristic of most important works of the period. Therefore, the music of Haydn's and Mozart's period is widely identified as **Classical** in style, the capital C serving here to distinguish the eighteenth-century period from more general applications of the term.

Music in America

Musical activity was stirring in eighteenth-century America, although the young nation had yet to produce an art music of its own. Indeed, Americans remained suspicious of art for its own sake, generally confining their artistic skills to giving useful objects aesthetic as well as functional value. Thus, landscape painting held little interest for them, but portraiture, which served before photography to preserve the likeness of important figures and loved ones, had an exalted place in American life. Among the most charming remnants of early America are folk paintings such as *The Sargent Family* (Color Plate 6), which are naive in perspective, but delightfully warm and expressive of the American experience.

Singing School Movement

Religious music had been important in the New World since the coming of the Pilgrims and Puritans and the even earlier arrival of Catholics from Spain and France, and psalm tunes and hymns continued to be sung in church and at home throughout the eighteenth century. However, the art of singing and the ability to read music had largely been lost during the rugged pioneer years. Late in the eighteenth century, a number of hardy, enterprising New Englanders who were merchants or craftsmen with little or no formal music training took it upon themselves to remedy this situation. Traveling from town to town, they set up temporary singing schools, where they offered lessons in singing and sight reading at modest fees. The singing schools were important social as well as pedagogical institutions that provided hard-working, somewhat isolated people with rare opportunities to enjoy each other's company. Thus, the **singing school movement** flourished, becoming the most important musical institution in late-eighteenth-century America.

Among the movement's accomplishments was the stimulus it gave native composers to write original music. Largely self-taught and characteristically independent in spirit, the singing school masters filled their teaching texts with sturdy tunes unfettered by traditional rules of harmony, and therefore uniquely American in character. These early Americans are sometimes referred to as members of the **First New England School** of composers. Like folk paintings, their music—conceived as teaching tools rather than art—is honest, unaffected, and often intensely charming. Many of the songs with which William Billings, Daniel Read, and other singing school masters filled their lesson books are found in psalters and hymnals today, and several have enriched the art (concert) music of recent American composers.

Over time, even as the singing school movement spread south from New England through New Jersey and Pennsylvania to the Carolinas, it declined in importance, and other types of musical activity replaced it in popularity in the nineteenth century. Yet much of this early American music has stood the test of time. Some of the songs introduced by the singing school masters are kept alive by city as well as rural folk, who sing the old American songs much as they were sung two hundred years ago; and the strong and simple tunes continue to inspire composers of modern art music.

Benjamin Franklin playing his glass harmonica.
AKG, Berlin

Art Music

In the late eighteenth century, art music became a part of life for many Americans settled in established urban areas. By this time, many middle-class families owned musical instruments, took music lessons, and entertained each other at home and in the presentation of amateur recitals. Orchestral music was not widely appreciated in eighteenth-century America, but nearly every village had its town band. It was during this period that America's first art songs (serious secular songs intended for concert performance) were composed (in imitation, however, of European models).

Since America as yet had no conservatories or facilities providing advanced music education, the only professional musicians were foreign immigrants who had brought their talent, experience, and musical instruments with them to their new country. Thomas Jefferson was among the many Americans who benefited from the teaching of foreign professionals and enjoyed their performances and those of visiting European artists. Though eighteenth-century Americans preferred light music to the masterpieces of Haydn, Mozart, and Beethoven, which they were not yet prepared to understand, America was beginning to participate in the world of serious music. Benjamin Franklin, who played the guitar very well, wrote perceptive and cogent criticism of the music of his day. He also invented a musical instrument called the **glass harmonica,** which Mozart enjoyed playing and for which he wrote some pieces. Thomas Jefferson played the violin, sometimes performing duets with Patrick Henry at the governor's mansion in Williamsburg, Virginia, and Jefferson is said to have kept musical instruments as he kept good horses—for their beauty and value as well as their usefulness.

Only the singing school masters, however, stayed independent of foreign influence at this time, the rest of America's eighteenth-century music remaining firmly under Europe's musical thumb.

Summary

Artists of the Classical period revered and sought to emulate the emotional restraint and balanced designs of the art of ancient Greece and Rome, replacing the fervent emotionalism of the Baroque with grace and simplicity. As prescribed by the leaders of the French Enlightenment, they accepted reason rather than emotions as the source of knowledge and truth.

The visual arts of the eighteenth century are referred to as Neoclassical in style, to distinguish them from the ancient models upon which they were based. Line and design were of more concern than color to the painters of this period; eighteenth-century architects designed buildings of simple grace and dignity.

The outstanding composers of the period, Haydn, Mozart, and the young Beethoven, lived and worked in Vienna, drawing inspiration from the spirit and culture of that city. The public audience for music grew steadily larger, and middle-class families produced avid amateur musicians. Women participated to an unprecedented degree in both amateur and professional musical activities. Composers increasingly resisted the system of support by church or noble patronage, relying more and more upon public approval of their works. For the first time in Western history, music became a significant part of the lives of a wide and varied audience.

In the late eighteenth century, the singing school movement improved the quality of singing in American churches and provided a stimulus for the composition of music for teaching purposes. Amateur singing masters composed America's first indigenous music, consisting of songs to be used in singing classes and for entertainment at home. Many of their strong and simple tunes survive today in psalm and hymn books and in modern religious and concert compositions.

Americans' interest in art music grew as their wealth and leisure time increased. Foreign musicians bringing European art music to the young country helped to expand America's musical experience and tastes. However, with the exception of the hardy New England singing masters, Americans nurtured their feelings of inferiority to Europeans in matters of art, including music.

Critical Thinking

• Why did the singing school movement become so strong in America at a time when there was little interest in concert or art music?

• Do we have many women conductors today? Composers? Performers? Do you think the opportunities available today to women in the music professions are equal to those for men? Explain your answers.

Terms to Review

Enlightenment   A movement led by eighteenth-century French intellectuals which advocated reason as the universal source of knowledge and truth.

fortepiano   The early piano, named for its range of dynamic levels.

many composers in Vienna

Viennese style   The term sometimes applied to the Classical style, to avoid the ambiguities of the word "classical."

Classical style   The emotionally restrained, formally balanced style of music from about 1750 to 1825.

singing school movement   A late-eighteenth-century effort to teach Americans to sing and to read music. The movement inspired the composition of America's first indigenous music.

First New England School   Singing school masters who composed music; America's earliest composers.

glass harmonica   A musical instrument invented by Benjamin Franklin.

Key Figures

Intellectuals	*Francois Marie Arouet de Voltaire*	*Denis Diderot*
	Thomas Jefferson	*Benjamin Franklin*
Artists	*J. B. S. Chardin*	*Jacques-Louis David*
	William Hogarth	*Sir Joshua Reynolds*
	Jean-Antoine Houdon	
Composers	*Wolfgang Amadeus Mozart*	*Franz Joseph Haydn*
	Ludwig van Beethoven	*Marianne von Martinez*
	William Billings	*Daniel Read*

18
Formal Design in the Classical Period

While Italy continued through the eighteenth century to reign over the world of opera, the main centers of serious musical activity moved north, especially to the cities of Berlin, Vienna, and Mannheim. Each important city-state or church-state, although under the nominal control of the emperor's court at Vienna, had its own patrons of music, and composers in each developed a style characteristic of their particular city, while all seriously explored the concept of form in music.

When the elements of music are organized into a musical composition, the overall design of the work is called its **form.** Of course, form is essential to every art. A novel, for example, is a literary form containing chapters, paragraphs, sentences, phrases, all of which are organized according to literary and grammatical principles. Similarly, each movement of a symphony has a formal design, but each movement, like each chapter of a novel or each act of a play, is ultimately related to the whole of the work.

Form in art is based upon the principles of *repetition* and *contrast;* repetition lends unity, symmetry, and balance to a composition, while contrast provides the variety necessary to keep the work interesting. Because music is a continuous process, it poses unique challenges to the listener, who must develop the technique of memorizing certain sounds in order to differentiate between the repetition of material and the introduction of new musical ideas. These signposts remind us where we have been and imply what lies ahead, helping to establish our musical bearings.

The Orchestra

During the eighteenth century, as instrumental music surpassed vocal music in both quantity and quality, composers expanded the Baroque conception of the orchestra, standardizing the number of instruments it included, the proportions of wind instruments to strings, and the melodic and harmonic responsibilities of each type of instrument in the ensemble. In Mozart's time, the standard orchestra balanced the string sections—including perhaps twenty violins and several violas, cellos, and double basses—with two flutes, two oboes, two clarinets, two bassoons, two horns, two trumpets, and two kettledrums. The harpsichord, which continued to be included in the orchestra throughout most of the eighteenth century, sometimes filled in harmonies not assigned to other instruments; however, as composers wrote more and more of the harmony parts for wind instruments and for some of the strings, the need for the harpsichord disappeared, and since it could hardly be heard among the larger group of more sonorous instruments typical by the end of the century, the harpsichord eventually disappeared from the orchestral ensemble.

In the mid-1700s, the German city of Mannheim developed an orchestra so outstanding that it attracted attention all over western Europe. Its director hired only the best musicians, who played with great precision and a beautiful quality of tone. Experimenting with dynamic expression, they achieved softer orchestral *pianissimos* and louder *fortissimos* than had ever been heard before. Even more significantly, they mastered the techniques of crescendo and decrescendo (or diminuendo), which were much better suited to the expressive eighteenth-century style than were the ter-raced dynamics of the Baroque.

Classical composers also expanded the Baroque concept of building a large composition from three or more separate movements; they standardized the number of movements included in certain forms of composition and used new or previously established formal designs to organize each movement of a multimovement work. For them, form represented a liberating rather than a confining influence, providing a stable framework without limiting the composer's creativity in any way.

Symphony

Among instrumental forms, the **symphony,** a multimovement composition for the symphony orchestra, experienced the greatest development and offered composers the widest field for creativity during the mid-1700s. The earliest multimovement or-chestral works called symphonies were quite short pieces written for a small number of instruments. They were based upon the introductory instrumental piece, or *over-ture,* played before an Italian opera, consisting of three sections in the order fast–slow–fast. Classical composers lengthened the three sections and generally added a fourth, organizing each movement according to the principles of a chosen in-strumental form. That is, each movement *within* a symphony (or other multimove-ment work) had its own formal design. This design was either inherited from an ear-lier period (such as the fugue or the theme and variations) or a new form introduced during the form-conscious Classical period (such as the *sonata-allegro*).

Sonata-Allegro

Composers have often found the **sonata-allegro** the ideal formal design for the first movement of a composition. It is, in fact, often nicknamed the "first movement form." The somewhat confusing name *sonata-allegro* derives from its association with the first movement of a *sonata* (see p. 121), which is normally *allegro* in tempo; however, the design, stable in structure but infinitely flexible in practice, has been used for the first movement, and sometimes other movements as well, of many sym-phonies, concertos, and string quartets as well as sonatas, and it is not necessarily *al-legro* in tempo.

The sonata-allegro is generally conceived as a three-part (*ABA*) structure: the **ex-position** introduces thematic material to be used throughout the movement; the **de-velopment** carries the themes and perhaps new material as well through many keys; and the **recapitulation** reviews the original material, presenting it in a new light (see figure 18.1 and table 18.1).

Exposition
The exposition contains two tonal areas, one tonic and the other usually the dominant or the *relative major* key—the major key having the same key signature as the minor key the movement is in. (*C major* is the relative major of A minor, for example, since neither has any sharps or flats in its key signature.) A **transition** or **bridge modulates,** or changes key systematically, from the tonic to the new tonal area, which may or may not include new thematic material, its primary significance has to do with its key. Unlike Baroque composers, who typically confined one section of a work to one mood or affection, Classical composers often considered the two tonal areas of the sonata-allegro exposition to be an opportunity to present two melodies of a contrasting nature: for example, one melody might be lyrical, the other motivic. The **closing section** remains in the new key.

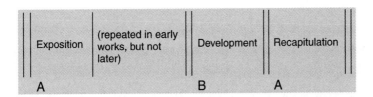

Figure 18.1

Ternary design of the
sonata-allegro form.

Table 18.1	The Sonata-Allegro Form
Exposition (*A*)	First section—tonic
	Transition—modulates
	Second section—new key
	Closing section—new key
Development (*B*)	Moves through several keys
	Ends with preparation for tonic
Recapitulation (*A′*)	First section—tonic
	Transition—does *not* modulate
	Second section—tonic
	Closing section—tonic
Coda	(optional)

In works of the Classical period, the exposition closed with a complete cadence and was repeated in its entirety.

Development

The development moves through several keys, generally using thematic material from the exposition, but sometimes introducing new melodies as well. Again, the significance of the section has to do with the keys it moves through.

Recapitulation

The recapitulation begins like the exposition; however, the transition does *not* modulate, but leads to presentation of the second section material *in the tonic key.* The closing section, also of course in the tonic, may end the movement, or the composer may add an extended closing passage called a **coda.**

The first movement of Mozart's Symphony no. 40 in G minor (Listening Example 18) is in sonata-allegro form.

Minuet and Trio

The third movement of many symphonies, sonatas, and string quartets is in the form of a **minuet and trio.** The minuet, a stately dance introduced at the seventeenth-century court of Louis XIV, became in stylized form a standard part of the instrumental suite, and it remained popular in instrumental music of the eighteenth century. The minuet is in triple meter, with a moderate tempo and rather heavy accents lending it a dignified, robust character.

The minuet and trio is actually a set of two minuets, played in the order *A B A;* the second dance, or trio (*B*), is lighter and more lyrical than the first (*A*), which is played by the full orchestra. Although the term *trio* was derived from Baroque dance pieces composed for three solo instruments, the instrumentation of the Classical trio varied, always including fewer instruments than the first minuet, but not just three.

1 56

LISTENING EXAMPLE 18

 1B 4

Sonata-Allegro

Composer: Wolfgang Amadeus Mozart (1756–1791)

Title: Symphony No. 40 in G Minor, K. 550, first movement

Composed: 1788

Form: Sonata

Rhythm: Molto Allegro; Duple meter

exposition

56	0:00	*first theme*	(tonic key, g minor)
. . . .		Main theme introduced in the violins (*p*); motivic in nature	
0:18	0:18	Repeated cadences (*f*)	
0:24	0:24	Main theme again	
57	0:33	*transition*	(modulates)
. . . .		A bold theme (*f*) containing **staccato** (detached) broken chords and rapid	
. . . .		scale patterns	
58	0:53	*second theme*	(Bb major)
		Highly chromatic theme in strings and woodwinds; lyrical in style (*p*);	
		is in the relative key of Bb major	
		("Relative" keys share the same key signature.)	
0:11	1:04	Theme 2 repeated by woodwinds and strings	
0:19	1:12	Transitional material (*crescendo*)	
59	1:28	*closing section*	(Bb major)
. . . .		Contains material derived from the first theme, expressed in long sighs in	
. . . .		the strings, while the woodwinds treat the original three-note motive.	
0:20	1:48	Descending scale passages end the exposition.	
60	2:02	*exposition repeated*	
2:01	4:03	The repeat of the exposition is followed by three bridging chords.	

development

61	4:07	Fragments of the first theme are heard in several keys.	
. . . .		Sudden changes in dynamic level contribute to the drama of this section.	

recapitulation

62	5:20	*first theme*	(tonic key, g minor)
63	5:53	*transition*	
		Developmental in nature, the transition touches other keys.	
64	6:34	*second theme* (in the *minor* mode this time)	(tonic key, g minor)
65	7:16	*closing section* (also in the *minor* mode here)	(tonic key, g minor)

coda

66	7:47	Fragments of the first theme in strings (*p*) bring the movement to a brisk close.	
0:10	7:57	Repeated cadences (*f*)	

Both the minuet and the trio contain subsections, which are repeated in the first presentation; then the minuet is played once more without repeats (see figure 18.2).

Listening Example 19 is the third movement from the same Mozart symphony as the sonata-allegro you heard earlier.

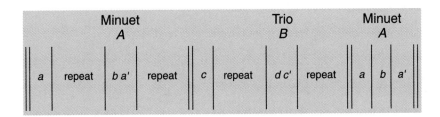

Figure 18.2

Minuet and trio.

 1 [67]   LISTENING EXAMPLE 19   📠 1B 5

Minuet and Trio

Composer: Wolfgang Amadeus Mozart (1756–1791)

Title: Symphony No. 40 in G Minor, K. 550, third movement

Composed: 1788

Form: Minuet and trio (A B A)

Rhythm: Allegro; Triple meter

Timbre: Classical orchestra (flute, 2 oboes, 2 clarinets—added later by Mozart, 2 bassoons, 2 horns, strings)

minuet (A)

[67]	0:00	**a** An intense, strongly syncopated theme (*f*)	(tonic key, g minor)
0:19	0:19	**a** First phrase is repeated	
0:37	0:37	**b** The second phrase begins in the relative major key.	(Bb major)
. . . .		The winds and strings move contrapuntally, achieving striking dissonances.	
0:55	0:55	**a′** The third phrase is similar to the first.	(g minor)
1:07	1:07	Ends quietly with winds (*p*)	
1:15	1:15	**b** repeat	
1:33	1:33	**a′** repeat	
1:45	1:45	Ends quietly with winds	

trio (B)

[68]	1:54	**c** Graceful and flowing in the parallel major key (*p*)	(G major)
0:25	2:19	**c** repeat	
0:51	2:45	**d** Low strings and winds	
1:12	3:06	**c′** Horns begin the varied repeat of **c**.	
1:26	3:20	**d** repeat	
1:47	3:41	**c′** repeat	

minuet (A)—The minuet is played again, without the internal repeats.

[69]	4:03	**a**
0:18	4:21	**b**
0:35	4:38	**a′**
0:47	4:50	quiet ending

1 70   # LISTENING EXAMPLE 20   1B 6

Rondo

Composer: Franz Joseph Haydn (1732–1809)

Title: Trumpet Concerto in E-flat major, third movement

Composed: 1796

Form: Rondo

Rhythm: Allegro; Duple meter

Timbre: Solo trumpet with standard Classical orchestra (two flutes, two oboes, two bassoons, two horns, two trumpets, timpani, strings)

70	0:00	**a**	The main theme, introduced by the violins (*p*), is bright and bustling, emphasizing rising intervals.
0:10	0:10		Main theme played again by the full orchestra (*f*)
71	0:21	**b**	A second theme, generally descending in direction, is introduced briefly by the violins.
72	0:36	**a**	Repeat of the main theme with added solo trumpet
73	1:04	**b**	Repeat of the second theme by the solo trumpet
74	1:43	**a**	Main theme in solo trumpet, followed by a statement in full orchestra
75	1:56	**c**	Developmental in nature; main theme passes through contrasting keys
76	2:28	**a**	Main theme (solo trumpet)
77	2:43	**b**	Second theme (solo trumpet)
0:30	3:13	**a**	Main theme (solo trumpet)
78	3:00		Coda (a)
. . . .			The coda, beginning with trumpet trills, rounds out the movement with a final reference to **A** following a grand pause.

Solo Concerto

After the Baroque, the concerto grosso declined in importance, becoming virtually obsolete by the time of Haydn and Mozart. By then, solo concertos were in great favor, and many were composed for a wide variety of solo instruments. The Classical concerto widely explores the colors and capabilities of the solo instrument, the virtuosity of the solo performer, and the effects achieved by combining the solo instrument with the orchestra.

A Classical concerto usually has three movements, occurring in the same order of tempos as the Italian overture: fast–slow–fast. There is usually at least one virtuosic passage, called a **cadenza**—a sort of extended cadence played by the soloist alone. The orchestra prepares for a cadenza, which normally occurs toward the end of a movement, by building to a loud and suspenseful chord and then simply dropping out. During the Classical period, cadenzas usually were not written out by the composer, but were improvised by the soloist, who indicated the end of the solo passage by a trill, summoning the orchestra to join in bringing the movement to a close. (Since the nineteenth century, composers have written cadenzas for their concertos and have even published cadenzas for earlier concertos, including those written by Haydn, Mozart, and their contemporaries.)

Rondo

The **rondo** form may be used for any movement of a piece, but often seems particularly appropriate for the last movement, since it usually is fast in tempo and merry in mood. Derived from an early French instrumental piece, the *rondeau,* the form is generally represented by the letters *A B A C A;* however, it may contain any number of sections, or "episodes," which alternate with the material of the opening section, *A.*

Like the sonata-allegro, the rondo is a versatile form that may be handled in many ways. The episodes interspersed between the *A* sections may be the same as each other (*A B A B A*), or different (*A B A C A*). The composer also may choose to include other material not part of the basic rondo form, rendering the design more complicated while retaining the basic stability of the form. Although the rondo is often easy to recognize because of the recurrence of *A* and its characteristic bustling mood, it may nevertheless be quite complex in the hands of a sophisticated composer.

Chamber Music

Chamber music is performed by a relatively small number of people, usually in a room (chamber) smaller than a full-sized concert hall. While the term "chamber music" is sometimes applied to vocal music performed by a small group, it usually refers to music for a small number of musical instruments, such as a string quartet, a woodwind quintet, or a small brass ensemble. The number of instruments in a chamber ensemble varies from two to about twelve, but there is usually just one instrument for each line of music, rather than several instruments for each part, as in a band or orchestra. Although the emphasis in chamber music is on the ensemble effect, each player must be an accomplished performer, since each is entirely responsible for one line of music. Chamber music is demanding of listeners as well, for one must be able to follow each instrument in order to fully appreciate the performance.

Of course, chamber music does not offer the full, rich sound of a band or orchestra; nor does it afford the color and drama of music theater. Rather, it appeals to its audience on an intimate, personal level. The special rapport established between players and listeners is an important source of the pleasure experienced through chamber music. The Classical period's appreciation for clarity of thought, purity of sound, and emotional restraint made chamber music one of the favorite means of expression.

Most chamber ensembles of the Classical period consisted of several instruments belonging to the same family, such as the **string quartet,** the most popular of all chamber ensembles. The term *string quartet* is used both for a particular ensemble of string instruments, consisting of two violins (each playing a different part), a viola, and a cello, and for the compositions that this ensemble plays. The first violinist serves as the leader of the group, indicating when to start and stop playing with a nod of the head, and keeping the ensemble together through expressive passages by subtle body movements and facial expressions.

The compositions called string quartets are multimovement works, usually consisting of four movements. Franz Joseph Haydn found the compositions and the ensembles that performed them particularly congenial to his remarkable ear.

Franz Joseph Haydn (1732–1809)

✲**Franz Joseph Haydn,** an early master of the symphonic form, was born in Austria near the border of modern Hungary. Showing musical ability as a child, he was accepted as a choirboy and student at a Vienna cathedral, where he remained until his voice changed in his late teens.

After several difficult years of studying composition on his own and earning a meager living by giving music lessons to Viennese children, Haydn entered the service of Prince Paul Anton Esterházy, a wealthy and powerful nobleman with a passion for music. For nearly thirty years, Haydn lived as a well-paid but overworked servant, composing many operas, symphonies, concertos, and chamber music pieces, besides performing arduous administrative chores. Although taxing, his position had

Franz Joseph Haydn.
E. T. Archive, London

inherent advantages; for example, it placed a fine orchestra and talented singers at his command.

A concerned and conscientious administrator and a modest and generous man, Haydn had a delightful, somewhat mischievous, personality. He never hesitated to praise others, calling Handel, whose *Messiah* overwhelmed him, "the master of us all," and insisting that Mozart was the greatest composer who had ever lived. Besides good humor, Haydn's music also reveals depths of feeling and an endlessly creative mind. Like Mozart, Haydn wrote nearly every conceivable form of music, including over a hundred symphonies. Several of his operas, long forgotten, are now being performed and recorded to appreciative review, and his oratorio *The Creation* remains a favorite of audiences today. His work was considered less interesting than Mozart's or Beethoven's during the Romantic nineteenth century, but Haydn—the very personification of the Classical composer—is one of the best-loved and most-admired composers today.

For the theme of the second movement of his "Emperor" String Quartet (Listening Example 21), Haydn used the melody he had written several years earlier when commissioned to write the Austrian national anthem. The stately tune later became the German national anthem.

An early nineteenth-century performance of Haydn's Creation.
Stock Montage, Inc., Chicago

Sonata

Another multimovement composition somewhat standardized during the Classical period was the **sonata,** understood by Classicists to be a composition of three or four movements performed by one or two soloists unaccompanied by other instruments. While sonatas exist for virtually every conceivable musical instrument, more sonatas have been written for the piano, on which a performer can achieve a great variety of melodic, harmonic, and textural effects, than for any other instrument. Also popular are sonatas for two solo instruments, such as a violin and a piano, which may be viewed as instrumental duets in which each instrument performs some soloistic or virtuosic passages.

2 [1]

LISTENING EXAMPLE 21

 2A 1

String Quartet

Composer: Franz Joseph Haydn (1732–1809)

Title: String Quartet in C Major ("Emperor"), op. 76, No. 3, second movement

Composed: 1797

Form: Theme and variations

Rhythm: Poco adagio; cantabile (rather slow; songlike); Duple meter

Timbre: String quartet (two violins, viola, cello)

Classical balance is apparent here in the symmetrical pattern of phrases, while the presence of the theme throughout the movement and the pause separating one variation from another lend Classical clarity to the music.

Theme   (The theme, *p,* has three melodic phrases, which occur in the order a a b c c.)

[1]	0:00	**a**	The theme is introduced by the first violin, accompanied by the second violin, viola and cello.
. . . .			
0:16	0:16	**a**	
0:31	0:31	**b**	(ends on the dominant)
0:50	0:50	**c**	
1:08	1:08	**c**	(ends on the tonic)

Variation 1 (*p*)

[2]	1:27	The theme is in the second violin, accompanied by a running pattern in the first violin. The texture is light and **contrapuntal,** or polyphonic, in texture.

Variation 2 (*p*)

. . . .		
[3]	2:47	The theme is in the cello, performed as a duet with harmonic support in the second violin. The first violin adds a new contrapuntal line.

Variation 3 (*p*)

. . . .		
[4]	4:11	The viola has the theme, while the other instruments perform countermelodies. The texture remains light and contrapuntal.

Variation 4 (*p*)

. . . .		
[5]	5:34	The first violin takes the theme once more, playing it sometimes an octave higher than before, while the other instruments play a basically chordal accompaniment. The texture is primarily homophonic, more dense than in the earlier variations. Slightly increased dissonance adds tension and harmonic interest to this section.

Coda (*pp*)

. . . .		
[6]	7:01	A short concluding passage ends the movement.

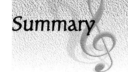

Summary

By the Classical period, the focus had changed from a vocal to an instrumental orientation, and from mostly religious to mostly secular music. The fortepiano became increasingly popular, eventually replacing the harpsichord as a solo and accompanying keyboard instrument. The instrumentation of the orchestra was standardized during this period.

As the Baroque was style conscious, the Classical period was form conscious. The classical concern with clarity of thought, order, and proportion led to the development of several important forms. Symphonies, concertos, sonatas, and string quartets were all multimovement works, each movement of which conformed to an old or a new formal design. Composers could organize any movement of a composition according to the design of their choice; but the first movement of a work was frequently in sonata-allegro form, and the last was often a rondo.

- Do you find that you are better able to understand form in music than you were when you began this course? What listening techniques have you developed that enhance your awareness of the form of a piece?

Critical Thinking

form   The organization and design of a composition, or of one movement within a composition.

Terms to Review

symphony   A multimovement orchestral form.

sonata-allegro   The "first movement form." The three sections—exposition, development, and recapitulation—form a ternary design.

exposition   In the sonata-allegro form, the first section.

development   The second section of a sonata-allegro, of the sonata-allegro; it moves through many keys.

recapitulation   The third section of a sonata-allegro, which reviews the material of the exposition, presenting it in a new light.

transition or **bridge**   A passage that modulates from the first to the second key area of the exposition.

closing section   End of the exposition.

modulate   To change key systematically.

coda   Literally, "tail"; a closing section.

staccato   Short, detached.

minuet and trio   *A B A.* Often the third movement of a symphony, sonata, or string quartet. Consists of two minuets, the second (trio) lighter and more lyrical than the first.

cadenza   An extended passage for solo instrument.

string quartet   A chamber ensemble consisting of two violins, a viola, and a cello.

rondo   *A B A C A.* A form in which various episodes alternate with the opening material. The tempo is usually fast, and the mood merry.

contrapuntal   Polyphonic.

sonata   (during and after the Classical period) A multimovement composition for one or two solo instruments.

Composers   *Wolfgang Amadeus Mozart*
                Franz Joseph Haydn

Key Figures

Mozart as a child,
accompanied by his
father and sister.
AKG, Berlin

19
Vocal Music in the Classical Period

Although the Classical period produced more instrumental than vocal music, a wealth of serious and comic operas as well as vocal religious music also appeared during this time.

Opera

Though it retained some devoted followers, the Baroque opera never fully recovered from the satirical drubbing it received in the 1720s. A composer named C. W. Gluck revitalized the threatened form of musical theater by introducing a new type of serious opera, thereby contributing to an already-smouldering war of operatic ideals.

Born in a German state and educated in Prague and Vienna, **Christophe Willibald Gluck** spent four years studying and composing operas in Italy. He then traveled to England, where he composed Italian operas in the Baroque style with little success. Finally, having returned to Vienna, he wrote several important "reform operas" that received high acclaim from enthusiastic Viennese and Parisian audiences.

Christoph Willibald Gluck (1714–1787)

Unlike his older contemporary, Handel, with whom he was acquainted, and who abandoned the composition of Baroque operas to write oratorios in the Baroque style, Gluck instead proposed to reform serious opera by imposing upon it classical restraint. He appreciated the demand of several Enlightenment leaders for a closer union between music and drama in opera. He also was impressed by a famous French opera composer, Jean-Philippe Rameau (1683–1764), who attempted with some success to integrate the ballet—an essential element of French opera—into the drama of his works. Eventually, Gluck met a fine Italian librettist who shared similar ideas, and they collaborated in 1762 to produce the first **reform opera,** *Orfeo ed Euridice.*

In response to the Enlightenment's call for a return to nature—that is, to a realistic, not a fantastic, style of art—in *Orfeo* Gluck lessened the difference between recitative and aria, writing expressive accompanied recitatives and lyrical arias with little or no embellishment of the simple melody line. The members of Gluck's ballet and chorus represented characters in the story of the opera, who enhanced rather than interrupted the dramatic development. Gluck's main characters were warm and believable. Even the orchestra added dramatic commentary, besides providing instrumental support for the singers. *Orfeo* made a great impression on a wide audience, and we still respond to its lovely music today.

Reform Opera

In later reform operas, Gluck further defined his intention to achieve operas of "beautiful simplicity" by writing music to serve, rather than dominate, the drama. Gluck avoided the *da capo* aria, which encouraged singers to hurry over the second section in order to repeat and embellish the first to exciting vocal, but no dramatic, purpose. He considered the introductory orchestral piece, or **overture,** an integral part of the work, setting the appropriate mood and introducing thematic material from the opera itself. He continued to avoid startling differences between arias and recitatives, making both as simple and natural as possible.

Next, in response to a statement by Jean-Jacques Rousseau (see p. 167) that the French language was entirely unsuited to singing, Gluck effectively set a French libretto to music (1774), and the Paris audience—including Rousseau—was charmed. Many had assumed that French operas could not successfully rival the delightful Italian comic operas Paris had been enjoying since 1752. When an operatic mischief-maker persuaded both Gluck and the favorite Italian composer of the day to set the same libretto to music, both the French and the Italian versions of the opera were well received; everyone in Paris (or so it seemed) entered the fray, fervently supporting either the French (Gluck's) or the Italian cause.

By 1780, Gluck was generally proclaimed the victor—but only in France. Most of Gluck's reforms suited the French taste, for the French believed in the supremacy of drama over music in opera, and in the importance of the chorus and the ballet. Of course, they also enjoyed hearing beautiful opera sung in their own lovely tongue. But although Gluck's reforms made a lasting impression upon composers, eventually most of the Western world resumed its allegiance to the Italian *bel canto* style, succumbing to the seduction of streams of arias and virtuosic vocal display and caring little whether the stories made sense.

Comic Opera

Gluck's reform operas were not the only constructive influences upon eighteenth-century opera: several ideas for opera reform were also embodied in the English, French, German, and Italian comic operas of the period. **Comic operas,** light in mood and concerned with everyday rather than mythical, historical, or make-believe characters and events, developed in several countries during the eighteenth century, their casts smaller, their staging simpler, and their productions altogether less elaborate than those of more serious operas. Audiences appreciated the fact that comic operas were written in their vernacular language, and that all comic operas except the Italian form used spoken dialogue instead of recitative.

English ballad operas (such as *The Beggar's Opera,* p. 112) contained popular English tunes of the day as well as parodies of famous opera arias. The French *opéra comique* also began by adapting popular French tunes, and by the middle of the century included imitations of Italian arias. Later *opéras comiques,* however, contained all new music, often had romantic rather than farcical stories, and offered amusing social commentary and parody on subjects other than Italian opera.

German comic operas, called *Singspiele,* began by copying English and French models, but soon developed a distinctive character of their own. Many of their folk-like songs became accepted as part of the German folk music repertoire.

Opera Buffa

Since the early eighteenth century, Italian audiences had enjoyed short comic episodes interspersed between the acts of a serious opera. These *intermezzi,* as they were called, were so well received that composers soon began to write independent works called *opera buffa* in this humorous style. An intermezzo titled *La Serva Padrona* (or *The Maid As Mistress*) by the young composer **Giovanni Battista Pergolesi** (1710–1736), the first opera buffa, is still performed and enjoyed today.

The delightful *opera buffa* made important and lasting contributions to serious opera, including use of the highly trained bass voice for both artistic and comic effect, which created a new sensation. The *opera buffa* also introduced the **ensemble finale,** a closing section in which several or all of the opera's soloists participate, each singing his or her own words and music, to bring an act or an opera to a musically and dramatically exciting close.

One of history's most tragic figures, **Wolfgang Amadeus Mozart** began his performing career as a child prodigy. He played the piano (still something of a novelty in his day), harpsichord, organ, and violin beautifully, and was taken by his father on a number of concert tours through several European countries. The young performer delighted his noble audiences, but was rewarded with flattery and pretty gifts rather than fees. Mercilessly prodded by his self-seeking father, upon whom he remained emotionally dependent most of his life, Mozart constantly sought to please his parent (who was never satisfied), his wife (demanding and ungrateful), his public (appreciative but ungenerous), and finally himself (who never doubted his own genius).

Though fun-loving, sociable, and generous to a fault, Mozart never learned the art of getting along with people. He could not refrain from offering honest but unsolicited criticism; nor could he bring himself to flatter a potential patron. Fiercely independent, he insisted upon managing his own affairs, although he was quite incapable of doing so. Few besides Mozart's great contemporary Haydn appreciated the true worth of this man who wrote such quantities of beautiful music in such a short time. Mozart lived a short and difficult life, and now lies buried in an unmarked grave.

Mozart was Austrian by birth, but his art is universal in its style and appeal. Among his greatest works are an *opera buffa, The Marriage of Figaro,* and a *Singspiel* called *The Magic Flute.* Firmly convinced that music was the supreme element of opera and that the text must always serve the music, never the other way around, Mozart wrote serious as well as comic operas, and some of his works are a curious combination of styles. *The Magic Flute,* for example, has many serious implications, while *Don Giovanni* is a serious Italian opera that includes several comic episodes.

Genuinely concerned with people and their plights, Mozart imparted such warmth to his operatic characters that for two hundred years audiences have continued to share concern for them. His operas teem with the passions of love and anger, with humor, wit, pathos, and revenge. Yet emotional expression is always under firm control, for no matter how unlikely the plot or improbable the resolution, Mozart never abandoned classical restraint. Soaring melodies and attractive harmonies, presented in a wide range of orchestral and vocal timbres and effects, provide unfailing entertainment in these masterpieces of music theater.

Mozart based *The Marriage of Figaro* upon a politically volatile play by the French writer Beaumarchais (1732–1799) concerning the adventures of a former barber who has become the valet to a Spanish count named Almaviva. One of the most touching characters in *The Marriage of Figaro* is Cherubino, a youth (his name implies "cherub") who has recently discovered the charms of women and is simultaneously in love with several of them, to his own great confusion. His part is written for a female singer in what is called a **pants** or **trousers role,** based on the premise that a female's voice and figure could best portray the youth and innocence of an adolescent boy.

Much of the opera's plot concerns the amorous Count's flirtations with his wife's maidservant Susanna, Figaro's pretty fiancée. Her wit in foiling the Count's illicit advances, and the eventual humiliation of this member of the nobility by his servants Susanna and Figaro, were devoutly appreciated by the newly emerging middle-class audience of late-eighteenth-century Vienna.

*Wolfgang
Amadeus
Mozart
(1756–1791)*

The Overture fairly bubbles with suppressed excitement and infectious good humor. Listening Example 22 begins as the curtain opens to reveal Figaro and Susanna in the room that is to be theirs when they are married. He is methodically measuring to be sure their bed will fit, while she gaily admires her own appearance in a new hat. Susanna finally captures Figaro's attention, and they join in a rapturous duet.

Mozart also wrote many other kinds of music besides opera. He was an extremely prolific composer who wrote quickly and easily from the time he was a child, producing masterpieces in virtually all vocal and instrumental forms.

LISTENING EXAMPLE 22

2 ⑦   📼 2A 2

Opera Buffa

Composer: Wolfgang Amadeus Mozart (1756–1791)

Title: *The Marriage of Figaro* (1785–1786), excerpt from Act I
(Duet *"Cinque . . . diece";* Cavatina *Se vuol ballare*)

Timbre: Soprano voice (Susanna), baritone voice (Figaro), and classical orchestra
(two flutes, two oboes, two bassoons, two horns, strings)

Duet: Allegro; Quadruple meter

⑦	0:00	Orchestral introduction (*p*)	
⑧	0:32	FIGARO (*misurando*)	FIGARO (*measuring*)
(*orchestra*		Cinque . . . dieci . . . venti . . .	Five . . . ten . . . twenty . . .
continues)		trenta . . . trentasei . . .	thirty . . . thirty-six . . . forty-
. . . .		quarantatre . . .	three . . .
⑨	0:53	SUSANNA (*guardandose nello*	SUSANNA (*looking in the mirror*)
. . . .		*specchio*)	
(*a simple*		Ora si ch'io son contenta;	How happy I am now;
melody)		sembra fatto in ver per me.	you'd think it had been made for
. . . .			me.
. . . .		(*Figaro continues to measure as Susanna sings*)	
. . . .		Guarda un po', mio caro Figaro	Look a moment, dearest Figaro,
. . . .		guarda adesso il mio cappello.	look here at my wedding cap.
⑩	1:27	FIGARO	FIGARO
(*same*		Si, mio core, or è più bello:	Yes, dear heart, it's better that
melody)			way;
. . . .		sembra fatto in ver per te.	you'd think it had been made for
. . . .			you
. . . .		(*Figaro and Susanna sing previous lines together*)	
⑪	2:00	FIGARO E SUSANNA	FIGARO AND SUSANNA
(*melody*		Ah, il mattino alle nozze vicino	Ah, with our wedding day so near
harmonized)		quanto è dolce al tuo/mio tenero	how pleasing to my/your gentle
. . . .		sposo,	husband
. . . .		questo bel cappellino vezzoso	is this charming little cap
(*ends*		che Susanna ella stessa si fe'!	which Susanna made herself!
forcefully)			

Next, in recitative (or sometimes today in spoken dialogue), Figaro admires the convenient location of the room, between those of the Count and the Countess; but Susanna warns him that the Count is as likely to call upon *her* "services" as Figaro's. Figaro responds with a short, sarcastic song, simple and straightforward in form, manner, and text: "Se vuol ballare" ("If you wish to dance"). Alone on the stage, he metaphorically informs an imaginary count that he, Figaro, will foil any illicit designs the Count may have upon Susanna.

Cavatina:		Modified *da capo* form (A B A′)	
. . . .		**A** (Figaro plots his plan.)	
. . . .		Allegretto; Triple meter	
. . . .		FIGARO	FIGARO
. . . .		*(begins with a pizzicato string accompaniment, imitating the sound of a guitar)*	
12	2:46	Se vuol ballare,	If you would dance,
. . . .		signor Contino.	my pretty Count,
. . . .		*(repeats in sequence at a higher level of pitch)*	
. . . .		il chitarrino	I'll play the tune
. . . .		le suonerò.	on my little guitar.
. . . .		*(orchestral accompaniment changes)*	
. . . .		Se vuol venire	If you will come
. . . .		nella mia scuola,	to my dancing school
. . . .		la capriola	I'll gladly teach you
. . . .		le insegnerò.	the capriole.
. . . .		Saprò, ma piano,	You will learn quickly
*(on a single		meglio ogni arcano	every dark secret,
pitch)*		dissimulando	you will find out
. . . .		scoprir potrò.	how to dissemble.
. . . .		**B** (shows Figaro's wit and temper)	
. . . .		Presto; Duple meter	
13	4:13	L'arte schermendo,	The art of singing,
. . . .		l'arte adoprando,	the art of conniving
*(rising		di qua pungendo.	fighting with this one,
sequences)*		di là scherzando,	playing with that one,
. . . .		tutte le macchine	all of your schemes
. . . .		rovescierò.	I'll turn inside out.
. . . .		*(words repeat with different music)*	
. . . .		**A′** (a brief reminder of the first section)	
. . . .		Allegretto; Triple meter	
. . . .		*(return of the pizzicato string accompaniment)*	
0:28	4:41	Se vuol ballare,	If you would dance,
. . . .		signor Contino.	my pretty Count,
. . . .		il chitarrino	I'll play the tune
. . . .		le suonerò. *(Parte.)*	on my little guitar. *(Exit.)*
0:56	5:09	Brief return in the orchestra to the Presto tempo and duple meter of **B.**	

As the opera proceeds, subplots emerge; new characters are introduced, and, in the tradition of comic opera, disguise themselves, hide from each other, and devise outlandish schemes. Mozart's musical characterizations render the figures warm and human, arousing our sympathy, outrage, amusement, and admiration.

Metropolitan Opera production of Mozart's *The Marriage of Figaro.*
Stock Montage, Chicago

Religious Music

Although the Classical period was primarily a secular age, the Church retained a strong influence in some areas of Europe, and many eighteenth-century composers contributed to the repertoire of religious music.

The religious music of the Classical period, like that of other times, was generally conservative in style, as eighteenth-century composers often found the *stile antico* of Palestrina and the fugal style of Bach appropriate for the church. They also wrote expressive passages in homophonic texture with lyrical melodies similar to those of a *bel canto* opera. But even here, instrumental concepts were paramount: the orchestral accompaniment to these religious works was extremely important, and the formal organization of many vocal sections was based upon instrumental forms of the Baroque and Classical periods.

After Bach and Handel, Protestant music declined, since many Protestant sects forbade the performance of accompanied music in church, and Protestants considered their religious music a functional part of the worship service rather than "art for art's sake." Music in the Protestant church was expected to enhance worship without allowing its inherent beauty to distract from the service. However, many beautiful hymns written at that time are still sung by congregations today.

But Haydn and Mozart, both Catholics, continued the well-established tradition of writing Masses, oratorios, and other religious compositions for church and for concert performance. Haydn, profoundly moved by Handel's *Messiah,* in his last years wrote two beautiful oratorios of his own, *The Creation* and *The Seasons.* Both Mozart's and Haydn's Masses contain passages for solo voice and for small ensembles, alternating with magnificent choruses—all accompanied by organ and orchestra. The solo passages are sometimes quite operatic, but the emphasis in these religious works is upon the choral sections. The irrepressible Haydn, criticized for writing religious music that was too "happy," replied that he did not believe the Lord minded cheerful music.

At the very time that the young Mozart's precarious health began to fail alarmingly, he was approached by a mysterious stranger who commissioned him to write a **Requiem,** the Mass performed for funeral or memorial services. Mozart, appalled, believed the stranger was a messenger from Death. (The stranger actually represented a wealthy plagiarist whose wife had just died and who intended to pass off Mozart's *Requiem* as one he had written himself in his wife's memory.) Mozart superstitiously postponed work on the *Requiem* and then set to work feverishly. He did not live to finish it, but the work was skillfully completed by a talented and well-taught pupil.

Summary

Recognizing some of the weaknesses of Baroque Italian opera, Gluck attempted to reform serious opera by imposing upon it classical restraint. He believed that instrumental pieces and ballet scenes should be integral parts of the drama, rather than irrelevant entertainments inserted at random. He also lessened the distinction between recitative and aria, rendering both as lyrical melodies of beautiful simplicity.

Comic operas reacted against the flaws of the Baroque Italian style. In England, ballad operas accompanied amusing stories with popular tunes of the day. The French *opéra comique* and the German *Singspiel* were also light works written in the vernacular. *Opera buffa* differed from the other comic styles by using recitative rather than spoken dialogue between the songs or arias.

Both Haydn and Mozart wrote quantities of religious music, although their primary interest was in music for the "chamber" or the concert hall. Haydn's oratorios and Mozart's *Requiem,* as well as individual religious pieces and several settings of the Mass by both composers, are major contributions to the repertoire of religious music.

Critical Thinking

- The excerpt from Mozart's comic opera *The Marriage of Figaro* is sung in Italian on your tape. Do you think you would prefer to see the opera performed in English, or in Italian with English supratitles? Why?

Terms to Review

reform opera   Eighteenth-century serious opera written to avoid the flaws of Italian Baroque opera. The reform movement was led by Gluck.

overture   An introductory orchestral piece.

comic opera   Another reaction against the Baroque style. Light in mood and modest in performing requirements, comic operas were written in the vernacular language of the audience to which they were addressed.

opéra comique   French comic opera of a satirical, or sometimes romantic, nature.

Singspiel   German comic opera, containing folklike songs.

opera buffa   Italian comic opera.

ensemble finale   A closing scene in which several soloists each sing different words and music at the same time.

pants or **trousers role**   A male role written for a female performer.

Requiem   The Mass for the dead.

Key Figures

Writer	*Pierre Beaumarchais*
Composers	*Christoph Willibald Gluck*
	W. A. Mozart
	Giovanni Battista Pergolesi
	E. J. Haydn

20
Toward Romanticism

The French Revolution introduced a long, turbulent period in which the middle and lower classes revolted against the ruling aristocracies of Europe. The Revolution began during the Age of Reason, but passions soon soared out of control, and the nineteenth-century revolutionary movement that followed was guided by a romantic spirit.

At first, the goals of the French Revolution seemed to match those of the Enlightenment: respect for individual rights, political and religious freedom, and a democratic or republican form of government. However, the nature of the Revolution changed from the time it erupted in 1789 to the time of resolution. Napoleon Bonaparte (1769–1821), hailed as the leader to replace authoritarianism with democracy, betrayed the very cause of the Revolution by crowning himself emperor. In addition, the much-needed social, political, and religious reforms achieved early in the Revolution were eventually overturned by Napoleon.

When Napoleon was finally defeated in 1815, Europe enjoyed a respite from war, but economies were shattered, lives were disrupted, and the previous orderly way of life was undone. Newly restored kings and prelates repressed freedom of expression in politics and the arts. Serious artists and intellectuals increasingly sought one another's company, sharing among themselves the revolutionary sentiments they dared not express in public. Many former Classicists began to doubt reason as a guide to truth and freedom, for all the reasoned philosophy of the Enlightenment had failed to produce an ideal society. Eventually, *feeling* replaced *reason,* and the nineteenth century became an age of sentiment, when intuition, emotions, and personal experience held sway over the intellect. The expression of individual and universal suffering became part of the artistic conscience.

The years around the turn of the nineteenth century witnessed a curious ambiguity of styles and an unusually long period of time when elements of both classicism and romanticism were apparent. Some artists and intellectuals changed during the course of their careers from a classical to a romantic approach; others preferred a classical style for certain types of work and a romantic style for others. While the members of the French Enlightenment continued to espouse their classical cause, other intellectuals, led by Jean-Jacques Rousseau, turned from a rational to an emotional approach to life and art.

Jean-Jacques Rousseau (1712–1778) deplored the materialism and atheism of the Enlightenment. He distrusted the intellect, placing his faith instead in the heart and emotions and declaring simply, "I feel, therefore I am." Rousseau advocated the abandonment of everything false, artificial, or contrived, and urged an immediate "return to nature." Rousseau's proposal was timely, for many Europeans, tired of confining manners and rules, were ready to place feeling above thought. In fact, Rousseau has been called the "father of Romanticism."

Literature

The poets of the late eighteenth and early nineteenth centuries were profoundly influenced by Rousseau. Their eloquence concerning universal love, reverence for nature, and revolt against authority inspired Beethoven, Schubert, and later Romantics in all the arts.

Johann Wolfgang von Goethe (1749–1832), one of the transitional figures of this significant period, was an important poet and dramatist who changed artistic styles not once, but twice, during his career. Goethe sandwiched a classical phase between a youthful and a mature romanticism. Early in his career, he wrote the sensational novel *The Sorrows of Young Werther,* as well as an impassioned drama about a heroic Medieval knight (encompassing the romantic rejection of authority, fascination with the Middle Ages, and trend toward nationalism). Then, Goethe spent some time in Italy, fell in love with Rome and with classical architecture, sculpture, and painting, and firmly rejected romanticism, which he called a "disease." Yet the romantic protagonist of his later, most famous drama, *Faust,* paraphrased Rousseau when he declared, "Feeling is all."

Painting

Around the turn of the nineteenth century, painters turned from classical subjects and styles to a subjective and highly emotional artistic expression. Eugène Delacroix (1798–1863) may be seen as a transitional figure who reveals a fascinating ambivalence between the classical and the romantic approach to art. His choice of subjects and his manner of rendering them on canvas reveal strong romantic inclinations. He depicted ancient, Medieval, and contemporary scenes of violence with a vivid emotionalism, and was more concerned with color and light than with form, design, or the classical unity of time. Delacroix's famous painting *Bark of Dante* (figure 20.1) depicts a scene from Dante's *Divine Comedy,* in which Virgil conducts Dante, together with others from the ancient and Medieval periods, to the underworld. Fires burn and damned souls rise around the terrified figures writhing in the small craft.

Figure 20.1

Bark of Dante, Eugène Delacroix.
RMN, Paris

Yet Delacroix, called the Great Romantic, always considered himself a classicist, and analysis of his paintings, which appear so romantic at first, indeed reveals the discipline and the firm intellectual control of the Classical artist.

Music

As music performance moved from the private chamber to the public concert hall, the quality and quantity of music changed. The range of volume increased significantly around the turn of the nineteenth century, as composers called for the very softest and very loudest effects. "Monster" performances were greatly appreciated, including festival oratorio performances with over five hundred people participating. The orchestra accompanying the first performance of Haydn's *Creation,* in 1798, had 180 instruments! Although these grandiose performances were exceptional, they indicated a significant change in taste and style.

The Viennese piano of which Mozart was so fond was a delicate instrument that could not take the weight and power required by Ludwig van Beethoven's sonatas and concertos, nor produce the volume necessary for participation with the nineteenth-century orchestra. Therefore, the piano now was made larger and stronger. Metal braces increased the amount of tension the strings could bear, and the piano was given a cast-iron frame, becoming, between 1800 and 1830, essentially like our modern instrument.

The harp, too, was improved at this time, acquiring the "double action" that allows it to play flat as well as sharp notes. Wind instruments were made in all sizes, in order to complete their "families." The effort to increase the capacity of various

A nineteenth-century piano.

brass instruments to produce rapid changes in pitch led to the addition of valves and pistons, which greatly enhanced their melodic capabilities.

In 1816, the metronome (p. 10) was invented, enabling composers to indicate exactly the tempo they desired for any composition. Beethoven was one of the first major composers to use metronome markings.

Thus Beethoven and his younger contemporary, Franz Schubert, inherited a well-established and richly endowed musical tradition. Solo and orchestral forms developed by Haydn and further explored by Mozart could now be carried to their limits of expression. A variety of instruments provided the range of colors Romantics desired in their orchestra, and notation became more precise than ever, as composers indicated the exact manner in which they wanted their music performed.

Ludwig van Beethoven (1770–1827)

Ludwig van Beethoven was a musical revolutionary, as effective in his field as Napoleon in his, and far truer than Napoleon to his revolutionary cause. However, unlike the political revolutionaries of his day, Beethoven neither denied nor abandoned his Classical heritage, but merely tempered it in his later works with a more Romantic orientation. The quality of Beethoven's music far surpasses that of any of his contemporaries, and his particular blending of methods and styles of composition is indeed unique.

Beethoven's father and grandfather were musicians, and Beethoven's early signs of talent led the family to hope for a prodigy on the order of Mozart, but these hopes

Ludwig van Beethoven.
Calmann & King Archives

were not fulfilled. The young Beethoven had a rather poor music education—in fact, he had little formal education of any kind, leaving public school when he was about eleven. His organ teacher encouraged him to publish a few compositions when he was about thirteen, and also helped him to find his first professional positions.

While still in his teens, Beethoven met and played for Mozart, who was impressed with the young man's potential. However, by the time Beethoven finally moved to Vienna from his home in Bonn, Mozart was dead. Beethoven studied briefly with Haydn, but as Beethoven's personality was as difficult and temperamental as Haydn's was sunny and sweet, the two musicians never achieved either a close friendship or a mutual understanding of artistic goals. Beethoven soon established a reputation as the best pianist in Vienna, and, although criticized for being "too original," was accepted as a composer on a par with Haydn and Mozart. He was well received by the aristocracy, whose company he disparaged, but whose support he sought.

Beethoven was a kind and generous man, but his life was filled with conflict, and he was also a man of stormy temper and changeable mood. He bowed to his fate no more than to his critics. He was afflicted in his late twenties with an ear disease that eventually led to total deafness, isolating him from society and making him feel lonely. Bitter family relationships, concern about the deteriorating revolutionary cause, poor health, and constant money problems all contributed to the emotional turmoil and unsettled conditions of Beethoven's life.

Steadfastly refusing to compose to order, Beethoven waited, in the romantic way, for inspiration and the inclination to create. He exerted rigorous demands and disciplines upon himself, but never sought to please any taste but his own. Unlike Mozart or Schubert, Beethoven composed with difficulty. He was a consummate craftsman, as concerned with form and logic as with the emotional content of his work. He wrote fewer compositions than either of the shorter-lived Viennese composers, but each of his creations was a masterpiece.

Beethoven built upon the accomplishments of Haydn and Mozart with regard to form, but felt free to alter well-established forms to suit his needs. Thus, for the third movement of his symphonies, he often replaced the traditional minuet and trio with the lighter, faster **scherzo and trio,** altering the tempo and mood of the movement while preserving the three-part design. *Scherzo* means joke, and Beethoven found the bright and happy mood of this form to be an effective contrast to the other movements of his symphonies.

Similarly, though he made frequent use of the sonata-allegro design, Beethoven often altered its traditional proportions. Instead of pausing at the end of the exposition and repeating that section, Beethoven usually disguised the "seams" between sections, moving smoothly from one to the next. His development was sometimes long in proportion to the exposition and recapitulation, while the coda, instead of being a simple finishing touch, sometimes had the proportion and significance of a second development section. Beethoven also liked to combine forms: the **sonata-rondo,** for example, retains the key relationships of the sonata-allegro, but alternates themes in the fashion of a rondo.

Beethoven's music reflects the conflicts of his personality and experience. His changes of mood were sudden; his humor was as robust as his suffering was intense. His concerns were universal as well as personal, and today his music speaks to all humanity as eloquently as it did almost two hundred years ago.

Beethoven contributed masterpieces to nearly every form of music, but his genius shines brightest in his instrumental music, particularly the symphonies. He wrote nine of them, each a towering masterwork, and each unique in form and style.

The
Symphonies

Beethoven's work is usually divided into three periods. The first, a time of learning and preparation that lasted until about 1802, included Symphonies No. 1 and 2, as well as several sonatas and some chamber music. Of all the symphonies, Symphony No. 1 is the one most closely related to Haydn's work, though even here Beethoven's originality is revealed in the colorful instrumentation, freer modulation, and preference for the scherzo over the stylized minuet.

The symphonies of Beethoven's second period—Symphony No. 3 through Symphony No. 8—alternate, like Beethoven's moods, between those that are light and happy and those that are filled with pessimism, foreboding, and tragedy. Symphony No. 3 astonished its first audiences with its musical and political audacity. Subtitled the Eroica (Heroic), it was originally conceived in admiration of Napoleon's conquests. When Bonaparte declared himself emperor, however, the disappointed Beethoven changed his dedicatory message to one in praise of heroism in general. This vivid expression of freedom and independence, professed in brave defiance of the Viennese aristocracy, had special meaning for the middle-class audience of Beethoven's day.

The good-humoured Fourth Symphony was succeeded by the famous Symphony No. 5, which seems to symbolize a huge struggle ending in glorious victory. The famous four-note motto, or **motive,** that dominates the first movement (Listening Example 23)—deceptively simple but pregnant with seemingly limitless material for development—recurs in later movements of the symphony as well. The Sixth Symphony (Pastoral) expressed Beethoven's feelings on his walks through his beloved Vienna Woods. Symphony No. 7 is long and serious and the smaller Eighth sophisticated and refined.

The Ninth Symphony (1823) belongs to Beethoven's third period, a time of retrospection and fulfillment. Some of the music from this period is meditative and extremely private. However, the powerful Ninth Symphony, with its choral fourth movement based upon Friedrich von Schiller's "Ode to Joy," roused its first audience to exultant applause and continues to thrill and profoundly move audiences today. Here chorus and orchestra join in glorious expression of Schiller's text describing the universal brotherhood of humankind, achieved through joy and with the blessing of an eternal and ever-loving God. Although Beethoven recognized the authority of the Church no more than that of the State, he celebrated in this last symphony the unity of the human family under the care of the loving God in whom he devoutly believed. Neither the first nor the last symphony to include passages of choral singing, Beethoven's Symphony No. 9 is the most famous such work. The memorable melody of the symphony's *Hymn to Joy* is known to millions as the hymn beginning "Joyful, joyful we adore Thee, God of glory, God of love."

Franz Schubert (1797–1828)

Franz Schubert, Beethoven's younger contemporary, was also a transitional figure who composed in both the Classical and the Romantic styles. During his tragically brief life, Schubert created an incredibly large and varied repertoire of music. The only "Viennese" composer actually born in that city, he inherited the Classical style characteristic of eighteenth-century Viennese music. He was, like Haydn, a choirboy through most of his childhood, and, again like Haydn, he held a position at the Esterházy court, although only for a short time. Schubert fervently admired the music of Beethoven, but was apparently too shy to seek personal association with the blustery, deaf, somewhat forbidding master he idolized.

LISTENING EXAMPLE 23

Beethoven Symphony (excerpt)

Composer: Ludwig Van Beethoven (1770–1827)

Title: Symphony No. 5 in C Minor, first movement

Composed: 1807

Form: Sonata-allegro

Rhythm: Allegro con brio; Duple meter

Timbre: Orchestra (two flutes, two oboes, two clarinets, two bassoons, two horns, two trumpets, timpani, strings)

exposition

14	0:00	*first theme*	(tonic, c minor)
. . . .		"Fate" theme (motive) stated dramatically, then repeated in melodic	
. . . .		sequence a whole step lower (*ff*)	
0:07	0:07	Motive is developed (without modulation)	
15	0:47	*transition*	(modulates)
. . . .		Abruptly, with consummate economy of means, a four-note	
		transition leads	
. . . .		to the second theme. Even this horn call (*ff*), rhythmically related to	
		the motive, introduces fruitful new melodic ideas—a descending fifth,	
		a rising half step.	
0:03	0:50	*second theme*	(relative key, Eb major)
. . . .		The graceful second theme (*p*) contrasts effectively with the	
		rhythmic motive.	
. . . .		(primarily based upon the notes of the transitional horn call)	
. . . .		Rhythmic motive is heard in lower strings as an accompaniment.	
16	1:21	*closing section*	
. . . .		Motive rises to dominate the texture once more and to bring the exposition to	
. . . .		a dramatic close (*ff*).	
17	1:32	***Exposition repeated***	

development

18	3:04	The development's melodic contour, key, mood, dynamic level, harmony,	
. . . .		timbre—all are dramatically changed in this stormy section dominated by	
		the first theme and by fragments of the horn call.	

recapitulation

19	4:32	*first theme* (motive returns)	(tonic, c minor)
0:20	4:52	A slow, recitative-like *cadenza* for solo oboe momentarily relaxes the	
. . . .		tension.	
20	5:25	*transition* (now played by bassoons)	
0:03	5:28	*second theme*	(parallel key, C major)
21	6:06	*closing section*	

coda

			(tonic, c minor)
22	6:13	The coda, nearly as long as each of the other sections, begins with material	
. . . .		similar to part of the development.	
0:17	6:30	Development of the *transition*	
23	6:46	Introduces a new, march-like theme, related to the motive	
0:37	7:23	Final statement of first theme (motive)	

Schubert (at piano) with his friends.
AKG Berlin

Unlike Beethoven, Schubert largely ignored Vienna's worsening political situation, divorcing himself from the real world and creating an imaginary, ideal world of his own. He hated teaching, the only practical means for a musician to earn an assured living in that time, and relied upon his friends, who supported him as best they could. Since he wrote and performed most of his music to please them, when Schubert died at the age of thirty-one he was not widely known or appreciated. His fervent wish to be buried near his idol, Beethoven, was honored by his grieving friends.

Schubert absorbed the Classical appreciation of form, and his chamber pieces are beautifully organized according to Classical principles. His symphonies, however, reveal a curious combination of styles: they are Classical in form but Romantic in content and expression. They generally conform to Classical proportions in the relation of sections within a movement or movements within a piece; but they are much longer than the symphonies of Mozart or Haydn. Schubert liked to build a whole musical section upon a single melodic phrase, often of a lyrical or songlike quality. He would repeat and vary the melody in the manner of later Romantics, rather than developing a motivic fragment in the intellectual style of Mozart or Beethoven. More interested in the sensuous beauty of sound than in formal organization, he was willing to abandon formal restraint for purposes of vivid emotional expression. Schubert's unique combination of lyrical melody and Classical form gives his symphonies a personal quality and style all their own.

Art Song

It is in his songs that the Romantic side of Schubert's nature triumphs. Composing lilting melodies characteristic of Viennese music came easily to him, and he wrote songs as naturally as he ate and slept. He virtually invented the **art song,** for although earlier composers had written a few of these, they attracted little attention and are hardly remembered today. The German word for "song" is *Lied* (plural, *Lieder*), and *Lieder* is the term universally applied to German art songs.

An art song is the setting of a poem to music, specifically conceived to enhance the meaning of the text. Both the poem and the music are by known artists, both are of equal importance, and the work is intended for concert or recital performance. Some of Schubert's most effective songs are included in sets, or **cycles,** of songs, with all of the texts in a particular song cycle by the same poet.

The singer of art songs must be able to alter his or her voice, appearance, and even personality in order to effectively portray various characters and events, since art songs often constitute small, self-contained dramas. Singers must also be able to sing in several languages, for art songs are seldom translated from the language in which they were written.

The art song exemplifies the Romantic appreciation for a blending of the arts, involving a close relationship not only between words and music, but also between the voice and the accompanying instrument. There is usually a significant piano accompaniment, which often portrays a character (such as a galloping horse) or an object (such as a spinning wheel), besides setting the mood of the piece and providing harmonic support for the vocal line.

Perhaps best-known of all Lieder is Schubert's setting of Goethe's ballad of the "Erlkönig" (Listening Example 24), which Schubert wrote when he was just eighteen. The ballad relates the legend of the mythical king of elves who lured children to their destruction in his dark habitat deep in the forest. The singer distinctively portrays in turn four characters—the Narrator, whose voice remains neutral and objective; the Father, who tries in low-pitched tones to calm his son; the Child, whose higher pitches suggest his youth and also his rising panic; and the ominously sweet-sounding wicked Elf King. The effective singer of Lieder changes not only vocal timbre but also facial expression and total demeanor in order to capture the personality of the characters in the drama. The piano, which often has a dramatic role of its own, here plays the fifth "character," the desperately galloping horse.

2 24   2A 4

LISTENING EXAMPLE 24

Lied

Composer: Franz Schubert (1797–1828)

Title: "Erlkönig" ("King of the Elves")

Composed: 1815

Rhythm: *Schnell* (fast tempo); quadruple meter

Genre: Lied for solo voice and piano

Form: Through-composed. Schubert wrote different or varied music for each of the eight stanzas.

Text: A narrative ballad by Johann Wolfgang von Goethe telling the story of a father riding through the night on horseback with his frightened child in his arms. The Elfking (representing death to anyone he touches) tries to persuade the child to come with him.

Accompaniment: The piano accompaniment contributes to the urgency of the song by its pounding repeated octaves in the right hand and sinister motive in the left hand.

There are four characters in Goethe's poem. Although sung by a single vocalist, the music Schubert wrote for each character is different:

Narrator:	objective
Father:	low pitched; trying to calm the son
Son:	higher pitched; becoming more frantic throughout the song
Elfking:	ominously sweet

24   0:00   Piano introduction (*contributes to a dark, tense mood with pounding octaves in the right hand and a gruff, low-pitched motive in the left hand*)

Narrator

Wer reiter so spät,	Who rides so late
durch Nacht und wind?	through night and wind?
Es ist der Vater mit seinem Kind;	It is a father with his child.
Er hat den Knaben wohl in dem Arm,	He has the boy in his arms,
Er fasst ihn sicher, er hält ihn warm.	he holds him close, he keeps him warm.

Father

25   0:55

"Mein sohn, was birgst du	My son, why do you so fearfully
so bang dein Gesichi?"	hide your face?
(*ascending chromatic line*)	

Son

"Siehst, Vater, du den Erlkönig nicht?	Don't you see, Father, the Elfking?
Den Erlenkönig mit Dron' und Schweif?"	The Elfking, with crown and train?

Father

"Mein Sohn, est ist ein Nebelstreif."	My son, it's a misty streak.
(*low pitch*)	

Elfking

26   1:27

"Du liebes Kind, komm, geh mit mir!	You lovely child, come, go with me!
Gar schöne Spiele spiel' ich mit dir;	Beautiful games I'll play with you.
Manch bunte Blumen sind an dem Strand,	Many colored flowers are on the shore.
Meine Mutter hat manch' gülden Gewand."	My mother has many golden robes.

		Son	
27	1:51	"Mein Vater, mein Vater,	My father, my father,
		und hörest du nicht	don't you hear
		Was Erlenkönig mir leise verspricht"	What the Elfking softly promises?
		Father	
		"Sei ruhig, beibe ruhig, mein Kind:	Be quiet, remain quiet, my child.
		In dürren Blättern sauselt der Wind."	In withered leaves rustles the wind.
		Elfking	
28	2:13	"Willst, feiner Knabe, du mit mir gehn?	Don't you want to come with me, you fine boy?
		Meine Töchter sollen dich warten schön;	My daughters will serve you well.
		Meine Töchter führen den nächtlichen Reihn	My daughters lead the nightly dancing.
		Und wiegen und tanzen und	And they rock you and dance
		singen dich ein."	and sing to you.

(note the change in piano accompaniment and extremely soft dynamics for this verse)

		Son	
29	2:30	"Mein Vater, mein Vater,	My father, my father,
		kund siehst du nich dort	and don't you see over there

(The son's melodic phrase is now a whole step higher in pitch.)

		Erlkönigs Töchter am düstern Ort?"	the Elfking's daughters in that place?
		Father	
		"Mein sohn, mein sohn, ich seh es genau:	My son, my son, I see it clearly.
		Es scheinen die alten Weiden so grau."	It's the shining of old grey willows.
		Elfking	
30	2:58	"Ich liebe dich,	I love you,
		mich reizt deine schöne Gestalt,	you have a beautiful form.
		Und bist du nicht willig,	And if you are not willing,
		so brauch' ich Gewalt."	I will have to use force

(The Elfking loses his patience; dynamics are extremely loud.)

		Son	
		"Mein Vater, mein Vater,	My father, my father,
		jetzi fasst er mich an!	now he has taken hold of me.

(The son's melodic phrase is yet another half step higher in pitch!)

		Erlkönig hat mir ein Leids getan!"	The Elfking has done me harm!
		Narrator	
31	3:22	Dem Vater grauset's er reitet geschwind,	The father shudders, he rides very fast.
		Er hält in Armen das ächzende Kind,	He holds in his arms the sobbing child.
		Erreicht den Hof mit Müh und Not;	He reaches the courtyard in anguish.

(The pounding accompaniment comes to a halt.)

		In seinen Armen das Kind war tot.	In his arms, the child was dead.

(Dramatic pause before the text, "war tot")

Summary

Beethoven was born thirty years before the turn of the nineteenth century, and he lived for nearly thirty years after. This "age of Beethoven" was a prolonged transitional period in the arts, during which important elements of both Classical and Romantic styles existed side by side, each represented and defended by major figures in several fields.

Beethoven represents a bridge from the Classical to the Romantic period, for his early works are closely related to the music of Haydn, while those written after the turn of the century become increasingly Romantic in style.

Schubert's instrumental music is basically Classical in conception, although his symphonies are romantically lyrical and expressive. His Lieder, on the other hand, are entirely the products of a romantic imagination.

Critical Thinking

- What "revolutionary" influences do you recognize in the art, literature, and music of the early-nineteenth-century period? Do you think they were inspired by the political and economic revolutions of the time? Or were artists simply moved by the same ideas and ideals as the politicians?
- Has the twentieth-century American experience involved any revolutionary (as opposed to "evolutionary," or gradual) changes? Have significant changes in your own life occurred in a drastic or in a subtle manner?

Terms to Review

scherzo and trio A third-movement form, *A B A* in design, faster in tempo and lighter in mood than the minuet and trio.

sonata-rondo A combined form, based upon the key relationships of the sonata-allegro and the alternating themes of a rondo.

motive A brief melodic phrase, often with strong rhythmic interest, appropriate for extended development; often serves as a motto or recurring theme throughout a movement or a composition.

art song The setting of a well-known poet's work to music by a serious composer.

Lieder German art songs.

song cycle A set of songs by one composer, often with texts by the same poet. The songs may be related by subject and/or by melodic material as well.

Key Figures

Revolutionary figure	*Napoleon Bonaparte*
Intellectuals	*Jean-Jacques Rousseau*
	Johann Wolfgang von Goethe
Artist	*Friedrich von Schiller*
	Eugène Delacroix
Composers	*Ludwig van Beethoven*
	Franz Schubert

21
The Romantic Style: Orchestral Music

So strongly was the nineteenth century oriented toward the romantic style of art that it is referred to as the Romantic age, the age that virtually exemplified all of the characteristics representing romanticism. Nineteenth-century writers, painters, and musicians were highly subjective in their approach to the arts, vividly expressing their most intimate and personal thoughts and experiences in the effort to assert their individual personalities. Indeed, individualism was one of the outstanding characteristics of the period, for Romantics were fascinated not only with their own psyches and any manifestations thereof, but also with the most personal expressions of others. At its worst, Romantic art is overly sentimental, trite, and superficial; but at its best, Romanticism produced a profoundly emotional, meaningful, and beautiful style of art.

Characteristics of Romanticism

Although it was the Classicists who sought to emulate ancient art, the Romantics actually achieved an intimate mating, or interpenetration, of the arts apparently similar to the ancient Greek ideal. The Romantics resisted boundaries of every kind, including those separating literature, painting, and music: Romantic poets spoke of words as "tones," musicians referred to the "color" of sounds, lyric poetry sought to be musical, and music of every sort was inspired by literary reference.

Fascination with the Unknown

The term *romantic* comes from *romance,* the name for a medieval story or poem of a heroic nature in one of the Latin-derived, or romance, languages. Thus, the term implies appreciation of the distant, the mythical, the ideal, the heroic, and the supernatural. The future as well as the past intrigued the Romantic imagination, and science fiction became an important genre during this period. Distant places held fascination, too, and exoticism was among the characteristics of Romantic art.

Love of Nature

The Romantic age was one of rampant materialism and, simultaneously, intensely emotional religious fervor. Even as several religious sects gained numerous converts, many Romantics replaced God with nature, or saw God in nature, worshipping their new idol as devoutly as their ancestors had worshipped God. The Romantics idealized nature, however, seeing it as they wished it to be rather than as it really was.

Revolutionary Spirit

The age of revolution continued throughout the first half of the nineteenth century. Romanticism itself was a revolt against Classicism. The Industrial Revolution entirely changed the face of society, causing country people to leave their rural environment to work in the growing cities. The middle-class standard of living rose as technology and machines replaced handwork and production greatly increased; but the lower classes suffered from exploitation in the factories, mills, and sweatshops.

Art for Art's Sake

Now art was largely supported by the middle class, who were willing and generally able to pay for what they appreciated, but whose taste was less sophisticated than that of the previous century's aristocracy. Many merchants and other businesspeople were more inclined to revere technology and the new machinery than to esteem art for art's sake, which was a nineteenth-century phenomenon; Romantic artists sought to please no one's tastes but their own. Thus, the gulf between artist and audience widened at the very time when artists came truly to depend upon public support.

History versus Science

History was of great interest during this period, which produced such works as Thomas Macaulay's *History of England,* John Ruskin's various art histories, and the historical novels of Sir Walter Scott. Late in the century, however, public interest turned to science, away from history as geological research proved how brief was the period of recorded history in comparison with the time humans had lived on earth. Anthropologists studied the remains of primitive cultures and explored the subject of human nature. Charles Darwin (1809–1882) published *The Origin of Species,* which was hailed by those who believed in the preeminence of natural and historical forces, but attacked by others who saw his theory of evolution as a challenge to religion and a denial of human individuality.

The Romantic Psyche

Unlike the healthy and well-integrated classical personality, the romantic psyche typically is divided by such conflicting desires and goals. And whereas the Classicists sought to resolve conflict with the application of truth and reason, keeping their emotions under firm control, the Romantics allowed their emotions to overwhelm reason. Further, they typically considered their extravagant goals unattainable. Many nineteenth-century artists suffered from physical or mental disorders brought about, or aggravated, by their frustrated emotional states.

Artistic Style

More impassioned than art of the Classical period, and more highly subjective, Romantic art can be overwhelming in its emotional impact. Literature, painting, and music dominated the art world, achieving a closer union than ever before.

Architecture, imitative rather than innovative, produced little that was new, interesting, or even attractive during the nineteenth century. Although cities grew rapidly at this time, builders were eclectic in their choice of styles, placing buildings of one style next to others entirely different. Churches, which often symbolized a kind of mystic faith during this period, were generally Gothic in style; opera houses exploited the more fantastic aspects of the Baroque; and public buildings often followed classical lines, more from a sense of convention than from artistic conviction. Innovation in sculpture, too, was rather dormant, although the nineteenth century produced the great sculptor Rodin.

Literature

The Romantics' strong literary orientation permeated every form of art, and nineteenth-century music was so closely married to literature that consideration of either without the other is inconceivable. Many Romantic composers were also critics and writers who handled words with expertise. The union of music and literature originated in their minds and was an integral characteristic of their style.

In 1798, two young poets, William Wordsworth (1770–1850) and Samuel Taylor Coleridge (1772–1834), produced a small volume of verse called *Lyrical Ballads,* in which Wordsworth eloquently expressed his romantic love for nature and Coleridge

The Thinker (Le Penseur), Auguste Rodin.

his fascination with the remote in time and place. Asserting their sense of individual freedom in a wide variety of unconventional verse forms, these young Romantics heralded a new style of literary art.

The next generation of English poets included Lord Byron (1788–1824), who died in Greece, where he was participating in the war of independence; Percy Bysshe Shelley (1792–1822), a radical, revolutionary idealist who drowned while living in exile in Italy (and whose wife, Mary, authored *Frankenstein*); and John Keats (1795–1821), the great apostle of beauty, who died in Rome of tuberculosis at only twenty-six.

A growing interest in nationalism produced as a by-product a spreading interest in the arts of other nations. As the first World Exposition, held in London in 1851, was succeeded by several others, England absorbed a strong foreign influence in the latter part of the century.

America, too, had its share of Romantic literary figures: James Fenimore Cooper wrote historical novels, and Washington Irving told the fantastic tale of Rip Van Winkle in *The Legend of Sleepy Hollow,* while Nathaniel Hawthorne filled his writings with Romantic symbolism and supernatural themes, and Bret Harte's sentimental stories idealized frontier life. Social reform became a matter of priority for some Romantics of various countries, including Charles Dickens (1812–1870), whose novels stirred the social conscience of his many readers.

Painting

Painting, proved a ready means of Romantic expression, and we turn once more to England to examine the work of two outstanding Romantic painters, John Constable and J. M. W. Turner.

John Constable (1776–1837)

As portraiture was the art of the Classical period, so landscape came to the fore in the nineteenth century when painters, like poets, responded to their Romantic love and reverence for nature. Constable and Turner, considered the greatest of all landscape painters, idealized nature much as Wordsworth, Keats, and Shelley did, expressing their delight in it in the same subjective manner.

Constable had a rather mystic side to his personality, and his paintings sometimes evoke a sense of mystery. Fascinated with clouds, he experimented with them on his canvases. Constable said that a painter must "become poetical," and indeed his paintings are subjective, poetic expressions of his interpretations of nature.

The wonderful cloudy sky dominates Constable's famous painting *The Hay Wain* (Color Plate 7), as the viewer looks down the winding River Stour through light-speckled trees to the distant fields. Constable, who liked to break colors into individual hues, used white highlights with an unusual effect. His work particularly appealed to the French taste, and the French Impressionist painters later in the century (p. 229) shared many of his ideas on light and color.

J. M. W. Turner (1775–1851)

Turner was an "atmospheric" painter, less mystical than Constable and interested in a wider variety of subjects. While Constable never left England, Turner traveled all over Europe and was moved by the changes being wrought on the countryside by encroaching industrialization. He also liked historical subjects, particularly those of a violent nature. Turner's work has one characteristic unusual in the age of individualism: his figures are quite insignificant, nearly swallowed up in the atmosphere, which is his true subject.

Rain, Steam and Speed (figure 21.1) shows a train crossing a bridge in a terrific storm; but as the title implies, the subject is not the train, but the atmosphere surrounding it. As the fog billows and the storm swirls around the approaching train, the viewer experiences the strong emotions aroused when viewing powerful phenomena of nature.

Figure 21.1

Rain, Steam, and Speed, J.M.W. Turner.

Unlike the artists of earlier periods, who performed as craftsmen in the service of wealthier and sometimes better-educated patrons, artists of the Romantic era considered themselves superior to other members of society, preferring their own company and forming in a sense a new class of people. However, not all composers felt alienated from society, and many enjoyed great adulation during their lifetimes. During this period, music became for the first time a lucrative business. Virtuosic soloists were in great demand during this age that exalted the individual, and music entrepreneurs, including P. T. Barnum of circus fame, brought music to a wider-than-ever audience by managing the careers of the great virtuosos of the day. There was indeed something of a circus atmosphere at some of their astonishing performances.

The nineteenth century also saw music included in many public education systems for the first time. As the public in both Europe and America became more musically aware, choral societies sprang up, and music festivals of various kinds proliferated. Instruments were more accessible and less expensive than ever before, and printed music cheaper and more widely available.

Romantic composers generally preferred long, lyrical melody lines to the motivic melodies Classical composers developed with such variety and skill. The varied repetition of expressive melodies, often associated with extramusical ideas, was a favorite means of unifying a Romantic composition. Composers sometimes subjected such melodies to *transformation,* or *metamorphosis,* altering their character with programmatic, or extramusical, intent. Recurrence of the same thematic material in two or more movements of a multimovement composition renders the work **cyclic.**

The concept of tonal harmony was greatly expanded during the nineteenth century, when composers used chromaticism more freely, and increasingly dissonant chords, on strong as well as weak beats, provided colorful and dramatic effects. The more frequent use of tones outside the major or minor scales not only varied the aural "palette," but suggested the restless seeking for something beyond tonal harmony—indicating yet further denial of established boundaries.

The Romantics' music reflects the high emotional level at which they lived. They expanded every means of expression—from the sounds of a larger-than-ever symphony orchestra to the most intimate expressions of the solo voice or piano. An understanding of the personality and experience of each of the great Romantics is essential to an understanding of his or her music, no one artist or composer serving to exemplify the period. Therefore, disregarding (in the romantic way) chronological and geographical boundaries, we shall consider the composers of this period according to the kinds of music in which they excelled: program music, **absolute** or abstract instrumental music, or music for the voice.

During the nineteenth century, many absolute monarchies were overthrown, as Europeans established popular states of various kinds. Although the Western world, including Russia and America, accepted the dominance of German Romanticism throughout much of the century, as their national consciousness developed various European countries turned inward and established national styles. Nationalistic writers, painters, and musicians turned to the colorful folk tales, legends, and sounds of their own countries, suddenly finding the peasant more interesting than the nobleman.

Romantic Music—An Overview

Melodic Techniques

Harmony

chord may not relate to specific key more ~~and~~ complex

Individualism

Nationalism and Internationalism

They also found the cultural styles of *other* countries to be exotic and refreshing, after so many years of German domination in the arts. Thus, **nationalism** became an important movement in the latter part of the nineteenth century, as European countries sought to establish their own distinctive political and stylistic identities. Although Karl Marx (1818–1883) urged the workers of the world to unite, even Marxists maintained strong national allegiance to their own countries.

While Russians had long based their art music upon European traditions, their folk and traditional religious music also reflected a strong Eastern influence, which finally was manifested in 1836 in an opera called *A Life for the Tsar,* by Mikhail Ivanovich Glinka (1804–1857). The Russian story and Slavic music, based on Russian folk tunes and Byzantine (an Eastern as opposed to Roman style) religious chant, awoke Russia to long-neglected rich national resources, and a strong wave of nationalism swept the country.

Five Russian musicians closely associated with the nationalistic movement (Alexander Porfirevich Borodin [1833–1887], Mili Alekseyevich Balakirev [1837–1910], César Antonovich Cui [1835–1918], Modest Petrovich Mussorgsky [1839–1881], and Nikolai Andreyevich Rimski-Korsakov [1844–1908] became known in the Western world as **The Five.** Only two, Rimski-Korsakov and Mussorgsky, became outstanding professional composers; but all of The Five wrote operas, symphonic poems, and orchestral suites based upon historical Russian themes and mythology, utilizing the melodies and rhythms of Russian folk songs and dances and adapting the chants and harmonies of Russian religious music.

The modal scales and irregular rhythms of Russia's folk music provided fertile material for other Europeans, too, who saw those scales and rhythms as exotic alternatives to tonality and to overworked Western styles. Soon composers in other countries, moved by Russian achievements, adapted characteristics of their own folk and religious music. As nationalist composers, viewing the folk music of their own and other lands as the spontaneous expression of a national soul, used it as the basis for their compositions, Spanish dances, Italian capriccios, and Turkish marches came from the pens even of French and German composers.

Thus, the wave of nationalism that swept Europe in the latter part of the nineteenth century strongly affected European art music. The music of the Norwegian composer **Edvard Grieg** (1843–1907) often reflects the influence of his country's folk songs and dances. **Bedřich Smetana** and **Antonin Dvořák** borrowed or imitated the folk tunes of their native Bohemia (modern Czechoslovakia). And although Frederic Chopin (pp. 202–203) seldom quoted Polish folk music directly, its influence often shows in the rhythms, harmonies, forms, and melodies of his music. However, nineteenth-century nations, like Romantic individuals, conceived themselves to be integral parts of a greater whole, and the sphere of Western interest slowly broadened to include other areas of the world. Consequently, the Romantics' concern to achieve universal kinship made their century an age of internationalism as well.

Orchestral Program Music

Most Romantics, more interested in expression than in form, found the Classical rules of formal design confining and freely adapted forms to suit their romantic needs, or built their orchestral compositions upon literary or other extramusical ideas, called *programs*. Romantic program music includes incidental music, expressing dramatic events in musical terms, that was written to be played during the performance of plays. Examples of such music that has entered the concert repertoire include Edvard Grieg's *Peer Gynt Suites* and the music Mendelssohn wrote for *A Midsummer Night's Dream.*

The major contribution of Romantic composers to orchestral music, however, was the introduction of three programmatic orchestral forms: the concert overture, the program symphony, and the symphonic poem.

The Romantics' taste and talent for mating literary and music concepts led them to create a new symphonic form, called the **concert overture.** Derived from the overture that served as an instrumental introduction to a dramatic work, the concert overture is an independent piece, often inspired by a literary or a dramatic idea, but unattached to any other work, and intended for concert, rather than theater, performance. The single-movement concert overture expresses through music the excitement and tension inherent in the dramatic subject that inspired it.

As a concert overture proceeds, the listener can recognize references to characters and events suggested by the title of the work and explained in the concert program or in the liner notes of a record album. Such references organize the work and give it dramatic meaning; but a great concert overture usually has a Classical design as well. The structure and the key relationships of a sonata-allegro, or the alternating thematic scheme of a rondo, for example, often reveal for those who care to pursue such analysis an intellectual as well as subjective conception of the concert overture.

Several effective concert overtures were composed by the Russian composer Peter Ilich Tchaikovsky, who tempered his Romanticism with a Classical appreciation for form.

Concert Overture

While many of **Peter Ilich Tchaikovsky**'s Russian contemporaries were learning to exploit their rich national heritage in their composition of art music, Tchaikovsky became a cosmopolitan composer more strongly influenced by the West than by his native land. Certainly his early music reveals a nationalistic flavor, and he never lost his flair for writing folklike melodies accompanied by rich, sometimes exotic, harmonies; but Tchaikovsky's music was strongly affected by Italian opera, French ballet, and especially German Romanticism.

Having studied law with the intention of going into government, at twenty-three years old Tchaikovsky finally entered a music conservatory, where he made rapid progress and was soon appointed a professor of harmony. An extremely sensitive, even neurotic, young man, Tchaikovsky disliked the discipline of teaching and longed to devote himself to the composition of music, a luxury finally afforded him by a sympathetic widow who became his benefactress for many years (although they never met).

Some of Tchaikovsky's most delightful music occurs in his ballets, especially *The Swan Lake, The Sleeping Beauty,* and *The Nutcracker.* The ballets must be seen to be fully appreciated, but selections from each of them have been organized into effective **orchestral suites,** among the favorite concert fare today.

Unhappy and repressed in life, Tchaikovsky poured all his romantic "feeling" into his music. He wrote some attractive songs and one very fine opera, *Eugene Onegin,* but most of his music is for the symphony orchestra. The concert overture was a particularly congenial medium for him, adhering as it does to some of the classical principles he admired. Tchaikovsky's symphonies and concertos also were based upon Classical traditions, but they, too, often have programmatic associations that Tchaikovsky sometimes revealed in his personal letters. Tchaikovsky's emotional expression is sometimes exaggerated, and he has been criticized for being too sentimental. Nevertheless, his lyrical melodies, brilliant orchestrations, and lush harmonies have made him one of the best-loved Romantic composers.

Peter Ilich Tchaikovsky (1840–1893)

A scene from Tchaikovsky's The Nutcracker.
Martha Swope Photography Inc., NY

Program Symphony

The literary and programmatic orientation of some Romantics extended even to the composition of symphonies, called **program symphonies,** organized according to programmatic rather than formal principles. The leading exponent of the program symphony was the Frenchman Hector Berlioz.

Hector Berlioz (1803–1869)

Sent to Paris to become a doctor, the impressionable young **Hector Berlioz** met and was inspired by several members of the Romantically inclined cultural elite. He fell in love with music, abandoned his medical studies, and entered the Paris Conservatory. Upon eventually winning the prestigious Prix de Rome, he left Paris for a year of study in Italy.

Madly in love with a famous Shakespearean actress named Harriet Smithson, and depressed by her lack of interest in him, Berlioz composed while in Italy his remarkable *Symphonie Fantastique* (*Fantastic Symphony*), a program symphony based upon his feelings while in the throes of unrequited love. This cyclical work in five movements is unified dramatically by the program and musically by the recurrence in each movement of a theme called the **idée fixe,** a melodic reference to the Beloved (Harriet). Longer and more complete in itself than the fragments usually referred to as motives, Berlioz's idée fixe—a concept he used in other orchestral works as well—also lends itself to incredibly varied interpretation.

The Fantastic Symphony's program concerns the Artist (understood to be Berlioz himself), who, unhappy in love, swallows an overdose of opium. He survives the powerful drug, but in his delirium experiences wild, impassioned dreams of his unfaithful Beloved. **Thematic transformation** of the idée fixe throughout the symphony dramatically reflects changes in the Beloved's personality and in the Artist's conception of her. In the first movement, "Reveries and Passions," she appears as a lovely figment of his unhappy dreams. She waltzes through the second movement, "A Ball," and appears in a pastoral setting in the third, "Scene in the Country." In the fourth movement, the Artist has killed his Beloved and is led to his execution.

listening report due in one week

LISTENING EXAMPLE 25

Program Symphony Movement

Composer: Hector Berlioz (1803–1869)

Title: *Symphonie Fantastique,* fifth movement, "Dream of a Witch's Sabbath"

Composed: 1830

Form: Free, rhapsodic, or "fantasia" design

Rhythm: Larghetto: Allegro

Timbre: Romantic orchestra (piccolo, flute, two oboes, E^b clarinet, clarinet, four bassoons, four horns, two cornets (with valves!), two trumpets, three trombones, two tubas, timpani, bass drum, chimes, piano, strings)

Key: C and E^b major

Introduction

| 32 | 0:00 | An array of weird or eerie sounds is dominated by the witches' gleeful chortling. |
| 33 | 1:20 | The beginning of the idée fixe is heard, but interrupted by the rest of the orchestra. |

. . . .   Idée Fixe

| 0:17 | 1:37 | The idée fixe (E^b clarinet) is terribly distorted, nasty and vile, a travesty of the attractive melody previously associated with the Beloved (first movement). |
| 1:29 | 2:49 | Distant church bells toll (chimes). |

. . . .   *Dies irae*

. . . .		The rhythm, tempo, and instrumentation (tuba and four bassoons) of this Gregorian chant for the dead are bizarre, suggestive of sacrilege.
34	3:13	First phrase of the *Dies irae* played by tuba and four bassoons.
0:22	3:35	Same phrase played by horns and trombones, twice as fast.
0:32	3:45	Same phrase played by woodwinds and pizzicato strings, again doubled in tempo—a vulgar parody reminiscent of idée fixe.
0:37	3:50	Second phrase of the chant presented in each of the three versions
1:01	4:14	Third phrase of the chant presented in each of the three versions
35	4:49	Transition

Witches' Round Dance

36	5:05	A frenzied dance loosely following the structure of a fugue (four entrances of the subject)
1:37	6:42	Fragments of the *Dies irae*
2:37	7:42	Witches' Round Dance and *Dies irae* combined
3:03	8:08	Strings played *col legno* (with the wood of the bow)—skeletons dancing?

Coda

| 37 | 8:44 | The *Dies irae* is heard in three versions one final time. |

The fifth movement (Listening Example 25) describes the Artist's dreams of a Witches' Sabbath, a mad and eerie celebration of unholy sport. Here Berlioz makes programmatic reference to the famous Gregorian chant for the dead, the ***Dies irae*** (Day of Anger), a theme often heard in vocal, orchestral, and dramatic music as a reference to the Day of Judgment. (Further examples of such reference include the *Totentanz,* or Dance of Death, by Franz Liszt, and innumerable movie scores, among them *Close Encounters of the Third Kind* and *Citizen Kane.*) By doubling the tempo of the solemn chant (a technique called **diminution**) and then doubling it again, Berlioz turns it into a vulgar parody suggestive of a devilish dance.

Berlioz directing an
orchestra.
AKG, Berlin

The *Symphonie Fantastique* became such an immediate success that even Harriet was impressed with it, or at least with Berlioz's sudden fame. They eventually married, but (predictably) their marriage was a tempestuous and unhappy affair.

Berlioz wrote several concert overtures, some vocal music (including some songs and operas that were not successful on the stage), and some very attractive program symphonies, each of his works different from the others. But despite the popularity of the *Symphonie Fantastique,* Berlioz was not generally well understood in his day. His harmony was unusual for the time, for Berlioz freely used dissonance, as he occasionally used a chorus or an exotic instrumental combination, for color and dramatic effect. Berlioz's music was, and is, sometimes considered overdone, yet he generally used his resources with sensitivity. His oratorio *L'Enfance du Christ* (*The Childhood of Christ*) is tender and delicate, and the quiet sections of his long *Requiem* are as moving in their way as the loud sections are in theirs.

However, the composer's livelihood largely depended upon writings about music, conducting assignments, and transcriptions he made of other composers' music. Fortunately, like many Romantics, he handled words well, producing critical essays on music and contributing a regular column to a French periodical. His most important literary contribution was his *Treatise on Instrumentation and Orchestration* (1844), the first significant discussion of that subject. Berlioz had unique understanding of the capabilities of various instruments. His romantic preference for harmony and color over line and form led him to expand the size of the orchestra, achieving a wider range of volume and a wider variety of colorful sonorities than had been heard before. Largely due to his influence, orchestration (the technique of scoring, or writing, music for particular instruments) became for the first time an art in itself.

The **symphonic poem,** sometimes called a **tone poem,** is a one-movement orchestral work conceived as a kind of poem expressed in tones instead of words. It is admirably suited to the Romantics' desire for organization based upon programmatic principles and for a close wedding of literary and musical concepts. Whereas the program symphony was a modification of a Classical idea, the symphonic poem was an entirely Romantic conception.

While similar in sound and concept to a concert overture, the symphonic poem is generally longer than a concert overture and usually abandons any pretense of organization according to Classical forms. It consists of a number of sections distinguished from one another by differences in mood, instrumentation, thematic material, or rhythm, or by any technique devised by a composer's fertile imagination. Franz Liszt, who introduced the new form, based his symphonic poems upon a story, poem, myth, painting, or philosophical idea, indicating his source of inspiration in the title of the piece and describing the essence of the tale in the music.

Franz Liszt was a cosmopolitan figure, as Handel and Gluck had been before him and as was his contemporary, Tchaikovsky. Born in Hungary of an Austrian mother, Liszt received most of his education in Paris and was most comfortable speaking the French language. He was taken to Vienna at an early age to study piano, and at eleven began touring widely through Europe, playing the light and frivolous music popular with the unsophisticated audiences of the day. Eventually tiring of the concert circuit, Liszt accepted a position as court conductor at Weimar, an important German center of cultural activity. He taught, wrote, played the piano, and conducted at Weimar for several years, but his tastes were too progressive to be popular at the court, and he eventually gave up the position.

Hopelessly in love with a married woman, Liszt turned to the Church for consolation, taking minor religious orders while living in Rome for a time. He spent most of the rest of his life in Germany, Austria, and Hungary, composing piano and orchestral music as well as oratorios, Masses, songs, and some organ music. He was a kind and generous person whose closest friend, the composer Richard Wagner, turned to him repeatedly when in need. Liszt generously played the virtuosic piano music of his contemporaries Chopin and Schumann as well as his own, and dedicated some of his works to Wagner, Schumann, Chopin, and Berlioz.

The outstanding concert pianist of his day, Liszt combined a poetic expressiveness with demonic virtuosity in his music. He used chords that were unusual at the time, sometimes modulating suddenly or to distant keys. He was consummately skillful at integrating a program into an instrumental work, fusing the story and the music into a meaningful whole, and his best music is logically, though unconventionally, organized, making musical as well as programmatic sense. Liszt's creation of the symphonic poem was the Romantics' major innovation in the field of orchestral music.

We have seen that Tchaikovsky was a Romantic composer who retained some allegiance to Classical concepts of formal design. Certain other nineteenth-century composers, led by Mendelssohn and Brahms, were even more classically oriented than Tchaikovsky. Like the Classicists, they generally wrote absolute music—that is, instrumental music based upon abstract principles of music rather than upon a text or a program.

Symphonic Poem

Franz Liszt (1811–1886)
fine pianist
leaders in symphonic poem

Absolute Music

Liszt during a
performance.
AKG Berlin

Solo Concerto

The nineteenth-century concerto, like other forms of symphonic music, reflected the change from the Classical to the Romantic style; it had more lyrical melodies, more colorful orchestration, expanded harmonic resources, and less fidelity to Classical forms than concertos of the eighteenth century. Nineteenth-century composers wrote out their cadenzas, instead of leaving them to the improvisation of solo performers. Some even wrote cadenzas that could be used in the concertos of earlier composers. To emphasize the virtuosity of the solo performer, so thrilling to audiences of that (and our) time, many wrote extensive cadenzas that are technically demanding and brilliant in effect.

Felix Mendelssohn (1809–1847)

Felix Mendelssohn was born in Hamburg, Germany, in the same year that Abraham Lincoln was born in Hardin, Kentucky; but while Lincoln grew up in a log cabin and struggled to obtain a rudimentary education, Mendelssohn prospered as the privileged son of a wealthy, aristocratic family. His father, a banker, provided every advantage of education, travel, and experience to the talented young man. Through his grandfather, a respected philosopher, the young Mendelssohn met the elderly writer Goethe, and their relationship became a source of mutual delight. Gifted in painting as well as in music, well-versed in languages, an effective writer, and a charming and pleasant young man, Mendelssohn was admitted to the finest social circles and led a life relatively free from the tensions and frustrations of many of his contemporaries.

When only twenty years old, Mendelssohn discovered a copy of J. S. Bach's long-neglected *Passion According to St. Matthew,* and, greatly impressed with the magnificent choral work, organized and conducted its first performance in one hundred years. Mendelssohn's reverence for the Baroque master, and the fact that he did much to bring Bach's music and that of other earlier composers to public attention, indicate the classical side of his personality.

However, Mendelssohn failed to apply classical restraint to his strenuous professional life, accepting extensive conducting and administrative responsibilities and becoming a leading pianist and organist of his day as well as an extremely prolific composer. Mendelssohn died at thirty-eight, his early death due partly to exhaustion brought on by overwork.

Mendelssohn's music shows expert craftsmanship and a masterful control of resources. His romantic spirit is exemplified in his skillful and colorful orchestration and in the lyricism that pervades both his instrumental and his vocal music. Though some of his symphonies bear descriptive titles, the compositions are musical reflections of ideas and impressions rather than literal descriptions of experiences or events, and are clearly organized according to classical principles of form. Mendelssohn's chamber music especially reveals the classical side of his nature, while his set of piano pieces called *Songs without Words* is quite romantic in concept and expression. The first composer since the time of Bach to compose magnificent works for the organ, Mendelssohn also wrote songs and two fine oratorios, *St. Paul* and *Elijah.* His best-known orchestral composition is his Violin Concerto, and his incidental music for *A Midsummer Night's Dream* is also among today's concert favorites.

The young Mendelssohn at the keyboard.
AKG Berlin

Fanny Mendelssohn Hensel (1805–1847)

Felix's sister **Fanny Mendelssohn Hensel** was an outstanding pianist whose distinguished family encouraged her music studies, but disapproved of public performances for women. She often played duets with her famous brother, who frequently sought her advice about his compositions. Her husband, too, was supportive of her talent and encouraged her to compose as well as to play the piano, though not on the public concert stage.

She also had a genuine melodic gift and a talent for writing brief, virtuosic, charming pieces that sound much like some of her brother's compositions. However, society discouraged women from publishing music. Some of Fanny's works actually appeared under Felix's name, but much of her music was never published at all.

Symphony

Some composers, including Tchaikovsky, Schumann, Mendelssohn, and Brahms, continued even in the Romantic age to find inspiration in the Classical symphonic form. Though they sometimes provided their symphonies with programmatic titles, their works are basically as classical in form as they are romantic in expression and technique.

Johannes Brahms.
The Bettman Archive, NY

Johannes Brahms, in many ways a misplaced Classicist, nevertheless poured the warmest Romantic emotional content into his Classical forms. While some of his contemporaries were discussing "the music of the future," Brahms based his music upon models from the past, which he frankly sought to emulate. He admired the polyphony of Bach, the craftsmanship of Mozart and Haydn, the lyricism of Schubert, and nearly everything about Beethoven. A conservative composer content to build upon time-honored classical conceptions, Brahms was aware that his style was unfashionable, and sometimes remarked that he had been born "too late."

Brahms lived in Vienna, where he was a freelance composer for most of his life. He was devoted to, and spent a great deal of time with, the composer Robert Schumann and his wife Clara, one of the foremost pianists of the day. Brahms is said to have been in love with Clara; but whatever his feelings, he never allowed them to hurt his friend Schumann. Deeply shocked by Schumann's early death, Brahms, who never married, maintained a close relationship with Clara until her death just a year before his.

The discipline and restraint Brahms exhibited in his private life were also apparent in his music, which reveals a classical clarity of structure, although the warmth of Brahms's emotional expression is romantic indeed. Each of his four

[handwritten margin notes:] Johannes Brahms (1833–1897) mostly absolute music / 4 symphonies / German regium wrote from Prodestant point of view

symphonies has four movements, and each movement is clearly structured. He further indicated his classical orientation in his skillful use of counterpoint and motivic development. Brahms avoided descriptive titles and showed little interest in program music; he wrote only two concert overtures and no symphonic poems while producing a great deal of chamber music, a genre that did not appeal to most Romantics. Much of his piano music, except for the late works, belongs to the realm of absolute music, in contrast to the programmatic piano pieces of Schumann or Chopin. Brahms wrote songs and organ pieces, as well. His choral works include *A German Requiem,* a Protestant conception with words from biblical texts rather than from church liturgy.

Brahms showed a Romantic reverence for folk music, and his rich harmonies and colorful orchestrations, too, clearly belong to the Romantic period. He achieved subtle rhythmic effects and used chromaticism freely, though he never directly challenged tonality. His deep, somber tones and complex harmonies make Brahms's serious music somewhat less accessible than some of the lighter, more brilliant works of this age; but his masterpieces generously repay the patience and effort one may expend in coming to love them.

Music in Nineteenth-Century America

For the most part, nineteenth-century Americans remained in awe of European culture and art, yet seemed naturally inclined toward Romanticism themselves. Having fervently expressed their own individualism during the American Revolution, they were now aggressively expanding their young country's frontiers and settling its wide open spaces. Perhaps influenced by the lack of such boundaries as confine small European states, as well as by the freedoms with which they are richly endowed, Americans have often shown a romantic expansiveness in their approach to art.

While early Americans made no great distinction between popular and art music, by the late nineteenth century important differences were discerned between folk and popular music on the one hand, and art, or concert music on the other. Dedicated patrons built concert halls and opera houses, formed choral societies to perform the music of Handel, Bach, Haydn, Mozart, and Beethoven, and established music conservatories, where Americans received professional training in the composition and performance of (European) art music. Music first entered the American college curriculum at Harvard in 1875.

Bands

Bands provided popular entertainment during the late nineteenth century, as instruments that had been used by military bands during the Civil War became readily and cheaply available, and more and more people had the time, money, and inclination to learn to play them. **John Philip Sousa** (1854–1932), director of the United States Marine Band for many years, wrote stirring marches that soon became popular all over the Western world, where he was known as the March King.

Sousa organized his marches according to the well-established European march form, which would become even more familiar to Americans as the form of piano rags (p. 289).

Orchestral Music

Orchestras were not yet widely appreciated in America; however, **Theodore Thomas** (1835–1905), a German who immigrated to America as a child, devoted great energy and talent to improving the quality of orchestral performances in America and to raising the level of the audience's appreciation. He formed his own orches-

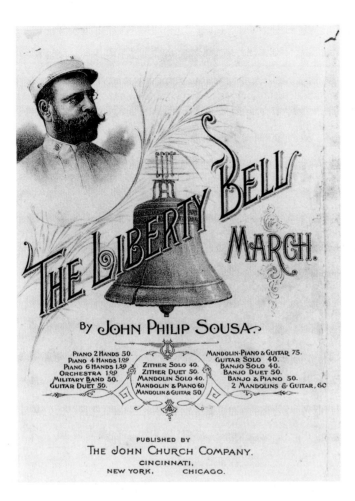

Sousa on a sheet music cover.
EKM-Nepenthe: 78 (Jean-Claude Lejeune)

tra, for which he hired only the finest and most dedicated players, and toured across the country, bringing orchestral music to people who had never before heard a professional music performance.

With great zeal and talent to educate, Thomas skillfully planned programs that challenged, but did not intimidate, his unsophisticated American audiences. Largely due to his efforts, schools and civic organizations in cities and towns across the country soon began to form their own symphony orchestras, and America quickly became enamored of the glorious orchestral sound.

Artists of the Romantic period asserted their individuality to an unprecedented degree, yet shared a wide range of ideals and achieved an amazing union of the arts. Fascinated with distant times and places, Romantics also worshipped nature and idealized it in their artistic achievements. They shared a strong literary orientation and expressed this, too, in various ways.

Summary

The Romantic period was fraught with paradox and contradictions. For the first time, art was largely dependent upon middle-class support, but the tastes of the artists and those of the unsophisticated public were widely divergent. The Romantic psyche was torn by conflicting emotions and goals, and the art of the period often reflects the emotional instability of its creators. Romantic literature reveals a love of nature and a fascination with history and science. Romantic painters preferred landscapes to portraiture and portrayed nature from highly subjective points of view. Music, too, was emotionally expressive and included many individual styles.

Nineteenth-century composers based most of their music upon programmatic rather than abstract principles, introducing three programmatic orchestral forms:

a. The concert overture, which combines programmatic and abstract principles of design. Tchaikovsky was among the composers who found this a congenial form.

b. The program symphony, which may be unified by the cyclic recurrence of thematic material, usually in altered form. The leading exponent of this form was Berlioz.

c. The symphonic poem, a one-movement work whose form is derived from its program. The symphonic poem was introduced by Franz Liszt.

Late in the century, a strong wave of nationalism spread among artists of many nations. Exploiting long-neglected characteristics of their own cultural heritage, they came to appreciate the native styles of other cultures and nationalities as well.

Some Romantic composers retained a classical appreciation for clarity of design, and most of their music can be analyzed according to the principles of absolute music. Even they, however, reflected the nineteenth century's broadened concept of tonal harmony and the expanded range of orchestral sounds. The symphonies and concertos of Mendelssohn and of Brahms are sometimes referred to as Classical in content but Romantic in expression, for their emotional expressiveness is far removed from the classical restraint of the preceding era.

The distinction between popular and art music did not become significant in America before the latter part of the nineteenth century. However, musical activity began stirring in the young country in the 1860s. Theodore Thomas began educating American audiences in the realm of orchestral music, but for a long time they preferred the stirring marches of John Philip Sousa to the symphonies of Mozart or Beethoven.

Critical Thinking

• What characteristics of Romanticism do you find particularly appealing?

• How do you think your own classicism or romanticism affects your decisions and your everyday experience?

Terms to Review

cyclic form   A multimovement form unified by the recurrence of the same or similar melodic material in two or more movements.

absolute music   Instrumental music based upon abstract principles of music theory and form.

nationalism   A late-nineteenth-century movement in which artists of many nationalities turned from the dominant German influence in the arts to the cultural characteristics of their own and of other countries.

The Five   Five Russian composers associated with Russian nationalism.

concert overture   A one-movement orchestral composition, often inspired by literature and dramatic in expression, yet generally subject to analysis according to classical principles of form.

orchestral suite   Several sections of varying character drawn from a larger work, such as a ballet.

program symphony   A multimovement orchestral work, the form of which is based upon programmatic concepts.

idée fixe   The term Berlioz used for the melody representing the loved one in his *Symphonie Fantastique.*

Listening
report

thematic transformation   The variation of thematic or melodic material for programmatic purposes. Sometimes called *metamorphosis.*

Dies irae   Gregorian chant for the dead.

diminution   Rhythmic technique in which note values are halved, doubling the tempo.

symphonic poem or **tone poem**   A one-movement orchestral piece, the form of which is based upon programmatic principles.

Key Figures

Socialist Leader	*Karl Marx*	
Historian	*Thomas Macaulay*	
Art Historian	*John Ruskin*	
Scientist	*Charles Darwin*	
Poets	*William Wordsworth*	*Samuel Taylor Coleridge*
	Alfred Lord Byron	*Percy Bysshe Shelley*
	John Keats	
Authors	*Sir Walter Scott*	*James Fenimore Cooper*
	Nathaniel Hawthorne	*Charles Dickens*
	Bret Harte	
Painters	*John Constable*	*J. M. W. Turner*
Sculptor	*Auguste Rodin*	
Entrepreneur	*P. T. Barnum*	
Composers	*Peter Ilich Tchaikovsky*	*Hector Berlioz*
	Franz Liszt	*Mikhail Ivanovich Glinka*
	Felix Mendelssohn	*Fanny Mendelssohn Hensel*
	Johannes Brahms	*John Philip Sousa*
	The Five:	
	Alexander Porfirevich Borodin	
	Mili Alekseyevich Balakirev	
	César Antonovich Cui	
	Modest Petrovich Mussorgsky	
	Nikolai Andreyevich Rimski-Korsakov	
Orchestral Conductor	*Theodore Thomas*	

22
Romantic Extremes: Solos and Vocal Ensembles

With romantic appreciation for opposite extremes, nineteenth-century composers divided their attention between increasing the size and the effects of the symphony orchestra, and writing music for the solo voice or piano. Song, one means of mating literature with music, was a favorite medium of Romantic composers. In Italy, song was closely related to opera on the one hand and to folk music on the other; Berlioz wrote some French art songs; but German composers clearly excelled in the composition of Romantic art songs.

Robert Schumann (1810–1856)

Robert Schumann may be seen as the prototype of the Romantic personality: restless, disturbed, alternately ecstatic and deeply depressed, incredibly talented but mentally unstable. This sensitive, loving man strongly affected the course of Romantic music. He wrote some symphonic works but was particularly attracted to, and successful in, the composition of piano music and Lieder.

Schumann studied law for a time, but, impressed with the astonishing virtuosity of the famous violinist Niccolò Paganini (1782–1840) determined to become a virtuoso pianist of comparable stature. However, in his romantic zeal he overpracticed, causing permanent injury to his right hand and ending all hope for that career. He turned then to the composition of music for the piano.

Schumann fell deeply in love with Clara Wieck, the daughter and prize pupil of his piano teacher. When they were finally wed, in 1840, Schumann celebrated his great joy by writing over one hundred beautiful Lieder in just one year. Finding the mating of words and music in the art song his ideal mode of expression, Schumann wrote several beautiful song cycles, in which all of the songs are related by narrative theme, key relationships, contrasts in mood or tempo, or certain recurring thematic material. Whereas Schubert's songs always retained a degree of classical restraint, Schumann's were impassioned outpourings of romantic feelings.

Schumann followed his year of songs with a year of symphonies (he wrote four), and then with a year of chamber music, often using cyclic relationships in his instrumental as in his vocal music. His special feeling for the piano is evident in most of his music: the piano accompaniment to his songs, for example, is even more important than Schubert's, carrying not only dramatic significance but often providing preludes, interludes, and postludes that contribute greatly to a song's effect. Schumann's music also reflects his restless personality. Fluctuating between extreme emotional states, he was able to express these human feelings beautifully in his art, but not to ease his personal torment. Terrified by his declining mental condition, Schumann attempted suicide for the second time in 1854, and was finally confined to a mental institution for the rest of his short life.

Throughout his brief but productive career, Schumann espoused the cause of the new (Romantic) style of music, which he believed should be free from the shackles of convention and Classical restraints. Gifted with words as he was with music, he became an effective music journalist, writing cogent criticism and commentary that

Robert and Clara Schumann.
AKG Berlin

was widely read and respected in his day and that still provides valuable insight into the music of his time. He founded his own influential journal, in which he included articles intended to raise the level of understanding and taste of the new middle-class audience.

Clara Wieck Schumann, a child prodigy carefully trained as a pianist by her father, established a highly successful career as a concert pianist and teacher at a prestigious conservatory of music. As the daughter and young wife of dedicated musicians, she was afforded opportunities unusual for women in her day to attend important music performances and to meet and associate on a par with other professional musicians. She composed a number of piano works and songs, as well as at least one piano concerto. Several of her virtuosic, well-constructed works were published and well reviewed, but she rather disparaged that facet of her career and is best remembered today as a brilliant performer.

Clara Wieck Schumann (1819–1896)

Song in America

The United States experienced a great deal of musical activity around the time of the Civil War (the 1860s). **Minstrel shows** featured the antics of white men, their skin darkened by cork or coal, caricaturing stereotypical African American figures, a form of entertainment we would find appalling today that nevertheless enjoyed great popularity then. Notwithstanding its offensive nature by today's standards, minstrelsy produced songs and dances whose tunes are as enchanting today as ever.

At home, people enjoyed playing simple "parlor music" on their pianos and singing sentimental songs. Tuneful Civil War songs could be heard in village band concerts or on the lips of people of every age and circumstance, and hymns and psalm tunes retained their popularity at home as well as in church.

Stephen Foster (1826–1864)

Stephen Foster, one of the world's greatest melodists, was born into the musically unsophisticated society of mid-nineteenth-century America. He had little formal music training and faced formidable opposition to his desire to become a professional composer, falling victim to the so-called "genteel tradition" of the mid-nineteenth century: the polite, superficial, conventional middle-class approach to life and art. His family appreciated music as a pleasant diversion from serious business, but could not conceive of a respectable man devoting his professional attention to it.

Foster's songs about love (including "Beautiful Dreamer" and "Jeanie with the Light Brown Hair"), home ("My Old Kentucky Home" and "Old Folks at Home"), and the Civil War were well received by his family and peers; but even he was ashamed of his own favorites, such nonsense songs as "O Susannah," "De Camptown Races," and "Nelly Bly," written for the minstrel stage. Foster gave away some of his best songs to enterprising publishers, who realized their worth as he did not; and he allowed other composers to claim some of his songs in their own names. Stephen Foster died, alone and impoverished, at the age of thirty-seven.

Stephen Foster's sensitive and sympathetic songs about plantation life—which he never experienced—tugged at the heartstrings of Europeans and Americans, Northerners and Southerners, alike. Simple in structure, with uncomplicated rhythms and harmony, Foster's songs have some of the loveliest melodies ever conceived and continue to be of nearly universal appeal.

Stephen Foster.

National Portrait Gallery, Smithsonian Institution Washington DC/Art Resource, NY

Choral Music

Since the Romantic period directed most of its energies along secular paths, neither Catholics nor Protestants added a great deal to their choral repertoires. However, the French enjoyed stirring choruses in their operas, and Romantic composers sometimes included choral movements in their symphonic works or wrote compositions for chorus and orchestra, often treating the chorus as an integral part of the instrumental ensemble rather than a separate entity. Berlioz wrote two gigantic works for chorus, soloists, and orchestra—a *Requiem* and a *Te Deum*—that were both quite theatrical but profoundly moving works.

The English have always been fond of choral music, and interest in the writing of oratorios centered there and in Germany during the Romantic period. Many works were composed especially for performance at English choral festivals. Mendelssohn's two oratorios contain lovely choruses, solos, and small ensembles appropriate for worship or concert performance, and Brahms shared with Mendelssohn the distinction of making the best use of the choral ensemble during the Romantic period, their classical concerns and interest in the forms of the past enhanced these German composers' understanding of the choral medium.

The Italian composers **Gioacchino Rossini** (1792–1868) and **Giuseppe Verdi** (1813–1901) are sometimes accused of having imbued their religious choral music with too many elements of the Italian opera. They were indeed men of the theater, as evidenced in all of their compositions. However, Rossini's *Stabat Mater* and Verdi's *Requiem* are sincere, if dramatic, expressions of religious faith, and both contain some of the loveliest choral music of any period.

Russian composers developed a new style of religious composition during the nineteenth century, writing for a large unaccompanied chorus, or for double chorus, and using the modal melodies and free rhythms of Russian Orthodox chant. The thick, rich textures and modal effects of these beautiful choral works are unique in the field of religious music.

Before and after the turn of the nineteenth century, Americans formed choral societies for the enthusiastic amateur performance of the great choral literature of Handel and Haydn, and later of the more "modern" works by Mendelssohn, Brahms, and other famous Europeans. American composers, too, included Masses, oratorios, and cantatas among their compositions. **Lowell Mason,** founder of American public music education, was a pioneer in the effort to foster appreciation for choral music in the young nation; and **John Knowles Paine** and **Dudley Buck** were among his best-known successors.

Piano Music

The piano was in many ways the ideal Romantic instrument, technological improvements having made it into a strong and versatile instrument similar to the modern concert grand. Its wide range of pitches and dynamic levels and the expressive possibilities afforded by the pedals made the piano equally effective in the concert hall and the private salon. Though technically a percussion instrument, the piano is capable of producing lyrical, singing tones, and under the hand of a sensitive performer it can produce the softest *pianissimos* or fill the largest hall with booming sonorities.

During the nineteenth century, pianists were in great demand, and the piano music of Mendelssohn, Schumann, and Liszt was widely appreciated. However, it was the Polish composer/pianist Frederic Chopin who eventually dominated that phase of Romantic composition.

Frederic Chopin (1810–1849)

Frederic Chopin was born in Poland. His father was French, and with the Russian takeover of Poland, Chopin moved to Paris, where he spent the rest of his life. He brought with him some of the moods, forms, and sounds of Polish music, though he seldom quoted actual Polish themes. Called the "poet of the piano," Chopin wrote melodies Italian in their lyricism, German in their melancholy, and French in their elegance and grace.

Chopin's life and personality exemplify those of the Romantic artist. Soon after arriving in Paris in 1831, Chopin became the idol of the aristocratic French public. Franz Liszt, creator of the symphonic poem and also an outstanding pianist, astonished his audiences with virtuosic and sometimes bombastic performances; but Chopin won them with the lyrical beauty of his songlike melodies, the rich accompanying harmonies, and the romantic spirit he perfectly captured and expressed. He eschewed Liszt's theatrical composing and performing style, instead writing small, intimate mood pieces as moving and meaningful today as when they first appeared.

Though successful as a composer, teacher, and performer in Paris society, however, Chopin was seldom happy. He formed a romantic relationship with George Sand, a successful French novelist who took a man's name to avoid discrimination against her work. However, she could not, or would not, devote herself to him entirely, and their love was troubled and largely unfulfilled. Chopin contracted tuberculosis when he was twenty-eight, and was often ill for the rest of his short life, suffering physically from his illness and emotionally from his exile from his beloved homeland. He carried a fistful of earth with him from Poland to France, and in his will he requested that his heart be buried in his native land. Much of Chopin's music reflects his delicate health, his sensitive feelings, and his longing for what he could not have.

Salon performance by Chopin.
AKG Berlin

Plate 6

American School, *The Sargent Family,* 1800. Folk artists, like the singing school masters, produce highly attractive art for practical purposes—here to preserve the likenesses of this young American family. Oil on canvas, 38 5/16 × 50 9/16 ins (97.2 × 127.8 cm). National Gallery of Art, Washington. Gift of Edgar William and Bernice Chrysler Garbisch.

Plate 7

John Constable, *The Hay Wain,* 1826. Dominated by the amazing sky, Constable's fields and trees shimmer with many hues of sun-dappled green and gold—of immense influence upon the later Impressionists. Oil on canvas, 56 ¹/₄ × 43 ins (1.43 × 1.09 m). National Gallery, London.

Plate 8

A scene from Verdi's Aïda, with the splendid costumes and staging effects characteristic of grand opera.
Performing Arts Library, London

Plate 9

Vincent van Gogh, *The Starry Night*, 1889. Van Gogh expressed in brilliant color and vivid design the disturbed perceptions that eventually drove him to suicide. Misunderstood in his own day (he sold only four paintings in his lifetime), Van Gogh is among the most popular of all artists today. Oil on canvas, 29 × 36 ¼ ins (73.7 × 92.1 cm). Museum of Modern Art, New York. Acquired through the Lillie P. Bliss Bequest.

Plate 10

Claude Monet, *Impression, Sunrise,* 1875. Working out-of-doors, the Impressionists captured the changing effects of sunlight on water and landscape. In this painting, which introduced the term "Impressionism" in art, Monet depicted the hazy atmosphere and watery light of a French sunrise. Oil on canvas, 19 × 23 ½ ins (48.3 × 59.7 cm). Musee Marmottan, Paris.
A. K. G. Berlin/Superstock

Chopin's Style

Chopin, like Schumann, was a melodist. His melodies are long and songlike, and he spun them out and repeated them with only minor embellishments, as a vocalist might embellish the line of a song. Such melodies do not lend themselves to motivic development, but one never tires of their repetitions, accompanied by Chopin's rich and imaginative harmonies and lush pianistic effects.

Chopin expanded traditional chords, adding dissonances for color and mood, as painters of his period expanded the color range of their palette. His use of chromaticism and his unusual modulations seemed bizarre to traditionalists, but Chopin's music is exquisitely organized, and his rich and varied harmonies appeal greatly to twentieth-century audiences.

Appreciation of Chopin's music requires understanding of a Romantic rhythmic technique called **rubato,** which literally means "robbing," and which refers to stealing from and adding to the tempo in a highly subjective manner. Whereas Classical composers intended the tempo of their compositions to remain generally steady, Romantics preferred to surge ahead in some passages and hold the tempo back in others for emotionally expressive effects. Chopin used two kinds of rubato in his piano music; in one, the left hand of the pianist keeps a steady tempo while the right hand, playing the melody, stretches and contracts expressively; in the other, certain passages are played faster and others slower, as suggested by their mood or character.

Unlike other Romantic composers of piano music, Chopin devoted nearly all of his creative attention to that instrument, exploring every color of sound, every technique, and every nuance of which the piano was capable. He wrote two piano concertos and several other works for piano and orchestra; but his most successful compositions were the intimate character pieces.

Character Pieces

Chopin's short, unpretentious, and highly subjective piano compositions called **character pieces** express in a few measures what other composers might hope to say in a lifetime. They include **nocturnes,** pieces about the moods and the atmosphere of night; **impromptus,** introspective pieces of an improvisatory character; **ballades,** narrative songs without words; and **preludes,** little mood pictures that move methodically through all of the major and minor keys, as do the preludes and fugues of Bach's *Well-Tempered Clavier.*

Another type of character piece at which Chopin excelled was the **étude,** a "study" or "exercise" that explores a particular pianistic technique, such as scale passages or **broken chords** (the tones of a chord sounded one at a time in succession, rather than simultaneously). Chopin's études are highly musical pieces well suited not only to enhance a pianist's technique but also for recital performance.

Chopin also wrote a number of stylized dance pieces. His **mazurkas** and **polonaises,** including his famous Polonaise in A♭ Major, (Listening Example 26) are based upon Polish dances, but each of these dazzling compositions has a style and character of its own. Chopin's waltzes, too, are interesting and varied in mood.

Piano Music in America

Piano music also enjoyed popularity in nineteenth-century America, where light concert pieces of an entertaining nature were greatly enjoyed. Famous nineteenth-century virtuosos included a number of women, who toured and concertized throughout the United States as well as Europe. Among the best-known pianists in America and abroad was a virtuoso performer from New Orleans, Louisiana, named Louis Moreau Gottschalk.

2 38   # LISTENING EXAMPLE 26   2A 6

Character Piece

Composer: Frederic Chopin (1810–1849)

Title: Polonaise in A♭ Major, Op. 53

Composed: 1842

Rhythm: Maestoso (majestic, dignified; hence, not too fast); Triple meter

Genre: Character piece for piano

Form: A B A´, with an introduction

Although the structure of this piece is ostensibly an A B A´ design, it is not the symmetry of that pattern that appealed to Chopin. The form merely provided a logical, though not necessarily balanced, framework for the melodic and harmonic experiences that interested the true Romantic.

Introduction

| 38 | 0:00 | Chromatic introduction leads into the main theme |

A Section

39	0:28	The stately opening theme is heard in the right hand, accompanied by octaves and chords in the left. The dotted (uneven) rhythms of the theme are characteristic of this aristocratic Polish dance. The bold chords are widely spaced, covering much of the range of the piano. The theme recurs, varied, interrupted, embellished, as the level of tension rises and wanes dramatically. As in all Chopin's music, the use of rubato is an essential expressive technique.
1:11	1:59	Contrasting material provides a brief diversion.
1:49	2:17	Bold return of the main theme

B Section

| 40 | 2:53 | Begins abruptly in the distant key of E major. (There is no modulation, just a sudden change of key.) The new melodic material is explored and expanded, accompanied by running octaves in the left hand. This accompanying figure, physically demanding on the pianist, is thrilling to hear. The bold, chromatic harmonies are sometimes surprising, always interesting. |
| 1:29 | 4:22 | A more relaxed melody leads into the return of the main theme. |

A´ Section

| 41 | 5:24 | Abridged repeat of the first section |

Coda

| 42 | 6:13 | Short yet dramatic closing section |

Louis Moreau Gottschalk (1829–1869)

Louis Moreau Gottschalk ~~was the first American composer/performer to establish an important reputation in Europe~~, where he lived and performed for several years. Astonished at the talent of this exotic young American, the European aristocracy welcomed him; and upon his return home, Americans considered his extensive stay in Europe to have made him worthy of their attention as well. He traveled across the United States, introducing light concert music to wildly enthusiastic Americans.

A showman as well as an artist, ~~Gottschalk well understood how to gauge his audience~~ and was content to play for them the virtuosic pieces they most admired, including some of his own pieces based upon Creole tunes he had heard as a child in Louisiana. While Gottschalk's delightful music was largely forgotten for a period, a recent revival of interest has brought it to the attention of a wide audience today.

American Music Comes of Age

Although still largely dependent upon Europe for guidance in the arts, America in fact was coming of age culturally. Music had been taught in American public schools since the early part of the century and was becoming an important part of life for many Americans, though most of the country's professional musicians were still Europeans. Toward the end of the century more and more Americans traveled to Europe—especially to Germany—to study composition, and they soon began to contribute serious works of their own to the concert repertoire.

The so-called **Second New England School** of composers (so named with respect to the First New England School of composers, p. 144) included a number of talented musicians who studied their craft in Europe and wrote quantities of serious music of every sort. Among them was a highly accomplished woman composer and virtuoso pianist, **Amy Cheney Beach.**

Amy Cheney Beach (1867–1944)

Mrs. H. H. A. Beach, as she preferred to be called, was a brilliant pianist who performed with Theodore Thomas's orchestra and other prestigious ensembles in the United States and, after her husband's death, in Europe as well. Her own compositions were performed on both continents and were generally well received, but she could not escape the inevitable references to her gender in reviews of her work: reviewers sometimes criticized her for trying to write music that sounded masculine, while praising her graceful melodies and more gentle symphonic passages as properly feminine in style.

Thus, although she handled the symphonic medium very capably, it is little wonder that Amy Cheney Beach composed more art songs than any other form, since they were readily accepted by her peers as fitting examples of feminine creativity. "The Year's at the Spring" (Listening Example 27) remains one of her best-known songs.

Edward MacDowell (1861–1908)

1st to step up College program

Like so many Romantics, Edward MacDowell was endowed with multiple talents, but lacked the stamina and emotional stability necessary to live a comfortable and healthy life. A fine painter as well as an outstanding musician, he had difficulty deciding his true vocation, but having studied both painting and music in Paris, finally chose music for his career and went to Germany to complete his music education. There he met and married a young American concert pianist.

When MacDowell and his wife returned to America after several years abroad, MacDowell began a hectic schedule of teaching, performing as a concert pianist, and writing music. He often prefaced his compositions with poems, most of which he wrote himself. His symphonic works include an orchestral suite based upon American Indian themes, but harmonized and orchestrated in the European way.

MacDowell was at his best in the composition of exquisite character pieces for the piano, in which he captured the sounds, the moods, the very essence of nature as he loved it. Delicate, intimate, and unpretentious, these modest miniatures perfectly express the sensitivity of the vulnerable Romantic soul.

Indeed, MacDowell's personality could not withstand the stress and strain of his professional life. Invited in 1896 to become the first director of the new music department at Columbia University, he proceeded to establish an integrated curriculum

2 43

LISTENING EXAMPLE 27

 2B 1

Art Song

Composer: Amy Cheney Beach (1867–1944)

Title: "The Year's at the Spring"

Composed: 1900

Rhythm: Allegro tempo; compound triple meter

Genre: Art song for solo voice and piano

Form: Modified strophic. The music of the second verse is similar, but not identical, to that of the first verse.

Text: Two verses by Robert Browning from his poem *Pippa Passes*

Accompaniment: The piano marks the triple division of the beats with rich chords that add interesting harmony and enhance the dramatic expression of the song.

The first melodic phrase is repeated sequentially at higher levels of pitch at the beginning of each verse. Notice how this, together with an expressive crescendo, increases the dramatic intensity of the song. Key phrases ("God's in his Heaven," "All's right") are repeated for emphasis. The highest note is reserved for the word "right" toward the end of the song.

43	0:00	The year's at the spring,
		And day's at the morn;
		(sequence at a higher level of pitch)
		Morning's at seven,
		(another sequence)
		The hillside's dew pearled;
0:17	0:17	(The year's at the spring,
		And day's at the morn;)
		(music is similar to first verse)
0:25	0:25	The lark's on the wing;
		The snail's on the thorn;
		God's in his heaven,
		(God's in his heaven,)
		(sequence at a higher level of pitch)
0:37	0:37	All's right (All's right) with the world.
		(highest pitch—"right")

in which music was taught together with other arts, implementing his ideal that the arts must be appreciated in relation to each other; but administrative opposition to this approach eventually broke his spirit, and MacDowell died soon after resigning from Columbia, when he was only forty-seven years old. His widow established the MacDowell Colony for painters, writers, and musicians at their estate in Peterborough, New Hampshire, where talented people continue to produce art in that nurturing environment.

Edward MacDowell.
*The Bettman Archive,
New York*

Summary

Romantic composers showed as much interest in music for solo voice and solo piano as in large orchestral compositions. German composers, especially Robert Schumann, excelled in the composition of Lieder, impassioned expressions of Romantic feeling in which the piano accompaniments have strong significance. Across the Atlantic, Stephen Foster wrote simple folk songs that retain their universal appeal.

With Romantic interpenetration of the arts, Americans and Europeans sometimes included choral music in their orchestral works, and accompanied their Masses and oratorios with significant orchestral music. Much religious music of the period is quite operatic in nature.

Franz Liszt, the outstanding piano virtuoso of the period, wrote and performed piano music of a showy, sometimes bombastic character. Schumann's wife, Clara Wieck Schumann, was among the most famous pianists of the period; but Frederic Chopin dominated the field of piano composition, devoting nearly all of his creative attention to it. Much of his music is tender and lyrical and should be performed with expressive rubato. Chopin greatly expanded the range of sounds the piano might produce. His intimate character pieces remain particularly effective today.

In America, the light concert music of Louis Moreau Gottschalk and the expressive character pieces of Edward MacDowell gained popularity. The music of piano virtuoso Amy Cheney Beach was generally well received, but she devoted most of her compositional efforts to writing art songs.

Critical Thinking

- Why do you suppose the Romantic style of art was dominated by Germany? Can you imagine France, England, or Italy as the leader of Romanticism? Why?

- Can you identify elements of romanticism in the American personality and experience? If so, is it different from the German style? How?

Terms to Review

minstrel show   A variety show, popular in the mid- and late nineteenth century, that included songs, dances, and comic repartee performed by white men who blackened their skin to resemble stereotypical African American figures.

rubato   The Romantic technique of "robbing" from the tempo at some points and "paying back" at others.

character piece   A relatively short piano piece in a characteristic style or mood, including

nocturnes   Pieces thought appropriate to the night.

impromptus   Pieces of an improvisatory character.

ballades   Songlike pieces.

preludes   Short mood pieces of no prescribed form.

études   Studies or "exercises" based upon specific pianistic techniques.

broken chord   The tones of a chord sounded one at a time in succession, rather than simultaneously.

mazurka and **polonaise**   Stylized dance pieces for piano, based upon Polish dances.

Second New England School   A group of late-nineteenth-century New England composers who studied in Germany and contributed to every genre of art music.

Key Figures

Novelist   *George Sand*

Musicians   *Robert Schumann*   *Niccolò Paganini*
Clara Wieck Schumann   *Stephen Foster*
Gioacchino Rossini   *Giuseppe Verdi*
Lowell Mason   *John Knowles Paine*
Dudley Buck   *Frederic Chopin*
Louis Moreau Gottschalk *Amy Cheney Beach*
Edward MacDowell

23
Music Theater in the Nineteenth Century

The integration of music, drama, and the visual arts made music theater a favorite form of Romantic expression. Indeed, for many Romantics, opera seemed the ideal art form, and the period produced a wide variety of serious and comic opera styles.

In mid-nineteenth-century France, serious works known as **grand operas** became widely popular. Usually based upon dramatic historical events, they emphasized grandeur and spectacle. Battles, storms, fires, shipwrecks, and murders vied with festive wedding scenes and triumphal marches to entertain the largely middle-class audience, who attended the opera for fun and excitement.

Grand Opera

opera / music drama

Hardly comic, but shorter, more realistic, and more modest than grand opera in performance requirements and techniques, the nineteenth-century *opéra comique* competed with grand opera for popularity. This type of opera also typically included some spoken dialogue. One of today's best-loved operas, *Carmen,* by Georges Bizet, originally known as an *opéra comique* because of its use of spoken dialogue in some scenes, has a serious story involving realistic characters caught up in social and romantic affairs beyond their control. The Spanish setting and musical characteristics indicate the French composer's appreciation for nationalistic art and exotic effects. Although *Carmen* ends tragically, the vivid scenes, colorful dances, brilliant stage effects, and irresistible music still render it a supreme entertainment and a particularly effective introduction to the world of opera.

Opéra Comique

o´pā-rah co-mĕk´
Bē-zā´

Early-nineteenth-century Italian composers brought the pure bel canto style of opera to its peak. One of the most famous examples of bel canto singing occurs in the so-called mad scene from *Lucia di Lammermoor,* by **Gaetano Donizetti** (1797–1848). In this scene the heroine, quite out of touch with reality, sings a series of wordless passages including rapid scale passages, elaborate embellishments, and incredibly high notes. This kind of virtuosic singing, called **coloratura,** provides some of opera's most rewarding experiences for lovers of the singing voice.

Italian Romantic Opera

Daw-nē-tzeht´-tē
kol-or-a-tu´-rah

Giuseppe Verdi also paid homage to the bel canto tradition in works of even greater stature than those of Donizetti. Verdi was a master of theater techniques, well versed in the Italian tradition of beautiful singing, and the finest Italian composer of the nineteenth century. A musical and political nationalist who believed that nations should cultivate their own artistic styles free from foreign influence, he used his early operas as thinly veiled calls for the political unification and independence of Italy. Verdi possessed the Italian gift for melodic invention, as well as a powerful dramatic sense and keen insight into human emotions. He was not opposed to using

Giuseppe Verdi (1813–1901)

Vair´-dē

spectacle to enhance a dramatic effect, but in his operas, the music reigns supreme over every other element, including the text.

Perhaps his own suffering made Verdi particularly sensitive. He and his young wife, whom he adored, lost one, and then a second, baby; when his wife, too, died, he was desolate with grief, with no heart to compose music for several years. Finally, a friend persuaded him to write an opera, and in 1842 he produced *Nabucco* (*Nebuchadnezzar*), a great success that finally launched him on his long and illustrious career.

Na-bu´-ko

Verdi's famous opera *Aïda*, written for the inauguration of the Suez Canal in 1871 and set in ancient Egypt, was Verdi's version of a grand opera: it contains great pomp, overwhelming spectacle, and magnificent pageantry. (See Color Plate 8.) The opera ends with the live burial of the hero and heroine in the Egyptian catacombs. Verdi's characters are warm and human; as heard in Listening Example 28, his beautiful music triumphs over the extreme pathos of the drama, drawing us deeply into the situation and involving our deepest sympathies and emotions.

I-ē´-dah

Unlike so many of the Romantics, Verdi led a long and fruitful life. In his later works, Verdi narrowed the distinction between recitative and aria, avoiding interruptions in the drama by writing a more continuous style of music. His harmony became richer than that in his earlier works, and the orchestra played a more significant role. He wrote one of the world's most passionate operas—*Otello*, based upon Shakespeare's tragedy—when he was seventy-four years old, and one of the funniest—*Falstaff*, based upon Shakespeare's comic character—when he was eighty.

Verismo

Like the French composers of *opéra comique* (and unlike Verdi in his grand opera *Aïda*), some Italian composers of the late Romantic period portrayed realistic, everyday characters in their operas. Called realism or naturalism in art and literature, this effect in opera is referred to as **verismo.** *La Bôhemia*

Pu-chē´-nē

Giacomo Puccini (1858–1924) was a leader in this movement to capture reality and express it through opera. The young, impoverished artists (bohemians) in his beautiful opera *La Bohéme* are based upon people Puccini knew and lived among as he struggled to become successful. Some of them, like the young heroine of *La Bohéme,* were doomed to early illness and death. The opera's characters are warm, living people involved in believable situations, and Puccini's soaring melodies, colorful orchestration, and effective ensemble scenes continue to evoke a fervent emotional response from audiences today. (The emotions roused by the current rock musical *Rent,* inspired by *La Bohéme,* are heightened by knowledge of the death of its English composer Jonathan Larson at age 35, after watching the final dress rehearsal of his show on January 24, 1996.)

La Bo-aim´

Music Drama

The late-nineteenth-century German music theater was dominated by Richard Wagner, who fervently espoused the Romantic doctrine of the intermingling of the arts. Wagner called the form of music theater he envisioned, in which the words and the music were of equal importance—or in which the music served simply to enhance the drama—**music dramas.**

Rē´-kart Vahg´-ner

Richard Wagner (1813–1883)

A poet before he became a musician, **Richard Wagner** had little formal music education. He turned to writing music only to enhance the emotional effect of his dramas; yet he revolutionized the course of Western music history, affecting in some way nearly every composer who followed him. Wagner was influenced by the liter-

2 44 # LISTENING EXAMPLE 28 2B 2

Scene from Aïda

Composer: Giuseppi Verdi (1813–1901)

Title: "Celeste Aïda" from *Aïda*

Genre: Recitative and aria from an opera set in ancient Egypt

Melody: Beautifully expressive melody; voice is most important

Rhythm: Recitative—quadruple meter; Aria—compound duple meter

Tempo: Andantino

Timbe: Solo tenor voice with Romantic orchestra

Radames, a young warrior, hopes he might be chosen to lead the Egyptian army against the invading Ethiopians. In addition, he hopes to free Aïda—an Ethiopian slave of the Egyptian king's daughter, Amneris—and seek her hand in marriage. Little does he realize that Aïda is of royal birth or that Amneris herself is in love with him. The jealousy of Amneris forms the basis of the story and leads to its tragic ending.

Radames

44	0:00	DRY **RECITATIVE** (*Simple string introduction ends before the voice begins singing.*)
		Se quel guerrier io fossi!	If I were that warrior!
		se il mio sogno si avverasse!	If my dreams were to come true!
0:24	0:24	ACCOMPANIED **RECITATIVE** (*brass fanfare; fast tempo; mostly loud*)
		Un esercito di prodi da me guidato,	A valiant army led by me,
		e la vittoria, e il plauso	and victory and the acclamations
		di Menfi tutta!	of all Memphis!
(*softly string		E a te, mia dolce Aïda,	And to return to you, my sweet Aïda,
accomp.*)		tonar di lauri cinto . . .	crowned with laurels . . .
		dirti: per te ho pugnato,	to tell you: for you I fought,
		per te ho vinto!	for you I conquered!
		(*brass fanfare followed by a sustained high pitch in violins*)
45	1:10	**ARIA** (*an expressive melody that repeatedly begins low and ascends to a high pitch; begins softly*)
		Celeste Aïda, forma divina,	Heavenly Aïda, form devine,
		mistico serto di luce e fior,	mystical garland of light and flowers,
		del mio pensiero tu sei regina,	of my thoughts you are the queen,
(*tremolo*)		tu di mio vita sei lo splendor.	you are the light of my life.
0:50	2:00		
(*oboe;*		Il tuo bel cielo vorrei ridarti,	I would return you your lovely sky,
minor mode)		le dolci brezze del patrio suol . . .	the gentle breezes of your native land . . .
(*return to*		un regal serto sul erin posarti,	A royal crown on your brow would I set,
major)		ergerti un trono vicino al sol	build you a throne next the sun.
		(*climax on "trono" ["throne"]*)	
		Ah!	Ah!
1:33	2:43	Celeste Aïda, forma divina.	Heavenly Aïda form divine,
(*varied*		mistico raggio di luce e fior,	mystical ray of light and flowers,
repeat)		del mio pensiero tu sei regina,	of my thoughts you are the queen,
		Tu di mia vita sei lo splendor.	you are the light of my life.
2:21	3:31		
(*softly on a		Il tuo bel cielo vorrei ridarti,	I would return you your lovely sky,
single pitch;*		le dolci brezze del patrio suol . . .	the gentle breezes of your native land . . .
minor mode)			

LISTENING EXAMPLE 28

Continued

2:32	3:42		
(*crescendo*		un regal serto sul erin posarti,	A royal crown on your brow would I set,
to high climax)		ergerti un trono vicino al sol.	build you a throne next the sun.
(*softly*)		un trono vicino al sol,	a throne next the sun,
		un trono vicino al sol.	a throne next the sun.
		(*high pitch on "sol" ["sun"]*)	
3:09	4:19	(*high strong tremolo with low strings and horns imitating a distant call; dying away*)	

ary movement called realism, which succeeded Romanticism; as we have mentioned, realism dealt with both tragic and mundane situations in an objective, nonjudgmental manner.

Fred´-rik Ne´che

Wagner also was impressed with the uncompromising teachings of the German philosopher Friedrich Nietzsche, who advocated the pursuit of human perfection by the practice of severe self-discipline. For a time, Nietzsche saw in Wagner the "Superman" who would unite all of the arts into one perfect form, but he later found Wagner's style too theatrical and "insincere."

Wagner, who had a fine sense of drama, composed almost exclusively for the stage. He wrote his own librettos, often based upon German or Nordic mythology or legend, thus uniting his Romantic fascination with the past and the supernatural with his nationalistic fervor. His early, not very successful, works were much like grand opera, with all of the pageantry and spectacle associated with that form. Wagner's dramas often relied upon supernatural intervention—unlike Verdi's, which dealt entirely with human situations.

During the revolutionary years 1848–1849, Wagner became a political activist, publishing some inflammatory articles that provoked a warrant for his arrest. Seeking refuge with his friend Franz Liszt, the unhappily married Wagner fell in love with Liszt's illegitimate daughter, Cosima—who was married at the time to the outstanding conductor of the day, Hans von Bülow. (She and Wagner eventually were happily wed.) Wagner fled over the border into Switzerland, where he lived in exile for over ten years, writing his theories about the "music of the future" and beginning

Ne´-beh´lun´gehn

the composition of a cycle of music dramas called *Der Ring des Nibelungen* (The Ring of the Nibelungen). These operas, as everyone but Wagner called them, depict the downfall of the Nordic gods (whose pantheon resembles that of the ancient Greeks) brought about by the curse of gold and by the lust for power, subjects close to the hearts of the literary realists.

No major minor key

Tris´-tahn; E¯-sol´-deh tonality

While still in Switzerland, Wagner wrote the music drama that was to change the course of music history: *Tristan und Isolde.* Based upon a medieval romance, this largely actionless opera evokes an unrelieved intensity of emotion through the close interaction between voices and orchestra, the ambiguous tonality caused by the extreme use of chromaticism, the unusual harmonies and colorful sonorities of Wagner's orchestra, and the unprecedented emotional intensity of the continuous music, all of which profoundly shook the nineteenth-century musical establishment. Wagner's highly original chromatic concepts stretched tonality to its very limits, inaugurating the disintegration of Romantic harmony. Musicians either loved or hated the work, but none could ignore it.

Wagner's theater at Bayreuth.

Always in financial difficulty, Wagner borrowed his friends' money (and sometimes their wives), remaining notoriously ungrateful for all favors, impervious to scandal, and supremely convinced of his innate superiority to the rest of humankind. Quite simply, Wagner considered himself the greatest poet, dramatist, and composer of all time. He believed, in the German way, that opera should be morally uplifting, whereas the French expected opera only to entertain, and the Italians reveled in the sensuous appeal of the singing voice. Not all of Wagner's ideas concerning music drama have stood the test of time, but his finest works are among the most powerful and most beautiful manifestations of Romanticism.

Eventually Wagner returned to Germany, where he designed a theater at Bayreuth specifically for presenting his own colossal productions. He placed the orchestra in a pit over which the audience had an unobstructed view of the stage, as has become the custom in music theaters and opera houses today. The eccentric and influential composer was buried at Bayreuth, which remains the site of widely attended annual festivals of his music dramas.

Bī´-royt

The orchestra had unprecedented significance in Wagner's dramatic works, weaving melodic fragments and chords called *Leitmotifs* (leading motives) throughout the

Leitmotifs

Līt´-mo-tēf

orchestral texture in Wagner's version of thematic transformation. Usually introduced in the orchestra with reference to a particular person, event, or idea, a *Leitmotif* recurs with dramatic significance throughout the music drama. Wagner's *Leitmotifs* express more than spoken language: they "speak" on an emotional and psychological level, relentlessly building to highly emotional climaxes.

In fact, certain portions of Wagner's music dramas may be effectively performed by instruments alone, the music so powerful and the dramatic message so clearly carried by the *Leitmotifs* that one scarcely notices the absence of the singing voice. Though he insisted that drama must be the supreme element of opera, Wagner's dramatic works more than those of any other composer are dominated by their music.

Wagner shared the belief of Monteverdi and Gluck that separate pieces, such as arias or ballets, destroyed dramatic integrity. Whereas Verdi gradually minimized their occurrence, Wagner simply eliminated them by writing a kind of endless melody, sometimes almost speechlike, sometimes soaring into impassioned lyrical lines and then returning, without pause or break, to the speechlike style. To enhance the effect of continuous music, Wagner avoided cadences, often covering a pause in one voice with a continued phrase in another. Neither recitative nor aria, Wagner's melody has a style all its own.

Lē´-behs-tōd

The "Liebestod," or Love-Death scene, from *Tristan und Isolde* (Listening Example 29) beautifully illustrates the manner in which Wagner contradicted his own insistent beliefs that the words, the drama, superseded music in great opera: in passages like this one, Wagner interwove the singing voice so closely among the other instruments that the voice can be (and sometimes is) replaced in performance by an orchestral instrument with little or no loss of artistic integrity.

LISTENING EXAMPLE 29

🔘 2 46   📼 2B 3

Music Drama

Composer: Richard Wagner (1813–1883)

Title: "Liebestod" (Love-Death") from *Tristan und Isolde*

Composed: 1859 (premiered 1865)

Genre: Aria from a music drama

Form: Through-composed

Melody: The "endless" melody of the Lietmotifs and Wagner's continuous harmonic instability evoke a level of emotional response unprecedented in art of any kind.

Harmony: Intensely chromatic and highly dissonant; harmonic resolution is persistently denied until the very end.

Dynamics: Long, expressive cresendos and descrescendos enhance the emotional atmosphere of this piece. Dynamic levels are sometimes extreme, from the loudest fortissimo to the softest pianissimo.

Timbre: Solo soprano voice with romantic orchestra (three flutes, two oboes, English horn, two clarinets, bass clarinet, three bassoons, four horns, three trumpets, three trombones, tuba, timpani, harp, strings). The voice is used as one thread entwined with the orchestra, rather than as a solo instrument with orchestral accompaniment.

The piece begins softly from a low pitch, gradually climbs to an incredibly powerful climax, and subsequently subsides.

Three *Leitmotifs* are particularly prominent in this selection.
"Love-Death" *Leitmotif* (heard at the beginning and throughout the selection)
"Ecstasy" *Leitmotif* (heard in the middle)
"Yearning" *Leitmotif* (heard in the middle and at the end)

46	0:00	Mild und leise wie er lachelt. (*Love-Death motive heard in voice: pianissimo;* *low pitch string tremolos, trombones in orchestra*)	How softly and gently he smiles,
0:16	0:16	wie das Auge hold er öffnet, (*varied sequence—Wagner repeats the musical* *idea on a higher pitch*)	how fondly he opens his eyes.
0:29	0:29	seht ihr's. Freunde? Seht ihr's nicht? Immer lichter, wie er leuchtet, (*quick crescendo; high pitch on "leuchtet" [shines]*) stern-umstrahlet hoch sich hebt? (*another quick crescendo; high pitch on "hoch" [high]*)	See, friends? Do you not see? How he shines ever lighter, Borne on high, stars glistening around him?
1:10	1:10	Seht ihr's nicht? Wie das Herz ihm mutig schwilt, Voll und hehr im Busen ihm quilt? (*orchestra plays "Love-Death" motive*)	Do you not see? How his heart swells proudly And, brave and calm, pulses in his breast?
1:40	1:40	Wie den Lippen, wonnig mild, süsser Atem sanft entweht. Freunde! Seht! (*orchestra alternates statements of the "Love-Death" motive and the "Ecstasy" motive; voice* *presents "Love-Death" motive on "süsser Atem"*)	How softly and gently sweet breath Flutters from his lips: See, friends!
47	2:35	Hore ich nur diese Weise Die so wundervill und leise, (*There is a sense of return to the beginning as the voice presents the "Love-Death" motive* *softly and sweetly.*)	Do I alone hear this melody which, so tender and wondrous,
0:23	2:58	Wonne klagend, alles sagend, mild versöhnend aus ihm tönend, (*voice and orchestra alternate statements of "Ecstasy" motive*)	in its blissful sighing, revealing all, pardoning gently, issuing from him,
0:46	3:21	in mich dringet, auf sich schwinget, hold erhallend um mich klinget? Heller schallend, mich unwallend, (*gradual rise in pitch and dynamics; brief climax on "Heller"*)	pierces me through, rises up, Blessedly echoing, ringing around me? Are they waves of refreshing breezes
1:19	3:54	sind es Wellen sanfter Lufte? Sind es Wogen wonniger Dufte? Wie sie schwellen, mich umrauschen, Soll ich atmen, soll ich lauschen? (*mood becomes more and more agitated.*)	Resounding clearly, wafting about me? Are they clouds of heavenly perfume? As the swell and roar around me, Shall I breathe them, shall I listen to them?
1:49	4:24	Soll ich schlürfen, untertauchen? Suss in Duften, mich verhauchen? In dem wogenden Schwall, in dem tönenden Schall In des Welt-Atems wehendem All (*long crescendo to the largest climax of the piece*)	Shall I sip, them plunge beneath them, Breathe my last in sweetest fragrance? In the billowy swell, in the ocean of sound, in the vast wave of the world's spirit—
2:35	5:10	entrunken, versinken, unbewusst höchste Lust! (*diminuendo; last word, "Lust" ["bliss"] is on a high pitch and seemingly floats heavenward; slower* *version of "Ecstasy" motive is heard in orchestra*)	to drown, to sink Unconscious—greatest bliss!
3:54	6:09	*Orchestra states the* *"Yearning" motive; harmony finally resolves.*	

A scene from Gilbert and Sullivan's H.M.S. Pinafore.

According to a Medieval Celtic legend, Tristan and Isolde fall helplessly, hopelessly in love, their doomed passion leading inevitably to their early deaths. At the end of the music drama, as she sings the famous "Liebestod," Isolde ecstatically embraces the body of her dead lover, with whom she joyfully contemplates reunion in the dark, private, eternal afterworld. The eloquent *Leitmotifs* express at an intellectual and emotional level far beyond that of spoken language all that the tragic heroine remembers, feels, and longs for.

Operetta

Periods of innovation or reform in serious opera seem to encourage the composition of light operas, or **operettas,** of a humorous nature. Comic operas were important in several countries during and after the reform-conscious period of Gluck, and nineteenth-century operetta reached a peak of popular appeal and artistic quality during the age of Verdi and Wagner. These lighter, less serious works poke fun at the conventions of serious opera, while exploiting some of the very musical and dramatic techniques they purport to ridicule.

While the *opera buffa, Singspiel,* and *opéra comique* found favor in their respective homelands, Gilbert and Sullivan created their own hilarious brand of operetta for appreciative English audiences.

Gilbert and Sullivan

Arthur Sullivan (1842–1900), an Irishman, became one of England's favorite composers, mainly by writing music of which he quite disapproved. He had already established a modest reputation as a composer of church and concert music when he met a talented librettist and comic poet, **W. S. Gilbert** (1836–1911), whom he never really liked, but with whom he wrote some of the world's most beloved operettas. To their romantic stories, exotic settings, good humor, and occasional parody of nineteenth-century music theater, Gilbert and Sullivan added a biting wit, social and political satire of an unusually caustic nature, and lilting melodies with rollicking rhythms that continue to delight audiences around the world.

Gilbert filled his hilarious librettos with outrageous rhymes and puns, irreverently poking fun at Victorian society. At the same time, Sullivan's music ridiculed the conventions of serious opera, including excessive vocal display—which he parodied in some lovely coloratura arias of his own. The team's delightful **patter songs** (tuneful settings of ridiculous multisyllabic texts delivered with incredible rapidity) have served as models for composers of every kind of humorous musical entertainment.

Music Theater in America

Other forms of music theater flourished besides the minstrel show in nineteenth-century America. Women, readily admitted to newly established music conservatories, participated widely in opera and concert performances. Popular **vaudeville** shows, unsophisticated productions including jokes, dog acts, and juggling as well as highly entertaining songs and dance routines, provided career opportunities for all entertainers, male and female, black and white. Though Americans admired and often imitated Italian opera and English music theater, throughout the century the American theater became increasingly independent of foreign styles, and a number of American entertainments actually traveled to England and received acclaim there.

Summary

Many Romantics considered the integrated visual, literary, and musical effects of opera to be the ideal art form, and their period produced several significant operatic styles, each associated with a particular nationality. The French enjoyed grand opera, which featured spectacular visual and dramatic effects, and the *opéra comique,* which included spoken dialogue. The Italians continued to exploit the sensuous beauty of the singing voice, writing melodic operas in the virtuosic *bel canto* tradition. Verismo was an important element in some of their works. The German composer Richard Wagner introduced a new type of opera called music drama, in which he intended text and music to be of equal importance, though his dramas are in fact dominated by their glorious music.

Operettas continued to be popular throughout the nineteenth century. In England, Gilbert and Sullivan produced comic operettas characterized by attractive visual effects, comic satire, rollicking tunes, and colorful orchestrations. This and other forms of music theater were also popular in America, where minstrel and vaudeville shows provided light entertainment and sophisticated Italian opera appealed to a growing audience.

Critical Thinking

- Why do you think Americans have been slow to cultivate enthusiasm for opera? And why do you think operas are enjoying increasing popularity here now?

- Many popular movies (*Fatal Attraction, Moonstruck, A Room with a View, Someone to Watch Over Me, The Untouchables, Prizzi's Honor, Hannah and Her Sisters,* and *Philadelphia* to name a few) include scenes from well-known operas. Some television commercials also use famous opera themes. Why is opera now being incorporated in these ways into our popular culture?

Terms to Review

grand opera   The nineteenth-century French serious opera style, which particularly emphasized spectacular visual effects. Ballets and stirring choruses were important components of grand opera.

opéra comique   In the nineteenth century, French works that were shorter, more modest, and more realistic than grand operas, but not necessarily humorous.

coloratura   A virtuosic singing style, including rapid runs, elaborate ornamentation, and extremely high pitches.

verismo   Realism in opera.

music drama   Wagner's concept of music theater, in which the drama and the music were theoretically of equal interest.

Leitmotif   A recurring melodic fragment or chord bearing dramatic or emotional significance, introduced by Wagner in his music dramas.

operetta   A comic or romantic form of music theater, sometimes called "light opera." It includes some spoken dialogue.

patter songs   Settings of humorous words sung very rapidly, with comic effect.

vaudeville   A variety show, popular in the late nineteenth century, including jokes, stunts, and skits, as well as song and dance.

Key Figures

Composers	*Georges Bizet*	*Gaetano Donizetti*
	Giuseppe Verdi	*Giacomo Puccini*
	Richard Wagner	*Arthur Sullivan*
Librettist	*W. S. Gilbert*	

PART FOUR
Twentieth-Century Concert Music

D uring the late nineteenth and early twentieth centuries, several important and influential styles contributed to the development of twentieth-century art. Each generation of artists beginning with those born about 1860 expressed different ideas, and even within each generation several styles existed concurrently, some individuals exploring and adopting more than one style during the course of a productive lifetime. Thus, it is not possible in this section of our text as in our discussions of earlier music to apply one label to the music of a significant period of time; nor can we consistently pursue a chronological ordering of events. Some significant developments were short-lived but influential upon future art, while others have continued to evolve concurrently with quite different means of artistic expression.

Social and political events have vitally affected the arts throughout this century. Russian composers either had to temper their expression to accommodate the demands of the regime ruling their country from 1918 to the fall of communism in the 1990s or, like Stravinsky, accept a life of exile. In the 1920s, political events in many countries and a stultifying cultural atmosphere in America caused artists from all over the Western world to gravitate to Paris, where they found a stimulating milieu of intellectual freedom and artistic independence. By 1940, the Nazi menace had forced many Europeans to immigrate to the United

States, where they taught and composed, strongly affecting the art of this country and leading America to become the new center of progressive music activity.

It seems paradoxical that in this age of increased mass education, audiences are actually less prepared than ever before to appreciate the music of their own time. Recordings, cassettes, CDs, radio, and television often turn the living room into a concert hall; recent research has brought to light (and sound) the music of earlier ages and other cultures, for us to enjoy and learn from; we can even hear recorded performances of composers, conductors, and virtuosos now long dead. But music education at the grade school level virtually ignores contemporary composers, and most of the art music presented on radio stations, on television programs, and even at concerts was written during the eighteenth and nineteenth centuries. Today composers receive commissions from new as well as old sources: ballet and opera companies, music foundations, orchestras, individual performers, film studios, churches, wealthy music lovers, and universities, among others. But in spite of this, most modern composers find it necessary to teach, write, conduct, and/or perform in order to make a living. Music has become for us at the same time ever-present and easy to ignore. Musicians might well counter the often-heard expression "Less is more" with the response that for them more—more technology, more sounds, more listeners, more commissions—means less: less appreciation, less understanding, less reward.

Of course, the three-part process of making music—of making music work—remains the same as ever: someone creates a composition, someone performs it, someone listens; and lack of dedication, effort, or appropriate preparation on the part of anyone involved in the process necessarily lessens the quality of the experience. The study we have made of earlier periods is excellent preparation for approaching the music of our own day, for we have seen the manner in which significant changes have occurred throughout the history of Western music. A sense of style enhances our appreciation for the art of any period; an understanding of history assures us that the art of every age challenges the audience before rewarding; a sense of adventure leads us to meet the challenge of our own time and become enthusiastic advocates of, and participants in, the art and music of our day.

Music is more varied, more fascinating, and more accessible than ever before. The sounds have changed, but the joy of fully experiencing great music has not.

24
Toward a New Music

A prolonged period of **post-Romanticism** succeeded the long dominance of German Romanticism in the arts, as composers confronted Wagner's ideas to either adopt or reject them. So strong was his influence that none could ignore him, though many espoused a return to classicism in the arts.

The great post-Romantics Richard Strauss and Gustav Mahler clearly wrestled with conflicting romantic and classical ideals. Three other distinctive styles bridging the turn from the nineteenth to the twentieth century—Impressionism, Primitivism, and Expressionism—helped to break the strong bonds of the Romantic movement, but each had strong romantic characteristics as well.

Richard Strauss (1864–1949)

Rĕ´kart Strauss

The paradox of **Richard Strauss,** a leader of the post-Romantic composers, lies in his nearly equal admiration for Mozart the Classicist and Wagner the Romantic. Strictly educated in the Classical style, Strauss never lost his affinity for Mozart, whose music he conducted with unique sensitivity and understanding, and who remained his ultimate idol. Yet he soon discovered that he also adored the music of Wagner, many of whose Romantic techniques he in fact adopted.

Some post-Romantics looked back to the old Church modes as a source of renewed inspiration. Others looked East and discovered pentatonic scales, upon which much of the folk music of the world is based, and the whole-tone scale, which is often heard in the music of East Asia. Still others followed the example set by Wagner in *Tristan und Isolde,* basing entire compositions upon the chromatic scale.

Strauss was one of several late-nineteenth-century composers who worked within the system of tonal harmony, expanding its concepts to their very limits. His melodies frequently include wide leaps, and his rhythm, like the twentieth century itself, is restless and filled with variety and conflict. His was a liberal, expansive concept of tonality, with extreme chromaticism, frequent modulations, and unresolved dissonances that lessen perception of a tonal center, just as the continually shifting rhythmic patterns obscure the sense of meter. Indeed, his complex harmonies strongly influenced those composers who eventually abandoned the tonal system.

Strauss's several tone poems, which show the influence of both Berlioz and Liszt, are quite theatrical in expression. (Listening Example 1, p. 8, is an excerpt from Strauss's tone poem *Also Sprach Zarathustra.*) In fact, in the early twentieth century, Strauss's major interest turned from the composition of purely orchestral works to opera, though his orchestral music, even in the operas, became ever more important. The ultimate master of orchestration, Strauss surpassed even the great pioneer in that field, Berlioz, for Strauss understood as no one had before him the ultimate capabilities of each orchestral instrument.

Strauss's opera *Salome* caused a scandal when it was first produced in 1905, for it presaged that most extreme of Romantic styles, Expressionism (p. 225), in a scene in which a crazed young girl kisses the lips of a severed head. Yet in his later music, Strauss called for small orchestras, indicating a new classical restraint. The singing voice became more important in his later operas than in his earlier works, where—as with Wagner—it had sometimes simply constituted one line of melody among others in the orchestral web of sound. Individual numbers were more clearly defined in his later works, as in the operas of the Classical period. Eventually, the twentieth-century return to classicism came quite naturally to this essentially romantic composer whose idol, after all, was Mozart.

Another post-Romantic composer, Gustav Mahler, probably is best known for his nine powerful symphonies, though he wrote beautifully for the voice as well as for the orchestra. He sometimes included choral sections in his symphonies, most of which have or suggest programmatic content; and he composed several very attractive song cycles.

> ## Gustav Mahler (1860–1911)
>
> *Gus´-taf Mah´ler*
>
> *expressive dramatic style*

Mahler's orchestra, like that of Strauss, was huge, and his range of orchestral colors extensive, for Mahler shared with Berlioz and Strauss a genius for using orchestral instruments to achieve astonishing variety and beauty of sound. His music expresses his own widely changing moods, from sunny cheerfulness to funereal gloom in startlingly sudden order. The extreme chromaticism, occasionally ambiguous tonal centers, strong emotionalism, and sense of magnitude associated with post-Romanticism all are characteristic of Mahler's music.

Expressionism

The early years of the twentieth century were highly traumatic for millions of people, who felt their lives in the new Machine Age to be dominated by machinery and totally out of their control. Many were forced to leave a comfortable rural life to find work in crowded, frightening cities. Mass production, while efficient, was terribly cold and impersonal. Even science seemed to have changed from a means to serve the needs of humankind to something that existed and progressed inexorably as if for its own sake. A sense of hopelessness in the face of impending disaster, and of the inherent meaninglessness of life, affected sensitive people everywhere.

The writings of the famous psychologist Sigmund Freud (1856–1939), who examined dreams and slips of speech in his effort to probe the secrets of the disturbed mind, had profound influence on many artists in late-nineteenth- and early-twentieth-century society. Like Freud, certain novelists, playwrights, painters, sculptors, and composers of the period also were intrigued by impulses of the subconscious mind, especially those of a dark and abnormal nature, which they sought to express artistically. Theirs is the style we call **Expressionism.**

Painting

van Go´ (French) or van Gok´ (Dutch)

A strange and tormented genius who might well have benefited from Freud's expert attention was the Dutch painter Vincent van Gogh (1853–1890), who is famous in our day but was virtually unknown in his. Possessed of strong religious and social convictions that absorbed his attention in early life, he eventually devoted himself to painting in a style the world had never before seen and was not prepared to understand. Mentally and emotionally tortured, van Gogh once cut off part of his own ear in a fit of self-loathing and despair. He was confined for a time to an asylum, and he shot and killed himself soon after his release from that institution. However, his genius was with him to the end.

One of the earliest artists to abandon the concept of "correct drawing," van Gogh found more meaningful and potent expression in inexact forms and vivid, though unrealistic, colors. While some of his "happy" paintings produced in southern France glow with the warmth and light of that country's brilliant sunshine, van Gogh

Figure 24.1

The Scream, Edvard Munch.

Kahn-din´-skē
Moonk
Keerk´-ner

used color to express despair as well. One of the first paintings to presage the style later called Expressionism was *The Starry Night* (Color Plate 9), van Gogh's highly emotional representation of stars as he perceived them.

The later Expressionist painters, including the Russian Wassily Kandinsky (1866–1944), the Norwegian Edvard Munch (1863–1944), and the German Ernst Ludwig Kirchner (1880–1938), portrayed the frustration, terror, and guilt suffered by humanity during the tortured periods around the two World Wars. The subject of Munch's terrifying picture of a poor creature strolling along a waterfront (*The Scream*) (figure 24.1) is the pictorial equivalent of Sigmund Freud's detailed analyses of neurosis and despair.

Literature

Many literary artists, too, were drawn to this emotional and often morbid style. In Sweden, August Strindberg (1849–1912) wrote "dream plays" dominated by fantasy, eroticism, and perversion. The Irish novelist James Joyce (1882–1941) used his "stream of consciousness" technique to expose the innermost thoughts of the characters in his stories. Franz Kafka (1883–1924), who was born in Czechoslovakia and trained as a lawyer, became all too well acquainted with the frustration and despair that characterize life controlled by a bureaucracy. One of his characters was condemned by the courts without ever knowing what he was accused of; another believed himself transformed into a cockroach, symbolic of the dehumanization and senselessness of life in that time and place.

Music

She(r)n´-berg

The ultimate example of Expressionistic composition probably is the song cycle titled *Pierrot Lunaire,* with words by a Symbolist poet and music by **Arnold Schoenberg** (1874–1951) (p. 246), who pushed Romanticism to its farthest extremes and in the process abandoned tonality. In the early 1900s, Schoenberg began to write **atonal,** or nontonal, music, in which no note served the function of tonic, and harmonic and melodic relationships based upon tonal concepts did not exist. Schoenberg disliked the term *atonality,* because it describes what the music is not, without saying what it is. He preferred *pantonality,* or music that is "inclusive of all tonalities." *Atonality,* however, has become the accepted term.

Pĕ-eh-ro´ Lu-nehr´

In 1912, Schoenberg wrote *Pierrot Lunaire (The Moonstruck Pierrot).* The words, a German translation of twenty-one poems by a Belgian Symbolist, are highly Expressionistic, and Schoenberg's music strongly enhances their strange, almost otherworldly effect. The songs are performed by a reciting female voice accompanied by a flute, piccolo, clarinet, bass clarinet, violin, viola, cello, and piano; however, only a few of the instruments play together at one time, producing a delicate, transparent texture. The voice declaims in a dramatic—indeed, a melodramatic—style called **Sprechstimme,** or "speech voice." In *Sprechstimme,* the durations, dynamic levels, and directions (higher or lower) of the pitches in relation to one another are notated, but the pitches themselves are only implied, and the singer—or declaimer—glides expressively from one inexact note to another.

Sprehk´-shtim-meh

A common Expressionistic technique is to distort visual, literary, or aural images for emotional effect. The strangely "distorted" melodies of *Pierrot Lunaire* contribute to the sense of unreality about the piece, as the listener feels the mystery of the moonlit atmosphere and shares the drunken, disoriented sensations of Pierrot. Extreme and constant dissonance maintains a level of tension and anxiety appropriate for the expression of the dramatic text. The form of the songs generally depends upon the form of the poems, and many, including "Mondestrunken" (Listening Example 30), are through-composed. Schoenberg sometimes used traditional techniques, including imitation and ostinatos, to lend a sense of organization to this atonal composition. However, the music is hardly intended to be pretty, or even realistic, but rather to evoke in the listener the senselessness and distortion of life as Pierrot experiences it.

Impressionism

Even as Austro-German post-Romantics and Expressionists were producing art of an increasingly emotional and exaggerated nature, strong reactions *against* German Romanticism appeared, especially in Paris. During the 1860s, an anti-Romantic movement began in France, known as **Symbolism** in the field of literature and **Impressionism** in painting and music. Symbolist poets and Impressionist painters and

2 48

LISTENING EXAMPLE 30

 2B 4

Expressionism

Composer: Arnold Schoenberg (1874–1951)

Title: "Mondestrunken," from *Pierrot Lunaire*

Composed: 1912

Genre: Song cycle (21 poems)

Text: Poems by the Belgian poet Albert Giraud, a follower of the Symbolists

Form: The text is a *rondeau* (some lines repeated), but the music is through-composed

Style: Expressionism

Timbre: Voice (using *Sprechtstimme*) and five instrumentalists (violin/viola, cello, flute/piccolo, clarinet/bass clarinet, piano)

48	0:00	(*Introduction—delicate, almost bell-like; piano [flute and violin later join the accompaniment]*)	
0:03	0:03	Den Wein, den man mit Augen trinkt,	At night the moon drenches thirsting
. . . .		Giesst Nachts der Mond in Wogen	eyes and a flood wells up on their
. . . .		nieder,	still horizon.
. . . .		Und eine Springflut überschwemmt	
. . . .		Den stillen Horizont.	
49	0:39	Gelüste, schauerlich und süss,	Tremulous sighs travel up through
. . . .		Durchschwimmen ohne Zahl die Fluten!	the swell.
. . . .		Den Wein, den man mit Augen trinkt,	Waves of wine for thirsting eyes
. . . .		Giesst Nachts der Mond in Wogen	gush forth from the moon at night.
. . . .		nieder.	
50	1:02	Der Dichter, den die Andacht treibt,	The poet, deep in devotion,
. . . .		Berauscht sich an dem heilgen Tranke,	grows drunk of the holy draught.
. . . .		Gen Himmel wendet er verzückt	His head turns heavenwards in
. . . .		Das Haupt und taumelnd saugt und	ecstasy and, reeling, slips and
. . . .		schlürft er	slurps the wine that slakes his
. . . .		Den Wein, den man mit Augen trinkt.	thirsting eyes.
. . . .		(*The sparse accompaniment simply winds down and stops.*)	

composers sought, paradoxically, to achieve realistic effects by denying realism and expressing only the suggestion, or impression, of an object, an idea, or an experience. Their approach was not objective, as that of the realists or naturalists purported to be; rather, it reflected their personal observations and perceptions in a most subjective manner. Indeed, the art of the Symbolists and Impressionists had several romantic characteristics—but this French romanticism was of an entirely different order from the hotly emotional German style that had dominated Western art for so long.

Literature

Symbolist poets dealt with the suggestive qualities and sensual effects of words rather than their literal meanings. Avoiding the traditional methods of rhyme and measured rhythm, they wrote a kind of free verse unfettered by conventional rules of poetry. They eschewed direct statements in favor of pleasing sounds, using words as artists used paints and as Impressionist composers used musical sounds.

The forerunner of the Symbolist poets was Paul Verlaine (1844–1896), a sensitive, disturbed, but highly talented man who wrote verse of great delicacy and grace. The meaning in his poems is suggested or symbolized by the imaginative use of words for their sensuous effects, and his poetry is often described as "musical."

The leader of the Symbolist movement, Stéphane Mallarmé (1842–1898), also used words for their "tone color," often distorting their actual meanings to achieve special effects. He built each poem around a central idea or symbol, using images and metaphors to communicate their meaning.

Painting

Mo-nä´

The "romantic classicist" Eugène Delacroix (see p. 168) had illustrated the manner in which strong sunlight breaks up colors into their separate elements. Claude Monet (1840–1926) applied this principle even more liberally to his painting technique and, in 1874, he startled the art world with a painting of sunrise over water that he entitled *Impression: Sunrise* (Color Plate 10). This painting, together with those by several other artists sharing Monet's subjective ideas about light and color, scandalized the Parisian art public. Every tradition of Western painting seemed to have been abandoned, and the exhibit containing these works was greeted with derision, as critics scornfully applied Monet's own word, "impression," to the new style of art in their scathing reviews of the exhibit. They considered Monet's work a bad painting of boats on the water, void of form and substance.

But of course the subject of the painting is not boats at all, but a mere moment in experience. Monet was fascinated by the ever-changing effect of light not only upon color, but also upon the outlines of objects as they are perceived by a viewer. By applying only patches of pure color to his canvas, Monet forced the observer to supply the details of form and outline and to blend the colors in the mind's eye as traditional painters had blended them on their palettes.

The River, Claude Monet. The Art Institute of Chicago, Potter Palmer Collection.

The Impressionists also admired and sometimes emulated aspects of Eastern, especially Japanese, art; the delicate lines and sensitive colors of Japanese scrolls and woodblock prints (see Color Plate 18) had great appeal for them. They nearly always worked out of doors, recording the manner in which surfaces and spaces are transformed by light and appear different at different times of the day. Mist, haze, smoke, and moisture all affect appearances, and the Impressionists sought to capture these fleeting effects, too.

Music

Deh-bu-sē´

The musician first labeled an Impressionist—although he detested the term Impressionism—showed his affinity for the new French style by replacing musical statement with suggestion. He, too, was impressed by certain non-Western art, reflecting its influence in his unusual harmonies and exotic timbres. This first, and greatest, Impressionist composer was **Claude Debussy.**

Claude Debussy (1862–1918)

Although Debussy sought the company of Symbolist poets and Impressionist painters and shared many of their ideals, he also willingly acknowledged a great debt to Wagner, who represented the epitome of the style the Impressionists sought to depose. Debussy was wholly French in his conception of art, which he thought should be entertaining rather than morally uplifting, simple rather than pretentious, and pleasant rather than overly sentimental. He firmly rejected the incessant tension and emotionalism inherent in Wagner's highly chromatic music. However, like Wagner, Debussy sought a way out of the venerable tonal system.

Like the Symbolists and the Impressionist painters, Debussy expressed reaction to experience rather than the reality itself, steadfastly maintaining a cool and detached perspective. He shared with the young French artists (as with Wagner) a tendency to rebel against established rules. Thus, his aims were related both to those of Wagner, whom he admired but strongly criticized, and to those of the Impressionists, whose name he despised.

As he searched for a path away from tonality, Debussy often used the whole-tone and pentatonic scales of the East, and sometimes the Medieval modes; each of these, like the chromatic scale favored by Wagner and the post-Romantics, implies no "pull" to a tonic. However, they create an atmosphere—or *color,* to use an Impressionistic concept—that is cool and quiet in comparison with the tortured emotionalism of Wagner's chromatic style. Debussy experienced non-Western music on several occasions while still an impressionable young man. Invited to travel to Russia as a pianist for the same romantic widow who supported Tchaikovsky's composing career, he was strongly impressed with Russian music, whose timbres and intervals are related to Eastern styles. The light textures and exotic scales and timbres of the East seemed to him better suited to express the French temperament than the lush orchestration and emotional style of the Wagnerians. He also traveled to Rome to absorb the sounds of Gregorian chant and make a study of the Medieval modes.

Closer to home, Debussy visited the Paris Exposition of 1889, where he heard with fascination and delight performances by a Javanese ensemble called a *gamelan.*

Gamelan

gah´-meh-lahn

The typical orchestra of Indonesia, called a **gamelan,** differs from the Western string ensemble in that it consists mostly of percussion instruments, with some wind and string instruments to color the sound. The primary instruments are *metallophones* (metal keys suspended over a bronze or wooden frame and struck with a mallet), gongs of various sizes and materials, and drums. While some instruments play the

Figure 24.2

An Indonesian gamelan.

© *George Holton/Photo Researchers*

melody, others embellish it; the gongs strike at phrase and section endings to indicate the formal structure of a piece, and the drums regulate the rhythm and tempo. Visually and aurally spectacular, gamelans are becoming familiar in the West, where they increasingly may be heard playing the music of Java or Bali, or even participating in Western-style concert music or jazz.

Listening Example 31 presents a Balinese gamelan, louder and more brilliant (some say boisterous) in effect than the sedate and delicate Javanese music that impressed Debussy.

Debussy's Stylistic Techniques

In his orchestral piece *Nuages* (*Clouds*), Debussy adapted effects gleaned from the Javanese gamelan to capture the delicate, fleeting impressions he desired. In other works, Medieval modes have programmatic significance, suggesting antiquity or timelessness. In *La Cathédrale Engloutie* (*The Sunken Cathedral*), the use of parallel octaves, fifths, and fourths—forbidden in Western harmony since the advent of the tonal system—implies the earliest polyphony, parallel organum. For Debussy, neither traditional nor unconventional sounds were inherently right or wrong.

Debussy's harmony, like his scales and textures, was imaginative and often provocative. He never entirely abandoned tonality, but used it in unconventional ways. When using the major or minor modes, for example, he deliberately obscured the distinction between them to nebulous effect. Delighting in sound as Impressionist painters did in color, for its sensuous qualities, he added dissonant notes to chords because they added color and beauty to the sound; he had little interest in functional relationships between dissonant and consonant combinations. More concerned with effect than with its cause, Debussy adapted the elements of music to suit his own unorthodox ends.

The piano suggested to Debussy resources never conceived by earlier composers, and he wrote many sensitive, expressive piano pieces that were Impressionistic in flavor. Many of his songs are based upon texts by Symbolist poets and have the delicate, elusive quality characteristic of the Impressionist style. Debussy's only opera, *Pelléas et Mélisande* (1902), considered the epitome of Impressionist art, is one of the great masterpieces of twentieth-century music.

Peh-lā-ahs´;
Mehl-ē-sahnd´

2 51   2B 5

LISTENING EXAMPLE 31

Gamelan Music

Title: "Kebjar Hudjan Mas"

Form: A series of variations evolves over relentless ostinatos, which provide stability and seem to anchor the composition.

Timbres: The performance here is of a Balinese gamelan, fuller and richer in sound than the delicate Javanese ensemble that so impressed Debussy. Perhaps this sound has more appeal for the modern Western audience; in any case, it seems to be more prevalent in the United States.

The metallic timbres of the gongs and metallophones dominating the beginning of the piece suggest the meaning of "kebjar": to flash or flame, as in a burst of light. Soon the full gamelan joins in the joyous peals of sound.

Notice the irregular phrase lengths, relaxed rhythms, frequent pauses, ostinato accompaniment figures, pitches lying between the tones of the tonal scales, and expressive changes in dynamic level.

Debussy's approach to form, too, was of a subjective nature. More interested in mood and expression than in motivic development or key relationships, he gave most of his compositions programmatic titles; however, Debussy's programs are vague and suggestive rather than literally descriptive. His art, like Mallarmé's and Monet's, is one of mood and atmosphere, in which details never intrude, but rather are left to the imagination and taste of the audience. Finding it unnecessary to add to the size of his orchestra, Debussy rather expanded the range of orchestral colors by using conventional instruments in unusual ways. He sometimes required instruments to play notes above or below their normal ranges of pitch, and often muted instruments, altering their timbre and softening their dynamic range. Debussy's music evokes a hazy, dreamy atmosphere, but his orchestration and his meticulous notation reveal a scrupulous attention to details.

Debussy's famous tone poem *Prélude à l'après-midi d'un Faune* (*Prelude to the Afternoon of a Faun*—Listening Example 32), based on a poem by the Symbolist poet Mallarmé, concerns the musings of a sleepy mythical figure, half-man, half-goat, uncertain as to whether his delightful visions are recollections of an experience or only of a dream. His pleasant drowsiness is reflected by the opening flute solo, a melodic line vague in contour, rhythm, tonality, and even timbre, since it is played in the velvety lowest register of the instrument. This chromatic figure recurs in various guises, presented with changing harmonies and varied sonorities, rather than developed in the Classical way.

Other Impressionists
extra musical ideas

While Debussy is acknowledged the outstanding composer in the Impressionistic style, others followed his lead and used aspects of Impressionism in their compositions. The music of **Maurice Ravel** (1875–1937) is often compared with Debussy's, for Ravel used some of the techniques that enhanced the Impressionistic effect of Debussy's music, though Ravel was primarily a Classicist. His melodic phrases are longer and more clearly defined than Debussy's and his rhythms stronger and more clear-cut. Ravel's compositions often have classical design, and he used functional harmonies based upon traditional key relationships.

LISTENING EXAMPLE 32

2 52   2B 6

Impressionism

Composer: Claude Debussy (1862–1917)

Title: *"Prélude à l'aprés-midi d'un Faune"*
(*Prelude to the Afternoon of a Faun*)

Composed: 1894

Rhythm: Constantly changing tempo and meter

Genre: Symphonic poem

Form: A loosely organized A B A′ pattern

Style: Impressionism

Timbre: Orchestra (three flutes, two oboes, English horn, two clarinets, four horns, antique cymbals, two harps, strings)

A Section

52	0:00	Chromatic melody played by solo flute (*p*); answered by harp and horns
0:44	0:44	Flute melody repeats; answered by the oboe.
1:36	1:36	Flute melody is expanded and varied
2:49	2:49	Clarinet plays a variation of the chromatic melody
3:17	3:17	A new theme is introduced by the oboe.

B Section

| 53 | 4:14 | Woodwinds introduce an expressive theme, legato with longer note values. |
| 0:54 | 5:08 | Legato theme is repeated in strings; builds to a climax |

A′ Section

54	6:24	A variation of the original chromatic melody returns in the flute, accompanied by harp and strings.
0:36	7:00	Chromatic melody; English horn
1:16	7:40	Chromatic melody; two flutes

Coda

| 55 | 9:05 | Begins with both harps playing |
| 0:07 | 9:12 | Horns present a final, brief statement of the chromatic melody. |

Charles Tomlinson Griffes (1884–1920) became known as the American Impressionist. His compositions titled "The White Peacock" and "Pleasure Dome of Kubla Khan" are among the best known and most popular in the concert repertoire today.

Primitivism, while serving fewer artists and composers than Impressionism and having less far-reaching influence, nevertheless was a significant movement during the second decade of the twentieth century. Further, it produced one of the masterpieces of modern music. The term as it is used today has no derogatory connotation but is the accepted name for this style of art, which exalts the beauty of a simple, unaffected way of life and revels in the glories of color.

Although Primitivism had certain romantic characteristics, including "exoticism" or a fascination with the distant in time and place, it represented a far stronger attack on Romanticism than that wrought by the Impressionists. Primitivists saw Impressionism merely as a French romantic style—anti-Wagner rather than anti-

Primitivism

heavy rugged rhythm
stru

romantic, in other words. Besides, they deemed Impressionism overly refined and affected. Rebelling against the cultural atmosphere of early twentieth-century Europe, which they found restrictive and confining, Primitivists were inspired by recently excavated art works of the primitive non-Western world and by the relaxed, unstructured life of uncivilized cultures.

As Germans prepared for war in the second decade of this century, the state of the economy, as well as intense political involvement, precluded their creative activity in the arts. Paris then became the hub of artistic enterprise. The outstanding Primitivist painter was Paul Gauguin, a Frenchman who eventually left the overly civilized environment of that city, however. The musical masterpiece in this style was composed by Igor Stravinsky, a Russian who escaped *to* Paris and composed *Le Sacre du Printemps (The Rite of Spring)* before becoming recognized as one of the greatest and most influential composers of the twentieth century.

Painting

Go-ganh´

Paul Gauguin (1848–1903) was for a time a respectable businessman who indulged his interest in art by providing financial and moral support to young Impressionist painters, whose work he greatly admired. He finally became an amateur painter himself, working in the Impressionists' style and exhibiting with them for several years before suddenly abandoning wife, children, and business career to devote the rest of his life to art in the Primitive style.

Gauguin had been a sailor in his youth, and the wanderlust never left him. Feeling stifled in the sophisticated atmosphere of Paris, he traveled to Brittany, a province in northern France, where life seemed relaxed and free in comparison with the civilized society he detested. He also spent time in southern France, where he lived with Vincent van Gogh. Eventually he traveled to Tahiti and finally to the remote Marquesas Islands, where he died lonely and destitute, having produced there many beautiful paintings in the style we call Primitive.

Gauguin loved to paint the rich, warm colors he found in the South Sea Islands—the sands, the vegetation, the skin of the Islands' people. Yet the colors in his paintings are seldom natural or realistic. His highly subjective use of color must be seen as a romantic characteristic, as is the exotic nature of his subjects. His rather flat style reveals his reverence for Japanese painting and woodblock prints; yet he never abandoned linear perspective, however unconventionally he applied the technique.

Gauguin's painting *The Day of the God* (Color Plate 11) beautifully reveals his appreciation for the island colors, for the grace of the women as they worked and played, and for the relaxed life they led. It is hard to imagine that this painter was once an Impressionist, for the figures are strongly outlined, almost like those in an Egyptian frieze. The island scene, the dominant presence of the ancient god, the bold colors, and the denial of traditional Western perspective are all "primitive" aspects of this work.

Music

Stra-vin´-ské

In music, the characteristics of Primitivism include strong, "savage" rhythms, dissonant combinations of sound, narrow melodies such as those that might have been played upon a simple reed pipe, and sometimes a story or a program drawn from a primeval subject. All of these apply to the masterpiece of Primitive music *Le Sacre du Printemps* (*The Rite of Spring*) (Listening Example 33) by Igor Stravinsky.

The Rite of Spring

Dé-ah´-gih-lev

In 1913 Stravinsky (see pp. 272–273) collaborated with Sergei Diaghilev (1872–1929), the famous director of the Russian Ballet, to produce *The Rite of Spring,* a savage, brutal portrayal of a prehistoric ritual in which a young girl is sacri-

Plate 11

Paul Gauguin, *The Day of the God* (Mahana no Atua), 1894. From the linear patterns, brilliant colors, and sensuous effects of primitive art, Gauguin evolved his own vibrant style, which, like Watteau's, is primarily decorative. Oil on canvas, 26 7/8 × 36 ins (68.3 × 91.5 cm). Art Institute of Chicago. Helen Birch Bartlett Memorial Collection 1926.198

Plate 12

Jacob Lawrence, *Tombstones,* 1942. Committed to portraying scenes from Black American life, Lawrence exaggerates or simplifies shapes for emotional impact, producing a style of silhouetted patterns in vigorous, often harsh colors. Gouache on paper, 28 3/4 × 20 1/2 ins (73 × 52.1 cm). Collection of Whitney Museum of American Art, New York.

Plate 13

Pablo Picasso, *Three Musicians,* 1921. This joyous painting readily evokes a smile, stirring the viewer to tap along with the happy rhythms. Completely unrealistic, the painting yet communicates clearly the essence of its meaning. Oil on canvas, 6 ft 8 ins × 6 ft 2 ins (2.03 × 1.88 m). Philadelphia Museum of Art: The A. E. Gallatin Collection.

Plate 14

Jackson Pollock, *Number 1, 1948,* 1948. Though Pollock splashed and dripped his colors, his art, like that of effective chance musicians, reveals a sense of structure. Hardly random, the colors are arranged in hues and densities to evoke aesthetic appreciation and emotional reaction. Oil and enamel on unprimed canvas, 5 ft 8 ins × 8 ft 8 ins (1.73 × 2.64 m). Museum of Modern Art, New York. Purchase.

2 56

LISTENING EXAMPLE 33

2B 7

Primitivism

Composer: Igor Stravinsky (1882–1971)

Title: Excerpts from Part I of *Le Sacre du Printemps*
(*The Rite of Spring*)

Composed: 1913

Rhythm: Constantly changing tempo and meter

Timbre: Orchestra (piccolo, three flutes, alto flute, four oboes, English horn, E♭ clarinet, two clarinets, two bass clarinets, four bassoons, contrabassoon, eight horns, piccolo trumpet, four trumpets, three trombones, two tubas, percussion, strings)

Genre: Ballet

Program: Scenes of Pagan Russia; Part I—"The Adoration of the Earth"

Introduction (Lento; tempo rubato)

56	0:00	A solo bassoon (*p*), played in a higher-than-normal register, introduces a plaintive melody, narrow in range and haunting in mood. A French horn and clarinets join the bassoon in evoking the atmosphere of awakening spring in a primeval Russian forest.
0:45	0:45	English horn solo
1:16	1:16	Oboe and E♭ clarinet combine with each other; music continues to build
2:55	2:55	Return of the bassoon solo
3:08	3:08	Violins play with the **pizzicato** technique (plucking instead of bowing the strings), introducing the accompanying ostinato figure of the next section.
		Omens of Spring—Dance of the Youths and Maidens (Tempo giusto)
57	3:30	Strings and brass instruments (*f*) produce the pounding, savage sound of primitive drums. Strong irregular accents enhance the wild flavor of the music.
58	4:17	Dance I; bassoons and contrabassoon
0:36	4:53	Return of introductory ostinato; English horn
59	5:09	Dance II; French horn, flutes
60	5:42	Dance III; trumpets, triangle
61	6:05	Dance II; flutes; music becomes increasingly frenzied

Ritual of Abduction (Presto)

62	6:37	An ominous chord is briefly sustained under a disjunct trumpet line.
0:11	6:48	Frantic horn calls
0:57	7:34	The extreme level of tension is heightened by brutal drum strokes in violently irregular metric patterns.
1:13	7:50	Flute and string trills lead directly to the next section, "Round Dances of Spring," which is significantly more quiet and peaceful.

ficed to the god of spring. The story and the means of relating it scandalized the proper Parisian audience, which staged a riot at the opening performance that has become one of the most famous stories in the history of music. Shocked at the "primitive" brown burlap costumes, the angular movements of the dancers, the brutal rhythms, harsh dissonances, and striking orchestral effects of this ballet, some people angrily shouted their disapproval, while others in the audience yelled for them to be quiet, rendering the poor dancers quite unable to hear the music. The composer, seated in the audience and humiliated by the uproar, went home before the performance was over.

Costumes such as these worn by the Ballet Rambert performing Stravinsky's *Rite of Spring* alienated early viewers, who expected ballet dancers to appear in conventional, softly-colored, tights, tutus, and gowns.
Hulton Getty/Tony Stone Images

But the shock was soon absorbed, and *The Rite of Spring* became, and remains, a favorite in the standard repertoire of dance performance. The music is often performed as an orchestral composition in two parts, to correspond with the two acts of the ballet: Part I, "Adoration of the Earth," and Part II, "The Sacrifice."

Summary

Post-Romantics and Expressionists carried the ideas and ideals of the late German Romantics even further. Expressionism must be seen as the ultimate romantic style, since it deals with emotion itself rather than with the experience of it or the reaction to it. Furthermore, the emotions portrayed by the Expressionists were not only exaggerated, but highly disturbed—emotions experienced by those who felt threatened by machines, by the wickedness of an immoral society, and by the advent of a terrible, inevitable calamity.

As post-Romantics and Expressionists exaggerated the German Romantic style, Impressionists and Primitivists reacted strongly against it. The Impressionists, holding the French view that art should be elegant and entertaining rather than profound or morally significant, criticized the emotionalism and exaggeration of the German Romantic style, though their own art had strong romantic overtones. Their love of nature, as seen in the beautiful Impressionistic landscapes and the programmatic titles of Debussy's music; their appreciation for color, whether of paint or sound; and their rebellious insistence upon freedom from rules—all were romantic characteristics.

The Primitives shared the Impressionists' disillusionment with Romanticism and post-Romanticism but considered Impressionism too refined, pretty, and vague. They turned instead to a vivid, provocative, stirring style inspired by what they knew or imagined of the life and art of uncivilized cultures. Gauguin painted life in the South Sea Islands as he saw it. Stravinsky, in *The Rite of Spring,* remained conscientiously detached from his brutal subject, avoiding the sentimentality of the Impressionists. Nevertheless, the Primitives' subjective approach to color and perspective in painting, and their choice of exotic subject matter in all the arts, are romantic concepts.

Each of these transitory approaches to art suggested a restless search for new means of artistic expression, as the twentieth century came into its own.

Critical Thinking

- Does one of the styles of art discussed in this chapter appeal to you more than the others? Can you cite reasons for your preferences?

- Do you believe that your tastes might change in time? If so, what might cause such a change?

Terms to Review

post-Romanticism   A general term for several romantic styles that succeeded the dominance of German Romanticism and preceded the return of classicism to the arts.

Expressionism   A highly emotional style in art that sought to express disturbed states of the mind.

atonality   The avoidance of a tonic note and of tonal relationships in music.

Sprechstimme   Literally, "speech voice." A style of melodramatic declamation between speaking and singing.

Symbolism   A literary movement sharing the ideals of the Impressionists.

Impressionism   A style of painting and of music that avoids explicit statement, instead emphasizing suggestion and atmosphere.

gamelan   An Indonesian percussion ensemble.

Primitivism   A style inspired by primitive works of art and by the relaxed life of uncivilized cultures.

pizzicato   The technique of plucking instead of bowing string instruments.

Key Figures

Poets	*Paul Verlaine*	*Stéphane Mallarmé*
Literary Figures	*August Strindberg* *Franz Kafka*	*James Joyce*
Psychoanalyst	*Sigmund Freud*	
Ballet Impresario	*Sergei Diaghilev*	

Artists	*Claude Monet*	*Paul Gauguin*
	Vincent van Gogh	*Wassily Kandinsky*
	Edvard Munch	*Ernst Ludwig Kirchner*
Composers	*Richard Strauss*	*Gustav Mahler*
	Arnold Schoenberg	*Alban Berg*
	Claude Debussy	*Maurice Ravel*
	Charles Griffes	*Igor Stravinsky*

25
Twentieth-Century Arts: General Characteristics

Although much twentieth-century art reveals a significant return to classical ideals, we have seen that certain individuals have chosen to express raw emotion to an extent unprecedented in Western history. Despair colors the literature of Gertrude Stein, T. S. Eliot, George Bernard Shaw, Eugene O'Neill, and Jean-Paul Sartre as it does the art of the Expressionist painters and musicians. The cataclysm of World War I hardly sprang full-blown upon an innocent and unsuspecting society: the unrest, desire for power, greed, suspicion, tension, and despair culminating in that tragic military confrontation developed over a long period of time and was reflected in countless works of art.

Some artists responded to the trauma of the time by adopting a light, even trivial, style; some turned to irony. The nonsense of *Dadaism,* the incongruities of *Surrealism,* and the abstraction of *Cubism* all were indicative of the disorientation and depersonalization experienced in the twentieth century.

Visual Arts

The outstanding sculptors of the early twentieth century, finding in the classical ideals of symmetry, balance, repose, and restraint the essence of beauty in art, replaced the exaggerated expression of the late Romantic period with simplicity and understatement. Architects, on the other hand, succumbed to the tastes and demands of the Machine Age, devoting more attention to function than to aesthetic appeal in designing their factories, office buildings, apartment houses, and department stores. Indeed, the famous and influential school of architecture called the Bauhaus preached the maxim that "form follows function." Members of this school drew attention to the basic structural elements of their buildings rather than disguising them in the more traditional fashion.

[handwritten margin note: 3 to 5% Educated in classical music]

In violent and bitter protest against the horrors of World War I, some artists joined a nihilistic movement called **Dadaism,** whose express purpose was to demolish art as they believed civilization itself was being destroyed. When the Armistice finally was signed, the Dadaists became more optimistic, delighting in their own nonsense before the movement petered out about 1920.

Many former Dadaists then turned to **Surrealism,** a more viable and lasting movement in literature and painting, which juxtaposed the most unlikely images upon one another in an attempt to achieve a "super" realism. Freud's interpretation of the peculiar ways in which the unconscious mind works strongly influenced this style of art, as it had influenced Expressionism a decade or so earlier.

Among the painters who used their medium to express strong social views was Jacob Lawrence (b. 1917), a member of the so-called Harlem Renaissance. This was a movement of the 1920s in which African American painters, sculptors, poets, playwrights, musicians, novelists, and essayists broke from convention, declaring their intention to "promote racial advancement through artistic creativity." Lawrence beautifully adapted African effects and the techniques of modern art to paint eloquent depictions of the African American experience. (Color Plate 12).

Pablo Picasso (1881–1973)

The career of the great painter Pablo Picasso runs parallel to that of the great composer Igor Stravinsky, composer of *Le Sacre du Printemps*. Picasso and Stravinsky knew and respected each other and collaborated on some important works. Each of these groundbreaking artists introduced several new styles and made important contributions to others; yet both returned most often to the formal design and emotional restraint of Classicism. Although Picasso was a leader in the movement toward abstraction in art, he approached abstraction, unlike the emotional Abstract Expressionists (p. 258), by exploring pure *form* instead of *feeling*.

Picasso was born in Spain but, like Stravinsky, spent most of his adult life in France. The works of his earliest periods reveal his strong compassion for poor and suffering humanity, but even at this time, his emotions were held firmly under control. All of Picasso's paintings further illustrate his classical inclinations by the manner in which they are wholly contained within the limits of their frames, which Picasso never violated in the Romantic way.

The painting called *Les Demoiselles d'Avignon* (*The Young Ladies of Avignon*) (figure 25.1), which reflected a strong African influence, heralded the beginning of **Cubism,** one of the most significant movements in twentieth-century art. The Cubists had such interest in form that they imposed geometric planes upon subjects of every nature, creating an unrealistic but curiously expressive style of art.

Although Picasso used strong, even harsh colors in *Les Demoiselles,* the Cubists soon turned to muted, monochromatic schemes of cool tans and olive tones, for color held less interest for them than design. The same year (1921) that he painted his joyous

Figure 25.1

Les Demoiselles d'Avignon, Pablo Picasso.

© 1998 Estate of Pablo Picasso/Artist Rights Society (ARS), New York

Figure 25.2

Guernica, Pablo Picasso.
© 1998 Estate of Pablo Picasso/Artist Rights Society (ARS), New York

Gär´-nĕ-kah

Three Musicians, which is Cubist in form but brilliant in color (Color Plate 13), Picasso also painted *Three Women at the Spring,* in which the muted colors, symmetrical design, heavy outlines, and impersonal facial expressions all indicate a classical taste.

Yet one of Picasso's finest pictures is an impassioned expression of social protest, painted during the Spanish Civil War (1937). One cannot view *Guernica* (figure 25.2) without vicariously experiencing the agony, destruction, and terror of war.

Music: An Overview

The broad range of interests and activities of Picasso and Stravinsky is reflected by other artists throughout the twentieth century to date. Classical and romantic characteristics exist side by side, those terms no longer sufficing to describe the style of a significant period of time, or even of the entire body of work of some individuals. Many twentieth-century composers have created their own distinctive styles from materials that have served Western composers for a very long time. Some composers have abandoned traditional techniques to explore uncharted realms, challenging or denying long-established concepts of melody, harmony, form, timbre, and sometimes the very purpose of art. These people may be seen as musical revolutionaries. Others, meanwhile, have continued to work within the tonal system—adapting it, however, to suit their modern taste. In fact, most of the music of the twentieth century has been conceived in such an orderly, evolutionary manner.

Despite this unprecedented diversity of styles, certain generalizations apply to contemporary approaches to the elements of music, to texture, and to form: both composers within the progressive and experimental areas of composition and composers who belong to the mainstream of twentieth-century music tend to reflect certain new aspects of the art of composing music.

Melody

Melody is not absent from twentieth-century music, as misguided listeners sometimes charge, although it is relatively less important to many composers than it was in earlier periods. Contemporary melodies are sometimes more difficult to perform, and often more difficult to recognize, than are melodies typical of earlier styles. New melodies are sometimes based upon scales other than the familiar major and minor scales, many composers having found melodic inspiration in the Medieval modes,

Figure 25.3

Normal and disjunct
notation of the beginning
of "Three Blind Mice."

the whole tone and other scales of the East, various pentatonic folk scales, and even artificial scales created for specific compositions.

Another factor rendering some contemporary melodies challenging to performer and listener alike is their angular contour, especially in comparison with the lyrical, songlike melodies of the Romantic period. Since melodies with notes distant from one another are easier to play on an instrument than to sing, these melodies are sometimes referred to as "instrumental" in concept, although vocalists are now frequently required to master very difficult melody lines. Using the technique called **octave displacement,** composers sometimes select the notes of a melody from different octaves, requiring the performer to "leap" wide distances. (If, for example, the first three notes of "Three Blind Mice" are each selected from different octaves, the melody is much harder to recognize and to sing than it is when the notes are adjacent. See figure 25.3.)

Of course some composers continue to write tuneful melodies. The French, for example, who traditionally prefer entertaining music, and the Italians, who have always loved song, continue to produce lyrical melodies, while many Americans, romantic in a twentieth-century way, also continue to write songlike melody lines. However, many composers from Germany and from Eastern Europe have built upon the chromaticism initiated by Wagner and extended by Schoenberg, while others of various nationalities have simply found melody less interesting than certain other elements of music, especially rhythm and timbre.

Harmony

Renewed interest in the Medieval modes affects the harmony as well as the melody of some twentieth-century popular and art music. Even composers remaining committed to tonality often use the system in highly original ways. Chords may be constructed of any intervals, including fourths or even seconds, rather than the traditional, more consonant, thirds. Composers sometimes choose to establish a tonal center by emphasis upon, or repetition of, a particular pitch, without recognizing traditional relationships of other pitches to the tonic. The new interest in a wide variety of sonorities, encouraged by increasing awareness of the musical sounds of other cultures, often leads composers to minimize the significance of harmonic relationships and to use chords or combinations of sound for their color rather than for functional purposes.

It is, of course, the dissonance of much twentieth-century music that many listeners find particularly challenging. However, in our study we have observed a steady increase in dissonance from the time of the Renaissance through the nineteenth century. Not only were a greater number of dissonant combinations included in compositions of the later periods, but dissonances became stronger and sometimes were not resolved. Thus, the use by some contemporary composers of extreme dissonance is only a logical continuation of a long-established trend in Western music.

Stimulated by expanding awareness of the rhythmic subtleties and complexities of the music of other cultures, composers in the West have revitalized rhythm, giving it unprecedented significance in Western music. Contemporary composers usually write metered music, but they often mix meters, frequently changing the number of beats per measure. They sometimes combine two or more meters at one time in a technique called **polymeter,** and they may use irregular, or asymmetrical, meters, such as five or seven beats to the measure, instead of the duple, triple, and quadruple patterns common to earlier periods. Some composers write rhythmic patterns so complex that they are beyond the capacity of human beings to reproduce and must be "performed" using computers.

Rhythm and Meter

Timbre, too, has recently claimed unprecedented attention in the Western world, where particular sonorities or combinations of sound, beautiful or not, have become important means of artistic expression. American composer John Cage (pp. 258–261) suggested that the old argument regarding the relative merits of consonance and dissonance is about to be replaced by one concerning the difference, if any, between music and noise—and some contemporary composers recognize no inherent difference between them.

Timbre

Instruments from the East, from Africa, from remote areas of South America, and from aboriginal colonies in the South Pacific offer a wide and exotic array of sounds new and fascinating to the Western world. Instruments of early periods, too, including the harpsichord, recorder, lute, and viol, are called for in some new compositions and are becoming widely appreciated in performances of music from the Medieval, Renaissance, and Baroque periods. Interest in the qualities and effects of sound around the middle of the century led to the invention of the electronic synthesizer, which allows composers to create sounds virtually at will.

The twentieth-century orchestra is generally smaller than the large ensembles of the late Romantic period, and there is strong interest now in chamber music of many kinds. The Neoclassical trend toward a drier, less emotional sound has led to decreased emphasis upon the string section of the orchestra in favor of the metallic and wooden sounds of various percussion instruments. In some orchestral performances, string instruments actually accompany the brass in an interesting reversal of roles. Non-Western instruments sometimes included in the percussion section of the modern orchestra enrich the sonority of the ensemble, besides emphasizing rhythmic patterns.

Some orchestral composers, inspired by jazz techniques, require instrumentalists to perform expressive slides from one tone to another, called **glissandos,** and to play in unusually high or low registers. Experimentalists have created new sounds from traditional instruments by playing upon unusual parts, such as the strings of the piano or the bridge of the violin. Even the human voice is required to produce a wide variety of timbres, for whispers, shouts, and spoken sounds may be included in music compositions.

The return to classicism in the arts, the influence of jazz upon art music, and the new emphasis upon rhythmic effects and varied timbres all have affected the twentieth-century approach to texture. We have witnessed a renewed appreciation for counterpoint, although the modern approach to polyphony differs from that of earlier periods. From the seventeenth through the nineteenth centuries, polyphony was governed, as was all music, by the rules of tonal harmony: that is, polyphonic as well

Texture

as homophonic music revealed the composer's vertical (harmonic) awareness. Twentieth-century polyphony, on the other hand, is often linear in concept, as was the Medieval music of Machaut and his contemporaries. The smaller orchestras, chamber ensembles, and jazz combos of today contrast with ensembles of the Romantic period in their ability to allow individual melody lines to be heard independently and to interact effectively. In addition, **polyrhythms**—several rhythms sounded simultaneously—make it easier to distinguish one voice from another. Whereas the chamber ensembles of the eighteenth and nineteenth centuries were usually composed of instruments of the same family, the new chamber groups often include instruments of unlike timbres, such as a flute, a cello, and a piano, also enhancing recognition of different melodic lines.

Form

The return to classical interests has led many composers to rely upon principles of absolute music and to organize their works according to forms developed in earlier periods, rather than upon programs of any kind. However, this century's musical revolutionaries—romantics at heart—have explored creative new means of organization. Some compositions consist simply of several sections of contrasting timbres, tempos, or rhythms, while the form of some works is actually indeterminate, dependent upon the circumstances of each performance. The varied tastes of contemporary composers are evident in their approaches to this and to every other aspect of music composition.

Summary

There has been a significant return to classicism in the arts, though it has not been observed with any degree of uniformity. Some composers working within the mainstream of twentieth-century music have organized their works according to modified versions of forms established in earlier periods, maintaining in much of this music an emotional atmosphere that is restrained and relatively cool. The increased dissonance of the music of our age is a natural extension of the historical development of Western music, which has generally proceeded in an orderly, evolutionary way.

Non-Western concepts and certain jazz techniques have greatly enriched the art music of the Western world. The elements of rhythm and timbre have received unprecedented interest, leading to the expansion of the percussion section of the orchestra, to experiments using traditional instruments in unorthodox ways, and eventually to the invention of the electronic sound synthesizer. Voices and instruments of unlike timbre on each line of music enhance the linear emphasis of much twentieth-century polyphony.

Critical Thinking

• Why are certain combinations of sound more "pleasing" than others? Why do cultures vary in their concept of "pleasing" sounds? Why are the terms "pleasing" and "beautiful" not necessarily compatible from an artist's point of view?

• Why do many composers resist or deny distinctions between "musical" and "nonmusical" sounds? Do you find such distinctions necessary or valid? If so, how would you distinguish between these concepts?

Dadaism   A nihilistic movement intended to demolish art.

Surrealism   A movement in literature and painting that juxtaposed unlikely images.

Cubism   A style in which geometric planes are imposed upon subjects of every nature.

octave displacement   A melodic concept involving the selection of pitches from various, sometimes distant, octaves.

polymeter   Use of more than one meter at the same time.

glissando   An expressive "slide" between pitches.

polyrhythm   Two or more rhythmic patterns performed simultaneously.

Artist   *Pablo Picasso*

Terms to Review

Key Figure

26
The Revolutionaries

Some composers of the twentieth century have broken certain ties with the past, to establish new methods of composition, new performance techniques, and new concepts of the essential meaning of music. Some have abandoned the tonal system of harmony that for three hundred years was considered essential to Western music, their new methods of organizing musical compositions producing some of the most provocative works of the twentieth century. Some have altered the very concept of musical sound.

Among the most influential, and controversial, developments was Arnold Schoenberg's proposal that music be organized according to his *twelve-tone technique.*

Arnold Schoenberg (1874-1951)

Schoenberg was born in Vienna at a time when that city, fiercely conservative in its approach to art, was becoming increasingly anti-Semitic. A true son of the Austro-German tradition, he drew inspiration from the music of Wagner, Brahms, and Strauss; during his Expressionistic phase (p. 227), he also reflected the influence of another famous Viennese, Sigmund Freud. However, Schoenberg was a radically progressive composer (although he never saw himself as such) who was born a Jew (although he later converted temporarily to Catholicism) and came to view the city of his birth with animosity.

After 1905, Schoenberg turned away from the exaggerated emotional effects of his early music, tempering his romanticism with a classical concern for restraint, economy, and design, and writing intensely concentrated melodic and rhythmic patterns to be performed by relatively small ensembles. His melodies became fragmented, his rhythms complex, and his textures increasingly contrapuntal, as he sought to establish his mature style. He explored extreme ranges of vocal and instrumental pitch and used such unusual techniques as the *Sprechstimme* in *Pierrot Lunaire* (pp. 227–228). He advocated the "emancipation" of dissonant sounds, which he found to have their own integrity, with no need to "resolve" to a perceived consonance.

For Schoenberg, who never thought of himself as a revolutionary at all, the path opened by Wagner's extreme use of chromaticism in *Tristan* seemed to lead naturally and inevitably to the dissolution of tonality. But the need arose, then, for some new means of organizing musical sounds. While *Pierrot* and other atonal songs were held together, so to speak, by their texts, Schoenberg spent several years searching for some way to achieve formal integrity in his atonal, textless instrumental compositions.

Twelve-Tone Technique

Schoenberg devised his **twelve-tone technique** as a means of replacing tonal relationships with an even more highly structured system of organization. According to this technique, all twelve notes within an octave are arranged into a series, or **row,** which then provides all of the melodic and harmonic material upon which a given composition is based. The twelve pitches are of equal importance, related only to one another.

Figure 26.1

(a) A twelve-tone row. (b) The row transposed up a fourth. (c) The retrograde version (the row backwards). (d) The row inverted (upside down). (e) The retrograde inversion (backwards and upside down). (a) (Courtesy: Frederick Carl Gurney.)

No tone is repeated during the course of a composition until the other eleven have been used in proper order, so that no tone is emphasized or made to sound like a tonic.

A twelve-tone row, which differs from a scale in that its tones are organized in creative rather than stepwise fashion, may be transposed to begin on any note, but it always retains the same intervallic relationships between the pitches. The row may be used in its original order, or backwards, in what is called *retrograde* form. The intervals may be inverted (up a fifth and down a fourth, for example, instead of down a fifth and up a fourth); in the *retrograde inversion,* the row is both backwards and upside down. "Harmonic" combinations are formed by sounding two or more tones simultaneously, but in the order prescribed by one of the versions of the twelve-tone row (figure 26.1).

Twelve-tone music requires that the listener abandon all preconceived notions of melodic and harmonic relationships; for although a twelve-tone composition is highly structured and very orderly indeed, the listener's ear is unlikely to recognize the row or appreciate the complexities of variation involved. Yet Schoenberg retained many traditional aspects of Western music. His music often reveals a classical clarity of formal design and warmly expressive, even romantic, attributes. He used familiar contrapuntal techniques, including canon and fugal passages, which are not difficult to recognize. Radical as it appears, the twelve-tone technique was actually (as Schoenberg claimed) a logical extension of the extreme chromaticism used by Wagner in *Tristan und Isolde.*

Arnold Schoenberg at the University of California.
Corbis-Bettmann

Forced by the political situation to leave Germany in 1933, Schoenberg came to America and taught for many years at the University of California in Los Angeles. Never a popular composer, Schoenberg felt that his music was misunderstood, and in fact, though he remained a romantic at heart and emotional expression in Schoenberg's compositions is often warm and intensely personal, twelve-tone music has been perceived by the public as more difficult and less expressive than music based upon the major and minor scales. Nevertheless, Schoenberg's work was, and remains, greatly respected, having provided an important stimulus to many composers who have applied it in highly personal ways; some have explored and then abandoned the method, while others have borrowed only some of its principles, tempering them with more traditional techniques.

Total Serialism

0-lē-viay´ Meh-sē-anh´

A French composer, **Olivier Messiaen** (1908–1992), applied Schoenberg's concept of organizing tones to other aspects of composition as well, including timbres, rhythms, durations of tones, and dynamic levels. For composers who organized these and other elements of composition into series, or rows, the term *twelve-tone* no longer sufficed, and the advanced technique came to be called **total serialism.**

Anton Webern (1883-1945)

Va´-burn

Anton Webern, a student and close friend of Schoenberg's, developed his own highly individual style, his classicism quite untempered by romantic inclinations and his music lean, clean, delicate, and strong. Webern, who thought his teacher *had not gone far enough* away from tonality and from other nineteenth-century concepts of organizing music, applied rigorous logic and the strictest control to his intense, sensitive miniatures. There is nothing superfluous, nothing to clutter the perfect order and design in Webern's music.

Webern usually wrote extremely brief compositions for small ensembles or for solo voices or instruments, appreciating each sound for its own sake much as

Figure 26.2

Sunday Afternoon on the Island of La Grande Jatte, Georges Seurat. 1884–1886.
(The Art Institute of Chicago, Helen Birch Bartlett Memorial Collection.)

Impressionist, Expressionist, and certain post-Impressionist painters appreciated colors. He scored the sparse lines of his music for instruments of unlike timbre, enhancing the listener's ability to hear in the linear fashion Webern intended and minimizing the dissonant effect of his vertical combinations of sound. His distinct separation of sounds (leading Aaron Copland to refer to Webern's musical lines as "atomized") and his intense organization of resources are reminiscent of the visual technique called **pointillism** seen in Georges Seurat's famous painting *Sunday Afternoon on the Island of La Grande Jatte* (figure 26.2).

Each section of Webern's *Five Pieces for Orchestra,* (Listening Example 34), which lasts for a total of less than five minutes, has a mood or character of its own, only vaguely suggested by the titles Webern supplied: "Prototype," "Transformation," "Return," "Memory," and "Soul." The fourth piece—the shortest in the entire orchestral repertoire—has only 6½ measures and takes about nineteen seconds to perform. However, Webern's musical ideas are so intensely concentrated that each miniature piece provides a complete and meaningful statement, its whispers as eloquent as the shouts of another work.

Alban Berg
(1885–1935)

Bairg
Vah´-tzek

Schoenberg's pupil **Alban Berg** also adapted the principles he learned from Schoenberg to create his own personal style, more lyrical than either Schoenberg's or Webern's. Berg's powerful opera *Wozzeck* (1917–1921) concerns a young soldier (Wozzeck) who becomes a victim of his environment, as so many people felt themselves to be in this difficult period in modern history. Betrayed by his society, by his mistress, Marie, and by his own supersensitive personality, Wozzeck finally is driven

LISTENING EXAMPLE 34

Nontraditional Orchestral Piece

Composer: Anton Webern (1883–1945)

Title: *Five Pieces for Orchestra,* Op. 10

Composed: 1911–1913

Rhythm: Constantly changing rhythm and meter

Melody: This work is almost entirely melodic in conception; that is, there are no significant chordal or harmonic progressions. The melodies are not governed by traditional tonal relationships, but the varied timbres and the clarity of the texture enhance the listener's ability to follow melodic phrases from one instrument to another.

Timbre: Chamber orchestra (clarinet, muted horn, muted trombone, harmonium, mandolin, guitar, celesta, harp, bass drum, snare drum, chimes, sheep bells, violin, muted viola, muted cello)

1	0:00	I. Prototype (*Very calm and delicate*)
		Clarinet has the longest melodic line among various solos; note the flutter tonguing in the flute.
2	0:42	II: Transformation (*Lively and delicately agitated*)
		The busiest movement, ending *fortissimo*
3	1:20	III: Return (*Very slow and extremely calm*)
		Bell-like accompaniment to melodic fragments in the solo violin, muted horn, clarinet, solo viola, and muted trombone
4	2:48	IV: Memory (*Flowing, extremely delicate*)
		Only 6½ measures long; begins with a mandolin solo; the middle features muted trumpet and trombone; ends with a solo violin
5	3:15	V: Soul (*Very flowing*)
		Begins quietly, builds quickly to a brief climax; immediately returns to very soft dynamics and ends quietly.

beyond reason and endurance; he murders Marie and drowns himself. The final scene, or **ensemble finale,** in which Wozzeck and Marie's little boy remains unaware of their deaths and therefore unmoved by the cruel taunts of his playmates, is one of the most poignant in all the literature of music.

However, the opera is concerned not so much with the facts of Wozzeck's downfall as with the psychological effects of his mental and emotional deterioration. *Wozzeck,* written before the twelve-tone technique was fully developed, clearly indicates Berg's romantic inclinations; and although Berg later mastered the twelve-tone technique, he often based his music upon rows that imply a tonal center.

Experimentalism

Some composers have combined the serial technique with electronic instruments and the magnetic tape recorder to create entirely new sounds. Those who radically altered not only the traditional methods of composing and presenting music, but also the very concept of what constitutes music as opposed to noise, are called **Experimentalists.**

Early Experimentalists extended the ranges of traditional music instruments (including the voice) to produce sounds that previously had not been considered desirable, and by the 1950s, electronic instruments enabled composers to create entirely new sounds and effects of various kinds. The Experimentalists, who have produced a prodigious diversity of styles, are united only by their endless curiosity and inventiveness. Some have striven for total control of the performance of their works, while others have written *indeterminate* music that leaves important decisions to the performers, to the audience, or simply to chance. Their creative exploration of unknown aspects of sound greatly expanded the concept of music.

Perhaps it is not surprising that the center of Experimentalism has been the United States, for the New World is naturally less tied to tradition than the Old, and a pioneering spirit has been a part of the American character since the nation's birth. Two American composers, one from the East Coast and one from the West, broke new ground for musicians everywhere as they embarked on new paths and devised new ways of treading them.

Charles Ives (1874–1954)

An inventive nature and an unconventional upbringing destined Charles Ives to become a music Experimentalist. His father, who had been a bandmaster in the Civil War, was fascinated with the qualities and effects of sound. He conducted acoustical experiments with various instruments and objects never previously associated with music, and used **quarter tones** (those that lie between the half steps of the major and minor scales) and **polytonality** (two or more keys at the same time) with impunity. Long before Europeans had expressed interest in polytonality, his father was teaching the young Charles Ives to sing a song in one key and accompany himself at the piano in another.

Thus this hardy, independent Connecticut Yankee never felt either constrained by tradition nor intimidated by stubborn opposition. Aware upon graduation from Yale that few listeners would approach his music with the same spirit of adventure with which he conceived it, Ives entered the insurance business and soon became financially successful. Thus assured that his family would not "starve on his dissonances," he composed music in the evenings, on weekends, and during vacations—ignored, as he expected to be, by most of the world. By the time the public slowly became acquainted with his music, and even more slowly learned to admire and finally to enjoy it, Ives's health had failed, preventing him not only from composing but even from attending the very belated premieres of his works. In 1947 Ives was awarded a Pulitzer Prize for his Third Symphony, which he had completed in 1904. Several of his other works won prestigious awards, also decades after they were written.

Like many romantic composers (for he was an inveterate romantic), Ives believed in and practiced the integration of the arts. Interested in literature as well as music, he wrote about relationships between the two and about their relevance to life. He penned provocative essays about important literary figures, including Ralph Waldo Emerson and Henry David Thoreau, and he portrayed some of them musically in his piano composition called the Concord Sonata. He was filled with ideas about art, sound, and the meaning of music and of life. Nationalism formed an inherent part of his makeup: fascinated by old American hymns, minstrel songs, Stephen Foster melodies, Sousa marches, barn dance fiddle tunes, and ragtime, he incorporated snatches of all of these in his symphonies, sonatas, organ music, and songs.

Ives combined his melodies in dense layers that sometimes produce very dissonant sounds, scoffing at those who disliked dissonances and charging that they were addicted to comfortable sounds as if to drugs. He pointed out that if sounds do not bother us, we tend to call them beautiful, and he warned against listening to twentieth-century music with nineteenth-century ears. Ives not only accepted but reveled in the imperfections of life and art: orchestras playing slightly out of tune, conflicting performances by two or more bands parading down a street, and the odd melodic turns, irregular phrases, and unconventional harmonies of some old

Charles Ives
The Bettman Archive, New York

American tunes were sources of delight and inspiration to him. He never tried to correct such irregularities, but exploited them for their unusual, sometimes amusing, and always interesting effects.

Most of Ives's instrumental music is programmatic, and much of it describes his own familiar New England milieu. One very famous piece, *The Unanswered Question,* is a strangely mystic conception leaving unusual decisions to the determination of the performers. In his prefatory instructions for the piece, Ives suggested that a solo trumpet pose "The Perennial Question of Existence"—a strangely nontonal melody—to which a woodwind ensemble is to respond while string instruments positioned offstage play their own quiet, mysterious, hymnlike music, quite oblivious of the squabble taking place on stage. However, Ives also noted that any instrument able to play the trumpet's pitches might play the role of questioner, and the woodwinds might be either all flutes or a combination of instruments from that family. He also declared that the "Answers" need not begin at the points notated in the score but could, at the performers' will, begin a bit early or late, inevitably changing the combination of sounds. Thus, *space* and *chance* have significant roles in this fascinating piece, which has earned a distinguished place in the American repertoire. (The Moody Blues ended their album *Knights in White Satin*—(the words are " . . . we decide which is right,/ And which is an illusion???")—with a brief but unmistakable quotation of "The Question"; and *The Unanswered Question* was performed with haunting significance at President John F. Kennedy's memorial service.)

Ives also wrote a large body of songs. "At the River," Listening Example 35, is his highly original setting of a hymn tune widely familiar in his day, as it is in ours. Ives's slight alteration of the famous melody at the end of the verse and the chorus immeasurably enhances the questioning, tentative mood of the lovely song, and with these and other techniques he made the piece his own original creation.

Henry Cowell (1897–1965)

Though the atmosphere in which he was born and reared also precluded allegiance to musical orthodoxy, in other respects **Henry Cowell's** childhood was entirely different from that of Charles Ives. Cowell, born in California to rather impoverished Irish-American parents, had little opportunity to hear or to study European concert music as a child, but loved the Chinese music he heard in the homes of Chinese neighbors and the modal church music performed by an organist friend. While Henry was still quite young, his family moved to the Midwest, where the young musician added to his store of Irish folk tunes, Chinese opera, and modal chant increasing familiarity with country fiddle tunes and early American hymns. Even as a child, he improvised highly original music at the piano, performing some of his own compositions in public when he was only fifteen.

In "The Tides of Mananaun," a piano piece about the legendary Irish "maker of the tides," Cowell introduced **tone clusters:** large groups of successive notes played with the flat of the hand or the arm. For this particular piece, Cowell used clusters from the lowest tones of the piano, which merge to disguise any particular tone and can easily be imagined to represent the roaring, rolling sound of the ocean tides. Conceived for this simple programmatic effect, clusters were soon recognized simply as chords built upon seconds rather than the traditional thirds, and Cowell later developed a system of harmony based upon them. As it happens, Charles Ives was using tone clusters in his music at about the same time that Cowell introduced them, but since Ives's work was not known at that time, Cowell was long considered their sole inventor.

3 ⑥

LISTENING EXAMPLE 35

 3A 2

Art Song

Composer: Charles Ives (1874–1954)

Title: "At the River"

Composed: 1911–1913

Genre: Art song

Form: Verse-chorus. The song on which Ives based his piece is strophic in form, each verse ending with a chorus, or **refrain,** in which the words remain the same with each repetition.

Tune and text: By Robert Lowry. Though Ives essentially retained the original tune, his altering of the ends of the verse and the chorus effectively enhance the questioning, tentative mood of his piece.

Rhythm: Quadruple meter. However, the rhythm is quite flexible, again in keeping with the mood of the song.

Accompaniment: Having set the rather plaintive mood in the introduction, the piano accompanies the familiar hymn tune with richly dissonant chords, adding an element of surprise to the piece. Toward the end of the verse, the piano offers the voice competing melodic interest, and then plays a brief interlude between verse and chorus.

Timbre: Voice (baritone) and piano

⑥	0:00	**Introduction;** piano
0:13	0:13	**Verse**
. . . .		Shall we gather at the river
. . . .		Where mighty angel feet have trod,
. . . .		With its crystal tide forever
. . . .		Flowing by the throne of God?
. . . .		Gather at the river
		Chorus
. . . .		Yes, we'll gather at the river,
. . . .		The beautiful, the beautiful river.
. . . .		Yes, we'll gather at the river
. . . .		That flows by the throne of God.
1:02	1:02	**Brief interlude;** piano
1:08	1:08	Shall we gather, shall we gather at the river?
. . . .		*(The music ends abruptly in a questioning, tentative manner.)*

Cowell's most far-reaching experiments, however, addressed a growing, and widely shared, restlessness at the perceived limits of musical sound. Having access in his youth only to the piano, he vastly extended the range of timbres of that readily available instrument, exploiting its possibilities as a member of the string family by stroking, plucking, striking, or strumming the strings with the hands, the fingernails, or various implements to produce an enormous variety of sounds.

The methods of directly manipulating the piano strings in "The Banshee" (Listening Example 36) correspond to those described in Chinese manuals of string-playing techniques, reflecting Cowell's increasing knowledge of and admiration for the music traditions of the East. Recognizing the wide range of timbres offered by instruments of China, Japan, India, and other non-Western cultures, he became one of the first Western musicians to advocate the merging of Eastern with Western sounds, and of old techniques with new.

3 7   # LISTENING EXAMPLE 36   3A 3

Experimental Piano Music

Composer: Henry Cowell (1897–1965)

Title: "The Banshee"

Composed: 1925

Form: The form of the piece, much like that of many later electronic compositions, is derived from changes in dynamic levels and contrasts in timbre

Timbre: Piano

One performer sits at the keyboard depressing the damper pedal, while another stands in the crook of the piano and manipulates the strings. The various techniques include sweeping the strings from the lowest note to a specified note with the flesh of a finger; sweeping the strings up and back; sweeping the length of one string with the flesh of a finger; plucking the strings; sweeping the strings with the back of a fingernail; and sweeping them with the flat of the hand.

7	0:00	A sweep with the flesh of the finger from low to high, followed by a sweep lengthwise along the string of a given note (or notes); (*pp, crescendo; diminuendo*)
0:32	0:32	Sweep up and down
0:38	0:38	String plucked with flesh of finger (*p*)
. . . .		*crescendo*
0:47	0:47	Sweep lengthwise along the string with back of fingernail (*f*)
1:06	1:06	String plucked with flesh of finger (*mf*)
1:24	1:24	Sweep with nails of both hands together (*ff*); presto
1:33	1:33	Sweep with flat of hand (*diminuendo*)
1:39	1:39	String plucked with flesh of finger (*p*); slow
. . . .		*Diminuendo* to end

Henry Cowell.
The Bettman Archive, NY

It is hard to imagine a more effective portrayal of the fairy-woman of Irish lore who foretells an individual's death by materializing near the doomed one wailing her dreaded, howling cry than the one Cowell achieved with his unorthodox piano techniques in "The Banshee."

Cowell finally received a formal music education, but never lost his curiosity about the unknown, his inventiveness, or his interest in non-Western and nontraditional sounds. Together with Leon Theremin, inventor of one of the first electronic instruments, the *theremin* (used with vibrant effect in the Beach Boys' recording "Good Vibrations"), Cowell invented a machine called the *rhythmicon* that was capable of reproducing rapid and complex rhythmic patterns beyond the capacity of human performers. Cowell became an ardent admirer and close friend of Charles Ives, whose background and experience could hardly have been more different from Cowell's, but who proved his soulmate indeed. Cowell's own difficult life included a (probably undeserved) term in jail; yet this prolific composer, writer, teacher, and critic remained a steadfast friend and generous advocate for young composers both in Europe and America.

Edgard Varèse (1883–1965)

Many musicians desired and envisioned electronic instruments long before they finally materialized. Among the most frustrated advocates of new musical sounds was **Edgard Varèse,** who tired of working with "ordinary" instruments by the 1920s and began even then to express his need for equipment that would allow him to create new sounds at will. He had to wait, however, for nearly three decades before the technology he envisioned arrived.

Varèse, who was born in France but emigrated to America, considered a career in engineering before his fascination with musical sound led him to become a composer instead. Of all the elements of music, timbre most appealed to Varèse, who remained interested in the physics as well as the aesthetics of sound. In a phrase reminiscent of Schoenberg's "emancipation of the dissonance," Varèse advocated the "liberation of sound." He defined music simply as *organized sound,* avoiding traditional distinctions between "musical sounds" and "noise."

Edgard Varèse.
The Bettman Archive, NY

Early in his career, Varèse wrote several compositions for a wide variety of percussion instruments, organizing his pieces largely upon principles of contrasting sounds. He scrupulously avoided reference to the major or minor scales and preferred using a pitch continuum, containing every gradation of pitch within a given interval, to any scale at all. He often called for glissandos on the few melodic instruments (his favorite was a siren) included in his works.

Ultimately frustrated by his inability to achieve with existing music instruments the sounds he conceived in his mind, Varèse stopped composing in about 1937, until his dreams came true more than a decade later with the inventions of the electronic sound synthesizer and magnetic recording tape. Then, although he was nearly seventy years old, Varèse plunged with unbounded enthusiasm into the new world of musical sounds.

Concrete Music

The invention of the magnetic tape recorder in the late 1940s provided Experimentalists interested in timbre as an element of expression with an important new tool and made possible a new type of composition, developed by composers working in France shortly after World War II, called *musique concrète.* They recorded and then manipulated sounds chosen from every conceivable source, organizing them into compositions that people could only "perform" by playing their recorded work: hence the term **concrete music.**

Composers of concrete music, considering all sounds valid material for music composition, combined the sounds of nature and of machinery with those of traditional musical instruments and the human voice. They also discovered that the many ways in which recorded sounds may be manipulated enormously expanded their realm of timbres. Altering the speed of a recorded sound, playing a tape backwards, and combining various altered sounds are only a few of the techniques available to the composer of concrete music.

Milton Babbitt (b. 1916)

The influential, if controversial, American composer **Milton Babbitt** combined the technological resources of the electronic synthesizer (pp. 35–36) and the tape recorder with the mathematical logic of total serialism. Having received an undergraduate degree in music from New York University and a graduate music degree from Princeton, Babbitt became a composer of twelve-tone pieces and a leader in the movement toward total serialism. In some of his compositions he mathematically interrelated tones, rhythms, durations, timbres, intensities, and textures, while in others each series is independently conceived and the relationships between them are of a musical, rather than a mathematical, order.

Babbitt derives aesthetic as well as intellectual satisfaction from orderly relationships, and his music is entirely rational. He prefers to retain total control over his compositions, which, devised by a brilliant mind, require brilliant performance rather than subjective interpretation. One of four codirectors who established America's first synthesizer (sponsored by Princeton and Columbia Universities and located at Columbia, in New York City, in 1959), he has taken full advantage of the resources of that remarkable instrument to invent, produce, and preserve exactly the sounds he requires.

Babbitt's composition *Ensembles for Synthesizer* (Listening Example 37), written in 1962, has become an early classic of the electronic music repertoire, a piece all the more remarkable when one considers its pioneering, revolutionary nature. Using the most sophisticated electronic techniques of the early 1960s, Babbitt eliminated the need for interpretation (performance) of the work by recording the *Ensembles* on tape as they were composed.

LISTENING EXAMPLE 37

3 ⑧   🎞 3A 4

Electronic Music

Composer: Milton Babbitt (b. 1916)

Title: *Ensembles for Synthesizer* (excerpt)

Composed: 1962–1964

Genre: Electronic music

Timbre: Synthesizer

The *Ensembles* are very short sections distinguished from one another by different timbres, ranges of pitch, rhythmic patterns, dynamic levels, and textures. The composition's outstanding characteristics are the wide variety of timbres and the complex rhythms.

Babbitt programmed the synthesizer to produce various metallic, wooden, and mysterious "airy" sounds, with occasional references to the tones of an electronic organ. The extremely rapid tempos sometimes supersede the ability of human performers to reproduce them or the human ear to distinguish them accurately.

⑧	0:00	Miscellaneous timbres combine with one another and end in a sustained sound. Three variations of this gesture are then presented. Listen to the change in tone color of each held sound.
0:07	0:07	High/low-pitched sustained sound
0:19	0:19	Medium-pitched sustained sound
0:33	0:33	High-pitched sustained sound
0:46	0:46	Low-pitched sustained sound
0:56	0:56	Various timbres and rhythms provide interest. Faster, more playful rhythmic movement; sustained tones combine with staccato articulation
1:27	1:27	Dance-like rhythms and percussive timbres combine with an occasional electronic organ "sound."
1:58	1:58	The last section of this excerpt is marked by extremely rapid rhythmic patterns, reminiscent of underwater "gurgling."

Milton Babbitt.
Courtesy Milton Babbitt

Because Babbitt's music is conceived and constructed differently from the music of other styles, it must also be approached differently by the conscientious listener. Although tightly organized and entirely logical, the complexity of Babbitt's structural conceptions often makes them difficult to recognize. This is, however, important music with its own personal style, and ultimately it is highly rewarding.

Indeterminate Music

At the same time that Babbitt and his like-minded colleagues were imposing the strictest control on their compositions, other Experimentalists reacted *against* the order imposed by serialists and composers of concrete music, moving in the opposite direction toward *minimal* control of their works. Indeterminacy—leaving significant components of a work to be determined by its performers—is not an entirely new concept: the Baroque figured bass required players to fill in harmonies; soloists playing concertos in the Classical period created their own cadenzas; and jazz composers expect interpreters of their works to include improvisation in each performance. However, in each of these cases, the performer's creative contribution is controlled by certain basic tenets of tonality and certain conventions of performance practice, whereas **indeterminacy** in the twentieth century means that some or many aspects of a performance are left entirely to chance. The melody, rhythm, harmony, and/or design of a composition may, in fact, be arbitrarily determined—by the throw of dice, for example, or the random operations of computers. Other names for this kind of music include **chance, random,** and, more technically, **aleatoric music** (the latter term derives from the Latin word *alea,* meaning dice).

Charts and graphs of many kinds often replace conventional notation for this new kind of music; curves, circles, other geometric patterns, and detailed verbal instructions may be the only "score" the composer provides. Live music performances are always unique in some respects, but performers of aleatoric music (the noun is *aleatory*) may be required to choose among so many alternatives that each performance of the same composition sounds like a different work.

The Unanswered Question, by Charles Ives, offers modest levels of indeterminacy, leaving limited choices of instrumentation and entrance times to the discretion of the performers. At the other extreme of indeterminacy, John Cage's *Imaginary Landscape No. 1* represents random music: it is "played" on several radios. The "score" indicates the radio frequencies to be used, the types of attack, and the durations and dynamic levels of each section, but the effect of each performance, of course, depends on what happens to be on the airwaves at that moment.

Random techniques are clearly related to the free jazz of Ornette Coleman and John Coltrane (pp. 306) and to the work of the Abstract Expressionists, or action painters, led by the American artist Jackson Pollock (1912–1956), who threw paint and then created art from the resulting patterns that randomly appeared on the canvas. (See Color Plate 14.) For all of these artists, the *process* of making art is more important than the finished product. Aleatoric music offers composers and performers alike a refreshing freedom from restraint or control. It is the very unpredictability of each performance that appeals to composers of indeterminate music.

John Cage (1912–1992)

John Cage studied composition with three important revolutionaries, Schoenberg, Varèse, and Cowell, each of whom introduced a fruitful area of experimentation that Cage explored and then adapted to his own particular designs. While he agreed with Schoenberg that music must seek new directions, Cage found the twelve-tone technique too closely tied to older traditions and soon abandoned it. From Varèse, he derived a fascination for sound and experimented with a wide variety of percussion instruments, including such unconventional items as automobile brake drums, cowbells, and metal sheets. In particular, Cage applied his inventive mind to the fertile area of research Cowell began by expanding the timbres and pitch capabilities of the piano.

Cage also was profoundly affected by the philosophies, religions, and aesthetic and cultural values of the East, finding himself particularly drawn to the concepts of Zen Buddhism. Thus liberated from Western traditions of form, tonality, and technique, he introduced startling new conceptions of the composition and performance of music. Endlessly creative, his inventive genius tempered by a keen sense of humor, Cage strongly affected the course of music history in Europe and America.

In the 1940s, Cage devised an economical means of expanding the range of a piano's sounds farther than even Cowell had conceived, by inventing the **prepared piano.** Positioning pieces of wood, metal, glass, or other material between the strings of a piano, thus altering both tones and timbres, he created a veritable ensemble of percussion sounds controlled by one performer at the keyboard. The effects are closely related to the sounds of the Indonesian gamelan (pp. 230–231), whose delicate and varied timbres particularly appealed to this American Experimentalist.

In some cases, the composer of a piece for prepared piano precisely defines the materials to be placed at particular locations on particular strings; in others, the directions are left deliberately vague. Each composition requires different individual preparation, which may take from a few minutes to an hour or more to accomplish. (Preparing a piano carefully does not hurt the instrument, but it is important to remove the foreign materials as soon as a performance ends to avoid putting the piano out of tune.)

At the beginning of the score for *The Perilous Night* (Listening Example 38), Cage indicated the precise manner in which the piano should be prepared, providing a meticulous chart showing which materials (nuts, bolts, weather stripping, etc.)

John Cage, leading Experimentalist composer.
Performings Arts Library, London

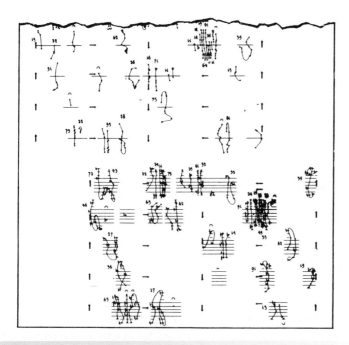

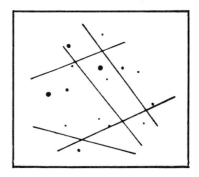

Nontraditional notation by John Cage.
© 1962, 1960 by Herman Press, Inc. Used by permission of C.f. Peters Corp.

3 9

LISTENING EXAMPLE 38

3A 5

Prepared Piano

Composer: John Cage (1912–1992)

Title: *The Perilous Night* (excerpt)

Composed: 1944

Form: Suite

Timbre: Prepared piano

Assorted nuts, bolts, washers, and pieces of bamboo and of weather stripping are placed between specific strings, thus creating a variety of wooden, metallic, and indeterminate sounds. As in so many twentieth-century compositions, exotic rhythms and timbres replace traditional melodic and harmonic patterns as the focus of aesthetic interest and the basis of formal design.

9	0.00	Section 1
		The composition begins with a loud, dramatic gesture that introduces to the listener the lowest and highest pitches of the piece.
		Unpredictable rhythms dominate this section.
10	0:26	Section 2
		A more steady rhythm is introduced with a melodic motive that alternates high and low pitches.
		This section leads into the next with a quick crescendo.
11	0:41	Section 3
		This section begins with a repeated note climax that sounds almost like a bongo drum. As in the opening, unpredictable gestures dominate this section.
12	1:34	Section 4
		Similar to Section 2, this last section begins with an even-note rhythm.
		Several loud outbursts from a high to a low pitch interrupt the steadier rhythm. These outbursts come closer together as the end of the piece is reached.

should be placed on particular strings and at what distance from the soundboard they should be applied.

His interest in unusual sounds also led Cage to experiment with electronic techniques as they became available; but ultimately, he was most interested in and committed to aleatory. One of his best-known compositions, *Aria and Fontana Mix,* combines a complex collage of taped sounds—musical fragments and amplified "natural" sounds, such as scraping on glass and swallowing—with a highly imaginative and aleatoric aria. *Fontana Mix,* which may be performed separately as an independent piece, consists of several tapes that may be played individually or together. *Aria,* which also may be performed alone, notes only the general contour of melodic shapes rather than specific tones, and calls for widely changing vocal styles, each to be determined by the singer.

Cage, who relished the experience of sounds—all sounds—also explored the realm of silence and its relationship to sound: after all, we notate rests as specifically as notes in traditional music. Having conducted several experiments that led him to conclude that absolute silence does not exist, at least in our world, he illustrated this controversial contention with *4' 33",* a piece that lasts for exactly four minutes and thirty-three seconds, during which a pianist sits quietly at the keyboard, raising and lowering the lid over the keys to indicate the beginning and end of three "movements." (Of course the piece may be performed on other instruments as well.) The sounds the audience hears—those occurring by chance during that time—Cage considered valid components of composition and proof of his theory that sound is always present, whether we pay attention to it or not.

Cage found the act of exploring and the science of inventing quite as intriguing as the art of composing—perhaps more so. Like Ives, who considered listening to music an adventure, and Varèse, who insisted that he was not an Experimentalist but that his listeners ought to be, Cage required of his audience a greater degree of participation and cooperation than has traditionally been expected. Performers of his music face unprecedented challenges as well, as they often are required to select among alternative directions rather than to reproduce a clearly structured concept.

While his ideas about music are certainly controversial, Cage did not impose them on anyone. His Eastern-inspired philosophy was gentle, his wit good-natured, and his inventiveness unquestionable. When his voice was finally stilled in 1993, ASCAP (the American Society of Composers, Authors, and Publishers) honored him with a full page in the Sunday *New York Times* reading simply: **SILENCE.**

European Revolutionaries

While Americans have led the field of Experimentalists, European composers also have produced many remarkable works, exerting their influence on Americans in turn.

Pierre Boulez (b. 1925)

Boo-lehz´

Like the other innovative composers discussed in this chapter, **Pierre Boulez** has derived his "new" ideas from a variety of earlier expressions. Strongly influenced by Olivier Messiaen (p. 248), with whom he studied harmony, Boulez also has been affected by Stravinsky's complex rhythms, Webern's varied timbres, and—especially—Schoenberg's twelve-tone technique. Like so many of his contemporaries, Boulez has been stimulated by the intricate and flexible rhythms of certain non-Western musics. His timbres, too, sometimes suggest the bell and percussion sounds of the East.

Serialism forms the basis for Boulez's approach to composition, the logic and the mathematical precision of that technique offering an attractive discipline to this composer who wishes to control (though not to suppress) emotional expression. Using serial technique in his own fashion, Boulez has created yet a new musical language. He rejects the tone row as the basis for composition, preferring an athematic (themeless) style, organized according to the ideals of total serialism.

Boulez, who often incorporates the element of chance in his music and, in fact, introduced the term *aleatory* into the music vocabulary, yet minimizes the amount of creative collaboration allowed the performer, simply offering a choice between limited and specified alternatives. He also has made important contributions to concrete music, to which he is drawn by his respect for control and his appreciation for exotic timbres. This famous conductor, innovator, and composer has emerged in recent years as one of the dominant figures of twentieth-century music.

Karlheinz Stockhausen (b. 1928)

Among the most revolutionary of composers, **Karlheinz Stockhausen** has derived many new ideas from older traditions and earlier styles. For example, one of his most famous scores, *Gruppen (Groups),* is written for three orchestras and involves spatial relationships reminiscent of the Venetians' sixteenth-century polychoral style (p. 90). His music reflects the influence of Messiaen's flexible and complex rhythms, Webern's approach to serialization, and Ives's experiments with sound.

Karlheinz
Stockhausen.

Often the performer of Stockhausen's music is required to master the composer's particular system of notation, in which tempo markings may be relative ("as fast as possible," for example) rather than absolute. His extremely detailed notation reflects a desire to control his work; yet like Boulez, Stockhausen also writes aleatoric compositions allowing the performer a limited creative role.

Stockhausen has applied his knowledge of physics and acoustics to the composition of some fascinating works. As the director of an early electronic sound studio, he had access to three sound generators with which he produced a combination, or spectrum, of tones called **white noise** (so named because white includes the spectrum of colors). Indeed, he has been involved in all phases of electronic techniques, including concrete music and the combination of live and taped music. (His "Electronic Studies" of 1953–1954 was the first published electronic music score.) Stockhausen believes that electronic music will eventually replace orchestral and other traditional concert music, since recordings and tapes make traditional music available to be heard at home, while electronic music's complex requirements of special microphones and spatial arrangements require group attendance at a concert hall.

Krzysztof Penderecki (b. 1933)

Kris-tof Pen-de-ret´-zkĕ

Krzysztof Penderecki combines traditional folk elements from his native Poland with various mainstream procedures and provocative avant-garde concepts to produce music with his own distinctive sound. His music often reveals a strong concern for human suffering, reflecting his experience as a child in Poland, where he experienced the terror of Nazi persecution of Jews. *Threnody for the Victims of Hiroshima* (1960), for example, scored for 52 shrieking string instruments, is an anguished cry that deeply moves Western audiences not only because of the subject addressed, but also through the warm, expressive style of composition.

The influence of Medieval and other early styles is apparent in much of Penderecki's music, which nevertheless is clearly of and about the twentieth century. Rather than exploiting electronic techniques, Penderecki has systematically extended the range of sounds that may be produced by traditional instruments, requiring the players of string instruments, for example, to produce quarter tones and other nontraditional pitches and to use a variety of unusual performing techniques. He sometimes combines voices in clusters of tones, producing unusual, moving effects. He also has introduced yet another notation system, inventing symbols to indicate his required durations, pitches, and playing techniques.

Penderecki, like Picasso, has been very radical, tried many different styles, and ultimately established his own, highly personal, artistic identity. But whereas Picasso was ever a classicist, Penderecki's warmly emotional music clearly lies on the romantic side of the imaginary style line.

Summary

The twentieth-century revolutionary composers share with each other little beyond their conviction that music must change in a radical manner rather than continue along well-worn paths. Some have abandoned tonality as the means of organizing their harmonic schemes. Melody has less interest for these composers than rhythms and timbres, which they have produced in a variety and complexity unprecedented in Western music.

Schoenberg's twelve-tone technique has proved adaptable to many highly personal styles of composition. Some composers, led by Milton Babbitt, have combined the advanced concept of the twelve-tone system, called total serialism, with electronic techniques to produce tightly structured and controlled compositions, while other revolutionaries share John Cage's preference to exercise minimal control over performances of their works. The latter require performers and audiences to share in the creative process of making music.

European revolutionaries include Boulez, who has his own athematic approach to serialization; Stockhausen, who introduced white noise and predicts that the concert music of the future will all be electronic; and Penderecki, who achieves warm, compassionate effects from musical instruments with a variety of nontraditional playing methods.

The music of the revolutionaries, challenging traditional concepts of the meaning of music, its substance, and its purpose (if any), offers boundless challenge and stimulation to the curious and receptive listener. It represents, however, a minority of twentieth-century composers of art music; by far the greater proportion of these composers may be analyzed and appreciated according to traditional methods and listening techniques.

Critical Thinking

- Are you more inclined toward art that is highly structured and entirely determined by the artist, or toward art that involves chance and to which an audience and/or performers contribute creative elements? Discuss the values and limitations of both concepts.

• Do you support or reject John Cage's contention that absolute silence is an absurd concept? How do you support your own conclusions on this matter?

Terms to Review

twelve-tone technique   The arrangement of the twelve chromatic pitches into a row that provides the melodic and harmonic basis for a music composition.

row   The series of tones on which a serial composition is based.

total serialism   An extension of the twelve-tone technique, in which other aspects besides melody and harmony are also arranged into series and systematically repeated throughout a composition.

pointillism   A painting technique in which colors and shapes are broken into tiny dots, which appear from a distance to blend.

ensemble finale   The final scene of a musical show, or of an act within the show, in which several soloists simultaneously express, in different words and music, their individual points of view.

Experimentalism   The exploration of previously unknown aspects of musical sound.

quarter tone   The interval halfway between half steps.

polytonality   Two or more keys at the same time.

tone cluster   A chord built upon seconds.

refrain   A section of melody and text that recurs at the end of each verse of a strophic song.

concrete music   (musique concrète) Music consisting of recorded and electronically altered sounds.

 indeterminate, aleatoric, random, or **chance music**   Music in which some elements of composition are left to the decision of performance participants or to chance.

prepared piano   A piano whose timbre and pitches have been altered by the application of foreign materials on or between the strings.

white noise   Sounds including the entire spectrum of tones, as white includes the entire spectrum of colors.

Key Figures

Artist	*Georges Seurat*	
Composers	*Arnold Schoenberg*	*Olivier Messiaen*
	Anton Webern	*Alban Berg*
	Charles Ives	*Henry Cowell*
	Edgard Varèse	*Milton Babbitt*
	John Cage	*Pierre Boulez*
	Karlheinz Stockhausen	*Krzysztof Penderecki*

27
The Evolutionaries

Provocative crosscurrents stir the wide and sometimes turbulent body of contemporary music, keeping it fresh and vital. Thus concurrent with the innovations of the Experimentalists and other "revolutionaries" runs the **mainstream** of twentieth-century music, which is *evolutionary* in the sense that its products represent a logical continuation of traditional Western techniques rather than a rebellion against them. Because the mainstream continues to flow, the present tense best expresses this general, introductory information. However, our concern in this chapter is ideological rather than chronological, for some of our most recent important works are best understood as contemporary versions of well-established and long-appreciated music styles. The date when a piece was composed no longer serves as a valid indication of its composer's stylistic ideals.

Mainstream composers believe Western music should evolve in an orderly and logical manner, enriched by a new awareness of other, non-Western, styles, but solidly based upon traditional concepts of the musical arts. Their means of achieving this goal, however, are highly individualistic. Many mainstream composers contain their art within classical ranges of expression and formal design, while others prefer the subjective, emotionally expressive style we call romantic. Some are inspired by folk, popular, and religious music of their own and other countries. Others find inspiration in the music of the past.

One significant aspect of twentieth-century music is a renewed appreciation for and application of certain Medieval concepts. Examples of this are found in two particularly attractive works: the modal effects, references to Gregorian chant, and mixture of the Old English and Latin languages in Benjamin Britten's Christmas work *A Ceremony of Carols* are Medieval concepts treated in a twentieth-century manner; and Carl Orff's *Carmina Burana,* based upon Medieval manuscripts of some Goliard songs discovered in a monastery after centuries of neglect, is a highly original treatment of Medieval material.

No single composer leads a specific movement identified as the dominant style of contemporary music, and no single work may be relied upon to classify a mainstream twentieth-century composer, for several have changed styles during long and productive careers.

Les Six

As certain painters adopted the nonsense of Dadaism, some composers, too, found nonsense and frivolity to be effective antidotes to the pomposity and pretentiousness of some late-nineteenth-century music. Six young French composers, sharing little beyond a distaste for Romanticism and for all the other "isms" of their day, found new inspiration in the popular music of the café, the theater, and the jazz band. They were Georges Auric, Louis Durey, Arthur Honegger, Darius Milhaud, Francis Poulenc, and a woman, Germaine Tailleferre.

The light, satirical style of Erik Satie (1866–1925), who supported his advocacy of simple, unpretentious music by writing attractive and witty compositions with

Sah-tē´

absurd, surrealistic titles such as *Three Pieces in the Form of a Pear,* pointed the way for these young French composers; like Satie, they wrote music to entertain, but hardly to challenge, and never to disturb, the listener. Dubbed **Les Six,** in half-humorous reference to the nationalistic Russian Five, these talented French composers wrote many significant works, never abandoning the French principle that art should be more pleasant than profound. Their music is characterized by a classical simplicity and a romantic warmth, without the intellectual or emotional flavor associated with either of these major styles.

Three of the group, Poulenc (1899–1963), Honegger (1892–1955), and Milhaud, are considered important twentieth-century composers, each having developed his own distinctive and sophisticated style of composition.

Darius Milhaud (1892–1974)

Mē-oh´

In many ways, **Darius Milhaud,** a prolific composer who worked within virtually every conceivable genre, including songs, symphonies, piano pieces, operas, chamber music, cantatas, and film scores, possessed a classical temperament. Sometimes satirical, even frivolous in his approach to music, Milhaud wrote attractive, logical compositions with lyrical melody lines. His music is often quite dissonant, but like Webern, Milhaud lessened the effect of harsh dissonances by combining voices of unlike timbres, thereby encouraging linear rather than "chordal" listening. In his search for new musical material upon which to base his compositions, Milhaud traveled widely, diligently exploring the "exotic" sounds of jazz in America and of folk music in Brazil. The melodies, rhythms, and timbres of popular music lend a fresh, invigorating flavor to his style.

First introduced to jazz by a traveling American jazz band performing in a London café, Milhaud was so thrilled with the exciting new sound that he left his dinner table to sit with the musicians and make detailed notes of their techniques. Later, on a visit to the United States, he went straight to Harlem, an African American district and important center for jazz musicians in New York City, where he steeped himself in the sounds of the new music. Upon his return to France (1924), he wrote a number of pieces based upon jazz, one of the most attractive of which is his ballet *La Créa-tion du Monde* (*The Creation of the World*). Certainly the rhythms, timbres, and harmonies of the piece reflect the influence of jazz, though Milhaud's composition clearly retains its identity as a European concert piece.

Darius Milhaud.
Corbis-Bettmann

While Milhaud was inspired by foreign sources, other composers found a wealth of ideas in the characteristic sounds of their own national music. The subjectivity of nationalism has had particularly strong appeal for Americans, the most romantic of twentieth-century composers. Yet Central and Eastern European traditions, too, offered rich materials for their own composers and also for Western Europeans, who early in this century became acquainted with the indigenous arts of these areas. As the folk music of many parts of the world stimulated composers of serious music, the field of **musicology,** or the scientific study of music, expanded to include the even newer science of **ethnomusicology,** the study of the music of specific cultures. These new disciplines broke through barriers of time and place, revealing the music of much earlier periods in European history and the folk and art music of the non-Western world.

Béla Bartók (1881–1945)

Bay´-la Bar´-tawk

For Béla Bartók, one of the most prestigious composers of this century, the folk music of Eastern Europe provided the most refreshing and provocative stimulus for his composition of art music. Bartók, whose mother was a piano teacher, was an accomplished pianist at an early age and performed widely as a child prodigy before becoming more interested in composing music than in playing it. Developing a strong interest in the folk music of his native Hungary and of other Eastern European countries, he made arduous journeys into the countryside, where he listened avidly to the music of the people—peasant music, as he called it—recording and analyzing it according to the most advanced scientific methods. One of the first and finest ethnomusicologists, Bartók never tried to "refine" or "correct" folk scales or the melodies based upon them, wishing instead to preserve their genuine, unique qualities. He became so thoroughly steeped in folk traditions that they virtually became a part of him, and he was eventually able to speak the folk music language as if it were his own.

Bartók wrote much of his music for the instrument he played, exploiting the piano's brilliant percussive characteristics as no other composer had before him. One of his early piano pieces, *Allegro barbaro,* has the narrow melodies, repetitive

In a documentary picture, young Béla Bartók , fourth from the left, is directing a young woman to sing into a wax cylinder recording machine on a field trip among Hungarian peasants in 1912.

© G. D. Hackett, New York

motives, and sharp, pounding rhythms associated with Primitivism; but that did not remain Bartók's characteristic sound. Like Beethoven, Bartók continued to develop until he arrived at a style uniquely and unmistakably his own.

Bartók never denied the essential integrity of the tonal system, though his use of folk and modal scales and complex harmonies often renders his tonality ambiguous. He disagreed with those Romantic composers who believed that the simple melodies of folk music should be accompanied by the simplest chords, insisting that, on the contrary, the simpler the melody was, the more complicated its accompaniment might be. Thus his harmony is often quite complex and may be very dissonant. Besides the triads of traditional Western harmony, he used chords built upon fourths and other intervals, seeking Henry Cowell's permission to use tone clusters, which he considered Cowell to have invented. Bartók sometimes combined melodies in linear counterpoint, producing the strong dissonances typical of that texture, but nearly always respecting a firm tonal center nonetheless. Bartók also showed the selective influence of other composers that he admired but with whom he disagreed on certain points. He shared Debussy's appreciation for beautiful sonorities, Stravinsky's fascination with driving rhythms, and Schoenberg's interest in chromaticism, without subscribing wholly to any of their philosophies of music.

It has been suggested that Bartók's stature as a composer ranks him with the three great "B's" of Western music. Like the first, J. S. Bach, he had pedagogical concerns; his *Mikrokosmos,* for example, is a set of six piano books of graded difficulty. Bartók's string quartets, considered the finest since those of the second "B," Beethoven, are often compared with those of that Viennese master for their strength and complexity. And like Brahms, Bartók wrote warmly expressive music that is yet held firmly under formal control. In fact, it is in the area of formal design that Bartók was least innovative, finding the established forms of earlier periods generally adaptable for his purpose.

Immigrating to the United States in 1940, Bartók became associated with Columbia University in New York City, where he continued his important research and his analysis and publication of various folk materials. Though desperately ill with leukemia and often hospitalized during the last months of his life, he wrote some of his most accessible music during that difficult period. Conceiving his Piano Concerto No. 3 (1945) as a kind of "insurance policy" for his wife, he wrote it so as to be readily understood and appreciated; and his stunning Concerto for Orchestra, also composed shortly before he died, remains one of Bartók's most popular works.

Aaron Copland (1900–1990)

Among American nationalists, who have exploited the folk, religious, and popular music of their broad land in varied ways, **Aaron Copland** is the best-known and most revered. A versatile composer with many interests, Copland revealed in several of his compositions strong, though intermittent, nationalistic inclinations.

At the turn of the twentieth century, American composers still suffered under the delusion of cultural inferiority to Europeans. Since American audiences had little interest in the serious music of their compatriots, American composers generally relied upon academic positions and performing careers for financial support.

Then, in the early 1920s, Aaron Copland led the first generation of American composers determined to devote their professional lives to the writing of music. To further their education and hone their technique, they traveled to France, which offered the young students flocking to Paris in the 1920s a new and refreshing freedom from pedagogical restraint. In particular, a gifted teacher named Nadia Boulanger pointed them in several provocative new directions. One of the greatest teachers of

Aaron Copland.

any time, Boulanger was a remarkable person who had the rare gift of teaching technique without imposing style. She encouraged young composers to "find themselves" and to learn to express themselves in individual and personal ways.

Having studied with Nadia Boulanger in Paris for three years, Copland returned to America an accomplished composer and—for a time, at least—a dedicated nationalist. Like many young musicians of his day, Copland was fascinated with the new popular style called jazz, to which, paradoxically, he was formally introduced while studying in Europe. He found many characteristics of jazz applicable to the composition of art music, and cross-rhythms, colorful timbres, and various instrumental techniques derived from jazz invigorated Copland's early compositions.

Perhaps the Great Depression of the 1930s sobered his approach; or perhaps by about 1930 Copland was simply ready to express a deeper, more introspective side of his inventive nature. His Piano Variations, composed during this period of economic austerity, is one of his finest though not one of his most popular compositions, a strong, uncompromising piece revealing Copland's keen intelligence and expert craftsmanship.

In the mid-1930s, however, disturbed by the apparent lack of effective communication between contemporary composers and the concert audience, Copland deliberately returned to a simpler style of composition. He became an influential lecturer and writer for the cause of new music, and together with another important American composer, Roger Sessions (1896–1985), organized a series of concerts for the purpose of promoting music by young, unknown American composers. Copland's own music of the 1930s and 1940s illustrated his belief that art music should appeal to a wide audience. Although he ceased to find jazz the stimulating influence it had been for him in the 1920s, he found new inspiration in other popular music of his own and other lands. He continued to use indigenous American materials—folk music, cowboy tunes, ragtime, and hymns—as a basis for much of his music; but like Bartók, he was interested in nationalism beyond that of his own country, and some of his compositions are based upon Mexican and Latin-American tunes.

Copland's asymmetrical and frequently changing rhythms show the influence of Igor Stravinsky as well as of various popular musics. He accompanied his attractive

Nadia Boulanger.
Stock Montage, Inc. Chicago

melodies with pungent dissonances, and the apparent simplicity of much of his music is quite deceptive. Though late in life he flirted with Schoenberg's twelve-tone technique, Copland's music is nearly always tonal, in the twentieth-century way. Copland believed in the composer's obligation to produce practical music, and in this vein produced some fine film scores, a children's opera, and a piece for high school orchestra.

Among the most famous of Copland's works is *Appalachian Spring,* a dance commissioned by the Martha Graham Dance Company, which won a Pulitzer Prize in 1945. Although called a ballet, *Appalachian Spring* is actually an example of **modern dance,** in which the steps, gestures, and costumes are more natural, or less stylized, than those of classical ballet. Copland originally titled the work simply *Ballet for Martha;* but Copland's music, which includes country fiddling and a set of variations on an early American hymn tune, reminded Martha Graham of a poem titled "The Bridge" by the American poet Hart Crane (1899–1932). Inspired by one section of this very long poem, "The Dance," in which the phrase "O Appalachian Spring!" occurs, the famous choreographer titled her dance, which depicts the daily activities of a bride and her farmer-husband, *Appalachian Spring.* A year later (1945), Copland extracted the most musically significant portions of *Appalachian Spring* to form an orchestral suite that has become one of his best-known and most popular works.

George Gershwin (1898–1937)

Whereas only a portion of Copland's music is nationalistic, **George Gershwin** always colored his music language with jazz-like effects, producing an unmistakably American sound. Gershwin wrote popular and art music with the same brilliant flair, flavoring both with a taste of jazz. Although he never wrote real jazz at all, many of his songs have become standards for jazz treatment by other musicians, while the jazzy timbres and rhythms of his *Rhapsody in Blue* have endeared that famous concert piece to music lovers all over the world.

3 13

LISTENING EXAMPLE 39

 3A 6

American Nationalism

Composer: Aaron Copland (1900–1990)

Title: Variations on "Simple Gifts" from *Appalachian Spring Suite*

Composed: 1944

Genre: Ballet suite

Form: Theme and variations

Timbre: Orchestra (piccolo, two flutes, two oboes, two clarinets, two bassoons, two horns, two trumpets, two trombones, percussion, two harps, piano, strings)

This set of five variations on a familiar Shaker tune forms the seventh (of eight) sections of the ballet. The folklike theme, to which early American Shakers sang a text beginning "'Tis a gift to be simple, 'tis a gift to be free," is introduced by a solo clarinet. The theme has two parts, the first half beginning with a rising inflection and the second half with a descending phrase.

		Theme; solo clarinet with simple accompaniment
13	0:00	a
0:16	0:16	b
0:29	0:29	brief transition
		Variation 1; played in a higher range by the oboe and bassoon; slightly faster tempo
14	0:33	a
0:13	0:46	b
		Variation 2
15	1:00	Ostinato accompaniment (harp and piano) introduces the next variation.
0:03	1:03	a Violas play the theme at half its former speed (a technique called **augmentation**).
0:17	1:17	a Violins and cellos play phrases of the theme in imitative polyphonic texture.
0:42	1:42	transition
		Variation 3
16	1:51	a Trumpets and trombones state the theme at twice the former speed (**diminution**), accompanied by rapid figures in the strings.
0:12	2:03	b
		Variation 4
17	2:15	b Slower and quieter, this variation gives the second part of the theme to the woodwinds.
		Variation 5
18	2:32	a The full orchestra plays the last variation, which is stately, majestic, slow in tempo, and fortissimo in volume.

Gershwin's *Porgy and Bess,* the best-known of all American operas, also is filled with the characteristic sounds of jazz, including syncopated rhythms, expressive vocal catches and slides, and imaginative instrumental timbres and techniques. The folklike character of this work—a white man's representation of the experience of poor southern blacks—and the rich variety of music it contains have made *Porgy and Bess* a worldwide favorite.

Throughout his tragically short career (he died of a brain tumor at age thirty-nine), Gershwin continued to bridge the gap between popular and art music. Other concert

A scene from
Gershwin's *Porgy
and Bess.*
Winnie Klotz, NY

works, including *An American in Paris* and a second *Rhapsody,* were followed by
more popular songs of the Broadway variety. His music has the warm expressiveness
of a romantic art, but his later works were more restrained and more clearly organized
than those of his youth. He was as impressed by the styles of Stravinsky, Schoenberg,
and Berg as he was by that of Beethoven. (Schoenberg indicated his reciprocal admiration for the young American composer by orchestrating Gershwin's Three Preludes for
Piano, composed shortly after *Porgy and Bess,* in 1936.)

Igor Stravinsky (1882–1971)

Igor Stravinsky found the plaintive sounds of his rich Russian folk heritage a source
of melodic, rhythmic, and harmonic inspiration. Born and reared in Russia during a
period of intense nationalism, Stravinsky neither forgot nor denied his Russian heritage, though he became a citizen of France and later of the United States.

The son of a well-known opera singer, Stravinsky heard serious European
music, as well as the folk tunes all Russian children know, from earliest childhood.
Forced by Russia's political atmosphere to leave his native land when he was
twenty-eight, Stravinsky traveled to Paris, where he became a part of the thriving
artistic community. In Paris he collaborated with Sergei Diaghilev (p. 234) to produce several short ballets, beginning in 1910 with *The Firebird,* based upon a Russian folk tale. The sensuous orchestration and exotic Russian nationalism of *The Fire-*

bird thrilled the sophisticated Paris audience; the next year, *Petrushka,* with its circus setting and fresh, intoxicating rhythms and harmonies, also captivated Paris. As we have seen, however, (pp. 234–235), the driving, restless rhythms, harsh dissonances, and unlovely story, costumes, and stage sets of *The Rite of Spring* caused a scandal when that ballet appeared, in 1913.

However, the Primitivism of *The Rite of Spring* had only brief relevance to Stravinsky's artistic intent, for like Picasso, Stravinsky continued throughout his long and productive life to seek new means of expression. Never satisfied with an accomplished success, he eventually explored nearly every musical idea of the twentieth century, including the rhythms and other characteristics of ragtime and jazz and—late in life—twelve-tone and serial technique.

This restless innovator and seeker of new paths generally is acknowledged as the father of the twentieth-century version of classicism in music, called **Neoclassicism.**

Neoclassicism

In 1919, Sergei Diaghilev suggested that Stravinsky write a ballet based upon some music of the eighteenth-century *opera buffa* composer Giovanni Battista Pergolesi, (p. 160), whose music strongly impressed Stravinsky with its clarity of design and economy of material and means. *Pulcinella*, the ballet inspired by this music of the Classical period, has been hailed as the introduction of the Neoclassical style, and although each of Stravinsky's compositions must be viewed in its own light, most of his later work reflects his undying faith in the principles of classicism. Even the several pieces Stravinsky wrote in the 1950s and '60s based upon twelve-tone technique represented only another means to Stravinsky's stated goal: the orderly and disciplined (or, the classical) organization of music.

Pul-chē-nel´-lah

Political, social, and economic problems during the second decade of this century encouraged the swing of the hypothetical style pendulum away from the excesses of Romanticism. Straitened circumstances forced composers to abandon the elaborate staging and grandiose conceptions of late Romantic works, as World War I strained budgets and rendered impractical the lavish production of operas and ballets. Consumers' tastes changed, too, during this period of apprehension, austerity, and deprivation, and a renewed interest developed in chamber music and in the great works of the pre-Romantic periods. The Neoclassical movement spurred an enthusiastic revival of the music of Haydn, whom the Romantics had not widely appreciated, and, paradoxically, of Bach, whose strong romantic characteristics have only recently been recognized. The highly structured forms, attractive melodies, firm tonal harmonies, and driving rhythms of the Baroque period particularly appealed to the Neoclassicists, who did not yet appreciate that period's romantic character. No one style has dominated the music of this century, but between World Wars I and II, Neoclassicism overshadowed all others.

Neoclassical composers, like the Classicists of the eighteenth century, preferred absolute, or abstract, music to programmatic concepts. The new discipline of musicology had produced more knowledge about the music of earlier periods than had ever before been available, and the Neoclassicists found the formal designs of the Classical, Baroque, and earlier periods well suited to their needs. The strong interest in form related the work of the Neoclassicists to that of the Cubist painters, whose work was also particularly important during this period.

In other respects, however, Neoclassical music had a refreshing, vigorous, twentieth-century sound. The Neoclassicists expanded the concept of tonality to include bitonal and polytonal chords and passages, and sometimes based their melodic and harmonic schemes upon modal or folk scales related to a tonal center. In other words, they respected the centrality of the tonic while abandoning the functional relationships of other notes to it. Orchestral works in the Neoclassical style were scored for relatively small ensembles, often containing more percussion and less string timbre than was typical of earlier orchestral music, and the new style of counterpoint was spacious and transparent in a manner related to the old style of the Middle Ages.

The small size of ensembles, clarity of formal designs, and basic simplicity of artistic concepts allowed a new intimacy to develop between composers, performers, and their audiences, who felt increasingly estranged from the music of their own time. Audiences appreciated the simplicity of melodic lines, the familiarity of tonal harmony, and the logic of orderly design offered by Neoclassical music. A preference for balanced designs and for emotional restraint was probably inevitable after the long period of Romanticism preceding the twentieth century, just as the renewed interest in counterpoint seemed inevitable after two centuries of predominantly homophonic music.

Sergei Prokofiev (1891–1953)

Pro-kaw´-fĕ-ef

Composers all over the Western world responded to Neoclassicism in their own way. As Russia expressly forbade outpourings of religious fervor, subjective commentary on the plight of the downtrodden Russian peasant, and experimentalism of any kind, many Russian composers adopted a restrained, basically classical approach to their art.

Sergei Prokofiev, composer of the delightful children's piece *Peter and the Wolf,* often revealed romantic tendencies in his music, for which he was chastised by critics and for which he dutifully apologized. However, his Symphony No. 1, subtitled *Classical,* is the prototype of a Neoclassical composition: the entire work lasts only about twelve minutes, each movement is clearly organized according to a Clas-

sical design, and the harmony is unquestionably—though unconventionally—tonal. Prokofiev claimed that he intended to write this symphony as Haydn would have written it in the twentieth century. Indeed, the orchestration is quite similar in size and instrumentation to that of Haydn's period, and Prokofiev has faithfully observed classical restraint and economy throughout the symphony. (The first movement, Listening Example 40, is a miniature sonata-allegro.) It is the character of the melodies and especially of the harmonies and certain harmonic progressions that identify the symphony as a modern work. One senses that Haydn might have been delightfully surprised, but not offended, at the twentieth-century characteristics of this charming piece.

Unlike the nineteenth-century Romantics, **Paul Hindemith** believed that composers bear specific responsibility to contemporary listeners. He therefore did not approve of music written purely for art's sake, or to serve the hypothetical pleasure of future generations, but advocated the composition of art music that would exist not only for its own sake but also to serve some need or desire of society. Hindemith wrote sonatas and solo concertos for instruments such as the tuba and the double bass, which seldom have solo opportunities, and composed music appropriate for amateur musicians and to be used for teaching purposes.

    The German word for Hindemith's concept of functional or useful music, ***Gebrauchsmusik,*** though coined in the twentieth century, could well have applied to the work of J. S. Bach two hundred years earlier; in fact, of all the composers in the history of Western music, it is to Bach that Hindemith was most closely related. Bach, too, was a practical musician who wrote to serve the needs of his church and community. Both Bach and Hindemith had diverse talents, performing, teaching,

Paul Hindemith (1895–1963)

Hin´-de-mit

Ge-browks´-mu-zēk

3 [19]

LISTENING EXAMPLE 40

 3A 7

Neoclassicism

Composer: Sergei Prokofiev (1891–1953)

Title: Symphony No. 1 *(Classical),* first movement

Composed: 1917

Rhythm: Allegro tempo; mostly duple meter

Form: Sonata allegro

Style: Neoclassicism

Timbre: Orchestra (two flutes, two oboes, two clarinets, two bassoons, two horns, two trumpets, timpani, strings)

exposition

[19]	0:00	first theme	(tonic key, D major)
. . . .		Main theme introduced in the strings (*ff, p*)	
0:12	0:12	Main theme again, in sequence, at a lower pitch level (C major)	
[20]	0:20	transition	(modulates)
. . . .		Begins with solo flute (*p*)	
0:09	0:29	Sequence (lower pitch level)	
[21]	0:48	second theme	(A major)
. . . .		Charming, elegant melody in violins that includes exhilarating two-	
. . . .		octave leaps; bassoon accompaniment (staccato)	
0:09	0:57	Theme 2 repeated	
0:21	1:09	Theme 2 a third time	
[22]	1:19	closing section (consists of repeated cadences, *ff*)	(A major)

development   (modulates)

[23]	1:31	First theme presented in minor mode.	
0:08	1:39	Transition material developed.	
0:26	1:57	Theme 2 developed (*ff*).	
0:48	2:19	Repeated cadences from the closing section lead directly to the	
. . . .		recapitulation.	

recapitulation

[24]	2:31	*first theme* (not repeated)	(C major)
[25]	2:39	*transition*	
[26]	3:00	*second theme*	(tonic key, D major)
[27]	3:25	*closing section*	(tonic key, D major)

writing prodigious quantities of music, and instilling in their music a warmth and intensity of feeling within rigorously controlled formal designs. Although Bach belonged to an essentially romantic age and Hindemith's style was predominantly classical, the two composers differed more in manner than in substance. Hindemith's skillful application of important forms of the Baroque era, including the fugue, the toccata, and the concerto grosso, led many to consider him the leader of a "back to Bach," or Neobaroque, movement.

Like so many of his colleagues, Hindemith explored more than one style of composition; but his basic philosophy of music was closely allied to that of the Classicists, and some of his compositions virtually exemplify the Neoclassical ideal. A superb craftsman who mastered every phase of his profession, Hindemith

Paul Hindemith.
AKG, Berlin

approached the composition of music more as a craft than as an art. He played many orchestral instruments well and therefore knew how to write effectively for them. A theorist as well as a practicing musician, he had strong opinions about harmony, about the proper role of the professional musician in society, and about the relationship between musicians and the audience and between music and the universe.

Hindemith's philosophy of music was related to that of the Greek and Medieval theorists, who believed that important symbolic relationships exist between music and various physical phenomena. He was interested in the doctrine of ethos (see pp. 52–53), and considered music to be part of a moral, spiritual, and physical universe. His famous symphony *Mathis der Maler* was taken from an opera he wrote concerning an artist's moral and ethical responsibilities to society. Tightly organized according to classical designs, the work is nevertheless romantic in expression and concept. Hindemith's *Kleinekammermusik* (*Little Chamber Music*), on the other hand, is clearly cast in the Neoclassical mold.

Klī-ne-kah´-mer-mu-zēk

Hindemith firmly believed that tonality was the natural, and the only rational, harmonic system, conforming to the laws of acoustics and to those of human perception. Since he believed that music was governed by moral and physical laws, he considered harmony a finite concept and held the continued search for something new in the field absurd. While Hindemith's tonality was clearly a twentieth-century concept, with biting, unresolved dissonances and unorthodox relationships between chords, nontonal systems held no interest for him whatever.

Neoromanticism

Meanwhile, romanticism was neither dead nor dormant. It remained particularly viable in America, where composers, unhampered by government restraint and accustomed to the relaxed manners and customs of their country, have often preferred an expansive, emotionally expressive style of music. While certain dissonances, a free adaptation of tonal principles, and nontraditional combinations of voices and instruments identify **Neoromantic** music as belonging to the contemporary period, the romantics of the twentieth century, like those of the nineteenth, prefer lyrical to motivic melodies and rich harmonies to a dry, contrapuntal texture. Their music, emotionally expressive and warmly personal, is often based upon a program, and their approach to design is less formal and more rhapsodic than that of classicists.

Samuel Barber (1910–1981)

Beginning in the 1920s, several American composers followed Aaron Copland to Paris to study with Nadia Boulanger; many of them were inclined toward the lyricism and subjectivity of a romantic style. **Samuel Barber,** who was a singer before he became a composer, wrote songlike melody lines for his instrumental and vocal compositions alike, which, together with his sensuous harmonies, sensitive text settings, and expressive orchestration, have made him one of the most accessible and appreciated composers of this century.

In particular, the slow movement of a string quartet written by Barber in 1936 aroused a warmly enthusiastic response from audiences. Barber therefore arranged that fervently expressive movement for a larger string ensemble, and it has become famous as an independent composition called *Adagio for Strings*. This quietly solemn piece, harmonically interesting but hardly bold, acknowledging tragedy while offering solace and rest, has taken a significant place in the American repertoire. It was played during the radio announcement of Franklin Delano Roosevelt's death in 1945, has been performed frequently at solemn state occasions since, and was used with outstanding effect in more than one recent feature film, including *The Elephant Man* (1980) and *Platoon* (Best Picture of the Year in 1986). It also remains a favorite piece of concert audiences.

Lukas Foss (b. 1922)

The music of Lukas Foss reflects the variety of interests and changes of style characteristic of many composers of this period. Born in Germany, Foss inherited a natural lyricism, a rich harmonic vocabulary, and the expansive, "boundaryless" approach to composition we associate with the German Romantic tradition; studying under Hindemith, he absorbed Neoclassic and Neobaroque characteristics of form and instrumentation; and arriving in America as a young man, he soon expressed appreciation for his new cultural setting by producing several "American nationalistic" compositions.

Foss, whose many works include operas, ballets, symphonies, cantatas, and piano compositions, has also written a kind of "controlled chance" music for the Improvisational Chamber Ensemble that he formed in the 1950s. The outlines of these compositions are clearly drawn in his own unconventional notation, but within these preplanned limitations the group, whose instrumentation varies, improvises freely. Yet the Romantic lyricism of his early works remains an apparent and endearing characteristic of some of his most recent compositions.

Minimalism

Many European and American composers have been influenced by the complexity of non-Western rhythms. But it is the systems that organize those rhythms (such as the tala, p. 318) that have intrigued the American composer **Philip Glass** (b. 1937), encouraging him to evolve a hypnotic, meditative style of music rooted in traditional Western concepts, but strongly affected by non-Western techniques. Glass studied in Paris with Nadia Boulanger, who, as we have seen, encouraged individualism in her students. He also traveled in North Africa and through parts of Asia, learning non-Western drumming techniques and absorbing the sounds of the Balinese gamelan

3 [28]   # LISTENING EXAMPLE 41   [📷] 3A 8

Neoromanticism

Composer: Samuel Barber (1910–1981)

Title: *Adagio for Strings*

Composed: 1936

Rhythm: Changing meter

Tempo: Adagio

Genre: Arranged for string orchestra from his String Quartet, 2nd movement

Form: Through-composed

Style: Neoromantic

Timbre: String Orchestra

[28]	0:00	Lyrical phrase (**a**) introduced by the violins; motive repeated in sequence at higher pitches; accompanied by soft and sensuous dissonances (*pp*)
0:23	0:23	Second phrase (**b**); ends on a lower pitch
0:49	0:49	Return to first phrase; altered to arrive at a higher pitch (**a´**)
1:11	1:11	These figures expand and evolve into an expressive melody consisting of long, asymmetrical phrases. The main phrases are heard in the violas (**a b a´**).
2:55	2:55	Beginning phrases presented (**a b**); cellos
3:40	3:40	The third phrase (**a´**) in cellos begins a buildup to the climax. Canonic imitation, consistently rising pitches, dramatic crescendos, and increasingly pungent dissonances steadily raise the level of tension.
5:18	5:18	Grand pause; immediate drop in pitch and dynamics
[29]	5:51	Return of opening phrases (**a b a**—abbreviated); violins and violas in octaves
[30]	6:10	Augmentation of main motive (violins) brings the piece to a peaceful ending (*pp*)

(pp. 230–231). As a result of these varied experiences and of his preference for a simple, direct, even naive musical language, Glass has evolved a style of music sometimes referred to by the term **minimalism.**

The hypnotic effect of Glass's music is achieved by the systematic repetition of short melodic and rhythmic phrases that change very gradually over a long period of time, evolving slowly into slightly varied patterns. (Compare Seurat's combination of dots of color in his famous painting of La Grande Jatte, p. 249.) Glass's melodies, narrow in range, are often accompanied by parallel harmonies, which add to the restful, meditative effect of his music. The composer has formed a distinctive ensemble, which he directs in performances of his own music, interpreting in practice and performance certain vague or ambiguous directions in his scores.

The music of **Steve Reich** (b. 1936), who is also often referred to as a minimalist, has an even more relaxed, soothing effect than that of Glass, because the alterations that evolve from repetition of the same and then of similar rhythmic and melodic patterns occur even more gradually. Although Reich, like Glass, has formed his own ensemble to perform his music, his scores differ from those of Glass in their exact notation and firm instructions. His refined, precise music often suggests an impersonal, detached attitude on the part of the composer as the music evolves inexorably from the patterns he has set in motion. Simple in conception, these patterns

Rīsh

Philip Glass.
Corbis-Bettmann

may become incredibly complex as two or more instruments (or tape loops, in some compositions) perform the same pattern out of phase with each other.

The Role of Women and Minorities

Women and members of various minority groups have made important contributions to the literature and performance of music of the twentieth century, as they have to the other arts. While still facing challenges irrelevant to their accomplishments in the arts, many have won the most prestigious prizes offered, and their gender, culture, or ethnicity is of less note than ever before.

Women have found acceptance as conductors, performers, and composers of music. Symphony orchestras have acquired large numbers of women players, and some are directed by women, although all of the major orchestras of the world have male conductors. The founder and conductor of the Boston Opera Company, Sarah Caldwell (b. 1928), was also the first woman to conduct at the Metropolitan Opera House.

Beverly Sills (b. 1929), for years a leading opera singer, is now the director of the prestigious New York City Opera Company. Leontyne Price (b. 1927), one of the best-known and best-loved concert and opera singers in the world, came from a musical family and studied at the Juilliard School of Music in New York City. She sang the role of Bess in George Gershwin's *Porgy and Bess,* touring through Europe with that all-African-American company, and has sung many important operatic roles at the Metropolitan in New York City and other opera houses around the world.

Ruth Crawford Seeger, Elisabeth Lutyens, and **Thea Musgrave** are among many women recognized today as important composers. In 1983 **Ellen Taaffe Zwilich** (b. 1939), who began composing at the age of ten, became the first woman to win the Pulitzer Prize for music, for her First Symphony. **Joan Tower** (b. 1938) also has achieved an international reputation as an outstanding composer of an impressive body of works for solo instruments, chamber ensembles, and orchestra.

William Grant Still (1895–1978), who came from a racially mixed family, found it difficult in his day to be taken seriously as a composer; to make a living, he worked as an arranger of popular music and played the violin, cello, or oboe in theater and nightclub orchestras. Yet he became the first black American to have a symphony performed by a major symphony orchestra and the first to have an opera produced by a major American company. His important contributions to American music consist of an impressive body of serious music, including two operas, three ballets, and several symphonic works. Still's intention was to express the Negro experience in American music, as he termed it, and several of his works have specific African-American effects—such as the use of a banjo in the third movement of his *Afro-American Symphony*.

Dean Dixon (1915–1976), a violinist, became probably the first black musician to achieve international recognition as a conductor of major orchestras. When only seventeen, he organized his own symphony orchestra and a choral society, and at the age of twenty-eight (in 1943), he became the first African American to conduct the New York Philharmonic Orchestra. A frequent guest conductor of other important American orchestras but never able to secure a permanent position in this country, Dixon went to Europe, where he conducted extensively and finally received a permanent position as conductor of a radio symphony in Germany. In 1970, Dixon conducted the New York Philharmonic in a summer concert series, receiving enthusiastic reviews.

An opera by the African American composer **Anthony Davis** (b. 1951), concerning the black nationalist leader Malcolm X, premiered in 1986 at the New York City Opera Company to an audience that responded with a standing ovation. The solo, chamber, religious, and symphonic repertoires also include significant compositions by black composers today.

Summary

Much of the music of our period is the result of an orderly, evolutionary progression. Classical or romantic in conception, its roots are firmly embedded in the music of the past.

Folk and other vernacular music have had an unprecedented effect upon the art music of our century. Having conducted a scientific study of the folk music of his own and of other lands, Béla Bartók assimilated their sounds into his own music personality. Aaron Copland used folk music in a more subjective manner, often with programmatic purpose and nationalistic intent. Darius Milhaud and other Europeans recognized the stimulating effects offered to art music by jazz even before Americans became aware of them.

From about 1920 to 1940, Neoclassicism was the predominant musical style, led by Stravinsky and adopted at least for a time by many important composers. However, romanticism is evident in many works composed before, during, and since that period. Stravinsky's *Rite of Spring,* whatever the composer's antiromantic intent, evokes a highly subjective response. The romantic concern for relationships between art and life expressed in Hindemith's *Mathis der Maler* made it a politically as well as emotionally sensitive work, and many of Prokofiev's late works reveal a romantic warmth and expressiveness. The twentieth-century nationalists, too, have continued a romantic tradition in a modern manner, while the same romantic spirit that caused Americans to lead the Experimental movement is also evident in the work of many mainstream American composers. Samuel Barber represents a long line of Americans who have continued to write in the Neoromantic style.

Schoenberg's revolutionary twelve-tone technique remained influential during the second quarter of this century. Stravinsky and Copland respected and experimented briefly with that method, but found tonality more congenial to their evolutionary tastes. For Hindemith, twelve-tone music simply confirmed his conviction that tonality was the only meaningful harmonic system. The concept of *Gebrauchsmusik* articulated by Hindemith has spurred the composition of many useful works, including attractive film scores, music to accompany radio programs and dance classes, music appropriate for performance by children or amateurs, music with a pedagogical purpose, music for the recently conceived symphonic band, and solo pieces for instruments that normally perform only in ensembles.

As today's musicians increasingly integrate the concepts and techniques of earlier cultures into their own compositions, we see that the music timeline might best be drawn in a circle, for some of the most important new sounds reflect very old music traditions from all over the world.

Critical Thinking

- Do you believe the evolutionary or the revolutionary approach to art has been of more significance in the twentieth century? Which do you think is likely to have the most lasting effect upon the arts? Why?

Terms to Review

mainstream   Term for the main body of work of a given period.

Les Six   Six French composers who, in the 1920s, reflected the strong influence of popular styles in their music.

musicology   The scientific study of music.

ethnomusicology   The study of the music of certain cultures.

modern dance   Contemporary dance form, usually performed barefoot, with steps, gestures, and costumes freely designed for each work.

augmentation   Rhythmic variation in which note values are doubled, making a theme twice as slow as in its original presentation.

diminution   Rhythmic technique in which note values are halved, making a theme twice as fast.

Neoclassicism   The twentieth-century version of classicism in music.

Gebrauchsmusik   Hindemith's term for "useful" music.

Neoromanticism   The twentieth-century version of a romantic approach to music composition.

minimalism   A style of music based upon many repetitions of simple melodic and rhythm patterns.

Key Figures

Composition Teacher	*Nadia Boulanger*	
Conductors	*Sarah Caldwell*	*Dean Dixon*
Performers	*Beverly Sills*	*Leontyne Price*
Composers	*Darius Milhaud*	*Béla Bartók*
	Aaron Copland	*George Gershwin*
	Igor Stravinsky	*Sergei Prokofiev*
	Paul Hindemith	*Samuel Barber*
	Lukas Foss	*Steve Reich*
	Ruth Crawford Seeger	*Elisabeth Lutyens*
	Thea Musgrave	*Joan Tower*
	Ellen Zwillich	*William Grant Still*
	Anthony Davis	

PART FIVE
Music in the Vernacular

V ernacular music is music in the common music language of the people, as opposed to music requiring study and practice for performance in a structured setting. However, although we recognize differences of style, purpose, and performance practice between the music we call "popular" and that we call "art," the terms are not mutually exclusive, each having influenced the other. Some melodies popular during the Renaissance period survive only because they were used in a Mass or other serious composition. Similarly, popular dances are reflected in the minuets of Bach and Mozart and the mazurkas of Chopin.

Popular music today draws from recent developments in the field of art music, and many composers of concert music find a wealth of ideas in the melodies, rhythms, timbres, and performance practices of folk and popular styles. Indeed, some music defies classification as popular, folk, or art. For example, some songs that Stephen Foster wrote for the popular minstrel stage have many characteristics of folk music; yet because they reflect the distinctive style of their creator and have survived the test of time, they must be considered art.

During the present century, as art music has proved increasingly challenging to listeners, popular music has proliferated at an unprecedented rate. Further, much of the popular music of this century already has demonstrated its appeal to succeeding generations of listeners—a characteristic traditionally associated with so-called classics. Operas have been written for the Broadway audience, and popular musicals often dispense with spoken dialogue and are sung throughout. This growing rapprochement between popular and art music suggests a healthy awareness that music of quality may be found in the worlds of popular, folk, *and* concert music; that musicians in all fields benefit from the contributions of those in others; and that the listening audience need not choose between them but rather may enjoy each, in turn, for the immeasurable riches it offers.

28
American Popular Music

Popular music is as varied as the population that produces it. Thus the wide realm of folk and popular vocal music includes love songs, songs for work and for play, songs about social and political conditions, patriotic songs, sea chanteys, and songs with texts of a religious nature, while dances, marches, and fiddle tunes constitute only a few examples of instrumental music in the vernacular. Each period, within each culture, preserves some traditions and contributes something new to the field of "people's music," and the art music of every age is enriched by elements drawn from the various vernacular styles.

Folk Music

Though **folk music** is difficult to define, since it changes from culture to culture and from one period of time to another, we usually consider folk music to fit one or more of the following descriptions:

a. music that seems to have originated spontaneously, or the origins of which have been lost or forgotten.
b. music expressing certain national characteristics of melody, harmony, rhythms, and performance practice.
c. music that is transmitted orally rather than by notation.
d. music that is performed and enjoyed by general audiences and professional musicians alike.

Folk music may be purely vocal, purely instrumental, or a song with an instrumental accompaniment. It is usually secular but may have religious meaning, as in the gospel tradition of American music and the beautiful African American spirituals. Although the origin of much folk music is indeed anonymous, the folk repertoire includes some pieces by composers who are, or were at one time, well known.

Ballads

Anonymous story songs called **ballads** form a well-known body of folk music. Handed down from one generation to another by aural rather than written tradition, famous ballads often exist in several versions, varying slightly in words and melody to suit a particular culture, time, or situation. Ballads are strophic in form, often including many verses, the better to prolong the entertainment.

Ballads surviving from the Middle Ages continue to delight listeners with their strong, often modal or pentatonic, tunes and their stirring tales of heroic action or romantic love. Many so-called American ballads actually came from the British Isles or other European countries and have been more or less altered to express the American experience. Among these is "Barbara Allen," a very old English ballad, sung to an appealing pentatonic tune, that has been lovingly preserved and adopted into the American repertoire. "Streets of Laredo," on the other hand, also originally an English ballad; has altered in text and even somewhat in melody to become part of the American cowboy song repertoire.

Folk and Art Music

Folk song has long been an important source of inspiration to German composers of art music, who have incorporated folk or folklike tunes in their most serious compositions. Many songs written for eighteenth-century *Singspiele* were so simple and tuneful that the German people consider them part of their folk tradition. Haydn and Schubert wrote attractive arrangements of German folk songs, and the melodies in their symphonic and other instrumental works are often folklike in their beautiful simplicity. Brahms, who declared his "ideal" music to be folk song, composed sensitive and appropriate arrangements of several folk songs and often reflected the folk influence in his concert music.

Around the turn of the twentieth century, the collection and examination of the world's folk music became a matter of scientific interest, as new technology made it possible to record folk music in its natural environment. Modern musicians, including Béla Bartók (pp. 267–268), eschewed the Romantics' sentimental approach to folk music but examined it objectively, finding its irregularities, which the Romantics often "corrected," refreshingly different from tired musical cliches. Published collections of folk music became valuable sources of ideas for composers around the world.

Folk and Popular Music

Two strains of folk music, one from the British Isles and one from Africa, have strongly affected popular music in America. British traditions preserved virtually intact in remote hill regions of the eastern United States seeped into the urban experience beginning in the early 1920s, as ballads, country dances, and other folk pieces brought from mountain and rural environments into American cities were recorded for commercial purposes. They soon attracted a city audience, who found them refreshingly different from standard commercial fare. Popular musicians recorded the old music and soon began composing new songs and pieces in the country tradition, introducing a new kind of popular music, first called "hillbilly" and later called **country-western.** As cowboy songs and the music composed for movie westerns beginning in the late 1930s were incorporated into the new genre, people lost track of which were genuine folk pieces and which were recently composed songs in the folk style.

The British influence also had a strong effect upon the folk revival in the 1950s and 1960s, although this "folk" music was of a commercial, urban, and highly professional variety. Musicians involved in this popular movement, such as Joan Baez, Judy Collins, Bob Dylan, and Pete Seeger, composed and performed songs based upon the style of traditional English, Scotch, and Irish folk ballads, while Burl Ives presented traditional folk songs in his own inimitable manner. Popular groups such as the Kingston Trio; Peter, Paul, and Mary; and the Limelighters performed their own folklike renditions in concert halls and on college campuses to wildly enthusiastic audience response. Though not folk in the traditional sense, their music was similar in sound and spirit to the folk music from which it derived. This commercial brand of folk music declined in popularity during the 1970s but revived in the early 1980s and continues to entertain new generations of enthusiasts.

The music of black Africa also has contributed richly to the music of America. A traditional **call-and-response** pattern of singing, in which a leader sings the first line or a verse of a song to which a group responds with a chorus or refrain, formed the framework for the African American **spirituals.** Some of these religious folk songs are hauntingly beautiful in their expression of the loneliness and pain of an oppressed people; others are filled with irrepressible rollicking good humor. Certain expressive vocal techniques, including swoops, slides, and shouts as well as melodically inflected **blue notes,** slightly above or below normal pitch, and the

characteristic "hot" rhythms of African music—all have had a profound effect upon jazz, gospel music, rhythm-and-blues, and eventually rock.

Ragtime, a popular piano music based upon black traditions, marked a particularly important step toward jazz.

Ragtime

During the 1890s, a number of gifted African American pianists began improvising a rollicking new music, consisting of a syncopated melody in the right hand accompanied by a steady beat in the bass. Soon they were publishing pieces called *rags,* which they intended to be played exactly as they were written. Therefore, since jazz normally involves improvisation, **ragtime** is generally considered a pre-jazz music rather than a form of jazz itself. (You may wish to review Listening Example 2, p. 12.)

The syncopated rhythm of a rag is related to that of a favorite dance of nineteenth-century blacks, called the *cakewalk,* whose characteristic pattern of beats— short-LONG-short—is often heard in ragtime compositions. Late-nineteenth-century minstrel shows, in which cakewalk dancing was a standard feature, also typically included banjo performances of plantation melodies played with the syncopated rhythm of the cakewalk, in a manner very close to that which came to be known as ragtime.

Although conceived as piano music, the irresistible rags were soon being played by informal street bands as well, and many Europeans were introduced to ragtime by the traveling United States Marine Band, led by John Philip Sousa. Ragtime in fact follows the form and has the steady duple meter of a military march. It is best performed at a moderate tempo, since a desperately fast pace lessens its dignity and dilutes its characteristic "strut." The king of ragtime, Scott Joplin, specifically marked his rags to be played "not fast."

Scott Joplin (1868–1917)

Scott Joplin, a talented and highly trained musician, was denied achievement of his fondest goals by the circumstances of his time. Although remembered today as the king of ragtime, Joplin's overwhelming desire in his later life was to produce a successful black-American opera.

Thus, having written and published many beautiful rags, Joplin composed at least two operas, one of which, *Treemonisha,* survives in its complete piano score.

Scott Joplin.
(1868–1917)
Corbis-Bettmann

(That is, we know the notes and the words, but his intended instrumentation has been lost.) Joplin used his opera, for which he wrote the words as well as the music, as a vehicle to preach his creed that African Americans must pursue education as a means toward prosperity and independence. Interestingly, he chose as the highly attractive and compelling leader of the people in his show a young African American woman.

The colorful, appealing *Treemonisha* was hardly known in Joplin's time, because audiences were not interested in operas by Americans and could hardly conceive of one by a black composer; however, the opera has been recorded and performed in recent years to appreciative audiences and reviews.

Ragtime had an important effect upon European composers of art music. Debussy found refreshment and stimulation in the exotic characteristics of ragtime, and "Golliwog's Cakewalk," from Debussy's piano suite called *Children's Corner,* is a humorous example of a European musician's appreciation for the new form. Other Europeans, including Eric Satie, Paul Hindemith, and Igor Stravinsky, also wrote piano rags or reflected their influence in some of their concert music. As talented pianists began to add improvisations to their performances of written rags, and as ragtime became more versatile and more sophisticated, it closely approached the music we call jazz. (See chapter 29.)

Evolution of Rock 'n' Roll

The sweetly sentimental songs of pre- and early World War II days meant nothing to American adolescents of the 1950s. More numerous and with more money to spend than any preceding teenage group in history, they needed their own music expressing *their* experiences, frustrations, and general rebelliousness. A fortuitous melding of two popular styles, one black and one white, produced an astonishing new vernacular music, as rock 'n' roll erupted in America, of and for American youth.

Both *country-western* and *rhythm-and-blues* were comprehensive terms encompassing a wide range of sounds. Country-western musicians had absorbed such various influences as the Hawaiian steel guitar, mariachi brass, Swiss yodel, Cajun dialect, bagpipe drone, and British ballad, finding all of these and more congenial to the country sound. The popular black music called **rhythm-and-blues,** combining twelve-bar blues with a strong "square" beat, a heavy **backbeat** (accents on two and four of the bar), and frank, earthy, even explicitly sexual lyrics, also had an intense, vibrant, highly distinctive character. Both country-western and r&b—rooted in the South, glorifying the guitar, featuring frank lyrics delivered in an earthy style in dialects different from that of the standard white urban population—lay outside the mainstream of American popular music.

As young blacks and whites experienced unprecedented association in the armed forces and in urban life during World War II, white youths found themselves attracted by the stirring sounds of rhythm-and-blues, to which they had not previously been exposed. Soon a few country-western musicians, led by Elvis Presley and Bill Haley, began to sing and perform in a style similar to rhythm-and-blues and to make recordings, called **covers,** of rhythm-and-blues hits. These were given wide exposure on major radio stations, as the original r&b hits were not, and the cover recordings soon became popular with a broad, mixed audience.

The term **rock 'n' roll** was coined by a radio disc jockey, who simply combined two sexually suggestive terms frequently used in rhythm-and-blues lyrics. The piano pounding of Little Richard, pelvic gyrations of Elvis Presley, and glittering costumes of growing numbers of rock 'n' roll performers thrilled mobs of screaming American youngsters, who indeed had found a music of their own.

The Beatles in 1963. Included left to right: bass guitarist Paul McCartney, guitarist George Harrison, guitarist John Lennon, and drummer Ringo Starr.

AP/Wide World

British Invasion

British youngsters were listening, too, preferring the roots of rock 'n' roll—the raw blues of the Negro past and the more recent rhythm-and-blues—to the tame white covers of r&b hits. By the mid-sixties, the music of the young Beatles—good-natured, exuberant, innocent ("I wanna hold your hand")—had become wildly popular on both sides of the Atlantic, revitalizing rock 'n' roll.

This unlikely group of largely untrained British teenagers proved to be incredibly talented musicians with genuinely eclectic interests, who matured into a highly polished, sophisticated, professional team. As they absorbed many of the influences affecting concert musicians of the time, including the sounds and styles of non-Western cultures and the theories of John Cage, their lyrics became less innocent, their rhythms more complex, their melodies modal, and their instrumentation widely varied.

From Rock 'n' Roll to Rock

As Elton John, The Who, the Rolling Stones, and numerous other English soloists and groups stimulated Americans, black and white, to return to the basics of rock 'n' roll, the new music matured to the broad field of music collectively called *rock*. Like country-western and rhythm-and-blues, rock has become a generic term embracing a wealth of sounds and styles; but certain characteristics distinguish rock from jazz and other popular music.

For example, in the 1950s and 1960s, rock was dominated by performance groups rather than the solo idols of jazz, country, and pop. Rock musicians wrote much of their own material instead of relying upon professional songwriters. Their melodies were often modal, their lyrics characteristically asymmetrical, their instrumentation derived from country-western and rhythm-and-blues, their beat heavy and unvaried, and their volume loud. Whereas jazz musicians excelled as virtuosic

Redferns, London

The rap group Public Enemy in performance. The emergence of this popular urban style has once again raised questions about the relationship between art, politics, and public morality, first considered by the Greeks more than two thousand years ago.

interpreters of given music, rock musicians' talent lay primarily with the original material they composed.

Rap

A recent and controversial rock music that evolved in the 1970s, **rap** counts among its influences African chanting, James Brown's spoken blues, disc jockeys' patter, and the boasting poetry of Muhammad Ali. The music's basic element is, in fact, the spoken word delivered rapidly in rhymed verses. (Compare the patter song, p. 217.) **Hip-hop,** as the music behind the rapped lyrics is called, has its roots in "toasting," a manner of making music by speaking over records introduced by Jamaican disc jockeys.

Music appreciation students at Northeastern Oklahoma Art and Music College recently wrote to the author: "Rap contains all the passion, love, anger, and joy of human emotion. . . . Although the lyrics of some of today's groups are controversial, rap music, like any other music, is only a vehicle of expression, and the message depends on what the rapper is trying to convey, whether feelings of joy and humor, a political message, or frustration at . . . prejudice and discrimination [in society]."

Toward the Future

Dismissed by the unconverted in early days as a fad, scorned much as jazz had been scorned in the 1920s, rock soared in popularity and for a time virtually eclipsed other popular styles. Now a sense of balance seems finally to have been achieved, and jazz, country-western, folk, and middle-of-the-road pop are appreciated today, each for its own qualities.

Meanwhile, rock musicians have evolved a complex and increasingly sophisticated array of sounds; today rock instrumentation, which includes electronic techniques and non-Western effects, is virtually unlimited. So many styles exist that rock cannot be easily categorized, though a hard beat, loud volume, and dependence upon sound engineering technology generally distinguish rock from other forms of popular music.

Conceived as music by and for youth, rock now offers provocative inspiration to composers of music for film, dance, church, concert hall, and the theater.

The earliest **musical comedies** faced stiff competition, ranging from crudely hilarious vaudeville shows to sophisticated European and American operettas. But as American enthusiasm for European products waned during World War I, a new confidence developed in our own artistic talents, and the new musical comedies, combining the entertainment of vaudeville with the integrated plot characteristic of operettas, proved irresistible if unsophisticated fun.

The earliest musical to have made a profound and lasting impact on audiences and critics alike was *Show Boat,* with words by Oscar Hammerstein II (1895–1960) and music by **Jerome Kern** (1885–1945). Accustomed to musical comedies consisting of songs and variety acts barely held together by a loose plot, audiences and critics were amazed that *Show Boat* (1927), based on a novel by an established literary figure (Edna Ferber), dealt with a sensitive social topic: relations between blacks and whites. Jerome Kern's beautiful music for that show retains its appeal yet today, but it was not until the 1940s that the revolutionary concept of a literature-based musical became the norm for musicals. We can cite a few examples: *South Pacific* was based on a novel by James Michener; *Kiss Me Kate* and *West Side Story* on Shakespeare plays; *The King and I* on an autobiography; *Cats* on poems by T. S. Eliot; and *Phantom of the Opera* and *Les Miserables* on French novels. You could name many more.

Oscar Hammerstein later collaborated with the gifted and prolific composer **Richard Rodgers** (1902–1979) to produce another landmark show, *Oklahoma!* (1943), in which lyricist and composer demonstrated their shared concept that all elements of entertainment—songs, dances, instrumental pieces—should be closely integrated with the plot of a musical. They thereby ushered in a new kind of music

Evolution of Musicals

Golden Age of Broadway Musicals

Scene from Leonard Bernstein's *West Side Story.*
The Kobal Collection

3 31   # LISTENING EXAMPLE 42   3A 9

Music Theater Ensemble

Composer: Leonard Bernstein (1918–1990)

Title: "Tonight" Ensemble from *West Side Story*

Composed: 1957

Genre: Ensemble from a musical

Rhythm: Fast and rhythmic; changing meters

Melody: Several different melodies are heard, each representing the various emotions of the characters involved.

Timbre: Vocal ensemble with orchestra

In this quintet, Riff and Bernardo make their own plans for the rumble; Anita, Bernado's girlfriend, sings of her plans
for a "hot" date that evening, and Tony and Maria sing blissfully of their love for each other. In a setting similar to
that of operas, Bernstein allows each character to sing separately before combining them in an exciting ensemble.

Ensemble

31   0:00   *Brief orchestra introduction; abrupt, loud and syncopated*
RIFF (*mezzo piano*)
The Jets are gonna have their day
Tonight.
BERNARDO
The Sharks are gonna have their way
Tonight.
RIFF
The Puerto Ricans grumble,
"Fair Fight."
But if they start a rumble,
We'll rumble 'em right.
SHARKS
We're gonna hand 'em a surprise
Tonight.
JETS
We're gonna cut 'em down to size
Tonight.
SHARKS
We said, "O.K., no rumpus,
No tricks."
But just in case they jump us,
We're ready to mix
Tonight!
BOTH (*forte*)
We're gonna rock it tonight,
We're gonna jazz it up and have us a ball!
They're gonna get it tonight;
The more they turn it on, the harder they fall!
JETS (*fortissimo*)
Well, they began it!
SHARKS
Well, they began it—

BOTH
And we're the ones to stop 'em once and for all,
Tonight.

|32| 1:05 ANITA (*saxophone introduction*)
Anita's gonna get her kicks
Tonight.
We'll have our private little mix
Tonight.
He'll walk in hot and tired,
So what?
Don't matter if he's tired,
As long as he's hot
Tonight!

|33| 1:25 TONY (*expressive melody, lyrical, legato*)
Tonight, tonight
Won't be just any night,
Tonight there will be no morning star.
Tonight, tonight,
I'll see my love tonight
And for us, stars will stop where they are.

(strings
imitate
vocal
melody)
Today
The minutes seem like hours,
The hours go so slowly
And still the sky is light . . .
Oh moon, grow bright,

(*crescendo*)
And make this endless day endless night!
(*Orchestra interlude, fortissimo*)
RIFF (to Tony)
I'm counting on you to be there
Tonight.
When Diesel wins it fair and square
Tonight.
That Puerto Rican punk'll
Go down.
And when he's hollered Uncle
We'll tear up the town!

|34| 2:39 Maria sings the lyrical "Tonight" while Riff and Tony have their own discussion.

MARIA	RIFF
Tonight, tonight	So I can count on you, boy?
	TONY
Won't be just any night,	All right.
	RIFF
Tonight there will be no morning star.	We're gonna have us a ball.
	TONY
	All right . . .
	RIFF
	Womb to tomb!
	TONY
	Sperm to worm!
	RIFF
	I'll see you there about eight . . .
	TONY
	Tonight . . .
	BERNARDO and SHARKS
Tonight, tonight,	We're gonna rock it tonight!!!

3 35   # LISTENING EXAMPLE 42   3A 10

Continued

35	2:25	*Voices combine in ensemble; each presents his/her own emotion in the drama.*

Voices combine in ensemble; each presents his/her own emotion in the drama.

BERNARDO and SHARKS

We're gonna jazz it tonight!

(augmentation)   They're gonna get it tonight, tonight!

They began it, they began it

And we're the ones

To stop 'em once and for all!

(pianissimo;   The Sharks are gonna have their way,

crescendo)   The sharks are gonna have their day,

We're gonna rock it tonight,

Tonight!

ANITA

Tonight,

Late tonight,

We're gonna mix it tonight.

Anita's gonna have her day,

Bernardo's gonna have his way

Tonight, tonight.

(pianissimo;   Tonight, this very night,

crescendo)   We're gonna rock it tonight!

RIFF and JETS

They began it, they began it.

We'll stop 'em once and for all!

(pianissimo;   The Jets are gonna have their way,

crescendo)   The Jets are gonna have their day.

We're gonna rock it tonight,

Tonight!

MARIA

I'll see my love tonight.

And for us, stars will stop where they are.

Today the minutes seem like hours,

The hours go so slowly,

And still the sky is light . . .

(pianissimo;   Oh moon, grow bright,

crescendo)   And make this endless day endless night!

Tonight!

TONY

Today the minutes seem like hours,

The hours go so slowly,

And still the sky is light . . .

(pianissimo;   Oh moon, grow bright,

crescendo)   And make this endless day endless night!

Tonight!

All voices come together on the word "Tonight," fortissimo

theater. Rodgers and Hammerstein went on to write *Carousel* (1945), *South Pacific* (1949) , *The King and I* (1951), and *The Sound of Music* (1959).

Leonard Bernstein (1918–1990), a pianist, conductor, and composer primarily associated with concert music, also made significant contributions to the Broadway musical. Choreographer Jerome Robbins ingeniously worked the wonderful dance sequences in Bernstein's *West Side Story* (1957), a retelling of Shakespeare's *Romeo and Juliet,* into the drama, where they seem an integral rather than an interruptive element of the show. The story is set in the streets of mid-twentieth-century uptown New York City; and though this Juliet (Maria in Bernstein's show) does not die, the aura of tragedy is palpable from the moment the curtain rises at the beginning of the musical. The rough language, realistic characters, lyrical music, and stunning dance sequences had an overpowering effect on Broadway and have become familiar to untold numbers of people through the movie version of the show.

The ensemble finale, or final scene, in Act I of *West Side Story*, in which several characters express their individual points of view simultaneously (Listening Example 42), vividly illustrates the musical and dramatic impact of the music theater ensemble. A gang of assorted Americans, the Jets, have challenged the rival Puerto Rican gang, the Sharks, to a rumble (fight) "tonight." As the finale begins, the Jets and the Sharks, each gang singing in unison, make excited threats to destroy each other.

Search for New Directions

Several shows in the sixties and seventies, including *Grease* (1972), *Hair* (1967), and *Godspell* (1971), were based upon rock music, as were three English shows billed as rock operas: *Jesus Christ Superstar* (1971) and *Joseph and the Amazing Technicolor Dreamcoat* (1981), with music by the British composer Andrew Lloyd Webber and words by Tim Rice, and *Tommy* (1969), by The Who. Yet the rock audience and the Broadway crowd have not been generally congenial. *Rent,* a show whose British composer, Jonathan Larson, died just before its 1996 opening, intriguingly mixes and matches vernacular music (reggae, gospel, rhythm-and-blues, hard rock, and pop ballads) with classical forms. This retelling of the nineteenth-century Italian opera *La Bohéme* (see p. 210), which seems to appeal to members of both artistic spheres, won the 1996 Pulitzer prize for drama.

Black musical theater, strong in the 1920s but with only intermittent successes in succeeding decades, returned to the fore in the seventies and eighties. Shows included a black interpretation of *The Wizard of Oz* called *The Wiz;* an all-black version of *Guys and Dolls,* and the all-black revue *Bubbling Brown Sugar,* featuring fondly remembered melodies by "Fats" Waller, Duke Ellington, and Eubie Blake, among others; *Dream Girls,* and, opening in 1996, a version of African American history told in song and dance titled *Bring in 'da Noise, Bring in 'da Funk.*

The outstanding American composer of musicals in recent decades is **Stephen Sondheim** (b. 1930), whose **concept musicals,** such as *Pacific Overtures* and *Company,* intentionally leave audiences wondering about their meaning and resolution. Most popular on the Broadway musical stage today are shows by the British composer **Andrew Lloyd Webber,** whose *Cats, Phantom of the Opera, Aspects of Love, Starlight Express,* and *Sunset Boulevard* have broken all records on both sides of the Atlantic for attendance and recording sales.

Summary

Vernacular music of the twentieth century is of unprecedented quality and significance. While art music has long been enriched by reference to vernacular forms, we now witness even closer interaction between popular and concert styles. As definitions of music genres have become increasingly ambiguous, the difference between art and vernacular is not always clearly drawn. Folk music, traditionally of anonymous origin, may refer to published pieces related in style and subject matter to the spontaneous folk creations of earlier times. Folk ballads were incorporated into the popular music field, and the folklike ballads of country-western music were then composed for commercial purposes.

Ragtime has characteristics of jazz rhythms and moods, but does not involve improvisation and so constitutes a precursor of jazz.

Rock 'n' roll evolved from a combination of the effects of country-western music and rhythm-and-blues. As country-western musicians became rich on cover recordings of r&b hits, English groups and soloists revitalized rock, bringing it back to its roots. Today the instrumentation, forms, moods, and styles of rock are richly varied and increasingly influential upon other music, including music theater.

The earliest musical comedies blended the light entertainment of vaudeville with a loosely integrated plot; but led by the examples of *Show Boat* and *Oklahoma!,* the Broadway musical stage produced many sophisticated shows with music of lasting quality, especially in the 1940s and 1950s. Stephen Sondheim is the current outstanding American composer of musicals, but most popular on Broadway today are musicals by two English composers, Andrew Lloyd Webber and Jonathan Larson.

Critical Thinking

- Can you suggest some reasons why Americans seem to have less interest in their folk music than the members of many other Western and non-Western cultures?

- We often speak of concert music as a "cultural" experience. Do you think that vernacular music is also representative of a society's culture? Why do scientists speak of the growth of bacteria in a nurturing substance as a "culture"? To put it another way, what does the word "culture" mean to you?

- Why do you suppose England has been so influential upon both American rock and the Broadway musical stage?

Terms to Review

folk music   Usually music of unknown origin, transmitted orally, and enjoyed by the general population. Today the term is applied to some popular music that has the style or flavor of folk art.

ballad   A folk song, strophic in form, that tells a story.

country-western   American vernacular music rooted in the South, glorifying the guitar and featuring frank lyrics delivered in an earthy style in southern or country dialect.

call-and-response   A solo voice alternating with a chorus.

spiritual   A folklike religious song, with a simple tune, developed by African Americans.

blue notes Flexible tones, chosen subjectively from between the half steps of tonal scales.

ragtime A popular piano style in which a syncopated melody is accompanied by a regular duple pattern in the bass.

rhythm-and-blues Broadly, black popular music of the 1950s. More specifically, a black popular style in quadruple meter with strong backbeats and in danceable tempo.

backbeat Heavy accent on the normally weak second and fourth beats in quadruple meter.

cover A re-recording, for commercial purposes, as in a recording by white musicians of a rhythm-and-blues hit.

rock 'n' roll A popular style developed in the early 1950s from the combination of country-western and rhythm-and-blues characteristics.

rap Rapid spoken patter accompanied by hip-hop music.

hip-hop The music behind rapped lyrics.

musical comedy A musical show combining the entertainment of vaudeville with the integrated plot characteristic of operettas.

concept musical A musical show presenting ideas subject to the audience's interpretation and leaving situations unresolved.

Key Figures

Composers	*Scott Joplin*	*Jerome Kern*
	Richard Rodgers	*Leonard Bernstein*
	Stephen Sondheim	*Andrew Lloyd Webber*
	Jonathan Larson	
Performers	*Elvis Presley*	*Bill Haley*
	Beatles	
Lyricist	*Oscar Hammerstein II*	
Choreographer	*Jerome Robbins*	

29

Jazz

While other American music is plainly derivative, however characteristic of American culture it has become, **jazz** is often referred to as America's truly indigenous music, unique to its culture and influential upon those of other nations. The Broadway musical was modeled upon the European operetta, and even minstrel shows, which contributed to the evolution of the Broadway musical, were performed in England before they became popular here in the mid–nineteenth century. Jazz, on the other hand, originated in America and is considered uniquely representative of the American personality, or soul. Its deepest roots lie in African cultures, but it was black Americans who created the important pre-jazz styles of ragtime and the blues, and who developed jazz itself in the early years of the twentieth century.

Jazz, which represents the unique blending of certain rhythmic and melodic techniques and performance practices of West Africa with Western harmony and instrumentation, is a generic term encompassing an extremely broad range of music styles. It soon became a sophisticated, urban music, eminently suited to the hectic pre– and post–World War I years. Americans responded to its refreshing timbres and danceable beat, and many Europeans enjoyed its informal, irreverent, uniquely American sounds.

Each kind of jazz has unique characteristics, but they all share certain basic concepts. There is normally a regular meter, usually duple; there is usually syncopation or some other form (hesitations, anticipations) of "play against the beat"; the melodies often include flexible tones called blue notes; and there is some degree of improvisation. A jazz performance is often based upon a preexisting tune that the musicians alter or paraphrase as they follow a chart of predetermined patterns of chord changes. Jazz harmony is mostly tonal, although jazz musicians are constantly expanding their harmonic concepts, some recently having shown interest in the occasional use of polytonality and even certain modal effects. Jazz rhythms are exciting and may be quite complex, slight hesitations and anticipations immeasurably enhancing the rhythmic interest of a performance. While some rhythmic effects are subtle and restrained, others produce the intoxicating "hot" rhythms that nearly compel an overt physical response from the listener. The mood of jazz may be bright or blue, the tempo fast or slow, the instrumentation large or small, and the concept simple or highly complex. Their increasing awareness of characteristics of non-Western music and of contemporary developments in Western art music offers jazz musicians new sources of harmonic, melodic, and instrumental ideas.

Blues

The **blues** evolved in the American South sometime after the Civil War, as newly emancipated blacks struggling in a hostile environment lamented their hard lot in a new, highly expressive form of solo song. Closely related to certain West African folk traditions, the blues became a kind of black-American folk song, evolving eventually from its unpretentious beginnings to become an important, sophisticated, and

Statement: "Hard times here, worse ones down the road."

Repetition: "Hard times here, worse ones down the road."

Response: "Wish my man was here to share the load."

Figure 29.1

A typical twelve-bar verse.

Chords

Line 1	I	–	–	–
Line 2	IV	–	I	–
Line 3	V	–	(IV)	I

Figure 29.2

Chord structure of the twelve-bar blues.

highly influential American music. The blues also may be seen as an early manifestation of jazz.

The mood of the blues, usually one of lament, is often leavened by a wry humor; the words are frank and matter-of-fact, rather than sentimental or oppressively sad. The third, seventh, and occasionally fifth notes of the blues scale are variable in pitch, slightly flatted or "bent" subject to the interpretation of each performer. Their very elusiveness is one of the most expressive characteristics of these blue ("tired," "worried," or "bent") notes, which have colored many forms of Western art and popular music since African Americans introduced them to the West.

The classic form of the blues is strophic, with each verse or stanza containing the unusual number of three lines in the order A A B: statement, repetition, and response (see figure 29.1). A simple harmonic structure consisting of tonic, dominant, and subdominant chords has become standard. Although the chords of the pattern are the most basic chords in tonal harmony (see figure 29.2), the order in which they occur in the last line of a twelve-bar blues is distinctive: that is, IV often goes directly or through V to I, but V does not normally go to IV (review figure 4.2, p. 23).

In time, as the blues became recognized as a form of entertainment as well as self-expression, blues singers often were accompanied by one or more musical instruments. Each line of a blues stanza has four measures or "bars" of music, though the text requires only 2 or 2½ bars, leaving a "break," or extra time, at the end of each line when a singer may sing neutral syllables, or **scat,** or an accompanying instrument may improvise a response to or commentary on the vocal phrase.

The cornet's emotionally expressive commentary at the end of each line of "Lost Your Head Blues" (Listening Example 43) illustrates the interaction and competition between voice and accompanying instrument(s) that led to increasing contrapuntal complexities in blues performances.

Instrumental Jazz

As instruments assumed more and more significant roles in blues performance, the logical next step in the evolution of jazz was the development of an instrumental blues, in which piano players simply transferred the twelve-bar form and harmonic structure of the blues to their instrument. Unlike the vocal form, however, the piano blues, or **boogie-woogie,** is happy in mood, brisk in tempo, and eminently danceable. The syncopated melody of a boogie, which is freely improvised and embellished, is accompanied by a left-hand ostinato that subdivides the four beats of each measure into eight pulses, usually in the pattern LONG-short-LONG-short-LONG-short-LONG-short. Exciting cross-rhythms reminiscent of African music often result from combining the syncopated melody in the right hand and this "eight-to-the-bar" pattern in the left.

3 36   # LISTENING EXAMPLE 43   3A 10

Blues

Composer: Bessie Smith (ca. 1894–1937)

Title: "Lost Your Head Blues"

Recorded: May 4, 1926

Genre: Blues

Form: Strophic; twelve-bar blues (a a b)

Rhythm: Quadruple meter

Harmony: Entirely based upon the I, IV, and V chords

Accompaniment: The increasingly eloquent and virtuosic cornet emphasizes and enhances the poignancy of the text, while the piano's dissonant (bluesy) chords mark the rhythm and hold the tempo steady.

Performers: Bessie Smith, voice; Joe Smith, cornet; Fletcher Henderson, piano

36	0:00	**Introduction** (cornet, piano)
37	0:11	**Verse 1**
. . . .		a I was with you, Baby, when you didn't have a dime.
. . . .		a I was with you, Baby, when you didn't have a dime.
. . . .		b Now since you got plenty of money, you have throwed your good gal down.
38	0:43	**Verse 2**
. . . .		a Once ain't for always, two ain't for twice.
. . . .		a Once ain't for always, two ain't for twice.
. . . .		b When you get a good gal, you better treat her nice.
39	1:15	**Verse 3**
. . . .		a When you were lonesome, I tried to treat you kind.
. . . .		a When you were lonesome, I tried to treat you kind.
. . . .		b But since you got money, it done changed your mind.
40	1:47	**Verse 4**
. . . .		a I'm gonna leave, Baby; ain't gonna say goodbye.
. . . .		a I'm gonna leave, Baby; ain't gonna say goodbye.
. . . .		b But I'll write you and tell you the reason why.
41	2:24	**Verse 5**
. . . .		a Days are lonesome; nights are long.
. . . .		a Days are lonesome; nights are so long.
. . . .		b I'm a good ol' gal, but I've just been treated wrong.

Other jazz piano styles, often highly individualistic, soon evolved, concurrently with music for small jazz ensembles, or **combos.** Beginning soon after the Civil War, African Americans in the New Orleans area had been forming brass bands to play for parades, concerts, and even funerals. In time their instrumental techniques became more individual, the tempos faster, the mood high-powered and intense. Some of these musicians read music; most did not, but improvised freely.

Each player in a small jazz ensemble or combo has solo responsibilities, and together they form a tight, virtuosic group. The rhythm section, which improvises and accompanies at the same time, usually includes a string bass or electric bass guitar, drums and cymbals, and a piano and/or other instrument such as a guitar, banjo, or organ that plays chords. The role of the bass, traditionally plucked to emphasize the rhythm and to clarify the harmonies by playing important notes of the supporting

chords, has recently expanded to sometimes engaging in musical "conversations" with the other instruments. The piano emphasizes syncopated rhythms by playing chords that support and stimulate the improvising soloists. The drummer plays a variety of drums and cymbals, adding a wide range of timbres to the performance. The solo instruments may include saxophones, trumpets, trombones, clarinets, and, since the 1950s, flutes, as well as a wide variety of other instruments. (The saxophone, a single-reed instrument, comes in four common sizes: soprano, alto, tenor, and baritone. Invented in the mid-nineteenth century, the saxophone was first considered a band instrument and then became associated with popular music, especially jazz. Recently, some composers have included the saxophone in their symphonic music.)

New Orleans Jazz

The first important center of jazz was in New Orleans, Louisiana, where **"Jelly Roll" Morton** (1885–1941) and other talented black musicians led the way from ragtime to jazz. The free improvisations and hot rhythms of **New Orleans jazz** were performed by small, tight combos of three or four instruments plus some background percussion. **Louis Armstrong** (1900–1971) played his cornet and trumpet in New Orleans during this early period but moved to Chicago in the 1920s, when that city's greater population, wealth, and recording opportunities attracted jazz musicians from many areas. Having survived a violent childhood to become a gentle, kindly, good-natured person, Armstrong added the qualities of true melodic inspiration and sensitive musicianship to the virtuosic technique expected of the great jazz soloists, and the emotional range of his playing was extraordinarily wide. His improvisations were beautiful as well as technically brilliant.

Jazz Moves North

It was in Chicago in the 1920s that white musicians first formed combos of their own, imitating the New Orleans style in what became known as **Chicago** or **Dixieland jazz.** The public was slow to appreciate this hot, swinging style. It has been suggested that the white musicians, setting out to prove they could do something foreign to their own folk traditions, added a tension and drive not present in the more relaxed New Orleans style; or perhaps Dixieland simply reflects the more hectic pace of big-city life.

Many people preferred the quieter music called **sweet jazz,** consisting of lush arrangements of popular and even light classical pieces. Hardly jazz in the literal sense, involving only minimal amounts of improvisation, this music yet played a significant role in the history of jazz by preparing white, middle-class audiences to enjoy jazz of a more serious nature. **Symphonic jazz,** exemplified by George Gershwin's *Rhapsody in Blue,* involved no improvisation whatever, but also had much to do with conditioning the general public to accept the sounds of jazz. In 1924, Gershwin was commissioned to write a piece for concert performance that would reflect the character of jazz and yet be acceptable to a "cultured" audience. Thus, a year after the French Darius Milhaud wrote *The Creation of the World,* Gershwin's *Rhapsody in Blue* introduced Americans to the contributions jazz offered to concert music. Its original scoring for jazz band and its free, "rhapsodic" form gave *Rhapsody in Blue* a relaxed, informal air that audiences immediately enjoyed. Today the piece is usually performed by an orchestra rather than a jazz ensemble, but its haunting melodies and fascinating rhythms continue to enchant listeners around the world.

Benny Goodman made **swing** famous in the mid-1930s, as the long years of the Great Depression began to wane, and the new dance music rapidly swept the cautiously optimistic country. Highly improvisatory, with a fast tempo and a danceable beat, swing was really a **big band** version of what the early jazz musicians had been playing all along, but was better accepted now by an audience conditioned by sweet and symphonic jazz. Swing bands had from ten to twenty instruments: three or more saxophones, three or more trumpets, some trombones, and perhaps some clarinets, plus a rhythm section of piano, drum set, string bass, and often a guitar, produced a full, rich, and vibrant sonority. The written scores for big band performances were sketchy in comparison with those of the sweet jazz of the 1920s, and the instrumentalists improvised freely around familiar tunes. Swing became the favorite dance music of the 1930s and greatly enhanced the public's appreciation for other "hot" styles, such as boogie-woogie and the highly individual styles of the great blues singers.

Concert Jazz

Jazz, usually associated with music in the vernacular, has interacted closely and effectively with music for the concert hall. Almost from the start, certain European composers included the distinctive rhythms, timbres, and performance techniques of jazz in their concert music: to name a few, Darius Milhaud, Igor Stravinsky, Béla Bartók, and Maurice Ravel used jazz techniques in some of their compositions and wrote pieces for particular jazz virtuosos.

Certain American composers, too, found jazz a stimulating source. Charles Ives was impressed by good jazz as much as by any other music, classical, religious, or popular. Aaron Copland based some of his most successful early pieces upon the new popular music. Milton Babbitt has also been seriously interested in and influenced by jazz. Symphonic jazz, including George Gershwin's *Rhapsody in Blue*—perhaps the most famous American concert piece of all—has many of the melodic, harmonic, and instrumental effects of jazz.

The world of jazz itself drew closer to the concert than to the dance hall, beginning in the early forties, when the great saxophonist **Charlie "Bird" Parker** and the outstanding trumpet player **Dizzy Gillespie** reacted against the polished performances of written and rehearsed "jazz." Particularly, they resented the broad popularity of swing, so far removed from the original New Orleans style. Seeking a return to the early ideals of jazz—improvisation, virtuosity, close interaction between soloist and accompanying combo, and intimately shared appreciation among a select few—they introduced a provocative new style known as **bebop,** which is now considered to be the first modern jazz, the first jazz intended for serious listening. Like much of the concert music of the forties and later, bebop is music for a small ensemble of virtuoso performers in which each instrumental line retains independence, resulting in richly dissonant combinations of sound. Bop musicians often dispensed with a given melody, basing their improvisations upon a song's chord progressions instead.

We hear the complexity and virtuosity characteristic of bebop in a stunning performance of Parker's composition "Bloomdido," Listening Example 44.

 3 42   # LISTENING EXAMPLE 44   3A 11

Bebop

Composer: Charlie Parker (1920–1955)

Title: "Bloomdido"
Recorded in 1950

Genre: Jazz

Style: Bebop

Rhythm: Very fast 4/4 meter

Harmony: The improvisations are based on a 12-bar blues pattern

Performers: Charlie Parker (alto saxophone); Dizzy Gillespie, trumpet; Thelonious Monk, piano; Curly Russell, bass; Buddy Rich, drums

42	0:00	Introduction (piano and drums)
0:09	0:09	First chorus played by alto sax and muted trumpet; Repeats
0:34	0:34	Alto saxophone improvises for three choruses (12+12+12) accompanied by rhythm section
1:25	1:25	Trumpet solo for three choruses with very fast running passages
2:03	2:03	Piano, accompanied by bass and drums, plays two solo choruses
2:30	2:30	Drum solo
2:55	2:55	First chorus is repeated twice; trumpet and saxophone slide to ending.

Just as Parker and Gillespie intended, most people—unable to recognize melody lines or to dance to the complex rhythms of bebop—continued to prefer the big band sound of swing or the popular music of "crooners" like Bing Crosby and Frank Sinatra. **Cool jazz** offered the 1950s a subdued concert jazz, with melodies more lyrical than those of bebop and textures fuller and less complex. A cool ensemble often included instruments not traditionally associated with jazz, such as the French horn, cello, flute, and oboe, thus producing intriguing new sonorities. **Ornette Coleman** and **John Coltrane** were among the leaders of **free jazz** in the 1960s. Without conforming to traditional forms and chord structures, free jazz allows musicians to improvise in a manner independent of other ensemble members. There is less emphasis upon a regular beat or steady tempo than in traditional jazz styles, and the result is sometimes a "random" effect, related to the "chance" music being explored by concert musicians at about the same time. (See pp. 260–262.) **Third stream** music combines the instrumentation of concert music with the improvisation of jazz in a manner preserving the style and integrity of each. For example, a modern concerto grosso might be scored for a symphony orchestra and a small jazz combo.

Edward Kennedy "Duke" Ellington (1899–1974)

Big band leader **Duke Ellington,** who was also a jazz pianist, an arranger, and a composer of a number of impressive concert works, is recognized today as one of America's most outstanding musicians. His unique piano style was widely admired, and some of his popular songs remain in the standard repertoire today.

Ellington was known for his exotic "Afro-American" effects of instrumentation and the unusual playing techniques he included in his jazz performances. He also

Duke Ellington.
Val Wilmer, London

used innovative and sophisticated music techniques not characteristics of jazz at that time, such as chromaticism and unusual and sometimes unresolved modulations. While primarily associated with jazz and other popular genres, Ellington also wrote musicals, symphonic suites, ballets, and film scores, as well as an opera, *Queenie Pie,* left unfinished when he died but finally performed in Philadelphia in 1986 under the supervision of his son, Mercer, to very favorable reviews.

Country-western, rock, electronic music, symphonic music, and the music of other cultures all have affected jazz. Recently demonstrating a renewed vigor and vitality, jazz musicians continue to apply diverse influences to their dynamic, creative, and uniquely American music.

Summary

Jazz developed from a combination of black and white music traditions, but was predominantly influenced by the rhythms and performance practices of African Americans. The many kinds of jazz share the characteristics of a regular meter, intricate rhythmic effects, blue notes and other expressive performance techniques, and improvisation.

The twelve-bar blues began as a kind of black folk song that became a sophisticated part of jazz. Boogie-woogie, or the piano blues, carried the form and harmonic structure of the blues to the piano. Small jazz combos were formed before the turn of this century, and jazz instrumentation soon became varied and colorful.

Almost from the beginnings of jazz, important interactions have occurred between jazz musicians and composers and performers of concert music. Bebop, cool, and third stream are among several kinds of jazz intended more for listening than to be danced to, while many European and American composers primarily associated with classical music enrich their compositions with the timbres and rhythms, and the harmonic and melodic effects, of jazz.

Critical Thinking

- What differences do you recognize between symphonic jazz and third stream—both of which include characteristics of both jazz and concert music?

- Do you recognize jazz as a characteristically American style of music? Explain your answer.

Terms to Review

jazz   A popular music rooted in Africa that developed in early twentieth-century America. There are many styles of jazz, but they generally share a danceable beat, syncopated rhythms, and certain characteristic performance practices, including improvisation.

blues   A vocal style that originated as a kind of African-American folk song and has become a form of jazz. The classical form is strophic, with three lines (twelve bars) in each verse.

scat   Improvised singing on neutral, or nonsense, syllables.

boogie-woogie   "Piano blues." A piano style derived from the formal and harmonic structure of the blues, but bright in mood and fast in tempo. The left hand of the pianist plays a characteristic ostinato pattern.

combo   A small jazz ensemble.

New Orleans jazz   Music performed by a small jazz combo whose soloists take turns improvising on a given tune.

Chicago jazz (Dixieland)   An imitation by white musicians of the New Orleans style of jazz.

sweet jazz   A highly arranged style, with little room for improvisation.

symphonic jazz   Concert music with many of the sounds of jazz but no improvisation.

swing   A highly improvisatory style of jazz.

big band jazz   Another name for swing.

bebop   A complex, highly improvised style of jazz.

cool jazz   A milder style, performed by bands of a moderate size that often include instruments not traditionally associated with jazz.

free jazz   A style in which musicians improvise independently, sometimes producing a "random" effect.

third stream   The combination of jazz and concert music.

Key Figures

Bessie Smith   *"Jelly Roll" Morton*
Louis Armstrong   *George Gershwin*
Benny Goodman   *Charlie "Bird" Parker*
Dizzy Gillespie   *Ornette Coleman*
John Coltrane   *Edward Kennedy "Duke" Ellington*

PART SIX

Cultural Connections: Seven Musical Encounters

W e have necessarily limited most of our attention to the Western European music that forms our own musical heritage; but beginning with our chapters on the nineteenth century, we have referred increasingly to the music of other lands. Nationalist Europeans incorporated into their compositions the "exotic" sounds of Russian folk and religious music, gypsy dances, and Turkish marches. As knowledge and understanding spread, musicians and performers in the West craved further experience with the music of Japan, China, India, Africa, and—more recently—North American Indians. Islamic chant, African rhythms, the timbres and textures of Chinese and Japanese music and of the Indonesian gamelan—all offered exciting new means of musical expression to Western musicians feeling constrained within the limits of their own music traditions.

Today, our world having become too small for cultural isolation to be a necessary or desirable condition, we are blessed with unprecedented access to the music of other cultures and with seemingly unlimited means of performing or reproducing them. Increased travel and communication render suspect the definition of recent music as characteristic of *any* particular culture. Certainly, each area we encounter in this brief final section of our study has made rich contributions to the music we think of as "our own."

The brief encounters of a musical kind offered here introduce some of the characteristics of other music that has made rich contributions to our own. Perhaps even so brief an introduction to sounds that have served their own cultures for many centuries and that are belatedly becoming a part of our own experience in the West will enhance your understanding and broaden your concepts of *music*.

A muezzin calling the Muslim faithful to their prayers.
The Hutchinson Library, London

 3 45   # LISTENING EXAMPLE 47   3B 3

Call to Prayer

Melody: Most of the muezzin's brief phrases, performed for the express purpose of delivering an important message, fall within a narrow melodic range, and most involve a rising inflection. The microtonal intervals are characteristic of Islamic music, as is the elaborate vocal ornamentation (a sort of exaggerated vibrato), which serves here to help the sound carry for some distance. There is no accompaniment.

Rhythm: The rhythm generally follows that of the text as it would be spoken. Long, unmeasured pauses between phrases allow the muezzin time to breathe and enhance the clarity of the message. Such pauses occur in Islamic classical music as well, where they serve an artistic rather than a functional purpose.

Musical Instruments

The music of Islamic cultures, like that of India, generally revolves around the human voice, musical instruments serving primarily to accompany song or play instrumental versions of vocal pieces. However, string instruments are widely popular throughout Islamic regions. The same instruments may be known by different names in different areas; on the other hand, unlike instruments may share similar names. For example, *rabab, rubab, rebab, rebaba,* etc., are variously applied to a one-stringed bedouin spike fiddle, the classical fiddle of North Africa, a short plucked Afghan lute, a barbed lute from Chinese Turkestan, and a Sudanese lyre. *Tambura (tambor, tanbur, tampura,* etc.) is another widespread name

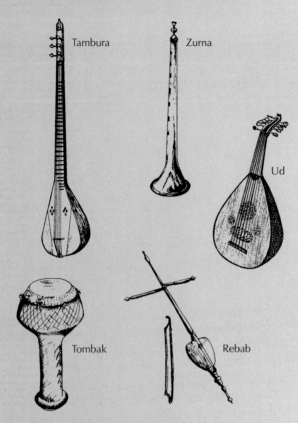

Tambura

Zurna

Ud

Tombak

Rebab

Musical instruments widely used throughout Islamic cultures.

Santur.

applied to different stringed instruments in various regions. The *ud,* a pear-shaped, plucked lute, is an important solo instrument that also is used in pan-Islamic orchestras, which play in unison or in mild heterophony rather than in the homophonic or polyphonic manner of the symphony orchestra.

Double reed instruments (related to the Western oboe) are also closely associated with Islamic music. Variously named *zurna, surnay, shahnay, sona,* or *saz* (among other names), these achieve a raucous, penetrating sound appropriate for festive outdoor occasions (weddings, festivals) and for military music. Flutes, such as the Iranian *nay,* are also important throughout Islamic regions.

Percussion instruments also exist in great variety. Most characteristic are drums of several sizes, shapes, and playing techniques, and a small frame drum surrounded by jingles that Westerners call a tambourine.

Iranian Classical Music

Unlike Western practice, which allows a performer to interpret expressive markings, tempos, and other aspects of a composition with a degree of subjectivity but generally requires the pitches to be performed as notated, the tradition of Iranian classical music requires extensive creative and interpretive responsibility of the solo performer. This music is based upon sets of melodic patterns called *gushes,* each related to a particular dastgah. Having memorized a gushe, a performer improvises upon it, embellishing the melody and bending pitches to make each performance unique. The result is a kind of extemporized chamber music, in which intricate melodic lines including microtonal intervals unfamiliar to Western ears are elaborately interpreted by masters of improvisational techniques. Much as a Western jazz audience encourages performers with applause and verbal exclamations, the approving sounds uttered by an Iranian audience enhance the evocation of musical ecstasy inherent in a successful performance of Islamic music.

The Iranian classical instrumental ensemble includes bowed string instruments, a *nay,* and a goblet-shaped drum *(domback),* as well as the *santur* (heard in Listening Example 48), a flat-bodied string instrument whose strings are struck by a pair of lightweight wooden mallets. (The Western dulcimer, popular with folk musicians in the United States, is a related instrument.)

Turkish Music

Ancient and modern classical music, religious music, and folk and popular musics of many kinds are heard in Turkey today. The most familiar ecstatic tradition in the West is probably that of Turkey's whirling dervishes, whose music reflects the relentless, steady rhythms and joyful improvisation of local folk

3 46

LISTENING EXAMPLE 48

 3B 4

Santur Piece

Title: "Mahur"

This light and happy piece describes a tiny mountain flower, the mahur, whose delicate petals are said to open at the sound of the music's joyful strains.

As the piece begins, one can imagine the flower's tentative response, and, as the music warms in intensity, the grateful opening of its petals to receive the warmth of the sun. The relaxed tempo, unmetered rhythm, and pauses at the end of the phrases—all characteristic of Islamic music—are programmatically appropriate here.

Notice that the dastgah on which this piece is based is very similar to the major scale—sometimes associated by Westerners with "happy" music.

---

traditions. Audiences dance and shout in response to this music, which may finally induce a state of trance—much as occurs in some gospel services in the United States.

Also familiar because of its influence on Western classical music is the Turkish military march tradition. Mozart and Beethoven were among the composers who labeled some of their compositions *alla turca*.

Critical Thinking

- *Why do you suppose the concept of the ideal singing voice varies widely from one culture to another? Upon what (besides familiarity) do we base our preference for one singing style over another?*

- *If you came to America from a non-Western country, what were your initial impressions of Western popular and classical music? Have those impressions altered with time?*

- *While both pan-Islamic and Western music reflect the influence of religious chant, why do you suppose Western art music based on chant generally has harmony, while pan-Islamic music does not?*

Music of China

A t the time of the Western Renaissance, China was ruled by the Ming Dynasty (ca. 1368–1644), whose early emperors sought to eradicate the disastrous results of so-called "barbarian" rule and revive the ancient arts of an earlier period, the Tang. Thus, as in the West, this historical period was one when artists inspired by the past made great strides forward.

An International Language?

Given the vastness of China's territory, the varied sources of influence it has absorbed, and the long duration of its history, it is easy to understand that there is no single tradition of Chinese music. Rather, local traditions and regional styles differ widely in history, theory, instrumentation, aesthetics, philosophy, and practice.

Yet these differences often escape Western listeners to whom Chinese music "all sounds the same." Westerners certainly find Chinese music quite different from their own—as foreign as any spoken tongue, giving rise to suspicion that music may not constitute the international language some would claim. Yet European and American music has reflected an Eastern influence for a century or more, and recently symphony orchestras and jazz and rock ensembles have sampled the timbres as well as the melodic and rhythmic concepts of the East.

Significance of Music

Traditionally, the Chinese have recognized in music powers beyond those that soothe or entertain. Ancient rulers expected music literally to move God to grant their requests. Having developed long before the Greeks a theory of relationships between the imperceptible sounds they thought were produced by the planets moving in space, the Chinese deemed it essential that music be in harmony with these sounds and with the forces of nature.

Like the Greeks, Confucius believed in the ethos, or powers, of music, which he considered an ethical as well as an aesthetic experience, to be conceived and

Chia-Ching wine jar from the Ming Dynasty (1522–1566). The stunning porcelain of this period is among the best-known of all Chinese art.

Chinese characters often have several meanings and are read different ways. Some of this character's meanings are "happiness," "serenity," and "joy." In an attractive association of ideas, it also may be read as yuo or yüeh, meaning "music."

performed only according to specific guidelines. Confucius recommended that music be serene; and in fact, *yuo* ("music") and *lo* ("serenity") are expressed by the same Chinese character.

Pitches and Scales

According to one legend, the notes, or *lus,* with which the Chinese construct their scales were the sounds of their inventor's voice when he spoke in reasoned tones. Another tale ascribes the lus to the sounds of birds imitating the tones of different lengths of bamboo pipes.

The Chinese name the tones for their position rather than their specific pitch (just as *do* can be applied to any note in the West and considered tonic). Each lu has extramusical connotations corresponding to planets, colors, substances, directions, and so on. Each also represents one month and one animal—tiger, hare, dragon, snake, horse, sheep, ape, cock, dog, pig, rat, and ox—a concept related to similar ideas in India, Greece, and Islamic cultures. The tones for a particular composition are selected from one of the sets of lus according not so much to musical considerations as to the season or other extramusical concepts; and the starting tones of a melody may be shifted monthly. A particular melody may begin in January on E and in February on F, for example.

Musical Instruments

The timbre of a Chinese instrument is of extraordinary significance. Performances of ancient music, at least, seem to have had more to do with single sounds than with melodies, and to some extent this is still true. Chinese and other East Asian musicians have developed an incredible number of ways in which an instrument can alter the quality of one tone—techniques clearly reflected in the manner Henry Cowell manipulated piano strings (p. 253), for example.

The Chinese recognize eight categories of musical instruments according to the material from which they are made: stone, metal, silk, bamboo, wood, skin, gourd, or clay (earth or pottery). Like the tones, each instrument has extramusical associations with a particular direction, season, substance, and power; the bell, for instance, represents the west, autumn, dampness, and metal, while the drum is associated with the north, winter, water, and skin.

Percussion instruments, made of an extremely wide variety of materials, are valued more for the colors of their sounds than for rhythmic importance.

Yu and whisk

Indeed, rhythm in Chinese music is less complex and receives less emphasis than in the music of India or Africa. There is no system such as India's talas; nor is rhythm as strongly marked as it is in much music of the West. Among the more exotic percussion instruments is the wooden *yu,* shaped as a crouching tiger. Along the animal's serrated backbone a bamboo whisk is swept to mark the end of a piece. The Chinese temple block, carved of camphor wood in the shape of a fish, adds exotic timbre to some contemporary Western orchestral works. Gongs and cymbals are important in Taoist ceremonies and also in opera, where the distinctive sound of wood clappers marks rhythmic phrases. Drums are of supreme importance for the variety of sounds they offer an ensemble.

Chinese wind instruments include panpipes and several kinds of flutes, as well as the *sheng* mouth organ, said to represent the oldest known organ principle in the world. String instruments include the *chin,* a very old zither that apparently originated in China, and that was later introduced to Japan, where it is known as the *koto* (see p. 333). The chin was originally a member of the "silk" category, but now brass as well as silk strings are used. Scholars were often pictured playing or listening to the chin, whose quiet and lyrical sound seems suited for classical music.

Another very ancient string instrument is the *pipa,* whose strings are strung over bamboo and ivory frets. The pipa, heard in Listening Example 49, may be tuned in different ways, has a very wide dynamic range, and can produce effects appropriate for both martial music and vivid pieces of a calm and lyrical nature.

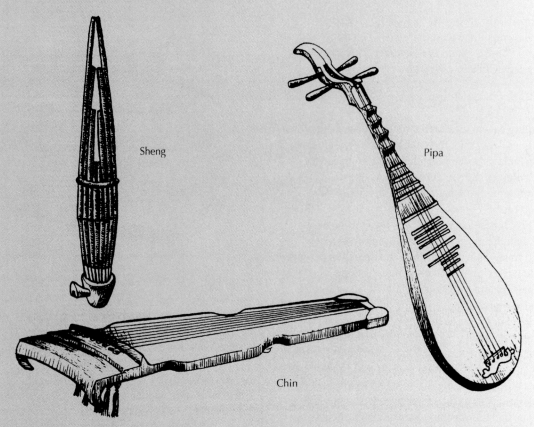

Sheng

Pipa

Chin

Ancient Chinese musical instruments.

 3 47

 3B 5

LISTENING EXAMPLE 49

Piece for Pipa

Composer: Lui Tsun-Yuen

Title: "The Running Brook"

This piece, which illustrates the many techniques the pipa player employs to achieve programmatic effects, begins rather tentatively. Distinctive "rolls" followed by expressive slides set the pastoral scene—perhaps the distant source from which the little brook emerges. After about twenty-five seconds of introductory music, we hear a melody plucked in higher pitches. The water splashes languidly over the rocks, dropping to the brook running below. The rhythm is appropriately relaxed and the tempo fluid.

Notice frequent drone accompaniments, consistently falling melodic phrases, and the increasing intensity as the water finds its path and rushes on. Notice, too, the variety of virtuosic techniques employed to achieve the restful sounds of the gurgling brook, the "drop-drop" of water falling on rocks, and the splashing effects of waterfalls.

Chinese Folk Song

Composer: Lui Man-Sing

Title: "The Choice of a Lover"

Lyricist: Samuel Tsoi

The girl sings of her plans to test a boyfriend's faithfulness. She will lightly bid him farewell if he fails to meet her standards of constancy.

Melody: The tune is based on the gapped pentatonic scale familiar in Western folk music.

Form: Modified strophic. Most of the phrases in each long verse consist of four "bars" (in Western terms), though some are irregular—as is typical of folk music around the world. We hear one stanza sung, and the example fades as the orchestra begins an instrumental version of the same music.

Orchestra: The instruments include a zither, banjo, fiddle, pipa lute, dulcimer, and several percussion instruments.

Notice the high pitch and straight tone of the singer's voice and the slides and bending of pitches heard in both the voice and accompanying instruments.

Vocal Music

Some of the languages of China, like some of those in Africa, are based on levels of pitch, and the Chinese traditionally have recognized close relationships between music and the spoken word. Certain forms of poetry are chanted to the basic tones of the language, and some secular songs also use the tones of speech. Small-scale performances such as shadow puppet plays, the singing of narrative songs (a kind of musical storytelling comparable to folk ballads in the West), and street and restaurant entertainments are highly popular.

Opera

Chinese operas vary from small, regional, folklike performances to those employing sophisticated urban styles, such as the famous Beijing (formerly Peking) opera, which in its turn actually reflects many regional styles. As in Western operas, arias are the most significant—or at least the most prominent—feature, though recitative and instrumental music also are important. The vocal style of Beijing opera is primarily a high, nasal falsetto, and until recently, all opera singers were male. Certain melodic phrases have specific emotional or other extramusical connotations, much as Wagner's *Leitmotif* (see p. 213) bears a wealth of psychological and programmatic significance.

Performances of Chinese opera often involve dancers, acrobats, dramatic staging effects, colorful costumes—in short, all that is required to produce excellent and highly entertaining theater.

Folk Music

While classical Chinese music sounds particularly foreign to unaccustomed Western ears, the folk music of this culture has ready international appeal. It includes dance pieces with lively melodies and bouncy rhythms; quiet, lyrical, sometimes erotic songs; and readily recognizable programmatic effects in instrumental accompaniments or solo works. The folksong heard in Listening Example 50 is characteristically good-humored.

Music in Modern China

In China today, one hears folk tunes, popular songs, choral music, film music, and several kinds of opera. Since the 1920s, Western music has been included in the Chinese education system, significantly affecting the instrumentation, vocal style, and other performance practices of Chinese music, though regional differences continue to be significant. Thus, choral singing, which has largely replaced instrumental performances in much of modern China, often includes Western-style harmony. Orchestras of traditional Chinese instruments exist in Hong Kong, Shanghai, Beijing, Taipei, and elsewhere in China, each using different combinations of instruments—sometimes including Western cellos and double basses to add low tones unavailable in traditional instruments—and sounding quite different from each other.

Exposure to Western music has opened new possibilities to Chinese composers, who have responded in highly individual ways, some composing for the Western symphony orchestra while others incorporate Western characteristics in compositions with traditional Chinese instrumentation. Ritual music, silk-and-bamboo ensembles, folk song, and Chinese rock all have their place in China today.

Critical Thinking

- *Having sampled the music of other cultures, do you accept the maxim that music is an international language? Do you feel you understand all that these musics are intended to communicate?*
- *Why do you think that folk music is usually more accessible to foreign listeners than the art music of the same culture?*
- *Why do you think the Chinese developed a wider variety of instrumental timbres than European musicians? Why do you think some Western composers have recently included Chinese and other non-Western instruments in the symphony orchestra?*
- *Can you suggest why several musicals have reflected a strong Eastern influence? Consider* South Pacific *(1949),* The King and I *(1951),* Kismet *(1953),* Teahouse of the August Moon *(1953),* Flower Drum Song *(1958),* The World of Suzie Wong *(1958),* Pacific Overtures *(1976), and* Miss Saigon *(1989).*

Plate 15

African musicians performing at a festival in Marrakech, Morocco, where music is heavily tinged with Islamic effects.

Dick Rowan Photo Researchers, NY

Plate 16

Bishan Singh, *Musicians and Dancing Girls Perform Before Sher Singh*, 1874. This exquisite nineteenth-century (Sikh) painting reveals the sensuous grace characteristic of much Indian art. Colored pigment on paper, 7 $\frac{1}{8}$ × 13 $\frac{7}{8}$ ins (18.2 × 35.3 cm).

Christie's Images, London

Plate 17

Illustration to the Shahnameh, Shiraz, Persia, A.D. 1539. This sixteenth-century Persian miniature of court musicians (bottom left and right) performing joyful improvisations captures the ecstatic mood characteristic of much Islamic music. Colored pigment on paper, 8 ¼ × 5 ins (20.9 × 12.7 cm).

Christie's Images, London

Plate 18

Ando Hiroshige, *Sudden Shower at Atake (Storm on the Great Bridge)*, 1857. Hiroshige's technique of depicting rain in sets of parallel lines was imitated by European artists, who called it "Hiroshige rain." Color woodcut, 13 × 8 ^{11}/$_{16}$ ins (33 × 22.1 cm). Toledo Museum of Art. Carrie L. Brown Bequest Fund.

Christie's Images, London

Plate 19

Chinese copy after Chou Fang, *Palace Ladies Tuning the Lute,* twelfth-century copy of T'ang Dynasty original. Handscroll, ink and color on silk, 11 × 23 ³⁄₈ ins (27.9 × 59.4 cm). Nelson-Atkins Museum of Art, Kansas City, Missouri (Purchase: Nelson Trust).

Plate 20

Velino Herrera, *Ceremonial Buffalo Dance,* 1948. The purpose of the dance is to appease the spirits of the animals that have been killed so that they will return in great numbers. Watercolor on paper, 21 × 28 ins (53.5 × 71.1 cm). Philbrook Museum of Art, Tulsa, Oklahoma.

Musical Encounter 5

Music of Japan

The 1889 World Exposition, held in commemoration of the French Revolution, brought performing groups from all over the world to Paris, where they caused a great sensation among those seeking something new—or at least different— in the musical arts. Europeans were particularly impressed with the delicate beauty of Japanese arts, which survived the brief flurry of furious popularity to exert a profound and lasting effect on the West.

General Characteristics

Though Japan absorbed a rich variety of music from other parts of Asia, especially China, early on the small island country developed many styles of music distinctive to its people's culture and experience. Serene instrumental pieces evoke images of the country's lovely forests, lakes, and gardens, and dramatic love songs, battle pieces, and lion dances belong to the various Japanese theater traditions. Among the most distinctive Japanese sounds are those of the ancient court music, or *gagaku*, sometimes referred to as the oldest orchestral music in the world. Performed today much as it was nearly a thousand years ago, this stately, dignified music creates a unique and compelling atmosphere.

The austere court music, performed for and appreciated by a limited audience, is only one of many kinds of music in Japan. Walking down a street, one may hear wafting from open windows the lilting melodies of Japanese folk songs, the hum of Buddhist chants, a pianist practicing pieces by Bach or Chopin, recordings of Beethoven symphonies, and a great wealth of popular music available day and night on radio and TV.

Scales and Pitches

The Japanese use several pitch systems, all derived from a chromatic scale of twelve uneven half steps. The particular scale on which a given piece is based depends on the instruments involved and the kind of music.

The two basic scales upon which most Japanese music is structured are pentatonic patterns called *yo*

and *in*. Neither is identical to the pentatonic pattern most familiar in the West, though the *yo* mode resembles it closely. Both the *yo* and the *in* scales emphasize the interval of the fourth, very characteristic of many Japanese melodies.

Japanese music is rich in melodic variety, though stereotyped melodic patterns are frequently used for programmatic reasons, especially in theater music. As in China, the tones of a melody are often slightly sharped or flatted in performance. In some cases, changes in instrumental timbre and dynamics are of more significance than changes in pitch.

Though traditional Japanese music is monophonic in texture, heterophony commonly occurs in performance, as when two or more instruments vary or embellish a melody they perform simultaneously.

Rhythm

Though a clearly discernible pulse may imply duple or quadruple meter, a relaxed, flexible beat is far more characteristic of music in Japan than of that in Western cultures. There are three basic rhythmic structures: an eight-beat pattern for slow portions of a piece, and four- and two-beat patterns for successively rapid sections. The patterns are sometimes mixed. Stereotyped rhythmic patterns recurring through a section or throughout a piece enhance the stability of the music.

Form

The form of a concert piece typically follows a principle known as *jo-ha-kyu,* with three sections differentiated primarily by tempo and rhythm. The *jo,* meaning "preface," is generally a rather brief introduction, slow in tempo. *Ha* means to tear or break apart, and this section is a development of thematic material, with a significant increase in tempo. The final section, *kyu,* meaning "to hurry," begins with an even faster tempo as it rushes toward the finish; but as the piece approaches its close, the tempo slows, rounding out the form to end somewhat as it began. This aesthetic conception is loosely interpreted and may be superimposed on pieces with two or four rather than three sections, or applied to a phrase or section within a piece, as well.

Musical Instruments

Several kinds of instruments are associated with particular Japanese musical traditions. For example, the *shamisen,* a long-necked instrument with three strings, accompanies the singing of geishas and is also heard in kabuki performances (see p. 335). A short bamboo double-reed pipe called a *hichiriki* produces a strident sound particularly associated with the court music of Japan. Court ensembles also include the fascinating *sho,* a set of seventeen bamboo pipes in a windchest, whose mysterious, ethereal chords have much to do with the elegant sounds of Japanese court music.

One of the most familiar Japanese musical instruments in the West is the *koto,* a zither with thirteen silk or nylon strings, whose name is an abbreviated form of *kami no nori koto,* "the oracles of the gods." A movable bridge on each string allows the player to readily change the tuning to one mode or another. Two shapes of plectrum are used: square, to produce a dramatic, resonant effect, or round, for a softer sound. While strumming the koto with plectra on three fingers of the right hand, the player "bends" pitches by pressing the strings with the left hand. The koto is well adapted either for providing simple accompaniments to folk songs or for playing elaborate, highly embellished solo or ensemble pieces. In some contexts the instrument is considered sacred: to pluck the string of a koto is to release its spirit/soul with its sound.

Folk Music

There are many folk music traditions, including work songs for planting, fishing, and other rural occupations; songs about the seasons; children's songs; and vocal and instrumental dance pieces. Each region of Japan has its own characteristic folk music, and though most Japanese now live and work in crowded cities, they continue to treasure these expressions of their former rural environment. It is still common practice at dinner parties and other social gatherings and on bus or car trips for people to entertain themselves and each other by singing the folk songs of Japan.

Folk songs are often sung in a high-pitched, tight-throated manner. Dance songs may be accompanied by simple clapping or drums, or by shamisen and/or koto. An instrumental group called *hayashi,* which includes drums and flutes and sometimes small brass gongs, may play a folk song or dance piece as an instrumental solo or accompany one or more singers. Listening Example 51 is a set of koto variations on a famous Japanese folk song.

Music for the Theater

Japan is rich in theater traditions, the best-known of which are the restrained choral dramas called *noh,* the

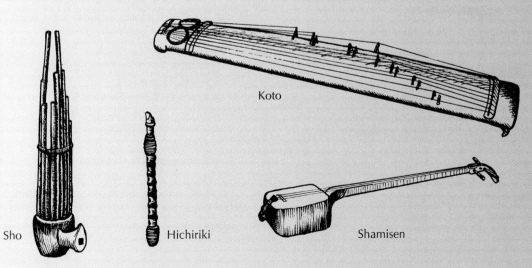

Sho

Hichiriki

Koto

Shamisen

Traditional Japanese musical instruments.

A graceful dancer in colorful kimono performs to the accompaniment of koto and shamisen.
Topham Picture Source, Kent

 3 49

LISTENING EXAMPLE 51

 3B 7

Japanese Folk Tune

Title: "Sakura" ("Cherry Blossoms")

Probably the best known and loved of all Japanese folk songs, this lovely melody celebrating the delicate cherry blossom lends itself well to koto interpretation. Here, after a brief introduction, the famous tune is heard, its first tones alone, then with a very simple harmonic accompaniment. (The first phrase is easy to identify if one thinks of the syllables "Sa-ku-ra, sa-ku-ra.")

Each verse has seven phrases. The first verse may be described as follows:

Phrase 1: solo melody line

Phrase 2: solo to last tones, when accompaniment begins

Phrase 3: melody plus simple homophonic accompaniment

Phrase 4: melody in octaves

Phrase 5: melody line embellished

Phrases 6 and 7: increasingly elaborate melodic embellishment. A slight ritardando marks the end of the first verse.

For his first variation, the koto player accompanies the melody with graceful running passages. The example ends as he begins yet another interpretation of the tune.

Colorful costumes and sets enhance the dramatic effects of kabuki.

more popular and sometimes even bawdy *kabuki* plays, and dramatic puppet plays called *bunraku.*

Kabuki

Kabuki began as a popular music theater with risqué connotations that now have been largely forgotten. Today's performances are colorful melodramas performed (generally) by all-male casts. Kabuki's elaborate sets and costumes and exaggerated acting style exploit theatricality to the fullest.

Several styles of music accompany a kabuki play. Onstage an ensemble of flutes, drums, and a shamisen accompany dances and the prevalent type of song, called *nagauta,* or "long song." Each instrument on the stage has distinctive responsibilities: the floor drum marks rhythmic patterns, while the voice and shamisen carry melodic lines. Stereotyped melodic patterns, often representing natural effects (snowfall, the sea), dramatic events (a battle), or simply an idea, are a frequent characteristic of kabuki and other Japanese theater music—reminding us of Richard Wagner's *Leitmotifs.*

An offstage ensemble, which also sometimes includes bells as well as other instruments to provide special sound effects, plays descriptive music through much of the performance.

Critical Thinking

• *Why do you suppose today's Japanese continue to enjoy their traditional folk music, while Americans are largely unfamiliar with theirs?*

Native American Music

E ven as Europeans explored the national characteristics of the music of their own countries and others, Americans remained largely unaware of the music of their own native inhabitants. The few interested composers (including Edward MacDowell, p. 205–206) who attempted to incorporate North American Indian effects in their music felt constrained to harmonize Indian melodies with tonal chords and orchestrate them in the European way.

General Characteristics

Native American music is never an independent concept but always a part of dance, celebration, games, work, or prayer. Not only is music thus intimately linked with ceremony, ritual, religion, and magic, but also it is understood to have strong powers. Songs enhance one's prowess for fishing, healing, gambling, and wooing, for example, and a basketweaver sings not only to ease the drudgery of work but to ensure that the resulting basket will be pleasing to supernatural spirits.

Music must, therefore, always be properly and respectfully performed and listened to, with full awareness of the function it is intended to serve.

Song

Native American music is basically song. Though there are as many kinds of songs as there are Native

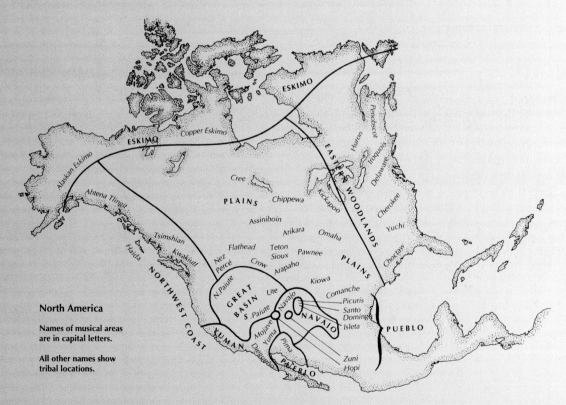

North America

Names of musical areas are in capital letters.

All other names show tribal locations.

A number of distinctive styles characterize Native American music. This map shows the most significant areas.

American cultures, many of the values of Native American song remain constant. For example, songs are not thought of as composed but as given to, or received by, an individual. Some songs, in fact, *belong* to one person and may not be sung by any other without express permission. Song texts may be in a native language (or recently, in English), or they may consist simply of a series of vocables, such as *hey, yeh,* or *neh.* Although there are significant regional differences in style and performance practice, song unites people as Native Americans, authenticates ceremonies necessary for their lives, and helps keep people in balance with nature.

Melody

Melodic phrases of many North American cultures generally begin on a relatively high pitch and descend, much in the manner typical of speech. Scale patterns vary, but most melodic intervals are narrow—that is, we do not often hear wide leaps in the melody line.

Form

Songs are generally constructed quite simply in strophic form, a strophe often consisting of a single short phrase or tune which is repeated several times. Particularly in the music of the Plains Indians, the first part of a song may not recur consistently in successive "verses," resulting in the form called *incomplete repetition.*

Texture

The texture of Indian music is generally monophonic, with male and female voices singing together in unison without harmonic accompaniment. However, one or more voices may provide a drone; or

Hopi dancers in Arizona.
Barnaby's Picture Library, London

sometimes a solo voice and responding chorus overlap, causing the unison to be inexact.

Dance Songs

The movements, costumes, melodies, and accompanying instruments of dance, an essential part of Native American life, vary from one culture to another. Indians dance in prayer, thanksgiving, preparation for war, and—as in Listening Example 52—celebration of victory, as well as in veneration of the animals with which they coexist in nature and which sustain them by providing clothing and food. Some dances are performed primarily as joyful social events.

 3 50   # LISTENING EXAMPLE 52   3B 8

Crazy Dog Song

Triumphantly reenacting their brave exploits, members of a Blood Tribe military society known as "Crazy Dogs" sing and dance, their voices doubled at the octave by women (who sound as if they may be standing in the background).

Melody: The phrases reflect the falling inflection typical of many tribes—as it is of speech in many languages, if not most. Notice the frequent repetition of tones.

Accompaniment: A hand drum and rattle accompany the singers and dancers. Though the instruments' rhythmic patterns appear largely independent of the melody, they in fact govern the progress of the performance.

Text: The text consists of vocables, or neutral syllables, sung in the tense, nasal quality characteristic of much Native American music. Vocal slides and microtonal intervals add to the expressiveness and dramatic character of the music.

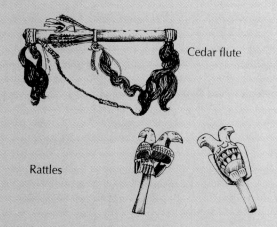

Cedar flute

Rattles

Symbolically decorated Native American sound instruments.

Sound Instruments

There is little purely instrumental music, but *sound instruments,* as Native Americans call them, sometimes "hold up" the songs, as in the example above. Most common are drums or rattles, which add percussive and rhythmic (not melodic) interest.

Musical instruments may be elaborately decorated, again not only for aesthetic reasons, but with symbolic purpose. The decorations on the rattles illustrated here, for example, might depict the closeness of the Northwest Coast Indians to nature, particularly to the sea.

The Native American flute, the only instrument for which there are solo pieces, emulates the sound of the human voice and is said to "sing" the melody. Traditionally associated with wooing a loved one, the flute is played by males only, though a woman may imitate the sound of the instrument when singing a love song. According to one old custom, the flute player positioned himself so that the wind would carry his melody to his beloved—a charming custom, but one intended not so much to please and attract the girl as to magically make her his bride.

While the flute is of less significance to North American Indian cultures today than it was in earlier times, its lovely, soothing sound has been used by Native American composers and others in recent compositions of concert music (see Listening Example 53, p. 341).

Recent Native American Music

The introduction of the horse and later the automobile greatly increased intertribal contact, enabling members of tribes from all parts of the country to travel many miles to share their dances, songs, and ceremonies in colorful celebrations called *powwows.* Soon pan-Indian song styles evolved, such as those of the peyote ceremony, which combines traditional music and religious elements with certain Christian rites and the powwow. (Banned for a long time by the United States government, celebration of the peyote ceremony in the Native American Church now has governmental approval.)

Increasing interaction between Native American and other musicians also has led to new mutual respect and influence. Besides their traditional songs, modern Indians sing others borrowed from European music, and a number of new vernacular musics have evolved on and off the reservations. Some Native American cultures incorporate elements of contemporary popular music, modifying them to suit their needs and tastes. Indian rock bands like Xit, country-western groups like the Navajo Sundowners, and gospel quartets flourish on many reservations today.

However, even borrowed music typically is performed so as to conform with prevailing cultural norms. Thus the *waila* (wy´-la), or chicken scratch music, borrowed by the Pima and O'odham cultures from northern Mexico, has become their own social dance music, but it is danced counterclockwise, beginning at sundown and ending at sunrise, expressly for the purpose of bringing happiness and joy to the people—all according to traditional North American Indian practice.

Concert Music

Some Native Americans are participating in today's concert music experience. John Kim Bell, a Caughnawaga Indian, is associate director of the New York Philharmonic Orchestra. R. Carlos Nakai, a well-known Navajo-style flute player (see p. 340, 341), fuses elements of jazz and concert music with traditional Indian concepts.

Other Native Americans compose concert music close to the European tradition. The best-known, Louis Ballard, often includes Native American instruments in his band and orchestra ensembles, thus mixing traditional sounds with those of the symphony orchestra.

Critical Thinking

- *Why has Native American music had little effect upon American composers, at least until very recent times?*

- *Why does the music of North American Indians sound so different from most American music?*
- *Do you see relationships between the manners in which Africans and Native Americans consider music? How do their concepts of the place of music in society differ from those of the European and Asian cultures we have encountered?*

The New Internationalism

Today we are blessed with unprecedented access to the musics of the world and seemingly unlimited means of performing or reproducing them. Increasingly, musicians of different cultures find fulfillment in collaborative experiences, both on the vernacular level (Paul Simon and Paul McCartney come to mind) and in art music as well. Large sections of music store shelf space are devoted to World Music, and it no longer seems unusual when a musician like Youssou N'Dour, from Senegal, sings with Paul Simon, or when the recordings of Hungarian Marta Sebestyen singing Irish, Greek, and Indian songs attract a wide listening audience in Western Europe and the United States.

Chinese-American composer Chou Wen-chung, whose music is widely available on CD, advocates something he calls "re-merger"—his concept of a fusion of Eastern and Western musical traditions. On the other hand, Chinese composer Tan Dun resists suggestions that his music brings East and West together, insisting there *is* no longer any East or West, and stating his purpose "to be flexible and freely flying around among all kinds of experience." Tan Dun's *Symphony 1997 (Heaven, Earth, Mankind),* written to commemorate the reunification of Hong Kong with China, was telecast worldwide July 1, 1997, and its recording debuted in fifth place on the Billboard classical chart. The eminent Japanese composer Toru Takemitsu (who died in 1996) also achieved a novel blend of East and West and of old and new in magnificent scores for film and concert. Takemitsu, who studied with Olivier Messiaen (p. 248), sought to merge ancient Japanese court music and traditional Japanese instruments with modern forms.

Left to right: Mark Sunkett, R. Carlos Nakai, James DeMars, Michael Hester, Xiaozhong Zheng.

Westerners reflect the recent consolidation of time and place as well. As early as 1937, Carl Orff's mock-Medieval cantata *Carmina Burana* (p. 265) seemed to transcend period, place, authorship, even meaning, and excerpts from that appealing work may be heard today in films (for example, *Badlands,* 1973), in advertisements, and accompanying the entrances of sports figures and, recently, of Michael Jackson. American composer Philip Glass (p. 278–279) drew the text for his opera *Satyagraha* from India's magnificent ancient epic the *Bhagavad-Gita* (Ba′-ga-vad Ge͂′-ta) and further examples of internationalism in music abound. So many pieces exhibit a finely wrought synthesis of two or more cultures, perhaps we may say music finally has achieved the status of an international language.

A Tapestry of Sounds

The fruitful collaboration of American composer James DeMars and Native American flutist R. Carlos Nakai has produced a stunning body of music combining characteristics of the music of European, Native American, and other cultures. They have, in fact, achieved the congenial collaboration of old and new, West and non-West, for which we have hoped in this text to raise a level of interest and excitement.

The poem (by Charles Baudelaire, an important precursor of the Symbolists) inspiring James DeMars's *Tapestry V* (Listening Example 53) suggests that the poet's vision moves "above the pools, valleys, mountains, clouds and seas," and expresses joy "for those whose thoughts, like larks taking flight in morning skies, soar upon life. . . ." Perhaps you will share the poet's vision as you hear this piece, in which African drums, Navajo flute, electronic synthesizer, cello, and saxophone combine in a stunning tapestry of sounds. Each instrument maintains its individual character and integrity, none is dominated by the others, and each is essential to the hauntingly beautiful effect the music achieves.

 3 51   # LISTENING EXAMPLE 53   3B 9

New Cultural Horizons

Composer: James DeMars

Title: *Tapestry V*

Melody: The flute, cello, and saxophone melodies are not confined to the pitches of the tonic scales.

Rhythm: The prevailing metric structure alternates 8 beats with 10 beats in the pattern $(3 + 3 + 2) + (3 + 3 + 2 + 2)$.

Texture: The texture is polyphonic; each line is melodically independent, and harmony occurs only as the result of passing combinations.

Form: Though freely rhapsodic in form, A-B-A is loosely implied, as a calm and slow passage occurs between pulsing, rhythmically intense sections.

African hand drums introduce a series of ostinato figures, varying in pattern but constant in their vibrant intensity. The cedar flute enters briefly with fluttery, birdlike sounds. With an upward gesture, the cello joins in, its repeated notes together with the drum ostinatos stabilizing the complex tapestry. Next the flute gives a joyfully independent cry, and, beginning tentatively, the saxophone soars upward in an expressive glissando. The cello's drone and the beating drums support the flute's further flight of fancy. As the cello and saxophone wax increasingly lyrical, the flute joins them. We hear occasional comments from the synthesizer, as the drums continue their constant, reliable support.

After a brief but dramatic crescendo, the sustaining instruments pause slightly; the cello plays a lyrical passage, which the saxophone joins in similar character. Suddenly the drum pattern changes dramatically. The flute and cello play briefly. In a passage of spiritual beauty, the haunting tones of the flute accompanied by mystical synthesizer chords introduce a slower section (B), romantic in mood, dominated by the warm tones of the saxophone and cello. The tempo picks up as the drums play new rhythms. Though consistently melodic in concept, the lines of the cello and saxophone in this expressive duet imply some harmonic consideration. The flute flutters delicate commentary.

As the rhythmic momentum of the beginning of the piece returns, notice the varied drum timbres. The flute, increasingly rapturous, flies above all other sounds. The saxophone and cello return with muted comment, and the saxophone, abandoning inhibition, soars to new heights.

But last we hear the haunting tones of the cedar flute, completing the tapestry of sound.

Codetta

T he stimulating linear counterpoint of the Middle Ages, the serene *a cappella* ideal of the Renaissance, the strong rhythms and dramatic contrasts of the Baroque, the clear designs and balanced phrases of the Classical period, the soaring melodies and sensuous harmonies of the Romantics, and the rich diversity of styles in the twentieth century—all have now become a part of your experience and understanding. You are well prepared to continue your exploration of the world of music.

As you continue your cultural quest, however, you will find as many questions as answers, and the answers are seldom definitive, for art is a relative concept. Even your personal tastes and preferences will change from time to time. The listening adventure never ends and is, as we have seen, fraught with paradox. The potential rewards are also endless, and they are rich beyond measure.

May your quest be fearless and bold, and your life enriched with the experience of great music.

Appendix: Chronology of Western Events

Musical Events	Dates	Composers

MIDDLE AGES AND RENAISSANCE

Musical Events	Dates	Composers
	1100	Hildegard of Bingen (1098–1179)
Development of Gregorian chant	1150	
Organum	1200	
Troubadour/trouvère music	1250	
	1300	Guillaume de Machaut (ca. 1300–1377)
	1350	
	1400	John Dunstable (ca. 1390–1453)
	1450	Josquin des Prez (ca. 1450–1521)
	1500	Giovanni Palestrina (1524–1594)
Rise of the Franco-Flemish school of composers	1550	Gioranni Gabrieli (c. 1555–1612)

BAROQUE

Musical Events	Dates	Composers
		Claudio Monteverdi (ca. 1567–1643)
		Thomas Weelkes (1575–1623)
Development of the monodic style	1600	
		Barbara Strozzi (1619–ca. 1664)
Development of opera and oratorio in Italy		Jean-Baptiste Lully (1632–1687)
		Dietrich Buxtehude (1637–1707)
Publication of Bay Psalm Book (1640)		
		Arcangelo Corelli (1653–1713)
	1650	Henry Purcell (1659–1695)
		François Couperin (1668–1733)
		Antonio Vivaldi (ca. 1675–1741)
Cristofori develops the piano	1700	Johann Sebastian Bach (1685–1750)
Development of equal temperament		Domenico Scarlatti (1685–1757)
Development of concerto grosso and orchestral suite		George Frideric Handel (1685–1759)
Bach's St. Matthew Passion (1729)		Carl Philipp Emanuel Bach (1714–1788)
Handel's Messiah (1742)		Christoph Willibald Gluck (1714–1787)

CLASSICAL

Musical Events	Dates	Composers
		Franz Joseph Haydn (1732–1809)
Mannheim orchestra at its height	1750	Wolfgang Amadeus Mozart (1756–1791)
Development of the string quartet by Haydn and Mozart		Ludwig van Beethoven (1770–1827)
		Niccolò Paganini (1782–1840)
		Carl Maria von Weber (1786–1826)
Mozart composes his last three symphonies (1788)		Franz Schubert (1797–1828)
		Gioacchino Rossini (1792–1868)
		Gaetano Donizetti (1797–1848)
	1800	Vincenzo Bellini (1801–1835)
Beethoven's Fifth Symphony (1808)		Mikhail Glinka (1803–1857)

ROMANTIC

Musical Events	Dates	Composers
		Hector Berlioz (1803–1869)
Invention of the metronome (1816)		Felix Mendelssohn (1809–1847)
Weber's Der Freischutz (1821) and origins of German romantic opera		Fréderic Chopin (1810–1849)
	1825	Robert Schumann (1810–1856)
Berlioz's Symphonie fantastique (1829); development of the program symphony		Franz Liszt (1811–1886)
		Richard Wagner (1813–1883)
		Giuseppe Verdi (1813–1901)
		Clara Wieck Schumann (1819–1896)
		Bedřich Smetana (1824–1884)
		Stephen Foster (1826–1864)
		Louis Moreau Gottschalk (1829–1869)
Wagner's Oper und Drama (1851)	1850	Johannes Brahms (1833–1897)
Liszt's Les Préludes (1854)		Alexander Borodin (1834–1887)
Wagner's Tristan und Isolde (1859)		Georges Bizet (1838–1875)
Balakirev, Cui, Borodin, Rimsky-Korsakov, and Mussorgsky form the "Five" (1862)		Modest Mussorgsky (1839–1881)
		Peter Ilyich Tchaikovsky (1840–1893)
		Antonin Dvořák (1841–1904)
First Wagner Festival held at Bayreuth (1876)	1875	Edvard Grieg (1843–1907)
Edison invents the phonograph (1877)		John Philip Sousa (1854–1932)
New York Metropolitan Opera founded (1883)		Giacomo Puccini (1858–1924)
Development of French Impressionistic music		Gustav Mahler (1860–1911)
Dvořák conducts first performance of "New World" Symphony (1893)		Edward MacDowell (1861–1908)
Debussy's Prélude à l'après-midi d'un faune (1894)		Claude Achille Debussy (1862–1918)
		Richard Strauss (1864–1949)
		Amy Beach (1867–1944)

Cultural Events Artists and Writers	Dates	World Events Political Leaders

MIDDLE AGES AND RENAISSANCE

Gothic cathedrals begun (St. Denis, Paris, 1144; Chartres, 1145)	1100	
	1150	
	1200	Magna Carta signed by King John (1215)
	1250	Marco Polo leaves for Cathay (1271)
Dante's *Divine Comedy* (1307)	1300	Hundred Years' War begins (1337)
Chaucer's *Canterbury Tales* (1386)	1350	
Botticelli (1444–1510)	1440	Battle of Agincourt (1415)
Gutenberg Bible (1456)	1450	Fall of Constantinople (1453)
Michelangelo (1475–1564)		Columbus discovers America (1492)
Raphael (1483–1520)		
St. Peter's begun in Rome (1506)	1500	Henry VIII King of England (1509)
		Martin Luther's ninety-five theses (1517)
		Council of Trent (1545–1563)
	1550	Elizabeth I Queen of England (1558)
		Spanish Armada defeated (1588)

BAROQUE

El Greco (1541–1614)		
William Shakespeare (1564–1616)		
Carvaggio (1573–1610)		
Peter Paul Rubens (1577–1640)		
Francesco Borromini (1599–1667)	1600	Jamestown settled (1607)
Cervantes, part I of *Don Quixote* (1605)		Thirty Years' War begins (1618)
Rembrandt van Rijn (1606–1669)		Mayflower Compact (1620)
Giovanni Lorenzo Bernini's *Ecstasy of St. Theresa* (1644)		Louis XIV King of France (1643)
Samuel Pepys's *Diary* (1660)	1650	Restoration of Charles II in England (1660)
John Milton's *Paradise Lost* (1667)		Reign of Peter the Great begins (1682)
Christopher Wren begins St. Paul's Cathedral (1675)		Salem witchcraft trials (1692)
Isaac Newton's *Principia Mathematica* (1687)	1700	War of the Spanish Succession begins (1702)
		Reign of Louis XV begins (1715)
Jonathan Swift's *Gulliver's Travels* (1726)		Age of Enlightened Despots (1740–1796)

CLASSICAL

Francisco Goya (1746–1828)		
Jacques Louis David (1748–1825)		
Pompeii rediscovered (1748)	1750	Franklin's discoveries in electricity (1752)
Voltaire's *Candide* (1759)		Seven Years' War; French and Indian War (1756)
William Wordsworth (1770–1850)		Beginnings of the Industrial Revolution (ca. 1770)
J. M. W. Turner (1775–1851)		American Declaration of Independence (1776)
Immanuel Kant's *Critique of Pure Reason* (1781)		French Revolution begins (1789)
Thomas Malthus's *Essay on Population* (1798)		Bill of Rights (1791)
Eugene Delacroix (1798–1863)		Eli Whitney's cotton gin (1793)
Goethe's *Faust, Part I* (1808)	1800	Louisiana Purchase (1803)
Jane Austen's *Pride and Prejudice* (1813)		Battle of Waterloo (1815)

ROMANTIC

Edgar Allen Poe (1809–1849)		
Goya's *Witches' Sabbath* (1815)		
Herman Melville (1818–1891)		Monroe Doctrine (1823)
Shelley's *Prometheus Unbound* (1820)	1825	Erie Canal opened (1825)
Victor Hugo's *Hernani* (1830)		July Revolution in France (1830)
Claude Monet (1840–1926)		Invention of telegraph (1832)
Ralph Waldo Emerson's *Essays* (1841)		Queen Victoria's reign begins (1837)
Alexander Dumas's *Count of Monte Cristo* (1845)		California Gold Rush; revolutions in Europe (1848)
Karl Marx's *Communist Manifesto* (1848)		
Harriet Beecher Stowe's *Uncle Tom's Cabin* (1852)	1850	Opening of Japan to the West (1853)
Vincent van Gogh (1853–1890)		American Civil War begins (1861)
Charles Darwin's *Origin of Species* (1859)		Emancipation Proclamation (1863)
Leo Tolstoy's *War and Peace* (1865)		Civil War ends; Lincoln assassinated (1865)
Karl Marx's *Das Kapital* (1867)		Franco-Prussian War begins (1870)
Henri Matisse (1869–1954)	1875	Invention of telephone, internal combustion engine (1876)
Pablo Picasso (1881–1973)		Irish Insurrection (1880)
Friedrich Nietzsche's *Thus Spake Zarathustra* (1883)		Wilhelm II, last Kaiser of Germany, crowned (1888)
Mark Twain's *Huckleberry Finn* (1883)		Nicholas II, last Czar of Russia, crowned (1894)
Brooklyn Bridge built (1883)		Dreyfus Affair (1894–1905)
Eiffel Tower completed (1889)		Spanish-American War (1898)
		Boer War (1899)

Musical Events	Dates	Composers

TWENTIETH CENTURY

Musical Events	Dates	Composers
	1900	
		Erik Satie (1866–1925)
		Scott Joplin (1868–1917)
German expressionism, represented chiefly by Schoenberg and Berg, developed before World War I		Arnold Shoenberg (1874–1951)
		Charles Ives (1874–1954)
		Maurice Ravel (1875–1937)
		Béla Bartók (1881–1945)
Stravinsky's *The Rite of Spring* (1913)		Igor Stravinsky (1882–1971)
Schoenberg announces his method of composing with twelve tones (1922)		Anton von Webern (1883–1945)
		Ferdinand "Jelly Roll" Morton (1885–1941)
First performance of Gershwin's *Rhapsody in Blue* (1924)		Alban Berg (1885–1935)
American jazz influences composers in the 1920s	1925	
N.Y. Philharmonic Orchestra first broadcast over radio (1928)		
		Edgard Varèse (1885–1965)
		Nadia Boulanger (1887–1979)
		Sergei Prokofiev (1891–1953)
		Darius Milhaud (1892–1974)
		Bessie Smith (1894–1937)
		Paul Hindemith (1895–1963)
		William Grant Still (1895–1978)
Many European composers emigrate to the United States during the 1930s and early 1940s, including Schoenberg, Stravinsky, Hindemith, and Bartók		Henry Cowell (1897–1965)
		George Gershwin (1898–1937)
		Edward Kennedy "Duke" Ellington (1899–1974)
		Aaron Copland (1900–1990)
Copland's *Appalachian Spring* choreographed by Martha Graham (1944)		Louis Armstrong (1900–1971)
		Richard Rodgers (1902–1979)
Early experiments in electronic music; development of *musique concrète* in Paris (1948)		
Introduction of long-playing records (1948)		Olivier Messiaen (1908–1992)
American experiments in electronic music at Columbia University (1952)	1950	Benjamin "Benny" Goodman (1909–1986)
		Samuel Barber (1910–1981)
John Cage develops chance music in the 1950s		
Beginning of rock 'n' roll (1955)		
Stockhausen's *Gesang der Junglinge* (1956)		Gian Carlo Menotti (b. 1911)
Boulez's *Improvisations sur Mallarmé* (1958)		John Cage (1912–1992)
Early Beatles tours (1963)		
Terry Riley's *In C,* first major minimalist work (1964)		
Woodstock Festival (1969)		Benjamin Britten (1913–1976)
Leonard Bernstein's *Mass* is opening work at Kennedy Center in Washington, D.C. (1972)	1970	Milton Babbitt (b. 1916)
		John "Dizzy" Gillespie (1917–1993)
		Leonard Bernstein (1918–1990)
		Charlie Parker (1920–1955)
		Ravi Shankar (b. 1920)
Milton Babbitt's *Phônemena* (1974)		Lukas Foss (b. 1922)
Philip Glass's *Einstein on the Beach* (opera) (1975)		Pierre Boulez (b. 1925)
		Bill Haley (1925–1981)
Krysztof Penderecki's *Paradise Lost* (opera) (1976)		Chuck Berry (1926–)
Nadia Boulanger dies (1980)		Karlheinz Stockhausen (b. 1928)
Ex-Beatle John Lennon murdered (1980)	1980	
Digital recordings become widely marketed (1980)		Stephen Sondheim (1930–)
Rap movement emerges (1980)		
One-hundredth anniversary of Metropolitan Opera House, New York (1983)		Elvis Presley (1935–1977)
Introduction of compact discs (CDs) (1983)		Steve Reich (b. 1936)
		Phillip Glass (b. 1937)
		Joan Tower (b. 1938)
Live Aid concert for Ethiopian famine relief (1985)		Ellen Taafe Zwillich (b. 1939)
		John Lennon (1940–1980)
		Bob Dylan (1941–)
		Paul Simon (1941–)
Pianist Vladimir Horowitz returns to Russia for a recital (1986)		John Adams (b. 1947)
John Adams's *Nixon in China* (1987)		Andrew Lloyd Webber (1948–)
A Chorus Line closes after a 15-year run on Broadway (1990)		
Pianist Vladmir Horowitz dies (1990)	1990	Wynton Marsalis (b. 1961)
Leonard Bernstein dies (1990)		
Dancer Martha Graham dies (1991)		Bruce Springsteen (1949–)
		Anthony Davis (b. 1951)
Aaron Copland dies (1900–1990)		Tan Dun (b. 1957)
Woodstock II (1994)		
Nirvana's Kurt Cobain commits suicide (1994)		
Selena killed (1995)		
Beatles first new music since 1970 (1995)		
Rap superstar Tupac Shakur shot to death (1996)		
The Lion King opens on Broadway, with new songs by Elton John (1997)		
Frank Sinatra dies (1998)		

Cultural Events Artists and Writers	Dates	World Events Political Leaders

TWENTIETH CENTURY

Cultural Events — Artists and Writers	Dates	World Events — Political Leaders
Ernest Hemingway (1899–1961) Fauvist and Cubist movements in painting George Bernard Shaw's *Man and Superman* (1903) Sigmund Freud develops psychoanalysis (1905) Albert Einstein develops relativity theory (1905) Jean Paul Sartre (b. 1905) Richard Wright (1908–1960) Frank Lloyd Wright designs Robie House (1909) Marcel Duchamp's *Nude Descending a Staircase* (1912) Marcel Proust's *Remembrance of Things Past* (1913) Albert Camus (1913–1960)	1900	Boxer Rebellion in China (1900) Queen Victoria dies; Edward VII crowned (1901) Wright Brothers' first successful flight (1903) First Russian Revolution (1905) San Francisco earthquake (1906) Model T Ford produced (1908) Panama Canal opened (1914) World War I (1914–1918) Bolshevik Revolution in Russia (1917) League of Nations founded (1919)
James Joyce's *Ulysses* (1922) T. S. Eliot's *The Wasteland* (1922) James Baldwin (b. 1924) The Bauhaus becomes important center for modern design and architecture (1925) William Faulkner's *The Sound and the Fury* (1929) John Barth (b. 1930) Toni Morrison (b. 1931) Picasso's *Guernica* (1937)	1925	Lenin dies (1924) Lindbergh flies solo across Atlantic (1927) New York Stock Market crashes (1929) Hitler assumes power (1933) Spanish Civil War begins (1936) World War II (1939–1945)
Andy Warhol (1931–1987) Development of abstract expressionism by Jackson Pollock and others (1940s) Norman Mailer's *The Naked and the Dead* (1948) Le Corbusier's chapel of Notre-Dame-du-Haut (1950)	1950	United Nations founded (1945) Korean War (1950–1953) Indochina War (1954) Sputnik launched (1957)
Pop art movement (1960) Minimal, conceptual, and super-realist movements Aleksandr Solzhenitsyn, *The Gulag Archipelago* (1974)	1970	John F. Kennedy assassinated (1963) Arab-Israeli Six-Day War (1967) Assassinations of Martin Luther King, Jr., and Robert Kennedy (1968) American astronauts land on moon (1969) Watergate affair begins (1973) President Nixon resigns (1974) End of U.S. involvement in Vietnam (1975) Mao Tse-tung dies (1976) U.S. and China establish full diplomatic relations (1978) Shah flees Iran, Ayatollah Khomeini seizes power (1979) Somoza government ousted by Sandinistas in Nicaragua (1979) SALT II treaty between U.S. and U.S.S.R. signed (1979)
Alvin Toffler, *The Third Wave* (1980) Umberto Eco, *Il nome della rosa* (1981) Bishop Desmond Tutu awarded Nobel Peace Prize (1984) Andy Warhol dies (1987) *The Closing of the American Mind* by Alan Bloom (1987) Salvador Dalí dies (1989)	1980	Mount Saint Helens erupts (1980) Ronald Reagan elected U.S. President (1980) Anwar Sadat assassinated; attempts made on Pope John Paul II and President Reagan (1981) Falkland Islands War (Britain and Argentina) (1982) Soviet Premier Leonid Brezhnev dies (1982) U.S. invades Grenada (1983) Indira Gandhi assassinated (1984) Major strikes by blacks in South Africa (1984) Union Carbide plant leaks toxic gas in India (1984) Mikhail Gorbachev becomes U.S.S.R. Premier (1985) Marcos regime overthrown in Philippines (1986) Nuclear accident at Chernobyl (1986) George Bush elected U.S. President (1988) Berlin Wall falls (1989)
Rabbit at Rest by John Updike (1990) Van Gogh *Irises* sold for 52 million dollars (1990) Elvis postage stamp (1993) Prince changes his name to a symbol (1993) Toni Morrison wins Nobel Prize for Literature for *Jazz* (1993) Edvard Munch's *The Scream* stolen, later recovered, in Norway (1994) Madonna stars in movie *Evita* (1996) Toni Morrison wins Nobel Prize for Literature for *Paradise* (1998)	1990	Clarence Thomas hearings (1990) Eastern Europe rejects Communism (1990) Persian Gulf War (1990–1991) U.S.S.R. rejects Communist Party (1991) Desert Storm, war in Iraq (1991) Rodney King verdict (1992) World Trade Center bombing, New York City (1993) Fire destroys Branch Davidian cult of Waco, Texas (1993) Richard Nixon dies (1913–1994) South Africa holds its first interracial national democratic election (1994) O. J. Simpson trial (1994–1995) Oklahoma City Federal building bombed (1995) Civil war in Bosnia (1995) Million Man march in Washington, D.C. (1995) TWA Flight 800 explodes (1996) Hong Kong reverts from British to Chinese control (1997)

Glossary

A

absolute music Instrumental music based upon abstract principles of music theory and form.

a cappella Unaccompanied group singing.

accent A strong sound. Accents may be achieved by stress, duration, or position of a tone.

acoustics The science of sound.

affections The Baroque term for human emotions or states of the soul.

Age of Humanism A period, characterized by a new optimism, that began in fourteenth-century Italy and spread throughout western Europe during the Renaissance.

aleatory *See* indeterminate music

alto (contralto) Low female voice.

answer Dominant version of the subject of a fugue.

antecedent The first of two balanced phrases, sometimes compared with a question.

aria A songlike vocal piece, musically expressive, with orchestral accompaniment; generally homophonic in texture.

ars antiqua The musical style of the thirteenth century.

ars nova The prevalent musical style of the fourteenth century.

art song A concert setting of a poem, usually by a well-known poet, to music.

athematic Themeless. Boulez's style of serialization, in which he rejects the tone row and avoids clear-cut themes.

atonality The avoidance of a tonic note and of tonal relationships in music.

augmentation Rhythmic variation in which note values are doubled, making a theme twice as slow as in its original presentation.

avant-garde Leaders in the development of new and unconventional styles.

B

backbeat Heavy accent on the normally weak second and fourth beats in quadruple meter.

ballad A folk song, strophic in form, that tells a story.

ballades Songlike character pieces.

ballad opera An English dramatic form in which humorous and satirical texts were set to popular tunes.

band An instrumental ensemble consisting of woodwind, brass, and percussion sections. A concert or symphonic band may include a few string instruments as well.

baritone Medium-range male voice.

Baroque The term, originally meaning irregular, applied to the dramatic, emotional style of seventeenth- and early-eighteenth-century art.

bass Low male voice.

beat The basic rhythmic pulse of music.

bebop A complex, highly improvised style of jazz.

bel canto "Beautiful singing." The eighteenth-century Italian singing style that emphasized the beauty and virtuosity of the voice.

berceuse A piece with the character of a lullaby.

blue notes Flexible tones, chosen subjectively from between the half steps of tonal scales.

blues A vocal style that originated as a kind of African American folk song and that has become a form of jazz. The classical form is strophic, with three lines (twelve bars) in each verse.

boogie-woogie "Piano blues." A piano style derived from the formal and harmonic structure of the blues, but bright in mood and fast in tempo. The left hand of the pianist plays a characteristic ostinato pattern.

brass Wind instruments that include the trumpet, trombone, French horn, and tuba.

break A dramatic, unstable, strongly rhythmic section, as in a march.

broken chord The tones of a chord sounded one at a time in succession, rather than simultaneously.

burlesque A variety show featuring satirical humor.

C

cadence A stopping point.

cadenza An extended passage for solo instrument; typical feature of a solo concerto.

call-and-response　A solo voice alternating with a chorus.

canon　A polyphonic composition in which all of the voices perform the same melody, beginning at different times.

cantata　A multimovement dramatic vocal work on a religious or secular subject, performed in concert style; shorter than an oratorio.

castrato　A male singer, castrated to preserve the unchanged soprano or alto voice.

chamber music　Music for a small instrumental ensemble with one instrument per line of music.

chance music　*See* indeterminate music.

chant, plainchant, plainsong, Gregorian chant　Music to which portions of the Roman Catholic service are sung by unaccompanied voices singing in unison.

character piece　A relatively short piano piece in a characteristic style or mood.

Chicago jazz (Dixieland)　An imitation by white musicians of the New Orleans style of jazz.

chivalry　A Medieval code of customs and behavior associated with knighthood.

choir　Usually, a vocal ensemble of mixed voices. Sometimes, an instrumental ensemble, as a *brass choir*.

chorale　A characteristic hymn introduced by Martin Luther.

chorale prelude　A prelude based on a Lutheran chorale tune.

chord　A meaningful (as opposed to a random) combination of three or more tones.

choreographer　The person who arranges the movements of dancers.

chorus　A vocal ensemble (choir); a composition for performance by a choral ensemble; in popular music, a refrain sung between verses of a song.

chromatic scale　The twelve consecutive half steps within the range of an octave.

chromaticism　The use of notes that are not in the scale upon which a composition is based.

classical style　A restrained, objective style of art. Spelled with a capital letter, the Classical style refers to Western music characteristic of the period from about 1750–1825.

classicism　The general term for objective art, restrained in emotional expression, emphasizing formal design.

clavichord　A keyboard instrument capable of subtle changes of volume and able to produce a slight vibrato.

clavier　General term for a keyboard instrument.

clef　A sign that fixes the tone represented by each line and space on the staff.

closing section　The end of the exposition of a sonata-allegro.

cluster　Chord, built upon seconds, containing any number of tones.

coda　Literally, "tail"; a closing section.

coloratura　A virtuosic singing style, including rapid runs, elaborate ornamentation, and extremely high pitches.

combo　A small jazz ensemble.

comic operas　Operas light in mood, modest in performing requirements, written in the vernacular language of the intended listening audience.

concept musical　A musical show presenting ideas subject to the audience's interpretation and leaving situations unresolved.

concert　A term describing any music performance, but usually one by an orchestral, band, or choral ensemble.

concertato principle　The principle of contrasting the sonorities of different performing ensembles.

concertino　A group of solo instruments in a concerto grosso.

concertmaster　The conductor's assistant, who is also the orchestra's first, or principal, violinist.

concerto　A multimovement work for orchestra and an instrumental soloist.

concerto grosso　A multimovement composition for orchestra and a small group of solo instruments.

concert overture　A one-movement orchestral composition, often inspired by literature and dramatic in expression, yet generally subject to analysis according to classical principles of form.

concrete music (*musique concrète*)　Music consisting of recorded and electronically altered sounds.

consequent　The second of two balanced phrases, sometimes compared with an answer.

console　Unit containing the keyboard, pedals, and stops of a pipe organ.

consonance　A passive sound that seems to be "at rest."

consort　An ensemble of several members of the same instrument family.

continuo　A group of instruments, including a lute or keyboard instrument and one or more sustaining bass instruments, that accompanied Baroque ensemble compositions.

contrapuntal　Polyphonic.

cool jazz　A mild style, performed by bands of a moderate size that often include instruments not traditionally associated with jazz.

Counter Reformation　The Catholic response to the Protestant Reformation; it proposed certain reforms, including some related to church music.

countersubject　In a fugue, thematic material, usually derived from or related to the subject.

country-western   American vernacular music rooted in the South, glorifying the guitar and featuring frank lyrics delivered in an earthy style in southern or country dialect.

cover   A re-recording, for commercial purposes, as in a recording by white musicians of a rhythm-and-blues hit.

crescendo   Becoming louder.

Cubism   A style in which geometric planes are imposed upon subjects of every nature.

cyclic form   A multimovement form unified by the recurrence of the same or similar melodic material in two or more movements.

D

da capo   "From the beginning." A *da capo* aria has an *A B A* design.

Dadaism   A nihilistic movement intended to demolish art.

decrescendo or **diminuendo**   Becoming softer.

development   The second section of the sonata-allegro; it moves through many keys.

Dies irae   Gregorian chant for the dead.

diminution   Rhythmic technique in which note values are halved, doubling the tempo.

dissonance   An active, unsettled sound.

Dixieland   A white musicians' version of New Orleans jazz.

dominant (V)   The fifth note of the major or minor scale.

downbeat   The first beat of a measure.

drone   A sustained tone.

duple meter   Two beats per measure.

dynamic level   Level of volume.

E

electronic synthesizer   A highly versatile electronic sound generator capable of producing and altering an infinite variety of sounds.

elements of music   The basic materials of which music is composed: rhythm, melody, harmony, timbre.

Enlightenment   A movement led by eighteenth-century French intellectuals that advocated reason as the universal source of knowledge and truth.

ensemble finale   The final scene of a musical show, or of an act within the show, in which several soloists simultaneously express, in different words and music, their individual points of view.

ethnomusicology   The study of the music of certain cultures.

ethos   The moral and ethical qualities of music.

études   Studies or "exercises" based upon specific pianistic techniques.

Experimentalism   The exploration of previously unknown aspects of musical sound.

exposition   The first section of a fugue or of a sonata-allegro.

Expressionism   A highly emotional style in art that sought to express disturbed states of the mind.

expressive style   An emotional style of music inspired by the German middle class of the second quarter of the eighteenth century.

F

figured bass   A system of musical shorthand by which composers indicated intervals above the bass line with numbers (figures) rather than with notated pitches.

first practice (*stile antico*)   The polyphonic, conservative style of the late Renaissance.

Five, The   Five nineteenth-century Russian composers associated with Russian nationalism.

Flanders (Netherlands)   Area of northern Europe where the musical Renaissance began.

flat   A sign (♭) that indicates that a tone is to be performed one-half step lower than notated.

Florentine Camerata   A group of scholars and intellectuals in Florence around the turn of the seventeenth century who promoted changes in the prevailing style of art.

folk music   Usually music of unknown origin, transmitted orally, and enjoyed by the general population. Today the term is applied to some popular music that has the style or flavor of folk art.

form   The organization and design of a composition, or of one movement within a composition.

forte   Loud.

fortepiano   The early piano, named for its range of dynamic levels; it was smaller and less sonorous than the modern instrument.

fortissimo   Very loud.

free jazz   A style in which musicians improvise independently, sometimes producing a "random" effect.

frequency   The rate of a sound wave's vibration.

fugue   An imitative polyphonic composition.

fusion   Combination of jazz and rock.

G

gamelan   An Indonesian percussion ensemble.

gavotte   French dance in quadruple meter, often included in a Baroque suite.

Gebrauchsmusik   Hindemith's term for "useful" music.

glass harmonica   A musical instrument invented by Benjamin Franklin.

glissando   An expressive "slide" between pitches.

Golden Age of Polyphony   Term for the Renaissance, when polyphonic texture was prevalent and particularly beautiful.

Gothic   Thirteenth-century style of architecture, characterized by lofty spires and pointed arches.

grand opera   The nineteenth-century French serious opera style, which particularly emphasized spectacular visual effects. Ballets and stirring choruses were important components of grand opera.

Gregorian chant   Term for Roman Catholic plainchant since the sixth century CE.

griot   African professional musician.

H

half step   The smallest interval on a keyboard.

harmony   The simultaneous sounding of two or more different tones conceived as a unit.

heterophony   Inexact unison, resulting from free embellishment of the melody by some voices or instruments.

hip-hop   The music behind rapped lyrics.

homophonic texture (homophony)   A melodic line accompanied by chordal harmony.

homorhythmic style   Polyphony in which all the voices move in the same rhythm, producing a chordal effect. (The chordal effect is achieved by the combination of melodic lines rather than by the addition of chords to one melody, as in homophonic texture.)

hymn   A religious song, with nonliturgical text, appropriate for congregational singing.

I

idée fixe   The term Berlioz used for the melody representing the loved one in his *Symphonie fantastique.*

imitative polyphony   A technique in which each phrase of a composition is addressed by all of the voices, which enter successively in imitation of each other.

Impressionism   A style of painting and of music that avoids explicit statement, instead emphasizing suggestion and atmosphere.

impromptus   Character pieces of an improvisatory character.

improvisation   The process of simultaneously composing and performing music.

indeterminate, aleatoric, random, or **chance music**   Music in which some elements of composition are left to the decision of performance participants or to chance.

interval   The distance between two pitches.

invention   Keyboard piece with two or three voices in imitative contrapuntal style.

J

jazz   A popular music rooted in Africa that developed in early twentieth-century America. There are many styles of jazz, but they generally share a danceable beat, syncopated rhythms, and certain characteristic performance practices, including improvisation.

K

kabuki   Highly stylized Japanese form of music drama.

key   The tonic note, and the major or minor scale, upon which a composition is based.

keyboard instruments   Instruments on which sound is produced by pressing keys on a keyboard.

L

leading tone   Half step leading to the final, or tonic, note of a scale.

Leitmotif   A recurring melodic fragment or chord bearing dramatic or emotional significance, introduced by Wagner in his music dramas.

Les Six   Six French composers who in the 1920s, reflected the strong influence of popular styles in their music.

libretto   The text of a dramatic vocal work.

Lieder   German art songs.

linear polyphony   Polyphonic music conceived without the intention that the combined melody lines should form chordal or harmonic combinations.

liturgy   The words of the Mass.

lute   A plucked string instrument; the most widely used instrument of the sixteenth century.

lyrical melody   A relatively long, songlike melody.

M

madrigal   A secular song introduced in Italy that became popular in England as well. Polyphonic in texture and expressive in mood, madrigals are written in the vernacular language.

madrigalism   Word painting used to enhance the expression of madrigal texts.

mainstream   Term for the main body of work of a given period.

major scale   The ascending pattern of steps as follows: whole, whole, half, whole, whole, whole, half.

Mannheim rocket   Rapidly ascending melodic phrase.

Mass   The Roman Catholic worship service.

mazurka Stylized dance piece for piano, based upon a Polish dance.

measure (bar) A unit containing a number of beats.

Medieval modes Seven-note scales modeled on, but differing somewhat from, those of the Greeks.

Medieval period or **Middle Ages** The period from about 500 to 1450 C.E.

melismatic chant Chant with several notes of music for each syllable of text.

melody A meaningful succession of pitches.

meter The organization of rhythm into strong and weak beats.

metronome Instrument to measure tempo.

mezzo Half, moderate, or medium.

mezzoforte Moderately loud.

mezzopiano Moderately soft.

mezzo-soprano Medium-range female voice.

microtones Musical sounds falling between half steps.

MIDI A system allowing composers to manage quantities of complex information, and making it possible for unrelated electronic devices to communicate with each other.

minimalism A style of music based upon many repetitions of simple melodic and rhythm patterns.

Minnesinger Noble poet-musicians of medieval Germany.

minor scale The ascending pattern of steps as follows: whole, half, whole, whole, half, whole, whole.

minstrel Traveling or resident entertainers and music performers.

minstrel show A variety show, popular in the mid- and late nineteenth century, that included songs, dances, and comic repartee performed by white men who blackened their skin to resemble stereotypical African American figures.

minuet Dance in triple meter, popular in the eighteenth century.

minuet and trio *A B A*. Often the third movement of a symphony, sonata, or string quartet. Consists of two minuets, the second (trio) lighter and more lyrical than the first.

modern dance Contemporary dance form, usually performed barefoot, with steps, gestures, and costumes freely designed for each work.

modes Seven-note scales within the range of an octave.

modulate To change key systematically.

monody Music for one voice with a simple accompaniment, introduced by the Florentine Camerata.

monophonic texture (monophony) One unaccompanied melodic line.

motet A polyphonic vocal form, usually consisting of two melodic lines, each with its own text, above a plainchant melody.

motive A short melodic phrase that may be effectively developed.

movement A section of a complete work, that has its own formal design and a degree of independence but is conceived as a part of the whole; usually separated from other movements by a pause.

Muses The nine Greek goddesses of the arts.

music In ancient Greece, "the art of the Muses," blending poetry, drama, and the visual arts with what we consider to be musical sounds.

musical bow A folk instrument, popular in many cultures, resembling in appearance the hunting bow, from which it may have derived.

musical comedy A musical show combining the entertainment of vaudeville with the integrated plot characteristic of operettas.

music drama Wagner's concept of music theater, in which the drama and the music were theoretically of equal interest.

musicology The scientific study of music.

music theater Staged drama including instrumental and vocal music and sometimes dance.

musique concrète Concrete music; music consisting of recorded and electronically altered sounds.

N

nationalism A late-nineteenth-century movement in which artists of many nationalities turned from the dominant German influence in the arts to the cultural characteristics of their own and of other countries.

Neoclassicism The twentieth-century version of classicism in music.

Neoromanticism The twentieth-century version of a romantic approach to music composition.

Netherlands (Flanders) Area of northern Europe where the musical Renaissance began.

New Orleans jazz Music performed by a small jazz combo whose soloists take turns improvising on a given tune.

nocturne Piece expressing the "character" of night.

noh Semi-religious, highly traditional Japanese music drama.

notation Written music.

note A tone; a specific pitch.

O

octave The interval of an eighth, as from C to C.

octave displacement A melodic concept involving the selection of pitches from various, sometimes distant, octaves.

opera A dramatic vocal form blending visual, literary, and musical arts, in which all dialogue is sung.

opera buffa   Italian comic opera.

opéra comique   (1) French comic opera of a satirical or romantic nature. (2) In the nineteenth century, French works shorter, more modest, and more realistic than grand operas, but not necessarily humorous.

operetta   A comic or romantic form of music theater, sometimes called "light opera." It includes some spoken dialogue.

opus   "Work." An opus number indicates the chronological order in which a piece was composed or published.

oratorio   A multimovement dramatic vocal work on a religious subject, performed in concert style.

orchestra   A mixed ensemble of string and wind instruments.

orchestral suite   Several sections of varying character drawn from a larger work, such as a ballet.

Ordinary   Portions of the Mass appropriate any time of the church year: the Kyrie, Gloria, Credo, Sanctus, and Agnus Dei.

organum   The earliest form of polyphony.

ostinato   A persistently repeated melodic and/or rhythmic pattern.

overture   Introductory orchestral piece.

P

pants (trousers) role   Male role written for a female singer.

passacaglia   Variations over a bass ostinato.

Passion   An oratorio based on the events leading to the crucifixion of Christ.

patter song   A setting of humorous words sung very rapidly, with comic effect.

pedal point   Pitch sustained, usually in the bass, under changing harmonies.

pentatonic scale   A five-note scale.

percussion   All instruments that may be played by shaking, rubbing, or striking the instrument itself. These include the timpani (tuned kettledrums), other drums, chimes, tambourine, triangle, cymbals, and various mallet instruments, such as the xylophone.

phrase   A section of melody, comparable to a section or phrase of a sentence.

pianissimo   Very soft.

piano   A keyboard instrument; also, soft in dynamic level.

pitch   The highness or lowness of a sound.

pizzicato   The technique of plucking string instruments.

plainsong, plainchant, chant, Gregorian chant   Music to which portions of the Catholic service are sung. The texture is monophonic, the timbre that of unaccompanied voices.

point of imitation   The introduction of a new phrase in imitative polyphony.

pointillism   A painting technique in which colors and shapes are broken into tiny dots, which appear from a distance to blend.

polonaise   Stylized dance piece for piano, based upon a Polish dance.

polychoral music   Music for two or more vocal and/or instrumental choirs, performed antiphonally. A characteristic feature of music of the Venetian school.

polymeter   Use of more than one meter at the same time.

polyphonic texture (polyphony)   The simultaneous combination of two or more melodic lines.

polyrhythm   Two or more rhythmic patterns performed simultaneously.

polytonality   Two or more keys at the same time.

post-Romanticism   A general term for several romantic styles that succeeded the dominance of German Romanticism and preceded the return of classicism to the arts.

prelude   A short independent or introductory piece for keyboard.

prepared piano   A piano whose timbre and pitches have been altered by the application of foreign materials on or between the strings.

Primitivism   A style inspired by primitive works of art and by the relaxed life of uncivilized cultures.

program music   Instrumental music that purports to tell a story or describe a scene, idea, or event.

program symphony   A multi-movement orchestral work, the form of which is based upon programmatic concepts.

Proper   Portions of the Mass performed only at certain times.

Protestant Reformation   A protest movement, led by Martin Luther, against certain tenets of the Catholic church.

psalm tunes   Tuneful settings of the 150 psalms in versions suitable for congregational singing.

psalter   A collection of psalms in rhymed, metered verse.

psaltery   Medieval string instrument.

Puritans   English followers of John Calvin.

Q

quadruple meter   Four beats per measure.

quarter tone   The interval halfway between half steps.

R

rag   A piece in ragtime.

raga   A melodic pattern with many connotations, including those of time, mood, and color, which provides a basis for improvisation in the classical music of India.

ragtime   A popular piano style in which a syncopated melody in the right hand is accompanied by a regular duple pattern in the bass.

rap   Rapid spoken patter accompanied by hip-hop music.

realize (a figured bass)   Improvise the inner voices according to a figured bass.

recapitulation   The third section of the sonata-allegro. It reviews the material of the exposition, presenting it in a new light.

recital   A performance by a soloist or small ensemble.

recitative   A speechlike setting of a text, with homophonic accompaniment by a keyboard (dry recitative) or an orchestra (accompanied recitative).

recorder   An end-blown wind instrument, sometimes called a "whistle" flute, developed in the Middle Ages and very popular in the Renaissance. The tone is soft and slightly reedy.

Reformation   Sixteenth-century movement, led by Martin Luther, protesting certain procedures of the Roman Catholic church.

reform opera   Eighteenth-century serious opera, introduced by Christoph Willibald Gluck, written to avoid the flaws of Italian Baroque opera.

refrain   A section of melody and text that recurs at the end of each verse of a strophic song.

Renaissance   The term, meaning "rebirth," refers to the period of renewed interest in the classical arts of ancient Greece and Rome. The Renaissance began in the early part of the fifteenth century and dominated the style of Western music from 1450 to 1600.

Renaissance motet   A religious vocal composition that is through-composed, polyphonic in texture, sung in Latin, and invariably serene and worshipful.

Requiem   Mass for the dead.

rest   A sign that indicates silence, or the cessation of musical sound.

revue   Variety show featuring lavish costumes and spectacular staging.

rhythm   The arrangement of time in music.

rhythm-and-blues   Broadly, black popular music of the 1950s. More specifically, a black popular style in quadruple meter with strong backbeats and in danceable tempo.

ripieno   The orchestral group in a concerto grosso.

ritardando   A gradual slowing in tempo.

rock 'n' roll   A popular style developed in the early 1950s from the combination of country-western and rhythm-and-blues characteristics.

rococo   An elegant, sometimes frivolous, style of art introduced during the French Regency and prevalent in France during the second quarter of the eighteenth century.

romantic style   An emotional, subjective style of art; Romanticism refers to the style of Western art prevalent in the nineteenth century.

rondo   *A B A C A.* A form in which various episodes alternate with the opening material. The tempo is usually fast, and the mood merry.

round   A melody that may be performed by two or more voices entering at different times, producing meaningful harmony.

row   The series of tones on which a serial composition is based.

rubato   The Romantic technique of "robbing" from the tempo at some points and "paying back" at others.

S

scale   An ascending or descending pattern of half and/or whole steps.

scherzo   "Joke." A movement, often the third, of a multimovement piece. The mood is lighthearted. The form is *A B A,* with a *trio* inserted between the scherzo and its repeat.

score   The notated parts for all the voices and/or instruments of a music composition.

Second New England School   A group of late-nineteenth-century New England composers who studied in Germany and contributed to every genre of art music.

second practice (*stile moderno*)   The homophonic, expressive style introduced by Monteverdi.

secular   Nonreligious.

sequence   A melodic phrase repeated at different levels of pitch.

serialism   *See* total serialism.

sharp   A sign (♯) that indicates that a tone is to be performed one-half step higher than notated.

singing school movement   A late-eighteenth-century effort to teach Americans to sing and to read music. The movement inspired the composition of America's first indigenous music.

Singspiel (plural, *Singspiele*)   German comic opera, containing folklike songs.

sonata   (1) In the fifteenth and sixteenth centuries, an instrumental composition to be "sounded" upon instruments rather than sung; (2) in the Baroque, a multimovement composition for one or two solo instruments accompanied by continuo; (3) after the Baroque, a multimovement composition for one or two solo instruments.

sonata-allegro   The "first movement form." The three sections—exposition, development, and recapitulation—form a ternary design.

sonata da camera   A light Baroque sonata intended for concert performance.

sonata da chiesa   A serious Baroque sonata, intended for performance in church.

sonata-rondo   A combined form, with the key relationships of the sonata-allegro and the alternating themes of a rondo.

sonatina   Multimovement solo form, shorter and often lighter than a sonata.

song cycle   A set of songs by one composer, often using texts all by the same poet.

soprano   High female singing voice.

spiritual   A folklike religious song, with a simple tune, developed by African Americans.

Sprechstimme   Literally, "speech voice." A style of melodramatic declamation between speaking and singing.

staccato   Short, detached.

staff   Five lines and four spaces upon which music is notated.

stile antico **(first practice)**   The polyphonic, conservative style of the late Renaissance.

Stile moderno **(second practice)**   The homophonic, expressive style introduced by Monteverdi.

stops   Levers, handles, or buttons that allow an organist to change timbres at will.

strain   A melodic section of a march or rag.

stretto   A section faster in tempo, or with imitative voices entering in closer succession, than earlier sections of the piece.

string instruments   Instruments that may be bowed, strummed, struck, or plucked. Orchestral string instruments include the violin, viola, cello, string bass (or double bass), and harp.

string quartet   A chamber ensemble consisting of two violins, a viola, and a cello.

strophic form   The most popular song form, which has two or more verses set to the same music.

style   Characteristic manner in which the elements of music, formal design, and emotional expression are approached by a composer.

subdominant (IV)   The fourth note of the major or minor scale.

subject   Principal melody of a fugue.

suite   A collection of stylized dance pieces for keyboard, or orchestral piece consisting of selections from a dramatic work or dance.

Surrealism   A movement in literature and painting that juxtaposed unlikely images.

sweet jazz   A highly arranged style, with little room for improvisation.

swing   A highly improvisatory style of big band music.

syllabic chant   Chant with one note of music for each syllable of text.

Symbolism   A literary movement sharing the ideals of the Impressionists.

symphonic jazz   Concert music with the sounds of jazz but no improvisation.

symphonic poem or **tone poem**   A one-movement orchestral piece, the form of which is based upon programmatic principles.

symphony   A multimovement orchestral form.

symphony orchestra   An instrumental ensemble consisting of members of the four families of instruments, dominated by strings.

syncopation   The occurrence of accents in unexpected places.

synthesizer   *See* electronic synthesizer.

T

tala   A repeated rhythmic cycle, characteristic of the music of India.

tempo   Rate of speed at which a musical piece is performed.

tenor   High male voice.

terraced dynamics   Abrupt changes of dynamic level.

texture   The manner in which melodic lines are used in music.

thematic transformation   The variation of thematic or melodic material for programmatic purposes. Sometimes called *metamorphosis.*

theme   A melody that recurs throughout a section, a movement, or an entire composition.

theme and variations   Instrumental form in which a theme recurs with modifications of melody, rhythm, timbre, meter, register, and/or other characteristics.

third stream   The combination of jazz and concert music.

thoroughbass   Strong bass line sounding continuously throughout Baroque ensemble compositions.

through-composed   A song form containing new music throughout.

timbre   The characteristic quality of the sound of a voice or instrument.

toccata   A rhapsodic, virtuosic keyboard piece.

tonality or **tonal system**   The system of harmony, based upon the major and minor scales, that has dominated Western music since the seventeenth century.

tone   A sound with specific pitch, produced by a constant rate of vibration of the sound-producing medium.

tone cluster (cluster)   A chord built upon seconds.

tone poem   *See* symphonic poem.

tonic The first and most important note of the major or minor scale, to which all other notes in the scale bear a subordinate relationship. The tonic is represented by the Roman numeral I.

total serialism An extension of the twelve-tone technique, in which other aspects besides melody and harmony are also arranged into series and systematically repeated throughout a composition.

transcription An arrangement of a piece so that it may be played by a different instrument or ensemble than that for which it was written.

transition, or **bridge** A passage that modulates from the first to the second key area of the exposition.

tremolo Violin-playing technique consisting of quick up-and-down movements of the bow on a single note.

triad A chord with three tones, consisting of two superimposed thirds.

trio (1) A composition for three voices or instruments; (2) a section of a composition lighter in texture, softer in dynamic level, and sometimes more melodic than the rest of the piece.

trio sonata A Baroque sonata for two solo instruments and continuo.

triple meter Three beats per measure.

troubadours, trouvères Noble French poets and composers of art (as opposed to popular) songs.

trousers role (See pants role.)

tune A melody that is easy to recognize, memorize, and sing.

tutti All; in orchestral music, refers to the full orchestra.

twelve-tone technique The arrangement of the twelve chromatic pitches into a row that provides the melodic and harmonic basis for a music composition.

U

unison Production of music by several voices or instruments at the same pitch, performed at the same or at different octaves.

upbeat The last beat of a measure.

V

vaudeville A variety show, popular in the late nineteenth century, including jokes, stunts, and skits, as well as song and dance.

Venetian School Late-sixteenth-century composers, including G. Gabrieli, who composed in the polychoral style.

verismo Realism in opera.

vernacular Common language; in music, refers to folk and popular pieces.

vibrato A rapid variation of pitch that lends "warmth" to the tone of a voice or instrument.

Viennese style The term sometimes applied to the Classical style, to avoid the ambiguities of the word "classical."

viol The most popular bowed string instrument of the Renaissance.

W

waltz Dance in triple meter.

white noise Sounds including the entire spectrum of tones, as white includes the entire spectrum of colors.

whole step An interval equal to two half steps.

whole-tone scale The six consecutive whole steps within the range of an octave.

woodwinds Wind instruments that include the piccolo, flute, oboe, English horn, clarinet, bassoon, and saxophone.

word painting Musical illustrations of verbal concepts.

Credits

Black-and-white prints

Color Plates

Index